THE
GLAMOR
GAME

THE
GLAMOR GAME

BILL CROMARTIE
and
JODY H. BROWN

RUTLEDGE HILL PRESS
Nashville, Tennessee

Published in Nashville, Tennessee, by Rutledge Hill Press, Inc.,
513 Third Avenue South, Nashville, Tennessee 37210.

Library of Congress Cataloging-in-Publication Data

Cromartie, Bill.
    The glamor game / Bill Cromartie and Jody H. Brown.
        p.   cm.
    ISBN 1-55853-036-3
    1. University of Notre Dame—Football—
    History.   2. University of Southern California—Football—
    History.   3. College sports—United States—
    History.   4. Football—United States—History.   I. Brown.
    Jody.   II Title.
GV958.N6C76   1989   89-10969
796.332'63'0977289—dc20   CIP

Manufactured in the United States of America
1 2 3 4 5 6 — 93 92 91 90 89

Table of Contents

Acknowledgements

A special acknowledgement is extended to both the University of Notre Dame and the University of Southern California for their generous cooperation in helping the authors gather material for this book.

We extend gratitude to the offices of Sports Information at both institutions, especially to Tim Tessalone at Southern Cal and to John Heisler and Jeff Spelman at Notre Dame.

Appreciation is expressed to the library systems of Notre Dame, Southern California, the University of Georgia and Georgia State University, as well as to the public libraries of Los Angeles, Indianapolis and Atlanta.

There were certain individuals who made contributions to this book, so a heartfelt "thank you" is offered to Bill Barner, Lyn Billings, Kay Cromartie and Ann Brown.

A book of this nature would have been impossible to compile without the newspapers files of the *Los Angeles Times,* the *Herald-Examiner,* the *Chicago Tribune,* the *Indianapolis Star* and *News,* as well as predecessor papers in these cities.

These newspapers were the source of the vast majority of the factual material included in this book. And to their sportswriters, past and present, we sincerely extend a grateful and admiring salute. They were the eyewitnesses to the drama and color as it unfolded year after year. They recorded the facts and quotations from which a large portion of this book has been drawn.

The Notre Dame athletic complex. The first game played in Notre Dame Stadium was in 1930. USC has played here 27 times through 1989.

To
NOBLE TROJANS, ALL,
and
FIGHTING IRISH, EVERYWHERE!

The Los Angeles Coliseum, home of Southern California football since its completion in 1923. Notre Dame and USC have played thirty-two games here.

THE
GLAMOR
GAME

For a long time Gwynn Wilson had dreamed of a Southern California–Notre Dame football series. His ideas took shape in November 1925 when he met Irish coach Knute Rockne in Lincoln, Nebraska.

1925

"Lady Luck" And Placards Brought ND-USC Together

Why would two colleges more than 2,000 miles apart consider even one football game, much less a long-term series?

Especially when you consider a grueling, week-long train trip there and back.

It was a bold move for the 1920s, but the University of Southern California and the University of Notre Dame did it.

And it was USC which lit the fire.

USC was in its 38th year of football but had played only eight games outside the state and no games east of Arizona. Furthermore, since the end of World War I, the Trojans had lost only nine of their 59 games. The athletic department, the alumni, the Los Angeles press and Angelinos in general felt it was time to schedule intersectional games with Eastern and Midwest grid powers of the time.

But why Notre Dame?

Following the 1924 season, USC had unceremoniously released six-year coach Elmer "Gloomy Gus" Henderson, despite his .866 winning percentage (45-7-0), still the best in the school's history. Henderson's undoing was an 0-5 record against the Trojans' hated rival, the University of California.

Ambitious USC then went after the nation's king of coaches, Notre Dame's Knute Rockne. And he would have accepted the offer, but Father Matthew Walsh, president of the school, quickly squashed any such thoughts, reminding both USC and Rockne that eight years still remained on his contract.

1

Rockne would remain in South Bend.

Rejected in their attempt to land Rockne, the next step was to play Rockne's team. The following year, 1925, Southern California began laying plans for a home-and-home series with the Irish.

Enter a fellow by the name of Gwynn Wilson, a 26-year-old graduate manager of the USC football team. Wilson had for some time been talking about such a series, but it only fell on deaf ears. Finally persuading school officials to pursue such a possibility, he was put in charge of getting the Fighting Irish inside the Los Angeles Coliseum.

Notre Dame was to play Nebraska in Lincoln on Thanksgiving Day that year. Wilson and his new bride, Marion, boarded a train on Monday morning and headed for the corn country, not necessarily to see the game, but to see Knute Rockne.

This was the 11th year of the Irish-Husker series and, strangely enough, nine of the games had been played in Lincoln. Nebraska won 17-0 to even the series at 5-5-1, and Notre Dame fans received some rude treatment from the townspeople, as well as from the local press.

This would also play a major role in getting the Irish in USC's date book.

Placards were displayed in downtown stores and in windows of homes throughout the city. The message was also published in the Lincoln newspapers. The placards read:

Now, altogether, loud and clear
Beat Notre Dame
Speak up so the whole world can hear
Beat Notre Dame
From South Bend rooters, take no sass
But boldly bellow out en masse
Those roughnecks Irish, shall not pass

Two weeks later, on December 9, Father Walsh announced that Notre Dame had broken off athletic relations with the University of Nebraska. There would be no ND-NU football game in 1926.

After the game, Wilson went to Rockne's hotel. They

2

COLUMBIA CLAIMS ROCKNE CONTRACT

| DEMPSEY MAY FIGHT WILLS ON MACKINAC ISLE | OVATION WINS HARNESS STAKE OF HORSE SHOW | Berlenbach Batters Down Delaney and Retains Title | BLOOD CLOT IN RED'S ARM; GRAVE RESULTS FEARED | SETS GRID WORLD AFLAME | 'I'LL STAY WITH NOTRE DAME,' KNUTE'S REPLY |

met. Wilson presented Rockne with his proposal. There's little doubt that it was ill-timed. Rockne could think only of the whitewash whipping that his team had just suffered. He invited Wilson to travel back to Chicago with him and the team. Mr. and Mrs. Wilson wholeheartedly accepted.

Following much discussion along the way, Rockne finally rejected the offer, giving as a primary reason the fact that Notre Dame officials had begun objecting to the team's extensive travel schedule. And they did have a legitimate point. In the last three seasons (1923-24-25), the Irish football team had made three trips to New York and three to Pennsylvania; two to Nebraska and two to New Jersey; one each to California, Georgia and Missouri; plus three other road games. It all added up to about 20,000 miles— on the railroads— not at the speed of today's jetliners.

The issue was dead. Gwynn Wilson had failed to land "the big game."

But wait. On the train also was Knute's wife, Bonnie Rockne. Whiling away the long hours, she and Marion Wilson struck up a close friendship. Marion kept insisting how great it would be for Notre Dame to play every other year in California. Bonnie, remembering Notre Dame's trip to the Rose Bowl against Stanford just two years earlier, began to like the idea.

The more Marion talked, the more Bonnie listened. Bonnie then talked to Knute. The rest is history.

Two weeks later, on Monday, December 7, 1925, the

3

SPORTS

The Los Angeles Times.

MONDAY MORNING, DECEMBER 7, 1925.

Notre Dame to Play U.S.C. Here Next Year

IRISH GRIDS
HERE NEXT
DECEMBER

Los Angeles Times' sports section carried a banner headline proclaiming, "Notre Dame to Play U.S.C. Here Next Year."

Marion Wilson and Bonnie Rockne had done it.

There would be three changes in Notre Dame's 1926 schedule. Drake would replace Baylor, and Indiana was taking the place of Lombard. The most important change, however, was that USC was "on" and Nebraska was "off." And what would soon become collegiate football's premier intersectional rivalry was booked.

"The Glamour Game" was on.

But it would be without Knute Rockne— and Bonnie— or so it seemed. Three days after the ND-USC announcement, the sporting world was shocked to learn that Rockne had signed a contract to become coach at Columbia University.

On Saturday, December 12, headlines across the country screamed the stunning and unexpected news:

The *Los Angeles Times*: "KNUTE ROCKNE QUITS AS NOTRE DAME GRID COACH....Columbia Gets Irish Mentor....Signs Three-Year Contract With University...Notre Dame Greatly Surprised at Loss of Coach."

The *Chicago Daily Tribune*: "COLUMBIA CLAIMS ROCKNE CONTRACT."

A full-blown and controversial crisis had exploded.

Rockne immediately said that he would remain at Notre Dame. The *Daily Tribune* reported, "Before word of Rockne's denial had reached South Bend, the city was thrown into great turmoil. 'Rock has quit Notre Dame,' was the word flashed through hotel lobbies, in business houses and over the campus of the Catholic university. 'Impossible' was the comment the report invariably brought forth. Students held impromptu mass meetings. Father Walsh was besieged with telephone calls from alumni. Newspapers from all over the country wired for verification."

The story hinted that the cancellation of next year's game with Nebraska had angered Rockne which brought on his signing a contract with Columbia.

Meanwhile, Columbia was rejoicing over having obtained the most outstanding football figure in the country.

The charges and counter charges continued between Rockne and James R. Knapp, a millionaire attorney and chairman of the football committee at Columbia, who had signed the coach to a contract in New York on Dec. 1. Rockne declared his agreement with Columbia was made contingent specifically upon his release by Notre Dame.

On December 7, Rockne had written Knapp that he could not obtain a release and that the agreement with Columbia was automatically cancelled. Knapp admitted receiving the letter but would not give an explanation of why he made the premature announcement.

Rockne told Westbrook Pegler of the *Daily Tribune*, "Knapp tried to blackjack me into signing a new and binding contract by giving publicity to our preliminary agreement after I told him that the deal was off....He was trying to drive me out of football if I refused to sign the new contract. Well, that's over. I hope to remain in football, but not at Columbia. I'd rather sweep the streets."

Pegler also wrote, "Knute K. Rockne, a wizard on his own home grounds, but something of a hick on Broadway, is bound for home convinced that the fountain pen is more deadly than the blackjack."

A few days later, Columbia University officially withdrew its offer. Rockne was back in Indiana, and the bizarre case was closed.

1926

GAME 1

Saved By A Little Southpaw

Notre Dame's despondent, dazed and dispirited players finished Monday classes and trudged off to Cartier Field for their next-to-last practice session of the season. They stood listless while their coaches lectured on the team's upcoming opponent.

Just three days earlier, however, this same squad had been atop the collegiate football world. They were in the driver's seat with a perfect record and charging toward a national championship. They had handed powerhouses Northwestern and Army their only losses of the season en route to an 8-0-0 record by an overwhelming score of 197-7.

The Irish, supremely confident, next traveled to Pittsburgh's Forbes Field to meet lightly–regarded Carnegie Tech. The Skibos, with losses to New York University and Washington & Jefferson, were coached by a real, live judge—Judge Walter Steffen, who on Monday would be back on another bench in Superior Court.

The Associated Press reported three days before the game, "Coach Knute Rockne will send his best team on the field when Notre Dame clashes with Carnegie Tech Saturday. Rumors that Notre Dame's first string men would be kept on the sidelines in order to have them for the contest the following week with Southern California brought vigorous denial from Rockne in a telegram to Carnegie Tech officials."

Rockne not only failed to start his first team against Carnegie, he failed to even go to Pittsburgh. Instead, he was at Chicago's Soldier Field with about 110,000 other

Quarterback Art Parisien's (left) *23-yard touchdown pass to halfback John Niemiec* (right) *led to Notre Dame's 13-12 victory in the series' first game. Niemiec returned the series' opening kickoff and also was the first to carry the ball from scrimmage.*

Notre Dame Gridiron Array Arrives in Tucson

SPORTS
The ⬛ Los Angeles ⬛ Times

THURSDAY MORNING, DECEMBER 2, 1926.

DEMPSEY POISONED ON DAY BEFORE TUNNEY FIGHT

IRISH PLAN TO STAGE WORKOUT	TROJANS LOOK GOOD IN DRILL	DOCTORED CREAM COST JACK TITLE, IS CLAIM
Searing Heat Wave Greets Men from South Bend	James Drives Team Through Final Scrimmage	*Jack's Generalissimo Hurls Charge of Black-Hand Stuff; Tunney's Win Slightly Off-Side*
Visiting Gridders Due Here Early Friday Morning	Devine Back With Report on Notre Dame Team	

people for the big Army-Navy game.

Meanwhile, back in Pittsburgh, assistant coaches Hunk Anderson and Tommy Mills later rushed Notre Dame's first team into the game, but....

Final score: The Fighting Irish 0, the Skibos 19. (What is a Skibo? It's the name of a castle in Scotland owned by Andrew Carnegie, founder of the school.)

Newspapers around the country received the score from wire services but refused to accept it. They either waited for a correction or phoned for verification. But the 19-0 score needed no correction nor verification.

It was an upset of stupendous proportions, an upset which is still considered by many as the greatest in collegiate football annals.

Rockne had a lot of explaining to do.

The numbed Irish squad now had to endure a rail ride back to South Bend, Monday classes, and then a four-day, four-night train trek all the way out to Los Angeles to play a rugged Southern Cal team.

On Monday night the 35-member squad pulled out of Chicago headed for Tucson, where it would hold a Thursday workout on the University of Arizona campus. Spending the night in Tucson, the team left Friday and arrived in Los Angeles that evening. It had been a long journey.

From Tucson, Bill Henry of the *Los Angeles Times* reported, "'We're just out to hold the score down, that's all,' said Rockne when he could make himself heard above the raucous strains of 'When Irish Eyes Are Smiling,' which were screeching from a brass-lunged calliope on the Southern Pacific platform. 'If we could have finished the season about a week ago, we'd have been all right, but the boys are pretty well fagged out now and we're just taking a chance. I don't know how the boys will hold up, but they'll try.'"

Meanwhile, Southern California's season had been a big success. The team won its first five games before dropping a one-point decision to Stanford. Three more wins followed and oddly enough, USC and ND would enter the first game of the series with identical 8-1-0 records. The Trojans' average score for the season was 34-4, Notre Dame's 22-3.

"NOTRE DAME ELEVEN DUE TO ARRIVE HERE TONIGHT," was the *Times'* sports headline greeting its Friday morning readers.

On Saturday, the *Times* said, "Two weeks ago Notre Dame was a 3-to-1 favorite over USC in the books of the betting commissioner in San Francisco. It wasn't quite that bad down here, but the Irish were top-heavy favorites. Now it's even money on the winner."

Braven Dyer, another *Times* reporter, was quite blunt in his appraisal of the game: "We like the Trojans. They are just as big as their rivals, just as fast and probably more experienced and just as smart."

George Shaffer of the *Chicago Tribune* said, "With most of the coaching talent in the country gathered here today, the consensus is that Notre Dame is just too

Before a Coliseum crowd of more than 74,000, USC's Morton Kaer picks up yardage in series' first game.

scrappy, too determined, and too skillful a football machine to lose two games in a row."

Notre Dame began playing football in 1888, Southern California a year later. When the two teams hit the Coliseum turf that December 4 before an official attendance count of 74,378 screaming fans, it would be ND's 282nd game and USC's 207th. The Irish had an all-time winning percentage of .815 (220-43-18), while the Trojans were .723 (142-50-14).

Southern Cal won the toss and elected to kickoff. The visitors defended the east goal. Brice Taylor kicked into the endzone, but the Trojans were offsides on the play. John Niemiec received the next kick at the 15-yard line and returned it out to his 33.

Almost to the day a year earlier (December 6), it had been officially announced that there would be a USC-ND series. Now, Gwynn Wilson's dream was a reality. "The Glamour Game" was on.

On the series' first play from scrimmage, USC team Captain Jeff Cravath hit Niemiec for a loss of two yards. Elmer Wynne gained five to the 36. Charlie Riley followed

Notre Dame's John Niemiec (left) *and USC's Morton Kaer* (right) *played important roles in the series' first game.*

with the series' first pass, and completion, a 13-yard strike to Bucky Dahman, giving the Irish a first down at their 49. A holding infraction stalled the drive and Niemiec punted to Morton Kaer, who returned it 21 yards to the USC 36.

Early in the second quarter, USC quick-kicked to ND's 26, and the first scoring drive of the series was launched. Christy Flanagan rammed for six, and Tom Hearndon got five for a first down at the 37. On second-and-nine, a Flanagan-to-Riley pass was good for 12 more yards and another first down at mid-field. Runs by Harry O'Boyle and Flanagan netted six, before O'Boyle burst through for a big gain of 28 yards to USC's 16. On the next play, Riley followed beautiful interference around his left end for a touchdown.

On the conversion attempt, O'Boyle's kick struck the outstretched arms of onrushing Cravath, and the ball ricocheted upward— and barely over the crossbar. It was reported that had the ball not hit Cravath, the kick, most likely, would have been too low. But it was good, and Notre Dame had taken a 7-0 lead.

Later in the period, USC began from its 34 and drove for a score. On third-and-15, Kaer rambled 29 yards and a first down at ND's 42. On second down from the 40, Kaer drilled a pass to Allen Behrendt, who caught it at the 15 and was racing for a touchdown—until Gene "Red" Edwards chased him down at the one-yard line. Kaer scored on the next play. Set to tie the game, kicker Taylor was slow in getting off the kick and it was blocked.

Neither team put up a serious threat for the remainder of the period and at the half, it was Notre Dame 7, Southern California 6.

In the third quarter, ND intercepted a pass and got down to USC's 27, but Flanagan missed a field goal attempt. Later, the Trojans' Albert Scheving blocked Flanagan's punt, setting in motion for USC to take the lead.

Starting from 56 yards away, Coach Howard Jones turned the show over to halfback Don Williams. He gained

Notre Dame quarterback Charles Riley scored the series' first touchdown, a 16-yard run in the second quarter.

eight and five yards, giving USC a first down at the Irish 43, as the third period came to a close. After a short break in the action to swap ends of the field, Williams was immediately at it again, ramming 10 yards and another first down at the 33. It was Williams to the 31, Williams to the 25, Williams to the 22 (first down) and Williams to the 18. After Manuel Laraneta ripped off a seven-yarder to the 11 and another first down, it was back to Williams, who could manage only two yards in two cracks, bringing up third-and-eight from the Irish nine. Williams scored on the next play. He had carried the ball all but once in the 11-play drive, including seven straight in one stretch.

The big majority of the huge Coliseum crowd were roaring their approval as their Trojans had scratched back to take a hard-earned 12-7 advantage.

And it stayed that way when Morley Drury's conversion try hit one of the goal posts and bounded back onto the field.

The game settled into a punting duel and, with six minutes left to play, Notre Dame received a punt at its own 41.

"Thousands of Trojan rooters, overjoyed at the prospect of victory, held back, waiting, pleading silently that the game, apparently won, would not be lost," reported Dyer.

Coach Rockne then made an ingenious switch. He replaced his star quarterback Charlie Riley with a little southpaw named Art Parisien.

"Few knew his name. Few had ever heard of him," wrote Dyer. "But Rockne knew his worth, knew that this was the right time to use him....It seemed suicidal to take Riley out....'Why remove the best player you have' was the

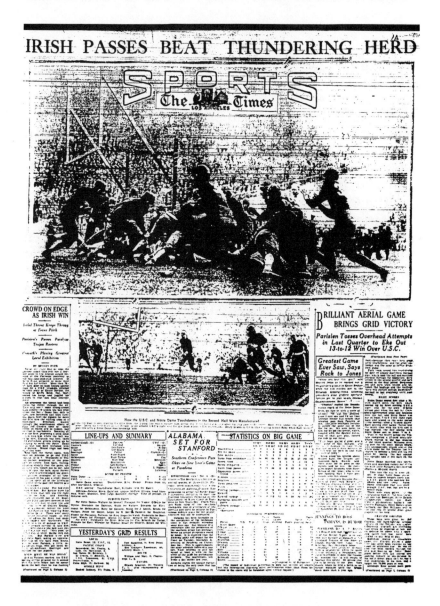

IRISH PASSES BEAT THUNDERING HERD

wail....out came Riley and in went Parisien, a little insignificant chap, who got down behind All-American center (Art) Boeringer and reached for the pigskin."

On first down, Parisien slid through the line for four yards. Parisien then connected on a 35-yard pass play to Niemiec to USC's 20-yard line. O'Boyle was stopped for no gain, and Dahman lost three, bringing up a crucial third-and-13 back at the 23 with just over two minutes left.

The Coliseum was in an uproar.

Parisien took the snap and ran far out to his left, sucking in the USC defense now expecting a run. Parisien then shot an aerial which a wide-open Niemiec caught at the five and waltzed into the endzone.

Notre Dame 13, Southern Cal 12. Cravath rushed in and blocked Niemiec's conversion attempt. But it didn't matter.

On first down after the ensuing kickoff, ND's Vince McNally intercepted Howard Elliott's long pass at the Trojan 41. The game ended two plays later with the Irish on USC's 18-yard line.

It was a crushing defeat for the Trojans, as they ended the season with an 8-2-0 record—both losses by a 13-12 score.

The Rose Bowl matched two undefeated teams for the fourth time in its 12-game history by booking Stanford (10-0-0) and Alabama (9-0-0). The Indians and Tide tied, 7-7.

Navy (9-0-1) was generally recognized as the country's top team, followed by Stanford, Alabama, Notre Dame

Morton Kaer scored USC's first touchdown against Notre Dame. He later became the first Trojan to earn All-America honors as a tailback.

and Lafayette, who posted the only perfect record (9-0-0) that year.

No doubt about it, then, Notre Dame's unbelievable loss to Carnegie Tech had cost the Irish the 1926 national title.

Meanwhile, the Irish took a 1-0 series lead over Southern California.

1927

GAME 2

"Luck Of The Trojans" Is No Luck At All

It was Tuesday afternoon, November 22, 1927. The USC football team was about to board train No. 4, destined for Chicago, where it would meet Notre Dame in the series' second game. Never before had a West Coast team gone so far to play on the gridiron.

"Amid the fanfare of trumpets and the raucous cheering of several thousand frenzied supporters, the University of Southern California football squad pulled out from the Arcade Station yesterday evening at 5 o'clock," reported Braven Dyer of the *Los Angeles Times*. "It was the greatest sendoff ever given a Trojan athletic delegation and the thunderous ovation will probably be ringing in the gridders' ears when they disembark in Chicago."

The official Trojan party, consisting of 33 players, five coaches, several managers and a trainer, departed Los Angeles on the Golden State Limited, the most luxurious, long-distance Pullman of the Rock Island Line.

The schedule routed the team through Tucson and Douglas, Arizona, to El Paso, Texas, up through Oklahoma and into Tucumcari, New Mexico, a junction point of the Rock Island. From there, ol' No. 4 steamed past Hutchinson and Topeka, Kansas, before rolling into Kansas City, Missouri. Next was Illinois, through Rock Island and, finally, Chicago.

The Golden State pulled into LaSalle Station at 10 o'clock Friday morning. The long rail run had covered more than 2,300 miles, and the team had spent three nights en route.

That afternoon, the Trojans held a spirited limbering-

up session at Stagg Field on the campus of the University of Chicago.

Southern Cal took a 7-0-1 record to Chicago, with victories over Occidental, Santa Clara, Oregon State, Cal Tech, California, Colorado and Washington State. The only blemish had been a 13-all draw with Stanford.

Notre Dame was 6-1-1. There was a 7-7 tie with Minnesota, and an 18-0 loss to Army, both national powers. The Gophers finished unbeaten, while the Cadets lost only to Yale, who lost only to Georgia, who lost only to Georgia Tech,

who lost only to Tennessee, who was tied only by Vanderbilt, who lost only to Texas in a string of head-on duels by a good portion of the country's top teams.

On the offensive side, USC was averaging 31 points per game, ND only 19. Defensively, both teams had surrendered just six points per outing. It looked on paper that the Californians were the stronger unit, but Notre Dame was officially made an 8-5 favorite to defeat Troy for the second straight year.

Saturday morning broke warm and overcast. Chicago

thoroughfares leading to Soldier Field were snarled by the crush of some 117,000 bodies struggling to arrive for the kickoff. It was reported that about 10,000 fans failed to find their seats in time, and about half of those failed to witness any of the scoring. All of the game's 13 points were posted in the first 10 minutes of action.

After receiving the opening kickoff, Notre Dame was quickly forced to punt, and John Elder sliced a short seven-yarder, setting up USC at the Irish 40-yard line. Morley Drury gained six yards in two carries. Drury was given the ball a third straight time, and he blasted through the line for 23 more yards before being knocked out of bounds by Elder at Notre Dame's 11. On fourth down from the seven, Drury pitched one into the endzone to Russell Saunders for a touchdown. A bad snap from center, however, spoiled Drury's conversion attempt, but the underdog Trojans had a 6-0 lead.

With their flubbed point-after attempt, the Trojans' frustrating afternoon of football had begun.

Another unlucky blow was soon to hit Southern Cal. The Irish faced a fourth-and-one at its own 34, and Coach Knute Rockne this time sent in Ray Dahman to punt, certain he could top Elder's seven-yard kick on the previous possession. But Dahman kicked it only six yards, as the ball fluttered out of bounds, once again at the Notre Dame 40.

But wait! There was a penalty on the play. The Trojans were called for holding and taxed 15 yards, giving Notre Dame a first down at its 49. Three plays later, Dahman was punting again, and this time he boomed one that backed USC to its five-yard line.

What a penalty it had been. It actually cost Troy 55 yards. Instead of having the ball 40 yards away from the Irish goal line, they were now 95 yards away.

Unable to knock out a first down, Drury got off a fine punt to Christie Flanagan, who slipped to the turf at his 46. Flanagan, on three straight carries, gained 21 yards and a first down at USC's 33. A play later from the 28, quarterback Charles Riley first faked a handoff to Flanagan, and secondly to Eddie Collins. Riley quickly retreated 10 yards and let a long one fly all the way into the endzone.

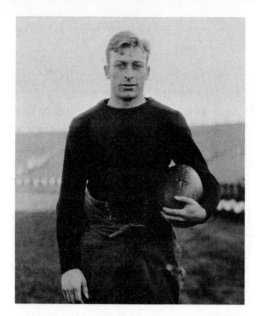

Halfback Ray Dahman caught a 28-yard scoring pass from Charles Riley, then kicked the PAT to pace Notre Dame's 7-6 victory over USC at Soldier Field in Chicago.

Dahman raced under the ball. Touchdown! Dahman also added the conversion and Notre Dame had a 7-6 lead with five minutes still remaining in the first period.

Each team punted on its next four possessions. Just before halftime, Drury's kick pinned the Irish back at their four, and Dahman answered with a boot out to the 24. Five plays later found the Trojans second-and-eight at the 11. Disaster struck USC again. Saunders passed complete to Lloyd Thomas, but the ball popped free from his grasp and bounded into the endzone where Notre Dame recovered for a harmless touchback.

The two teams continued playing "kickback" in the third quarter, or for most of it. Late in the period arose the series' first bona fide controversy. In whose favor did it go? Not Southern Cal's. Not on this muggy afternoon. This one was the crowning blow, the blow that finished off the Trojans.

Once again, Dahman was punting from his own endzone, and he got off a long kick which Drury returned 20 yards to the Irish 23. Three plays gained only a yard, and on fourth down Drury threw a pass intended for Lowry McCaslin. Riley, however, intercepted for ND at the three. Taking a few steps up field, he was smashed by Saunders with such force that Riley flew one way and the football flew

22

Chicago Sunday Tribune
THE WORLD'S GREATEST NEWSPAPER

0 CENTS PAY OR MORE
FINAL EDITION

VOLUME LXXXVL—NO. 48 .... NOVEMBER 27, 1937. A ★★★ PRICE: TEN CENTS

117,000 SEE NOTRE DAME WIN

W. FOCUSES ON SOCIETY INE FIELDS | NEWS SUMMARY | TROJANS FALL, 7 TO 6; DRURY, FLANAGAN STAR | **Poland Spurns Warning by Russia**
THE MASTER OF THE WORLD | On Your Mark, Good Fellows! Yuletide Calls | WILL TALK ONLY WITH LEAGUE ON LITHUANIA ROW

another. In fact, the football flew all the way out of the back of the endzone.

Safety! Two points. And, suddenly, the Trojans had grabbed an 8-7 lead.

Hold on! Umpire John Schommer rushed in and ruled the play an incomplete pass, saying that Riley never had possession of the "intercepted" pass.

Southern Cal players, coaches and fans vehemently protested Schommer's decision and a full-blown rhubarb was on. But to no avail. Schommer's decision stood firm. Furthermore, with the disputed play occurring on fourth down, the Irish took possession out at the 24-yard line.

John Schommer, referee George Varnell and head linesman Walter Eckersall (who was also a *Tribune* sports reporter) were all from Chicago, while field judge Pinkie Griffith was from Iowa.

Final score: Notre Dame 7, Southern California 6.

The controversy raged for days following the big game. It was reported that after Schommer viewed films of the play, he admitted that he had missed the call.

"Regardless of what the records show, regardless of what the official decided, the Southern California team will maintain forever that Riley had control of the ball when he intercepted Drury's pass," said the Sunday edition of the *Chicago Tribune*.

The *Tribune* also observed, "The Notre Dame band did its best to supply pomp— but somehow Notre Dame's band isn't that kind of band....The gangsters and detectives were

SPORTS

The Los Angeles Times

SUNDAY MORNING, NOVEMBER 27, 1927.

NOTRE DAME NOSES OUT TROJAN ELEVEN, 7 TO 6

Drake in Smashing Rally to Beat Bruins, 25-6

CADETS STAGE RALLY TO WIN

117,000 FANS JAM STADIUM

Under Leadership of Wilson, Soldiers Triumph

BULLDOG PUNCH DOWNS LOCALS

TWO SCENES FROM A DAY OF FOOTBALL THRILLS AT CHICAGO

Blind West Point Cadets is Outstanding Star

Cook, Johnson, Nesbit in Great Exhibition

Rival Teams Score in First Period of Struggle

Scores Two Touchdowns for Team in Third Period

Midwesterners Run / Hog Wild to Run Up Score

Chicago Game Lacks Thrills Seen in 1926 Brawl

Drury and Flanagan Heroes of Day in Windy City

out in full force and called off their shooting until after the game.... A few, who didn't have tickets, were left in jail, but all the bigshot hoodlums were at the game behaving just like gentlemen."

The winning Irish led in first downs (11-8), yards rushing (199-137), yards passing (31-18), and total yards (230-155). Each team was penalized 20 yards. ND's Flanagan pounded out 124 yards in 22 carries (5.6 average), while USC's Drury gained 100 yards in 28 attempts (3.6).

The disappointed Trojans left Chicago late Saturday night and arrived back home in Los Angeles on Tuesday morning, a week after leaving for the game.

And facing the weary Troy warriors was still another crucial game— in just four days against Washington— but at least this one would be played on the home grounds.

The strong Huskies had lost only once (13-7 to Stanford), given up just four touchdowns, and in the last six seasons had built an impressive 51-7-4 record.

A Southern Cal win would mean a share (with Stanford) of the Pacific Coast Conference title. The Trojans, undoubtedly forgetting their devastating defeat in Chicago, routed Washington 33-13, and USC captured the first official football championship in its 40-year history of playing the game.

No team in 1927 finished with a perfect record, although Texas A&M (8-0-1), Tennessee (8-0-1), Illinois (7-0-1) and Minnesota (6-0-2) were unbeaten.

In "the only bowl in town" during this particular era, Stanford edged Pittsburgh 7-6 in the Tournament of Roses.

Southern Cal finished 8-1-1, Notre Dame 7-1-1.

1928

National Champions!

It was the Roarin' Twenties, and the nation's sports horn of plenty was overflowing. The United States Olympic team won the most medals in both the 1924 and 1928 Summer Olympics at Paris and Amsterdam. In single seasons, Grover Cleveland Alexander won 27 games, Rogers Hornsby batted .424, Babe Ruth hit 60 home runs, and Lou Gehrig batted-in 175.

Red Grange, "The Gallopin' Ghost," and the Four Horsemen burst upon the scene on the same afternoon during the decade. Jack Dempsey lost the heavyweight boxing crown to Gene Tunney. Bobby Jones won four U.S. Opens and two British Opens, and Charles Lindbergh flew the *Spirit of St. Louis* nonstop across the Atlantic.

It was also a decade of Gallant Fox and Man o' War, crowds of 100,000-plus at college football games, flapper dresses, a new dance craze called the "Charleston" and, of course, the Model A Ford automobile.

The twenties were the entertainment heydays of Barrymore, Berlin, Chaplin and Caruso...Fairbanks, Jolson and Keaton...Laurel and Hardy...Will Rogers and Rudolph Valentino...along with the Great Garbo and Helen Hayes...Annie Oakley, Mae West and Mary Pickford.

The music world of that decade gave us such popular songs as "April Showers" and "Ol' Man River"..."Rhapsody in Blue", "Blue Skies" and "Am I Blue?"..."You're The Cream in My Coffee" and "I Found a Million-Dollar Baby in a Five-and-Ten-Cent Store." All are still being played more than 60 years later on modern-day radio.

The decade had now reached December 1, 1928, and

Los Angeles Times

NOTRE DAME vs SOUTHERN CALIFORNIA

Three Horsemen

Nathan Barra, center, Southern California

Charles Boren, guard, S. C.

Russell Saunders, full back, S. C.

Frank Anthony, tackle, S. C.

Lloyd Thomas, half-back, Southern California

E. Collins

Don Williams, quarter-back, S. C.

Jack Brady, right half-back, Notre Dame

Francis Tappaan, end, S. C.

Harry Edelson, half-back, S. C.

Bill Seitz

Tackle, Southern California

Galloping Irish

Capt. Jesse Hibbs, tackle, Southern California

"Moon" Mullins

South Pasadena High School graduate, who plays full-back for Notre Dame

time for the third game of the Notre Dame-Southern California football rivalry.

In March of that year, the St. Francis dam in Los Angeles collapsed, killing more than 400 people.

In June, Amelia Earhart became the first woman to fly across the Atlantic.

In August, Joseph Scheke, president of United Artists, said, "Talkies (movies) are only a fad."

In October, the powerpacked Yankees swept the Cardinals in the World Series, and Ty Cobb retired from baseball after 24 seasons and over 4,100 hits.

On November 6, Republican Herbert Hoover was elected president in a landslide victory over Democrat Alfred E. Smith.

And, four days later, November 10 at Yankee Stadium, Knute Rockne gave his fiery and famous halftime "Win One For The Gipper" speech. His Fighting Irish then stormed from the locker room and turned a scoreless game into a stunning 12-6 upset victory over undefeated Army.

Historians say that the Rockne-Gipp bedside incident of 1920 never happened. It's a great story, though, and true or not, George Gipp will forever be an American sports legend.

Except for two missed conversions in each of the 1926 and 1927 seasons, Coach Howard Jones' Trojans would be working on a 29-game unbeaten streak leading up to its game with Notre Dame. Troy would also be 1-0-1 against the Irish, instead of 0-2-0.

USC's '28 schedule called for only one road trip, the fourth game of the season at Berkeley. The Trojans opened with three wins, 40-12 over Utah State, 19-0 over Oregon State and 19-6 over Santa Clara. It was now time

for the road trip to meet hated California, which held an 8-3-1 series lead at the time. The game ended in a scoreless tie. Troy rebounded by downing Occidental, Stanford, Arizona, Washington State and Idaho by an average score of 32-5.

The Trojans were 8-0-1.

Except for its surprise triumph over Army three weeks earlier, Notre Dame's season had been sort of a washout. The Irish edged Loyola of New Orleans (12-6), Navy (7-0), and Penn State (9-0), plus there was a 32-6 win over Drake. On the other side, however, the Irish had lost to Wisconsin (22-0), Georgia Tech (13-0) and Carnegie Tech (27-7)— Notre Dame's first loss at South Bend in 23 years.

USC was a 7-5 favorite to whip ND for the first time.

The Trojans pretty much hammered on the Irish that bright December afternoon before a capacity Los Angeles Coliseum crowd of 72,632 (the stadium wasn't enlarged until 1932).

On the day of the game, Coach Rockne received word that his two-year-old son, Jack, was at St. Joseph's Hospital in South Bend in critical condition with a peanut lodged in his lung. The operation was successful, but hospital officials said there had been only a slight improvement in his condition.

The Irish threatened midway through the first quarter when Manny Vezie recovered Don Williams' fumble at USC's 26. But four plays gained only three yards, and the Trojans escaped early trouble.

Later in the period, USC's Jesse Hibbs blocked a punt and Williams recovered for the Trojans at his 36. The big play led to the game's first score.

Coach Jones then turned the show over to Don Williams and Russell Saunders. Saunders carried to the 42, Williams to the 44, Saunders to Notre Dame's 34, Williams to the 25, Saunders to the 12, Williams to the six, then to the three, and Saunders scored from there. But the ol' extra-point bugaboo continued, as Hibbs' kick went below the crossbar, and the lead stayed at 6-0.

After the ensuing kickoff, the game moved into the second period and, on first down, John Niemiec's pass was picked off by USC's Francis Tappaan at the Irish 42.

Stanford Machine Crushes Army, Score 26-0

SPORTS

Los Angeles Times

SUNDAY MORNING, DECEMBER 2, 1928.

TROJANS HUMBLE NOTRE DAME, 27-14

IRISH BAFFLED BY VARIED ATTACK OF JONES' SQUAD

Touchdowns by Saunders, Apsit, Steponovich Give Locals 20-0 Lead at End of First Half

SMOTHERING NOTRE DAME'S VAUNTED AERIAL ATTACK

WARNER'S BOYS SHOW AT BEST

Cardinals Romp to Easy Win at Yankee Stadium

Great Crowd Sees Western Team Whip Cadets

Ten plays later, Troy was fourth-and-four at the four, but Williams threw an interception into the hands of Jim Brady.

Notre Dame ran three plays before punting out to its 35. Here came the Trojans again. Williams' pass to Lowrey McCaslin was good for 11 yards and sparked a quick advance to the 19. From there, Williams hit Marger Apsit, who caught the ball at the two and scored. After Hibbs' conversion, Troy led, 13-0.

It would soon be seven more. The Irish were second down at their 29, and Niemiec's pass was batted into the air by end Tony Steponovich, who also caught it and rambled for a touchdown. Hibbs was again on target with the conversion and upped the score to 20-0, as Trojan faithful were going absolutely wild with their big lead.

Notre Dame scored midway through the third quarter on a 51-yard run by John Chevigny and Frank Carideo's conversion.

Both teams added touchdowns in the final period. USC faced second-and-15 at ND's 47 when Williams threw to Harry Edelson at the 25, and Edelson sped to the five before being hauled down by Chevigny. Williams came right back with another pass, this time to McCaslin, for a touchdown. Williams kicked the conversion for a 27-7 Trojan advantage.

Notre Dame posted its final points late in the game when Albert Gerbert plunged over from one yard out to cap a seven-play, 25-yard drive following a USC quick-kick. Gerbert also added the point-after.

Final score: Southern Cal 27, Notre Dame 14.

Jess Hibs, captain and two-time All-America tackle, admires USC's 1928 national championship trophy.

This was Notre Dame's 300th all-time game, and its record stood an impressive 233-48-19 (.808).

Immediately after the game, Rockne went directly from the field to Central Station, where he boarded a train for South Bend to be with his ill son.

"This was truly a Trojan year," wrote Braven Dyer of the *Los Angeles Times.* "In the past there has been much ballyhoo about Trojan years but some never materialized. This season, without the advanced hullabaloo, the Trojans went to work and as Saturday after Saturday passed, they bowled over hurdle after hurdle."

USC led in first downs 12-5, ND in rushing yards 145-141, USC in passing yards 116-21 and total yards 257-166. USC was 7-for-11 in the passing game, ND only 2-for-13. The leading ground gainers were Williams with 93 yards in 27 carries (3.4 average) and Saunders' 69 yards in 22 attempts (3.1). ND's Larry (Moon) Mullins carried 11 times for 53 yards (4.8). There were eight turnovers in the game with ND leading 5-3.

Notre Dame's final 5-4-0 record was its worst since an identical showing in 1905.

Even though USC won the Pacific Coast Conference

championship with a 4-0-1 record and had a better overall record than California, the Rose Bowl chose the Golden Bears as the coast representative to play Georgia Tech. In a game made famous by the infamous "wrong way" run by Roy Riegels, the Yellow Jackets edged Cal by an 8-7 score.

Both Georgia Tech (10-0-0) and Southern California (9-0-1) claimed a national championship in 1928.

The decade of the twenties had been ragtime and jazztime. It had been an era of good-time Charlies and high-flying Janes, big spenders and superheroes. By the time USC and Notre Dame would meet again in a year, the nation's outlook wouldn't be so kinky.

1929

Oh No, Not Again!

From one end of the United States to the other, financial uncertainty and fear fed on rumor and cascaded into panic today. Frightened investors ordered their brokers to sell at whatever the price, and the stock market crashed. Dazed brokers on the floor of the Wall Street exchange waded in paper and tried to add up their losses. This is a day that will be known for years as "Black Thursday."

It is hard to qualify the losses, but they are believed to rise into billions of dollars. Thousands of accounts were wiped out as a record number of shares were traded. It would not be an exaggeration to say that some stocks were almost given away. Nearly 13 million shares traded hands.

The Wall Street Journal
Friday, October 25, 1929

The Roarin' Twenties were roarin' no more. The decade had come in like a lion but was leaving like a lamb. The good times were over—for about the next 20 years.

Also in the autumn of '29, Knute Rockne was fighting for his life. He was stricken with phlebitis in early October. And the painful illness came at a time when Notre Dame Stadium, Rockne's "pride and joy," was rising near the site of old Cartier Field.

Notre Dame's football team throughout the decade had been known as "Rockne's Ramblers," simply because they traveled so much. The Irish gridders more than earned that tag in 1929.

Meanwhile, out on the West Coast, Coach Jones'

PART TWO
SPORTS
MARKETS

Chicago Daily Tribune

Superior 0100

FRIDAY, NOVEMBER 15, 1929.

N. DAME CONFIDENT; U. S. C. ARRIVES TODAY

Southern Cal team had also picked up a new nickname—"The Thundering Herd". And the Herd was leading the nation in scoring when it went to Chicago for the series' fourth game.

Following Notre Dame's "disastrous" 5-4-0 season of a year earlier, Rockne boldly predicted that the '29 Irish would be one of his best teams ever. They opened the season at Bloomington with a 14-0 win over Indiana, and the "road show" had begun. Next was a 14-7 win over Navy at Baltimore, then a 19-0 shutout of Wisconsin at Chicago. It was on to Pittsburgh and a 7-0 blank of Carnegie Tech. A week later the Irish were in Atlanta, where they tripped Georgia Tech, 26-6. Back "home" at Chicago, Drake was beaten by a 7-0 score.

The Thundering Herd was next.

USC, defending national champion, opened with a 76-0 smashing of upstart UCLA in the first meeting ever between these crosstown rivals. Troy followed with victories over Oregon State (21-7), Washington (48-0), Occidental (64-0) and Stanford (7-0). Not only were Jones' juggernauts riding the crest of a 16-game unbeaten streak dating back to 1927, his team was still ranked No. 1 in the nation by the *Dickinson* system, considered by the press as the top football rating system.

But Southern Cal's old nemesis, the University of California, went to Los Angeles and pulled off a 15-7 stunner, snapping the streak and knocking Troy from its lofty position. The Trojans then walloped Nevada, 66-0.

Who replaced Southern Cal at the top? Notre Dame. Who was Southern Cal's next opponent? Notre Dame.

The records: ND 6-0-0, USC 6-1-0. The season scoreboard: ND 99-20, USC 289-22. Average score: ND 21-3, USC 41-3.

On Thursday before the game, the *Chicago Tribune* reported, "They took Knute Rockne to Cartier Field in an

Inspired Santa Clara Team Upsets Stanford — SPORTS — Los Angeles Times — SUNDAY MORNING, NOVEMBER 17, 1929. — NOTRE DAME DEFEATS TROJANS, 13-12

ambulance again today (Wednesday) and he directed the last hard workout the team will have before meeting the Trojans on Soldier Field Saturday.

"Rockne's ailing leg, heavily bandaged, confined him to his wheel chair. Rockne should have been home in bed giving his leg the rest it needs. Each trip he makes to the football field sets back his recovery a week or two, doctors

34

say. But there is no holding back Rock this year. Southern California is regarded as the most formidable foe on a schedule bristling with strong opposition. Rockne plans to go to Chicago Friday night and will direct his team from a wheel chair at Soldier Field."

Russell Saunders, USC's fine quarterback, told the *Tribune*, "One thing worth remembering, we are at peak form for Notre Dame. Ever since we whipped Stanford we have been pointing to this battle. We lost to California because we played bad football in the first half. It was one of those days when nothing went right. But it will be different tomorrow. If we beat Notre Dame we feel that we still are somebody in national football. It we lose we are just a bunch of bums with two defeats in one season."

The paid attendance for the game was officially put at 99,351, but it was reported that about 120,000 fans jammed Soldier Field on November 16 to watch the two gridiron powers slug it out.

Notre Dame received the opening kickoff and after a quick exchange of punts, USC took possession at its 48. Don Moses rammed for four yards to the Irish 48. Marshall Duffield then shot a pass straight down the middle that Marger Aspit grabbed at the 25 and sped untouched for a touchdown. Once again in this series, however, Troy flubbed the conversion, as Duffield's kick missed its mark, and USC's lead remained 6-0.

Following another swap of punts, the Trojans began in good shape at Notre Dame's 37, but Tim Moyniham intercepted a pass at his 31, saving the Irish from possible disaster.

Keyed by a 40-yard pass from Marchmont Schwartz to Tom Conley and a 17-yarder from Schwartz to Marty Brill, the Irish were first-and-goal at the seven. Brill then burst through for six but fumbled the football away to USC's Moses at the one.

Early in the second quarter from USC's 24, ND's John Elder threw a pass into the endzone which struck Conley's shoulder pads and popped in the air and into the hands of teammate Frank Carideo for a touchdown— a touchdown which didn't count. A forward pass couldn't touch two offensive players.

USC's Russell Saunders scored touchdowns in three consecutive games (1927-28-29) against Notre Dame, including a 96-yard kickoff return in 1929.

It looked like a Trojan kind of afternoon. Not only did they have a 6-0 lead, the breaks were also going their way.

But not for long.

Later in the period, USC punted to the Irish 47. On first down, Elder faded back and heaved a long pass. Bulls-eye! Touchdown! Just that quick. It was a 53-yard strike. But Carideo missed the conversion, the score remained 6-6, and that's the way the first half ended.

Just before going back for the second half, Notre Dame's locker room was the scene of another one of Rockne's patented and eloquent orations— this one from his wheelchair.

Don Maxwell of the *Tribune* was there and described it this way:

Rock was looking them over. Then he spoke. The words came snapping out. He had raised himself in his wheelchair.

"Go on out there. Go on out there, and play 'em off their feet in the first five minutes." The command was explosive. Rock's voice was strident. He talked fast. "Go out there, play 'em off their feet in the first five minutes." He was shouting. "They don't like it. They don't like it. Play 'em. Play 'em. They don't like it. Come on, boys, Rock's watching."

The doors of the dressing room shot open. Savoldi

sprang to the front. No one looked left or right. They jumped through the open door.

Notre Dame kicked off, stopped the Trojans, and Ernest Pinkert's short punt was taken by Carideo and returned 27 yards down to Troy's 13. Elder was stopped cold, but he came right back with an end sweep down to the three. Savoldi smashed to the one, then into the endzone. Carideo kicked good this time and the Fighting Irish had fought back for a 13-6 lead to the absolute delight of the howling mass.

Moments later, however, the throng sat in stunned silence.

Saunders received the ensuing kickoff and, according to Braven Dyer of the *Los Angeles Times*, "....came roaring out into the open, shedding tacklers like a duck sheds water and being aided by fine interference as he gathered headway. At midfield, Saunders cut over sharply, eluded the last would-be tackler and sped across the goal."

It was a return of 95 yards.

Coach Jones took a long delay before the crucial conversion attempt that would tie the game. He chose Jim Musick. Musick missed. The Trojans still trailed by a point.

Two time All-America Frank Carideo scored on a 53-yard pass from John Elder and kicked a conversion in Notre Dame's 13-12 1929 win.

Late in the game, the battling Trojans desperately drove 60 yards to Notre Dame's 29, but their passing attack wouldn't click, and the Irish hung on for victory, 13-12.

What a strange set of circumstances:

If USC kicks two conversions in 1926, ND is beaten, 14-13.

If USC kicks one conversion in 1927, ND is tied, 7-7.

If USC kicks no conversions in 1928, ND is beaten, anyway.

If USC kicks two conversions in 1929, ND is beaten, 14-13.

That scenario gives USC a 3-0-1 series lead over the Irish. But that's all it is—a scenario. In reality, Notre Dame leads the Trojans, 3-1-0.

It seems unbelievable that USC missed all five of its conversion attempts in the three series losses.

After leaving Chicago, the Trojans still had three games remaining on their schedule, all at home. All were also easy prey. Idaho fell 72-0, Washington State 27-7, and Carnegie Tech 45-13. That gave USC a 9-2-0 record, its third straight Pacific Coast Conference championship and its first Rose Bowl bid.

Notre Dame, now firmly entrenched as the No. 1 team in the land, had games left with Northwestern at Evanston and Army at Yankee Stadium. The Irish won both, 26-6 over the Wildcats and 7-0 over the Black Knights, giving them a perfect 9-0-0 record and the national championship.

"Rockne's Ramblers?" In the decade of the 1920s, Notre Dame played a total of 97 games—38 at South Bend and 59 on the road—in 24 different cities covering 14 states. There had been 11 games in the state of New York, nine in Illinois, seven in Indiana and Pennsylvania, four in Georgia and Nebraska, three in California and Wisconsin, two in Michigan, Minnesota, Maryland, Iowa and New Jersey, and one in Missouri.

When pondering the countless hours those teams spent on the trains, plus the fact that they were playing some of the toughest competition the country could offer, it's astonishing that they were able to compile a 47-10-2

(.814) record. The Irish were almost perfect at home during the decade, posting incredible 36-1-1 figures.

The Pitt Panthers took a 9-0-0 record to Pasadena for its Rose Bowl clash with Southern California. Final score: Trojans 47, Pittsburgh 14. USC's final record was 10-2-0 and 492 points scored. The 41.0 average per game was the most since Cornell's 49.0 average in 1921.

In the four ND-USC classics, the Irish led 3-1-0, even though Troy had scored more points— 57-47.

1930

"It'll Be Unfortunate For Southern California If They Make Any Mistakes"

The 1930 edition of Notre Dame football had a heavy load to haul. It was the defending national champs. It was still ranked No. 1. It faced another rugged schedule. And, if that wasn't enough, the press declared this club as good, or maybe better, than the Four Horsemen/Seven Mules team of 1924.

The Irish opened with a thrilling 20-14 victory over SMU before a crowd of 14,751 in the first game played at Notre Dame Stadium. The following week was the official dedication of the new facility, and over 40,000 showed up to watch their team defeat Navy, 26-2.

The next five weeks produced five more wins. Carnegie Tech was beaten 21-6, Pittsburgh 35-19, Indiana 22-0, Penn 60-20, and Drake 28-7.

The Irish were 7-0-0. But Rockne and his boys had three bona fide powerhouses that must be dealt with over the next three weeks— all on the road. At that point in the season the three opponents had already combined for a 19-1-1 record.

There was nothing to do, as they say, but take 'em one at a time. First was 7-0-0 Northwestern at Evanston. Notre Dame won, 14-0. Next was 7-0-1 Army at Yankee Stadium. Before more than 103,000 fans, the Irish battled icy winds, rain and snow and escaped New York City with a 7-6 triumph by blocking a conversion attempt in the game's final seconds.

The final roadblock was 8-1-0 Southern Cal at Los Angeles. And, strangely enough, the No. 1-ranked team

found itself in an underdog role against an awesome Trojan scoring machine.

In the course of the season, USC had walloped UCLA, Oregon State, Utah State, Stanford, Denver, California, Hawaii and Washington by an overwhelming score of 376-39, an average of 47-5. The highlights of Troy's campaign had been a 74-0 bashing of Cal's Golden Bears and a 41-12 stomping of Stanford.

But there was also a lowlight, and it occurred in the season's third game, when Washington State handed USC a 7-6 setback. WSU used the big win as a springboard to a 9-0-0 regular season, a Pacific Coast Conference title, and a Rose Bowl bid.

Notre Dame's rail schedule to California called for a two-day break in Tucson, where the team held workouts before crowds reported to be as large as 5,000, including the Los Angeles press corps.

Five thousand people at football practice sessions in Arizona to watch a team from Indiana? "Rockne's Ramblers", ramblin' all over the country, had long ago captured the imagination of the sporting public.

There's little doubt that this era's two most popular teams were baseball's high-flying Yankees and football's unbeatable Fighting Irish, popular in that they were either the most loved or the most hated. And each team was led by the country's most dynamic personalities of the time—Babe Ruth and Knute Rockne.

A big welcoming party awaited Notre Dame's arrival in Los Angeles late Friday afternoon. "Five thousand cheering alumni and team followers greeted the squad at the station, and the hills of southern California echoed their mingled co-claim of the Irish hosts and defiance to the Trojan forces," reported George Shaffer of the *Chicago Tribune*.

Rockne could "pore mouth" with the best of coaches, and he had been doing plenty of it all week, especially in Tucson. Upon his arrival in L.A., he was asked, "Who's going to win the game?"

"Anyone would be foolish to say that Notre Dame is going to win," he declared. "But my boys are going to play sixty minutes of football and I don't think we'll make many mistakes. But I'll tell you another thing, it will be unfortunate for Southern California if they make any mistakes."

There had been a gigantic buildup all week for the big clash between the best of the West and the beast of the East. Game day, Saturday, December 6, was bright and cool. Just right for the huge crowd of 88,000 which crammed the Coliseum.

Well, the big game turned into a big dud, for the favored Trojans. Paul Lowry of the *Los Angeles Times* described it this way:

"The Irish won. And how!

"In an amazing game, one-sided from start to finish, punctuated by spectacular passing and scoring plays, Notre Dame vanquished Southern California 27-0, yesterday, and swept aside the last barrier to the Hoosier goal of a second successive unbeaten season....Pulling the strings of battle from his seat on the side lines, where a year ago he was pillowed in a sick chair back of Notre

NOTRE DAME CRUSHES TROJANS, 27-0

RAMBLERS ROUT TROY WARRIORS

Jones Gets Warm Licking in Career at SC

Irish Look Superb in Game and Coliseum Tussle

O'CONNOR HERO OF GRID CLASH

Substitute Fullback Scores Pair of Touchdowns

Southern California Squad Completely Outclassed

BUCKING ALONG WITH THAT O'CONNOR PERSON

Pic-a-shop was snapped into the Trojans portion rather unconcerned by "Bucky" O'Connor acquitted himself nicely. Here is the Notre Dame ace smashing off a bit of yardage through Troy's line at the Coliseum yesterday. Brian Smith has made the tackle. Sader and Sbar of the Trojans are on the left, with Arbelbide and Musick at the right. O'Connor later dashed 38 yards to Notre Dame's second touchdown.
[Photo by Fred Colley, Times staff photographer]

ROCKNE HAS TOUGH TIME
Poor Bald Knute Stumbles Along With Makeshift Fullback to Wreck, Ruin and Whip Trojans

BY BILL HENRY

IRISH FORWARD WALL PRAISED
Lieb Credits Linemen With Capturing Contest

BY TOM LIEB
Loyola Football Coach

STATISTICAL STORY OF NOTRE DAME'S TRIUMPH

"ROCK" USES SHIFT, TOO
K-Noot Yanks Fedora Out of Shape as Ambling Ramblers Amble in Coliseum Tussle

BY CHESTER G. HANSON

COACHES SING IRISH MELODY
Visiting Mentors Laud Play of Notre Dame Team

BY FRANK ROCHE

TROJANS NOT ONLY ONES FOOLED BY K. K. ROCKNE

BY EDWARD LAWRENCE

Chicago Gets Irish Contest
CHICAGO, Dec. 6

JONES INACTIVE DURING GIGANTIC

IRISH CONFETTI FOR TROY

Dame's bench, Knute Rockne unleashed a powerful running and passing attack that baffled and bewildered the Trojans at every stage and far surpassed the efforts of the Four Horsemen team which beat Stanford, 27-10, in the New Year's Day game at Pasadena in 1925."

George Shaffer of the *Tribune* typed: "Notre Dame's brilliant football warriors, who haven't taken defeat since 1928, crossed up the football world by crushing the University of Southern California's greatest eleven by the amazing score of 27-0."

The game's statistics were as lopsided as the outcome. The Irish led in first downs 14-8, rushing yards 331-89, passing yards 97-57, and total yards by a wide margin of 428-146. The game's leading rusher was ND's Paul O'Conner, who had 118 yards in only 10 carries.

Notre Dame received the opening kickoff and quickly marched from its 20 to USC's 20, where a fourth-and-one pass failed. The Trojans' first play from scrimmage vividly set the tone for their afternoon of futility. Stanley Williamson's snap from center was too low and ND tackle Alvin Culver rushed in and recovered the loose ball at Troy's 19-yard line.

On first down, Marchmond Schwartz drilled a pass to Frank Carideo, who snagged it at the seven and scored. Carideo kicked good, and the Irish had an early 7-0 lead.

With only seconds remaining in the first quarter, USC punted into the endzone, and the ball was brought out to the 20. Paul O'Conner, on first down, broke through the line and raced 80 yards for a touchdown. Carideo missed the conversion, but the Irish now owned a 13-0 cushion.

A great portion of the Coliseum crowd was aghast!

The score remained that way until early in the third period. Notre Dame kicked off to start the second half.

Troy ran two plays and quick-kicked out of bounds at the Irish 30-yard line. Schwartz broke through for 11 yards, and Marty Brill added two more to the 43. Schwartz then raced 45 yards to USC's 12 before being hauled down by Marger Apsit. A defensive penalty moved the ball to the seven. A play later, still from the seven, resulted in Schwartz throwing a quick pass across the field to O'Conner, who ran in for a touchdown. Carideo added another conversion, and the score was now 20-0.

Late in the game, Notre Dame posted its final points. Starting from their 11 after receiving a punt, the Irish scored in only five plays. The big gainer was a 66-yarder on a pass from Mohler to Daniel Hanley that carried to USC's 21. Two runs by Hanley gained seven, and Nick Lukats scored from the 14. Charles Jaskwhich converted, and the game ended two minutes later.

Final score: Notre Dame 27, Southern California 0. It would also be Knute Rockne's final score.

Notre Dame back March-mount (Marchy) Schwartz finds rough going in 1930 scuffle. USC's Jess Shaw (35) aids teammates on the stop.

A huge celebration awaited the national champs back home. The Golden State Limited pulled into Chicago Wednesday morning just after nine o'clock.

"Immediately after arrival the players will be escorted to automobiles for a parade through the loop," reported Arch Ward of the *Tribune*. "The lines of march will be decorated in the gold and blue of Notre Dame by the south park board. Police escorts will lead the athletes through the loop....For one hour Notre Dame will be Chicago's guest. The team then leaves for South Bend, where the home town folks have prepared a welcome that will be second only to Chicago's."

Things got a little out of hand in South Bend.

"For the first time in the memory of officials, student enthusiasm over a Notre Dame athletic victory threatened to develop into disorder tonight," reported the Associated Press. "More than 1,000 youths milled about the entrance of a film theater intent upon 'rushing' the place in celebration of the Irish conquest of Southern California, and police reserves were called out to break up the gathering....A

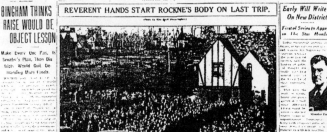

local bookmaker, who was reputed to have laid odds on Southern California, was cuffed about before the crowd gathered at the theater. A police squad, equipped with tear-gas paraphernalia, arrived on the scene shortly before 9 o'clock, and their captain warned the crowd to disperse."

Less than four months after the celebration, Knute Rockne was dead.

On March 31, 1931, Rockne boarded Transcontinental-Western flight 599 in Kansas City bound for Los Angeles to take part in a football demonstration movie. Shortly after takeoff, the plane flew into a storm, iced over, and crashed into a field near Bazar, Kansas. There were no survivors among the eight people aboard.

Rockne's tragic death was front page news all across the nation. He was only 43.

Rockne's head coaching career at Notre Dame spanned 13 seasons (1918-1930) and 122 games. His teams put a fabulous 105-12-5 record in the books, and his .881 winning percentage is *still* the highest of any coach at the college or professional levels.

What makes his record even more glowing is that he played top teams from all sections of the country— most away from home. Rockne's 13-year schedule called for

47

Notre Dame coach Knute Rockne holds all-time collegiate record for winning percentage (.881). He won four out of five games against Southern California.

only 48 games at South Bend and 74 on the road.

Just nine coaches beat Rockne. They were Bill Alexander (Georgia Tech), E.E. Bearg (Nebraska), Fred Dawson (Nebraska), Howard Jones (Iowa and Southern Cal), Biff Jones (Army), John McEwan (Army), Walter Steffen (Carnegie Tech) and Glenn Thistlethwaite (Wisconsin).

There would never be another Knute Kenneth Rockne.

1931

GAME 6

"The Glamor Game" Decides National Championship For Fourth Straight Year

Oddly enough, it was this same weekend only six years earlier that Gwynn Wilson, then a graduate manager at USC, went to Lincoln, Nebraska, to try to persuade Knute Rockne into a Trojan-Irish gridiron series.

What hath Wilson hatched?

In the short five-game span of its existence, this rivalry had seemingly grown bigger than the game of football itself.

Had Wilson, in 1925, envisioned such an instant and stupendous impact "his game" would have?

Had he envisioned three games settled by one point?

Had he envisioned an official paid attendance of 419,901, averaging almost 84,000 per game?

And had he envisioned three of the series' first five games deciding the collegiate football national championship?

Wilson, no doubt, had some big ideas in mind. But this big?

It was now November 21, 1931, and time for the series' sixth game, the first to be played at South Bend. It would be only the ninth game at two-year-old Notre Dame Stadium, where the Irish had attracted an average attendance of 25,871. But this was Notre Dame-Southern California, and the place would be at capacity— 50,731— for the first time.

Well over 100,000 tickets could have been sold— had there been that many seats available.

Was this a big game?

It was big enough that not one, not two, but three Los

50

Evening Express Sports

PAGE 12●   LOS ANGELES,   SATURDAY, NOV. 21, 1931

Sun Shines as Notre Dame, Southern California Clash

THE INSIDE TRACK	Harvard Is Favored Over Yale	Dry Field Promised Teams
WITH SID ZIFF	55,000 FANS	NEW BRUIN SIGNAL CALLER IN ACTION	Despite Rains of Past Days

Angeles radio stations would air the game back to the West Coast. On Friday, the *Los Angeles Times* reported, "Radio returns from the USC versus Notre Dame game at South Bend will be given to football fans through the public-address system at Westlake Park. Seats for 4,000 persons are available in front of the band stand where the broadcast will be made."

The game would also draw the largest radio audience in broadcast history up to that time—an estimated 10 million listeners!

Had Wilson envisioned such megafigures as that?

Heartley "Hunk" Anderson had inherited the Irish grid reins following the death of Rockne. Anderson won four football letters at Notre Dame (1918-21) and was named an All-America at his guard position his senior season. Since then he had played for the Chicago Bears, was head coach at St. Louis University for two years and a Rockne assistant.

Anderson's gridiron storm troopers picked right up where Rockne's had left off, extending a 19-game winning streak into a 26-game unbeaten string.

After a 25-0 win over Indiana in the season's opener, the Irish were held to a scoreless tie by Northwestern. Then came wins over Drake 63-0, Pittsburgh 25-12, and shutouts of Carnegie Tech 19-0, Pennsylvania 49-0 and Navy 20-0.

USC was next.

Howard Jones' Trojans were jolted in their opener, losing a 13-7 shocker to St. Mary's. But Troy rebounded with six straight successes by an overwhelming score of 215-6, including 6-0 and 19-0 victories over California and Stanford.

51

Southern Cal captain Stan Williamson puts brakes on plunge by Notre Dame's Steve Banas in 1930 game.

ND was next.

Jones, in the best spirit of "Scheduling 101," scheduled Open Date U, the week leading up to his team's trip to South Bend. Jones had also drilled his men behind closed doors for the entire two-week practice period. He remembered well last year's 27-0 humiliation.

The Irish were 6-0-1 by an average score of 29-2, the Trojans 6-1-0 by 32-3. Notre Dame had pitched six shutouts, Southern Cal five.

"Notre Dame versus Southern California! There is magic in those words," wrote Arch Ward of the *Chicago Tribune* the day before the game. "They conjure a parade of famous athletes, of thrilling competition, of colorless players blooming into headline stars...More than 150 newspapers from New York to Los Angeles and from New Orleans to Windsor, Ont., will be represented. Nearly a hundred radio stations will pick up on the broadcast...Notre Dame is conversationally rated a slight favorite to win but her rotaries are said to be a little timid when it comes to talking money...Tomorrow is another day, the Trojans have another powerful team, and there are thousands who feel they are about to make history."

The Southern Cal team, traveling in style aboard a special train with eight cars, arrived at Chicago's Englewood Station Friday morning. "They were met by an enthusiastic delegation of Southern California alumni and other Pacific coast colleges," said Harvey Woodruff of the *Tribune*. "After settling at the Hotel Windemere East, the players took a brief workout at Stagg Field, the sun kindly peeping forth for their benefit and surplanting the drizzle of their arrival."

That evening, actress Joan Crawford accompanied the team to the Chicago Theater. The team was bussed to South Bend on Saturday morning.

Howard Jones' brother, Tad, writing a syndicated column for the *Los Angeles Times* about the upcoming big game, observed, "Southern California sympathizers can hardly be looking for a victory. And should this by any chance come about, it could properly be called an 'upset'." Brother Tad predicted a two-TD defeat.

So much for all the talk. It was time to play ball!

Notre Dame won the coin flip and elected to receive, but after three plays was punting to USC's 44-yard line. The Trojans, keeping the ball for 17 plays, were first-and-goal at the three. Fumble! James Musick lost it, and Joe Kurth found it for the Irish at the two.

What a low blow for USC this early in the afternoon.

The game then turned into a complete standoff. ND's next five possessions all resulted in punts, while USC's offensive efforts produced three punts, a quick-kick and an interception.

Late in the half, however, somebody finally got something going. It was the home team. Receiving a punt at their 45, the Irish banged across the game's first score.

Running back Gaius (Gus) Shaver recorded both touchdowns to lead USC to an incredible fourth-quarter rally in 1931.

Steve Banas got it started with an 11-yard run into USC territory at the 44. Marchmont Schwartz then completed his team's only pass of the day, a 26-yarder to Charles Jaskwhich, down to the 18. Schwartz carried to the 17, Ray Brancheau to the nine, and Schwartz to the four, where it was first-and-goal. Schwartz was stopped for no gain. Banas cracked for four, or almost four. He was stopped a foot shy of the goal. It was Banas again, and the big fullback plowed into the endzone. Jaskwhich converted.

Halftime: ND 7, USC 0.

The Irish made it 14-0 on their first possession of the second half. Stopping Troy and forcing a punt, they began 53 yards away. Brancheau shot for nine, and Schwartz whirled around end for 15 to USC's 29. Banas then smashed through for a big gain of 26, all the way to the three. Banas got trapped on the next play and lost seven. Schwartz scored from there. Jaskwhich kicked good again.

Notre Dame Stadium was roaring with the big 14-0 Irish advantage. These gridiron heroes hadn't lost in three years, going all the way back to December 1, 1928 against USC. Now, the Irish fans were celebrating their "30th

straight game without defeat...."

Southern Cal took the ensuing kickoff and set in motion a 14-play drive that netted a first down at Notre Dame's 15. The next four plays lost six yards.

The frustrated Trojans soon had the ball again on a punt and, starting from the enemy 48, finally cashed in. On the 10th play of the drive, Gaius Shaver scored from one yard out, putting USC back into the game four plays into the final quarter. But Kurth slashed through and blocked Johnny Baker's conversion attempt.

"No! No! No! Not again!," screamed Trojan fans everywhere. "What's this conversion curse we have against those lucky so-and-sos! Even if we score again and do kick good, we'll still lose, 14-13! Drats!"

Notre Dame 14, Troy 6.

Southern Cal got the ball right back, this time at its 43, following another Irish punt. After an incomplete pass, ND was guilty of pass interference, giving USC a first down at the Irish 24. Orville Mohler pushed to the 21, Shaver to the 17, Mohler to the 10 for another first down. Mohler

MIDWEST STILL STUNNED BY TROJAN TRIUMPH

OLD HOODOOS GIVEN BOUNCE

Trojans, Bears Smash Hoets Pigh Bullion Victories

Baker's Final Goal Shivers One-Point Decision

Watches for Grid Heroes

Oak Gine Williams and young Baker, Trojan Same, and hereon, will be prominent in the fray of the historic Saturd Trojan flamon mottos molism Priday, starting. Oma Maple astonished and sinks.

THUNDERING HERD HEADS HOME FOR LOS ANGELES

Overthrowing of Notre Dame Wins Many Friends for S.C. Squad Among Big Ten Followers

MONDAY MORNING, NOVEMBER 23, 1931.

then lateraled to Shaver who scored his second touchdown of the game. Baker got his kick off this time, it was successful and the Trojans had pulled to within one, 14-13.

Southern Cal, now fired skyhigh, kicked off, held the opponents at bay, and went on offense again, this time at Notre Dame's 39-yard line. But Mohler fumbled, and ND's Edwin Kosky recovered at the 40.

The Irish knocked out a first down but were forced to punt. Schwartz kicked to USC's 27.

There were four minutes left in the game.

Mohler got nothing, and neither did an incomplete pass. Third-and-10. Shaver then faded all the way back to his 10 and unleashed a bomb. End Ray Sparling, racing at full speed, made a diving, desperation stab at the ball. Sparling caught it! First down at the Notre Dame 40. Even though the play gained "only" 33 yards, Shaver actually threw the football 50 yards. It was also USC's first pass completion of the game in 11 attempts. Mohler lost a yard. Shaver came back with another pass, this one complete to Bob Hall for 24 yards to the 17.

The clock was now down to two-and-a-half minutes.

Mohler slipped for no gain, but the defense was penalized five yards for offsides (this counting as a down), moving the ball to the 12. Sparling, on an end-around, lost a yard. Mohler's pass was incomplete.

Fourth down, game-to-go. Less than two minutes to play.

Coach Jones, not certain that Mohler, his signal-caller, was going for a field goal, rushed Homer Griffith into the huddle to make sure. Stanley Williamson, team captain, waved Griffith back to the side lines. They had already called the play. It *would* be a field goal.

The 50,000 or so souls were on their feet. Some were

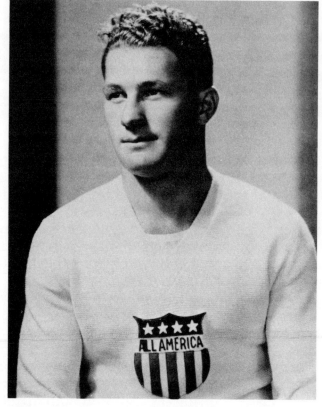

Johnny Baker's 33-yard field goal in the last minute capped USC's 16-14 triumph in the first series clash played at South Bend. His kick is still considered a highlight of Trojan gridiron history.

squealing and screaming. Some were stomping around crazily. Some stared numbly and silently into space. It was, most likely, too late for prayer, but some were trying it anyway, just in case. Notre Dame Stadium was a seething madhouse.

Mohler, the holder, knelt at the 23-yard line. Baker, the kicker, was set. Williamson, the center, sent back a perfect snap. Baker slammed the ball forward. Straight through the uprights! Johnny Baker had done it!

The small portion of Trojan fans in attendance were going absolutely mad, while the Irish faithful stood in dazed shock, wondering what had happened to their "insurmountable" 14-point lead.

Duke Millheam returned the ensuing kickoff out to his

35. Millheam, back to pass, slipped and lost 10 yards. The game ended on the next play when Gordon Clark intercepted a pass at the Irish 44.

Final score: USC, with 16 fourth-quarter points, 16, ND 14, marking only the second Irish loss at South Bend in 26 years.

The 26-game unbeaten streak was also history.

The conquering Trojans spent the night in Chicago, had the time of their young lives, and began the joyous and victorious ride back home Sunday night.

They would be welcomed as kings.

"Plans for a gigantic victory celebration, comparable in pride and spirit of welcoming ceremonies which have greeted heros of other battles on return to their native California today are consummated, for the arrival at the Santa Fe Station at 8 a.m. of the 34 Sons of Troy who last Saturday walloped Notre Dame's Fighting Irish in the outstanding classic of the year," reported the *Los Angeles Times*.

"When the Trojan Special comes to a halt it will be stormed by thousands of cheering boosters representing the USC student body, the Alumni Association, civic leaders, and citizens from all walks of life....It will be a demonstration unique in Los Angeles history....Headed by the famous Trojan Band, the entire student body is scheduled to roll up to the station in cardinal and gold decorated cars."

A ticker tape parade in the downtown area followed. It was reported that 300,000 people joined the wild celebration. Los Angeles had never seen anything like it.

TROJANS ACCLAIMED 'NATIONAL CHAMPS'

'My Greatest Triumph in 23 Years of Coaching,' Says Howard Jones

Washington, Georgia
Hurdles Ahead for
'Irish' Conquerors

By JACK JAMES
EN ROUTE HOME, SOMEWHERE IN KANSAS, Nov. 23.—University of Southern California Trojans today stood acclaimed as top-notch football team of these United States, as rated by the only system that pretends to any degree of scientific

Ray Sparling's Fight ✕ Proves Trojan Inspiration ✕ In Great Victory

ENTIRE SQUAD PRAISED BY HAPPY S.C. MENTOR

South Bend Victory Held Superior to Hawkeye Team's Great Win

USC still had two games to play, both at home. Washington arrived with a 5-2-1 record and was handled with ease, 44-7. Then, on December 12, a strong Georgia team rolled into the Coliseum sporting 8-1-0 credentials, losing only to undefeated Tulane. Troy hammered the Bulldogs by a score of 60-0, which still stands as the school's worst beating on the football field.

The Trojans, conquerors of mighty Notre Dame and champions of the Pacific Coast Conference, would meet Tulane (11-0-0) in the Rose Bowl.

Notre Dame, unable to shake the ills of its devastating defeat at the hands of USC, lost again a week later to Army, 12-0, at Yankee Stadium. How the mighty had fallen.

In the Rose Bowl, Southern Cal toppled Tulane from the ranks of the undefeated by a 21-12 count. Troy finished 10-1-0. Oh, that opening loss to St. Mary's!

Six officially recognized authorities of the era voted Southern California as the 1931 national champion. Thus, for four years in a row, the winner of the ND-USC game had been crowned No. 1 in the nation— USC in 1928, ND in 1929 and 1930, and USC again in 1931. Gwynn Wilson had indeed created a monster.

Even today, Southern California's victory over Notre Dame on November 21, 1931, is considered the biggest in the school's football history.

1932

Incredible.
USC-ND Winner Is National
Champ Fifth Year In A Row

It was 1932, and the hit song of the time was,"Brother, Can You Spare a Dime," while the slogan of the year was, "Hard Times Are 'Hoovering' Over US."

In November, Franklin D. Roosevelt removed Herbert Hoover from the White House by a 472-59 landslide margin, prompting the Associated Press to say, "Roosevelt's stunning defeat of Hoover came at a time when the nation is in a deep depression, a time of growing bread lines and soup kitchens, of bank failures, farm foreclosures and soaring unemployment."

In the winter of '32, the Olympic Games were held in Lake Placid, New York, Benito Mussolini met Pope Pius XI for the first time, and Charles Lindbergh's infant son was kidnapped.

Over 11,000 World War I veterans camped out in Washington, D.C. that spring, demanding a bonus for serving in the war. They became known as "The Bonus Party," and their camp site, "Tent City." Their efforts were wasted. The U.S. Army, led by Capt. Douglas MacArthur, routed them and burned their tents.

The summer months saw Jack Sharkey take the heavyweight boxing crown from Max Schmeling at Madison Square Garden; and out west, Los Angeles was bursting at the seams, hosting the Summer Olympics.

The World Series, made memorable by Babe Ruth's "called shot" home run off Charley Root at Wrigley Field, highlighted the Yankees' sweep of Chicago.

Both Shirley Temple (*Red-Haired Alibi*) and Johnny Weissmuller (*Tarzan*) made their first motion pictures in

1932, and Erskine Caldwell's *Tobacco Road* was published.

On the collegiate football scene, when time arrived for the seventh Irish-Troy clash, played on the late date of December 10, there were three teams with perfect records— Michigan, Colgate and Southern Cal's Thundering Herd.

Howard Jones' '32 edition was among the top on the strength of an awesome defense. His sporadic offense had sputtered on four occasions, but the defense bailed out all four. There were close wins over Oregon State (10-0), Loyola (6-0), Stanford (13-0) and Washington (9-6). But the other four games went Troy's way by an aggregate count of 115-7.

USC was 8-0-0, and the Irish were next on the menu.

But nobody had shed any tears over Notre Dame, as Hunk Anderson's boys had lost only once. Playing their first three games at home, the Irish smothered the Haskell Indians, Drake and Carnegie Tech by a 177-0 score. (Only 6,663 showed up for Drake, the smallest crowd that would ever attend a game at Notre Dame Stadium.)

Hitting the road for the first time, ND ran into a red-hot Pittsburgh team, and lost, 12-0. The Irish then defeated Kansas 24-6, and Northwestern 21-0. Navy was taken care of, 12-0, at bitter cold Cleveland Municipal Stadium before 61,000. A week later, it was on to Yankee Stadium and another shutout, 21-0 over Army, as 78,000 looked on.

Now, Anderson had two weeks to get his team ready for the long trip to Los Angeles and those rambunctious Trojans.

USC had surrendered only two touchdowns and 13 points, ND just three touchdowns and 18 points.

Notre Dame was favored. But only because of a betting battle cry of the time: "Never bet *against* the Yankees or Notre Dame!" Plus, it was said that the Irish had faced tougher competition than the Trojans.

On Thursday before the game, it was announced that the two schools had agreed to extend the series through 1935, putting to rest rumors that next year's game would be the last. Notre Dame had been thinking about drop-

ping USC and picking up either Michigan or Ohio State.

Depression? What depression! A crowd of 100,000 (93,924 paid) showed up at the enlarged Coliseum and watched the two rugged defenses butt heads throughout the afternoon.

Each team had eight possessions in the first half. Notre Dame punted all eight times, while Southern Cal kicked six times (three punts and three quick-kicks), scored once, and was stopped by the clock.

The Trojans' touchdown came just three minutes before halftime. Irvine Warburton made a fine 38-yard punt return to the Irish 44. Warburton, on first down, cracked for 24 more yards to the 20. It was Warburton twice more, to the 18, then to the 16. Quarterback Homer Griffith, back to pass, was sacked for a loss of five, bringing up fourth-and-11 at the 21. Halfback Robert McNeish, as a pass receiver, sneaked into the Irish secondary completely unnoticed, and sped for the goal. Griffith spotted the target, rifled one his way, and McNeish caught the perfect pass at the goal and scored. There was not a defender within 10 yards of wide-open McNeish. Ernie Smith converted.

NOTRE DAME INVALIDS TAKE TURN FOR BETTER
TROJANS SIGN WITH IRISH FOR 1934 AND 1935

Halftime: Trojans 7, Irish 0.

A big break in favor of USC led to another touchdown early in the third period. With the ball at mid-field, Griffith's quick-kick was partially blocked and picked up by ND's Mike Koken, who fumbled, and USC's Bob Erskine recovered at the Notre Dame 26. On third-and-nine, Griffith found a huge hole in the line and rambled for 11 yards and a first down at the 14. Gordon Clark rammed to the seven, then to the four. Griffith got two, bringing up fourth-and-one at the two. Griffith blasted straight ahead. Touchdown. Smith's point-after attempt was wide, but Troy's lead was now 13.

Midway through the final quarter, Notre Dame finally got its offense untracked. And it came via the air route—Charles Jaskwhich to Hugh Devore for 26 yards, Nick Lukats to George Melinlovich for 11, and another for 18—quickly moving the Irish to USC's 23-yard line. But the Trojan defense said, "enough," as Curtis Youel and Raymond Brown crashed through to drop Joe Skeeketski for a loss of six yards. Laurie Vejar fumbled on the next play, but picked up the ball, and threw a scrambling pass which Griffith intercepted at the nine.

Southern Cal punted out to its 37, and here came the Irish again. Lukats passed complete to Melinlovich for 25 yards down to the 12. But a dropped pass, a run for three, and two incomplete passes, finished off Notre Dame for the day. The game ended four minutes later.

64

Final score: Trojans 13, Irish 0. And the greater portion of the Coliseum's big crowd filed out happy.

Troy's defense kept the Irish backed up all day. Notre Dame's 16 possessions began, on the average, 78 yards away. Strangely enough, however, the losers led in first downs 11-7, and total yards 218-131. The two teams punted 25 times (13 by Notre Dame) and kicked the football a total of 861 yards.

Six recognized rating systems named Southern California as their national champion, while one chose Michigan.

Now, for five years in a row, the winner of the USC-ND game was crowned as No. 1— the Trojans in 1928, 1931 and 1932, the Irish in 1929 and 1930. Amazing.

Attendance-wise, it was a strange season for the 7-2-0 Irish. Their four home games averaged only 15,725, while their five road games averaged 61,368.

Southern Cal still had one game remaining, against Pittsburgh in the Rose Bowl. It wasn't even close— Trojans 35, Panthers 0— capping a perfect 10-0-0 season.

Notre Dame now led the series 4-3, and the scoring 88-86.

1933

GAME 8

A Tiny "Cottontop" Too Big For Irish

For the first time in the relatively short history of the series, Notre Dame versus Southern California was "just another game" played before "just another crowd."

Notre Dame, *mighty* Notre Dame, had sunk to the depths, and the Irish grid faithful across the country were screaming for the coach's ouster. Hunk Anderson, conservatively speaking, was roasting atop a red-hot stove. Under Hunk, it was said, "Notre Dame was learning how to lose."

There was an opening 0-0 stalemate with Kansas, a team which would also be shutout in its next four games. Then came an unimpressive 12-2 win over an Indiana club that posted only one win that year.

Horror of horrors! The Fighting Irish then suffered four straight shutouts, losing 0-7 to Carnegie Tech, 0-14 to Pittsburgh, 0-7 to Navy, and 0-19 to Purdue. Four blanks in a row? It's a school record that's still on the books.

The "streak" was broken, but barely. The Irish edged Northwestern 7-0, and this was a bunch of Wildcats good enough to beat only Indiana. Next on the rocky road was Southern Cal, followed by unbeaten Army.

While the Irish were wallowing in misery, the Trojans were churning out shutout victories over Occidental, Whittier, Loyola (USC's 200th all-time win), and Washington State, by a 141-0 tally. St. Mary's broke the shutout streak, but Troy prevailed, 14-7.

USC's first road test of the season was a journey up to Corvallis to meet just-as-tough-defensive-oriented Oregon State. The Beavers had also allowed just one touch-

66

Bill Henry
Says—

CALIFORNIA FALLS BEFORE INDIANS, 7-3; TROJANS SMASH NOTRE DAME, 19 TO 0

LENGTHY HEAVE IN LAST PERIOD TOPPLES BEARS

Norgard Scores on Long Pass

Los Angeles Times

SUNDAY MORNING, NOVEMBER 26, 1933.

As the Gael Blew the Bruin Over the Mountain

Boardwalker in Close Victory

FIGHTIN' IRISH OUTCLASSED BY WESTERNERS

Warburton Hero of Grid Game

down in their first five games. One would certainly expect this to be a low-scoring affair, and it was— 0-0.

USC next went to Palo Alto and scratched out a 6-3 verdict over California, and Coach Howard Jones' Thundering Herd was thundering along a 27-game unbeaten streak. But Stanford ended it a week later, 13-7, at the Coliseum. Troy then defeated Oregon by a 26-0 score.

It was now "Irish time" at South Bend.

USC was 7-1-1, ND 2-4-1. USC's average score was 23-3, ND's an incredibly low 2-7. A Notre Dame football team averaging just two points per game this late in the season? It was a statistic that Irish grid followers could hardly believe.

The official paid attendance of the series' first seven games had averaged 80,651. But in 1933, "The Glamor Game" had temporarily lost much of its glamor, as only 25,037 cared enough to show up at Notre Dame Stadium. It would also be the smallest crowd ever to see a USC-ND game.

There were two primary reasons for the paltry turnout— Notre Dame's sudden fall from glory, and the overall "hard times" endured by the entire nation. The resources for such frivolous fun as football were just not available for many people.

The game fit the doldrum environment as Southern Cal methodically punched out a nondescript 19-0 triumph.

"At no time during the contest did the Fighting Irish even feebly threaten," said John F. Gallagher of the *Los Angeles Times.*

Troy's consensus All-American halfback, Irvine "Cotton" Warburton, was just too much for the Irish. "The Cottontop", as he was also called, scored two touchdowns, and rushed for 95 yards in 18 carries (5.3). Warburton wore jersey number 13.

Jones, for some reason, didn't send his pint-sized superstar into the game until the beginning of the second quarter, but "Cotton" quickly cranked up. USC received a punt at its 47. Haskell "Inky" Wotkyns gained five. Warburton, all 5'6" and 147 pounds, then wiggled and wormed and dodged his way on a zigzag run of 39 yards to the Irish nine.

"As the teams lined up, a crashing roar arose from the west stands of 'Hold 'em Notre Dame.' For the next four downs it sounded like the Pacific rolling up at Long Beach," reported Gallagher.

The show was then turned over to "Inky" and "Cotton." Wotkyns went to the eight, Warburton to the five, and Warburton to the three, where it was fourth-and-goal. Warburton streaked around right end, was hit, but spun

Halfback Irvine (Cotton) Warburton scored two touchdowns and rushed for 95 yards in 18 carries as the Men of Troy blanked the Irish, 19-0, in 1933.

his way just inches into the endzone. Lawrence Stevens converted, and Troy led, 7-0.

It stayed that way until late in the third period, when USC received a punt at the Irish 49. Bob McNeish, who caught a TD pass in last year's game, threw a long one intended for Julius Bescos. The throw was a bit short, and Bescos was closely covered by Reyman Bonar and Raymond Brancheau. But Bescos went high in the air and outfought the two defenders for a big gainer to ND's eight-yard line. On third down from the three, McNeish tossed one into the endzone to a wide-open Homer Griffith. The conversion was flubbed due to a bad snap.

The Trojans scored their final points late in the game. Cal Clemens intercepted an Andy Pilney pass and returned 10 yards to the Irish 29. Warburton carried four times for 21 yards to spark a six-play drive, and it was "The Cottontop" scoring from the one. Stevens missed the conversion, but Troy still claimed its third straight win over Notre Dame.

Jones told the press afterwards, "Southern California played the best game of the season. I wanted them to win, of course, but I just asked them to put their hearts as well as their bodies into the game. I wanted the spirit that brought them that 16-14 victory on this same field two years ago."

Anderson said, "Warburton is the best back we have seen this year. He was the spark plug of a great team."

The winning Trojans led in first downs 9-4, yards rushing 164-107, yards passing 51-33, and total yards 215-140. Just as in last year's game, ND punted 13 times, USC 12. The Irish also had to fight 35 yards in penalties to the visitors' none. In the series' first eight games, Notre Dame had been penalized almost three times the yardage as Southern Cal— 310-105.

The series was now tied 4-4, and USC led in scoring, 105-88. The Trojans went on to defeat Georgia 31-0, and Washington 13-7, finishing 10-1-1, while surrendering only four touchdowns and 30 points.

The battered and bruised Irish, now with a 2-5-1 record and a mere 19 points scored during the season, limped off to New York to face Army's firing squad. The

Cadets were 9-0-0 and had given up just seven points. So here was an offense averaging 2.4 points per game against a defense averaging 0.8 points per game.

But there was an "unwritten rule" of this era that said, "Never bet against the Yankees or Notre Dame." And with Notre Dame playing at Yankee Stadium, maybe it carried double significance. Maybe it did.

Notre Dame 13, Army 12.

But even one of collegiate football's premier upsets couldn't save Hunk Anderson's job. It was his last game as coach at Notre Dame. Anderson's '33 team finished 3-5-1, the school's first losing season since 1888. His overall record was 16-9-2, a 36 percent losing ratio, which at Notre Dame "won't win" for any coach.

Like almost all coaches who follow legends, Heartley "Hunk" Anderson paid the same price. His biggest mistake was Rockne before him, his next biggest mistake was losing three years in a row to Southern Cal.

There was another major upset a month later in the Rose Bowl. At that time, the West Coast representative hand-picked its eastern opponent, and Stanford rejected such teams as Princeton (9-0-0), Duke (9-1-0), Pittsburgh (8-1-0), Nebraska (8-1-0), LSU (7-0-2) and Alabama (7-1-1). Instead, Stanford invited Lou Little's Columbia Lions, a 20-0 loser to Princeton.

Columbia 7, Stanford 0.

1934

The Coach's Little Brother Saves The Day

Elmer Layden, one of the famous Four Horsemen of the early twenties, was named Notre Dame's new coach in 1934. Since graduation, Layden had been head coach at Columbia College in Dubuque, Iowa, and Duquesne University in Pittsburgh.

Among the 63-member Irish squad was a substitute running back named Francis Layden— Elmer's brother.

At Southern Cal, Howard Jones was about to begin his 10th season as Trojan gridmaster. It had been a grand period, reflected by an 84-11-3 (.872) record. Jones had also captured five Pacific Coast Conference championships, four national championships, four wins over Notre Dame, including three in a row, and three Rose Bowl victories in as many tries.

It was indeed a high-flying time for USC football. But Jones and the Trojans were on the verge of a depression of their own. Most of The Thundering Herd had stampeded into history at last spring's graduation ceremony.

The Trojans handled three lightweights to open the season— Occidential (20-0), Whittier (40-14), and College of Pacific (6-0)— before the cylinders began to really gum up.

The next five games produced only a tie and four losses by a 62-8 score. But then came a huge upset of undefeated Washington, 33-0 at the Coliseum, leaving the Huskies in total bewilderment.

Notre Dame was straight ahead, and the Irish would be facing a losing Troy team (4-5-1) for the first time.

Outside of South Bend, neither had the Fighting Irish

71

Champ Avoids Puncher Pirrone

Teddy Yarosz, middleweight boxing champion, is steering clear of that Paul Pirrone guy. The Cleveland mauler packs a mighty wallop and he knows how to score with it. Mickey Walker was flattened by Paul recently, and Walker is tough.

IRISH AND TROJANS CLASH ON WEST COAST

| Indiana Cage Squad Scores 35-19 Victory | Crimson Tide That Will Roll Into Rose Bowl | N. D. Is 2-1 Favorite Over Southern Cal. |

Indianapolis Player Leads Crimson to Win Over Ball State.

By Jimi Harrold

BLOOMINGTON, Ind., Dec. 8 — Indiana University's basketball team hit its stride in the second half last night and defeated Ball State, 35 to 19, after trailing early in the game.

The score at half-time was 13 to 17. Indiana Led by Fred Frichtman, 6-foot 8-inch sophomore center from Indianapolis, the Crimson cagers

Both Elevens Out to Take Fifth Win in Annual Football Series.

By Paul Zimmerman

LOS ANGELES, Dec. 8.— One of football's greatest rivalries will be renewed in the Coliseum here today when Notre Dame and Southern California meet in their ninth annual battle. Each team is seeking its fifth victory in the series.

Notre Dame came in as a 2-to-1 favorite because of its 12-to-6 victory...

turned many heads. They were 5-3-0 with wins over Purdue, Carnegie Tech, Wisconsin, Northwestern and Army, and losses to Texas, Pittsburgh and Navy. Southern Cal was next.

Notre Dame's seasonal scoreboard read 13-7 on the average, compared to USC's 12-10. The West Coast press, however, reminded its readers that the Trojans had beaten only one quality opponent (Washington) all season.

For the second straight year the ND-USC game lacked its usual pizzazz, and the Coliseum attendance figures magnified that fact. The four previous series games in Los Angeles had averaged 78,725, but the '34 card would draw just over 45,000.

Notre Dame hopped on top late in the first period. Wallace Fromhart returned a USC punt 10 yards to his 49. Then came the play of the game, and here is the way Braven Dyer of the *Los Angeles Times* described it:

"Suddenly the Trojans realized that a long-legged individual was streaking like an antelope straight through the heart of their secondary defense.

"It was brother Mike Layden.

"Frantically they turned to chase him but those long legs were carrying him at blinding speed. Back far beyond midfield Shakespeare uncoiled the arm used by his namesake to pen immortal plays and fired a long arching pass with aim as true and fatal as any verbal barb hurled by brilliant Portia and bearded Shylark.

72

"Down at the 15-yard line Brother Mike reached into the sky, plucked down the pigskin projectile, hugged it to his bosom and scampered across for a touchdown that really meant the ball game."

It was a 51-yard strike from quarterback William Valentine Shakespeare, better known as Bill, to Francis Layden, better known as Mike. Fromhart kicked the conversion and the Irish led, 7-0.

Notre Dame's next series resulted in a first down at USC's 11, but the Trojans held. Getting the ball right back on a punt, again at their 49, the Irish clicked this time for their second score.

Layden hit for two to Troy's 49. Fred Carideo (whose cousin Frank Carideo scored in the 1929 and 1930 series games) rammed to the 46, and Layden broke through for 14 yards and a first down at the 32. Andy Pilney passed to Wayne Millner to the two, and Layden scored from

Number 80, big Don Elser (6-2, 215 pounds), halts USC's Cotton Warburton (5-6, 148 pounds) in 1934 action at the Coliseum. The Irish won, 14-0.

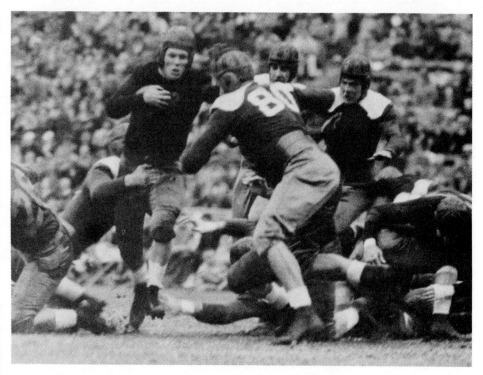

there. After another Fromhart point-after, ND's lead was 14-0.

Later in the period, Layden fumbled, and USC's King Hall recovered at the Irish 20-yard line. Coach Jones then went exclusively with his "WW" boys, Haskell Wotkyns and Irvine Warburton. Wotkyns carried to the 14, then to the 12. Warburton went to the nine, and a first down. After Warburton managed only a yard, Wotkyns hit down to the three, and on the next play was stopped at the one. Fourth down. Wotkyns crashed into the line again— but he was immediately met head-on by none other than Mike Layden. He had stopped Wotkyns literally inches short of the goal line.

The second half was hardly more than a game of "kick-back." The Trojans managed only two first downs, 66 total yards, and reached no closer than 44 yards of ND's goal. A rugged defense and Shakespeare's punting kept the Trojans backed in their own territory. USC's eight possessions in the last half began from its 20, 22, 14, 11, 20, 40, 46, and 20.

Final score: Notre Dame 14, Southern California 0, giving Elmer Layden a 6-3-0 record in his "rookie" coaching season.

The star of the game was Mike Layden, who scored both touchdowns and also kept USC out of the endzone with the aforementioned jarring tackle inside the one-yard line.

"Until yesterday's game, Mike had been a third-string left halfback all season, warming the bench," wrote Bob Ray of the *Times*. "It took a couple of injuries to make Coach Layden feel charitable and decide to give Mike his opportunity."

The game statistics were heavily in favor of Notre Dame. The Irish led in first downs 11-7, yards rushing 120-109, yards passing 109-24 and total yards 229-133. There was a total of 19 punts, 10 by USC. (The last three series games had produced 69 punts). Wotkyns, with 86 yards in 23 carries, was easily the game's leading ground gainer. Warburton, who rushed for 95 yards in last year's game, was held to only 16 (in 14 attempts).

Southern Cal finished 4-6-1, its first losing season

since 1915. The Trojans averaged just 10.9 points per game, their lowest offensive output in 16 years. It was a lousy year for USC football.

It was also a lousy year for some of the nation's most notorious and "Most Wanted" gangsters. In May, Bonnie and Clyde were riddled by a posse of Texas Rangers on a little-traveled road outside Shreveport, Louisiana...in July, John Dillinger, Public Enemy No. 1, was gunned down in front of a Chicago movie theater...in October, G-men wiped out Charles "Pretty Boy" Floyd with machine gun fire on a farm near East Liverpool, Ohio...and a month later, George "Baby Face" Nelson's body, pierced with 17 bullets, was found in a roadside ditch outside of Chicago.

Francis (Mike) Layden, brother of Irish coach Elmer Layden, scored both touchdowns in 14-0 win over Trojans in 1934.

Back to the lighter side of the news, even though the Rose Bowl had lost its exclusive status back on January 1, 1921, when little Centre College of Danville, Kentucky, trounced Texas A&M 63-7 in the Ft. Worth Classic, two of today's major bowls— Sugar and Orange— also opened for business after the 1934 grid season. Tulane topped Temple 20-14 at New Orleans, and Bucknell blanked the host Hurricanes at Miami 26-0.

Later that day in the Rose Bowl, 9-0-0 Alabama, featuring an end by the name of Paul Bryant, handed Stanford its first defeat of the season, 29-13.

Both the Crimson Tide and Minnesota claimed national championships that year.

Meanwhile, Notre Dame took a 5-4-0 series lead over Southern California. In points, the nine-year score showed: USC 105, ND 102.

1935

GAME 10

Wally Fromhart Caps A Career In High Style

It was like old times again at Notre Dame when Elmer Layden's '35 Irish team reeled off five straight wins to start the season. Next on the schedule was undefeated Ohio State, who had lost just three of its last 28 games. It was the first-ever meeting of these Midwest grid giants, and it had the undivided attention of the nation's sporting public.

Over 81,000 crazed fans jammed Ohio Stadium and watched the Buckeyes take a 13-0 lead into the fourth period. It became 13-6, then 13-12, with two minutes left to play, as Notre Dame missed both conversions. OSU recovered the ensuing on-side kick and only had to run out the clock. Fumble! And the Irish recovered at the Bucks' 40-yard line. Quarterback Andy Pilner, back to pass, couldn't find a receiver and scrambled all the way to the 19, where he was racked hard by three Bucks. Pilner didn't get up. He had severely damaged a knee and had to be taken from the field on a stretcher. There were 30 seconds left. Bill Shakespeare entered. His first pass was right into the hands of an Ohio defender. He dropped it. Shakespeare then threw a touchdown pass to Wayne Millner. Wally Fromhart missed another conversion. But who cared?

Notre Dame won the game, 18-13.

In 1951, sportswriters across the nation voted it the most thrilling football game of the first half of the Twentieth Century.

But a football, they say, takes funny bounces.

And there were some funny bounces a week later in

77

South Bend where Northwestern, with only a 2-3-0 record, pulled off a 14-7 ambush, breaking Notre Dame's nine-game win streak.

Another week brought another bruising game, this one against Army at Yankee Stadium. The Irish scored with only 00:29 on the clock but missed the conversion and settled for a 6-6 draw.

Exhausted and emotionally drained, Notre Dame still had to face Southern California in a week, but at least it would be at home. Also aiding the Irish cause was the fact that this would not be a typical Trojan team. These Trojans had won only three games (Montana, College of Pacific and Washington State) and had lost four (Illinois, Oregon State, California and Stanford).

On Troy's trip east they ran head-on into a blast of arctic air. Upon their arrival in Chicago, the team held a workout in frigid 22-degree temperature—the coldest weather any USC football team had ever experienced.

On game day, November 23, the country read about one of the strangest heavyweight fights ever, which had occurred at Boston Garden the night before. Jack Sharkey, a former champ on the comeback trail, knocked out an opponent known as Eddie "Unknown" Winston, within 70 seconds of the first round. After a near-riot of the 12,000 fans, Sharkey and his manager appealed to fight officials to permit Winston to re-enter the ring to "give the fans their money's worth." The officials agreed. Sharkey dropped "Unknown" twice more in the "second first round," and the fight was called.

It was now time for the 10th ND-USC classic.

Arch Ward of the *Chicago Tribune* wrote, "Probably no series in modern football has developed such widely celebrated players as Notre Dame and Southern California. Their glittering deeds marking the ebb and flow of past struggles spangle some of the grandest chapters in football history."

Braven Dyer of the *Los Angeles Times* observed, "Nobody back here (South Bend) gives the Southern California team any chance. Most of the critics figure Notre Dame is at least two touchdowns better...Not one writer has picked the Trojans...But I'm going to climb out

Halfback David Davis picks up yardage for USC. Irish prevailed, 20-13, in 1935 skirmish.

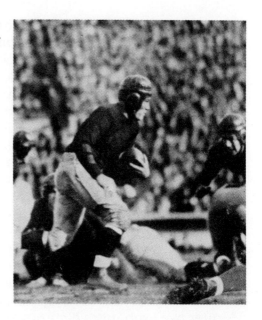

on a limb and pick USC to win, 13-7 or 10-0."

Both the Chicago and Los Angeles press reported that 50,000 attended the game, but the official paid count was 38,305. And what a game they'd see! This one would be a rock 'em, sock 'em affair in the real spirit of this young rivalry.

USC scored on its second possession after Clifford Propst recovered a Don Elser fumble at the Irish 19-yard line. Propst's lateral to David Davis on first down gained 11. Propst gained two to the six, and Davis scored from there. But on the conversion attempt, Max Belko's kick was blocked by Bill Shakespeare and Wayne Millner as Troy's woes is this phase of the series continued. USC had made only five of 15 conversion attempts against Notre Dame.

Later in the first quarter the Irish punted to USC's 17. On first down Lawrence Langley boomed a quick-kick all the way to ND's 17— a 66-yard boot. The strategy worked to perfection when, on first down, Mike Layden fumbled and Owen Hansen fell on it for the Trojans at the 18. But it went for naught. After an incomplete pass in the endzone, Propst dropped the football, and Marty Peters came up with it for Notre Dame.

After an exchange of punts, moving the game into the second period, the Irish were in punt formation at their 45. But Bob Wilke's kick was blocked by Ed Shuey. And what a block! The ball bounded all the way back to the three-yard line, where Belko recovered for USC.

What a break! What a play! The Trojans were on the verge of taking a two-touchdown lead over their heavily-favored foes, on their foes' home grounds no less. "What is happening?" pondered the Irish.

Davis, on first down, plowed into the line. He fumbled! And John Lautar recovered for Notre Dame.

Shakespeare, on first down, punted out to his 36, giving USC decent field position for another try. But Troy kept the ball for only one play as Davis threw an interception into the hands of Frank Gaul at the 14-yard line.

Notre Dame Stadium was going wild with all its good fortune, while it was the Trojans' turn to ponder.

After two exchanges of punts, the first half ended with Notre Dame luckily behind by only six points.

During intermission, the Rev. John O'Hara, president of Notre Dame, presented an honorary monogram, the first ever given to a non-athlete, to the Rev. Michael Shea, composer of "The Victory March," the school's famous fight song, which was first played on the campus on February 22, 1909.

The Irish received the second-half kickoff and, after an exchange of punts, began from their 39. Elser gained a yard. Shakespeare passed 10 yards to Victor Wojcihovski right at mid-field. Wojcihovski hammered to the 41 in two rushes, and Shakespeare hit Wayne Millner for 16 down to the 25. Shakespeare came right back with another pass, this one to Wally Fromhart, who made a spectacular leaping catch in the endzone for a touchdown. Fromhart also added the conversion, and Notre Dame had a 7-6 advantage.

Following another exchange of punts, Southern Cal drove 41 yards to a first down at Notre Dame's 28. But three plays gained only two yards, and James Sutherland was set to give his team the lead with a 43-yard field goal. It was blocked by Dick Pfefferle, and the Irish took over at USC's 44.

It turned out to be a *big* play.

On second down from the 43, Wojcihovski slipped the ball back to Fromhart, who threw deep, right into the arms of Millner. Touchdown. Fromhart kicked good, and the Irish were in command with a 14-6 lead.

What could possibly have been a 9-7 USC lead quickly became a 14-6 ND lead.

But the Trojans came back with a touchdown early in the final period. Glenn Thompson's 27-yard pass to Charles Williams put the ball at the three, and Thompson scored three plays later from the one. Homer Beatty converted, but USC still trailed by a point, 14-13.

Oh, those missed opportunities. All those missed opportunities.

Notre Dame passing ace William Valentine Shakespeare threw passes of 51 and 25 yards against USC in the 1934-35 games. He scored a touchdown in 1935 game.

Late in the game Southern Cal received a punt and moved to a first down at the Irish 36. After losing two yards, Thompson, going for it all, and victory, threw long. But that man Wally Fromhart stepped in front of the intended receiver, intercepted at the 10 and streaked all the way to USC's eight—a return of 82 yards. Shakespeare, on first down, swept around end for a touchdown against the discouraged Trojans. Marty Peters, subbing for the exhausted Fromhart, missed the conversion.

Southern Cal received the ensuing kickoff, ran five plays, and the game ended.

Final: Notre Dame 20, Trojans 13. But the game was much closer than that. The two teams had given the huddled fans little time to think about the bitter cold temperatures.

Wallace Fromhart, playing his last game for Notre Dame, caught a 25-yard touchdown pass, threw a 43-yard touchdown pass, kicked two conversions, and returned an interception 82 yards late in the game to seal Troy's doom.

This was the final game for the Irish, and they finished with a 7-1-1 record. But USC still had four dates remaining. The team left immediately after the game for Chicago, where they would board a train Sunday night for the long ride home.

There would be no celebration upon their arrival this time.

On December 7 the Trojans lost again, 6-2, to Washington. A week later they lost still again, 12-7, to Pittsburgh. That gave them a 3-7-0 record, and never before in the school's 47-year football history had there been seven defeats in a season.

Coach Howard Jones and his weary troopers later shipped out across the blue Pacific on a "Hawaiian Holiday," and while there, they would even play some football. Two games to be exact. USC defeated the University of Hawaii 38-6 and Kamehamella 33-7, bringing home a 5-7-0 record for the long 1935 season.

There was a mad scramble for the Pacific Coast Conference title that year, with UCLA, Stanford and California all deadlocked with 4-1-0 league marks. UCLA lost to

Cal (14-2), Stanford lost to UCLA (7-6), and Cal lost to Stanford (13-0).

Stanford got "the bid." And the Indians met SMU, which took the best record, before or since, to the Rose Bowl— 12-0-0. But Stanford's famous Vow Boys, now seniors and playing in their final game, pulled off a 7-0 victory. The Vow Boys vowed as freshmen *never* to lose to hated Southern Cal. And they never did.

After 10 ND-USC games, the Irish led 6-4 in wins, 122-118 in points, 2464-1793 in total offensive yards and had been penalized exactly twice as many yards as USC, 410-205. The Trojans, however, led in first downs 98-95, and in turnovers, 25-23.

Three months before the 1935 game, the nation was jolted by the tragic news that humorist Will Rogers, like Knute Rockne four years earlier, had been killed in a plane crash. Rogers and famed aviator Wiley Post went down in their small craft while touring Alaska.

1936

U-n-b-e-l-i-e-v-a-b-l-e

Notre Dame operated 94 plays, Southern California only 36. ND racked up 18 first downs, USC a measly one, and that via a penalty in the final period. ND amassed 406 total yards of offense, USC just 53. ND's leading back rushed for 157 yards, USC's 19.

But, unbelievably, Notre Dame did *not* win the game. It ended in a 13-13 tie, as once again Troy's failure to beat the Irish hinged on the simple act of kicking a successful conversion. If USC could go back and hand-pick six flubbed conversions, it would hold a commanding 7-3-1 series lead, instead of its actual 4-6-1 deficit.

A new feature became a part of collegiate football in 1936. It was the Associated Press' weekly sportswriters' poll. It would, in the years ahead, become a monster, but a wonderfully fun monster. It would seemingly be as much a part of the game as shoulder pads, penalty flags, fair-weather fans and grumblin' alumni.

The Irish won their first three games in 1936, topping Carnegie Tech, Washington of St. Louis and Wisconsin by a combined 62-13 score. During the same period, Southern Cal topped Oregon State, Oregon and Illinois, 88-13, before being held to a scoreless tie by Washington State.

On the Monday following the tie, October 19, the AP's first poll appeared in newspapers across the country. Thirty-five writers cast ballots in that initial poll, and all but three voted Minnesota as No. 1. Next came Duke, Army, Northwestern and Purdue, followed by No. 6 Southern California, and No. 7 Notre Dame.

USC then topped Stanford 14-7 but fell a notch to

seventh, while Notre Dame lost 26-0 to ninth-ranked Pittsburgh and tumbled all the way out of the Top 20.

Troy also disappeared, losing back-to-back games to California and Washington. Cranking back up its series with UCLA after a five-year hiatus, Southern Cal was fought to a 7-7 tie by the Bruins.

Meanwhile, Notre Dame defeated Ohio State 7-2, lost to Navy 3-0, and beat Army 26-6. That brought the season to November 21, and Northwestern, now No. 1, pranced into South Bend to meet the 11th-rated Irish. Wham-o! ND won big, 26-6, and the school's tradition of knocking off top-ranked teams had its beginning.

After a week off, it was time to head out to Los Angeles.

Notre Dame was 6-2-0, Southern California 4-2-2. On the morning of the game Braven Dyer of the *Los Angeles Times* reported, "Elmer Layden's squad rates a heavy favorite to scale the walls of Troy by a margin of anywhere from six to 20 points."

Nobody gave USC a chance. But why should they? The Trojans hadn't won a game in 44 days, and here were the Fighting Irish, fresh from a triumph over the land's No. 1 team.

It was reported that 40,000 tickets had been sold, but as many as 65,000 might show up should the rains stay away. The rains did stay away, and 71,201 found their way to the Coliseum that December 5 afternoon.

And what a whack-o game they'd sit through. But in the end nobody complained. Before the big crowd could say, "Beat Notre Dame," Notre Dame had a touchdown. Bob Wilke, who would be a workhorse all day, returned the opening kickoff 22 yards out to his 32. Keyed by a 36-yard pass from Wilke to Nevin McCormick, plus three McCormick runs for 13 yards, the Irish scored in 11 plays, capped by Wilke's three-yard burst. James Henderson blocked Andrew Puplis' conversion attempt, but a quick 6-0 score went on the boards.

Late in the second period the Irish were fourth-and-five at USC's 32-yard line. Jack McCarthy threw a pass that was intercepted by Gill Kuhn at the 10 and returned out to his 25. After a yard loss, the Trojans then electrified the big crowd with the ol' flea-flicker trick. Ambrose

85

Schindler broke through for 11 yards before being grabbed by three Irish defenders. Schindler then whirled around and lateraled the ball to Dick Berryman, but the ball hit the ground.

From this point, let the *Times'* Bob Ray describe what happened: "That Schindler-Berryman play was a planned lateral, but the Trojan quarterback said it was really a 'half-fumble.'

"'When I was trapped,' said Schindler, 'I heard Berryman call for me to lateral the ball to him. Just as I was about to throw, a Notre Dame player grabbed my arm. I half-shoved the ball, and it took one bounce on the ground before Berryman scooped it up and ran to the touchdown.'"

It was also reported that most of the Irish players thought the play was over when Schindler was caught. At any rate, it was a 76-yard touchdown—the first 11 yards by Ambrose Schindler and the last 65 yards by Dick Berryman.

(Editor's note: Undoubtedly, Berryman's 65-yard run didn't count as "yards gained from scrimmage," as the game's "box score" in both the *Chicago Tribune* and the *Times* showed USC with 34 net yards rushing, and 19 yards passing, for 53 total yards.)

Regardless, it counted as six points, and the game was tied at 6-6. Henderson missed the point-after. And it stayed tied.

Four minutes remained in the first half when Notre Dame received the ensuing kickoff. In seven plays the Irish quickly marched to USC's nine, where it was first-and-goal. Wilke drifted back and tossed a pass out to the left flank, but in shot Laurence Langley of USC, who intercepted in full stride at the four and streaked all the way, 96 yards, touchdown!

Henderson converted this time, and only 47 seconds remained before intermission. The underdog Trojans had snatched a 13-6 lead, and the Coliseum crowd was going absolutely crazy.

Langley's run matched Russell Saunders' (USC) 96-yard kickoff return in the 1929 game as the longest scoring play in the series at that time.

IRISH TIED BY TROY IN 13 - 13 THRILLER

Breaks Aid Trojan Cause

Notre Dame Outgains S.C., 406 Yards to 53, Before 70,000 Fans

'CROSS TROJAN GOAL LINE COMES HALFBACK WILKE WITH SIX POINTS FOR THE IRISH

Bob Wilke, hard-driving Notre Dame back, plunges over for a touchdown in the first quarter as Homer Beatty, Trojan back, hangs on. Southern California players shown include Nos. 20, Duboski; 73, Wilensky; 62, Hibbs, and 27, Davis (back to camera). Referee Tom Louttit at right. Wide World photo by Barrett Harter

| Abbott New Seattle Pilot | VERBAL WAR BREAKS OUT IN STORMY A.A.U. SESSION | "Troy Lucky," Says Jones | FEW THRILLS OMITTED AS TROJANS TIE NOTRE DAME |

Notre Dame had the option to start the second half and elected to receive. The Irish quickly reached USC's 39 but stalled, and Puplis sliced a short punt that went out of bounds at the 25. David Davis, on second down, blasted a quick-kick 64 yards back to the Irish 11.

On third-and-nine, Wilke rammed for 10 yards and a big first down at the 22. Facing third-and-seven, it was Wilke again, this time for the seven and a first down at the 32. Larry Danbom got one yard, McCormick broke loose for 12, and the Irish had another first down at their 45. After Danbom lost a yard, it was Notre Dame's turn to try the ol' flea-flicker. It worked to perfection, as Danbom gained 15, then lateraled to McCormick for 24 more yards, all the way to Troy's 17. On second down from the 15, the Danbom-McCormick combo clicked again, this time with a forward pass for a touchdown. Puplis converted, and the score was 13-13.

As the final period began, Southern Cal was fourth-and-five at Notre Dame's 35 and threw incomplete. But

87

wait! The Irish were penalized five yards, and the Trojans had their first (and only) first down of the game. But the next three plays gained exactly nothing, and they punted into the endzone.

After an exchange of kicks, Notre Dame knocked out a 16-play, 64-yard march to USC's 16, where it was fourth down. Puplis came upon the scene for a possible game-winning field goal. But Gene Hibbs blocked the kick, picked up the ball and rambled to his 37-yard line before being forced out of bounds.

What a game! Everybody was in a tizzy.

But the Trojans wasted the opportunity and were forced to punt. The Irish were fourth-and-eight at their 40. Puplis was standing in punt formation. Back went the snap. Too low! Puplis picked up the ball and managed to struggle back to the line of scrimmage.

Trojans' ball on Notre Dame's 40! Two minutes left in the game! And the big Coliseum crowd was reelin' 'n rockin' with all sorts of frenzied behavior.

Schindler, on first down, threw deep, and for a few breath-taking moments Southern California had a chance to pull out an incredible victory. But the pass was intercepted! Wilke got it.

Troy was crushed.

The game ended five plays later. Bill Henry of the *Times* reported, "Everybody got their money's worth out of the Notre Dame-Trojan football game because practically everything happened in a 13-13 tie that the law allows...A game with a 65-yard gallop on a bobbled bouncing lateral pass...A game with a run of practically 100 yards...Then there were the kids—hundreds of 'em—who rushed the field while the game was still in its thrilling last few seconds and proceeded to tear the goal posts down."

Coach Howard Jones told the press, "We were lucky, but it was an exciting game to watch." On the other side, Coach Elmer Layden said, "It was quite a ball game. No, there are no squawks from us. You have to be prepared to give and take in football. Sometimes the breaks go your way, and sometimes they don't."

McCormick set a series record with 157 rushing yards (only 13 attempts), topping the 124 yards by ND's Christie

Flannagan in the 1927 game. Wilke carried the ball 27 times (also a series record) and gained 74 yards.

Washington won the Pacific Coast Conference title in 1936 but lost to Pittsburgh, 21-0, in the Rose Bowl.

Notre Dame finished 6-2-1, USC an odd 4-2-3.

The final Top 10 in the AP's first poll in 1936 were: Minnesota, LSU, Pittsburgh, Alabama, Washington, Santa Clara, Northwestern, the Fighting Irish, Nebraska and Pennsylvania.

1937

Two Chicago Boys
Wreck Upset Bid

On a windy, rainy and cold Inauguration Day in Washington, Franklin Roosevelt, beginning his second term as President, said, "I see one-third of a nation ill-housed, ill-clad and ill-nourished."

In March, a devastating gas explosion at a school in New London, Texas, killed over 500 children. In May, the giant airship *Hindenburg* went down in flames in New Jersey. In June, Hollywood's first sex goddess, Jean Harlow, only 26, passed away. In July, Amelia Earhart and her navigator, Fred Noonan, were lost at sea attempting to fly around the world. In August, Germany opened Buchenwald, its fourth concentration camp. In September, Hitler reviewed 600,000 Nazi troops at Nuremburg in a massive rally amid an awesome display of military power.

But 1937 wasn't all gloom and doom.

Benny Goodman, "The King of Swing," was taking the country by storm, the Golden Gate Bridge opened in San Francisco, War Admiral won racing's Triple Crown, Joe Louis became the heavyweight champion, and that memorable movie of grand innocence, *Snow White and the Seven Dwarfs*, was playing at theaters everywhere.

When the first Associated Press football poll emerged a month into the '37 season, Southern California was No. 11, while Notre Dame was missing altogether.

But five weeks later, when time rolled around for the 12th ND-USC match, the Irish stood ninth, and Troy was nowhere to be found.

It had been a strange season for Notre Dame. After

90

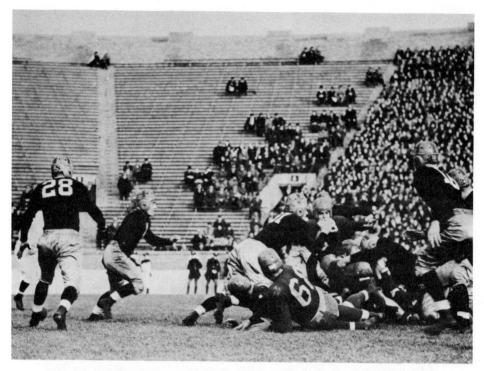

Action in the 1937 game at South Bend before only 28,920 fans, the third smallest crowd in series history.

opening with a 21-0 win over Drake, its other wins were by "close to the vest" scores of 9-7 (Navy), 7-6 (Minnesota), 7-0 (Army) and 7-0 (Northwestern). There was also a 0-0 tie (Illinois) and losses by scores of 9-7 (Carnegie Tech) and 21-6 (Pittsburgh).

It all added up to a 5-2-1 record, only 64 points scored, and just 43 points surrendered. That averages out to a lowly 8-5 score.

The Trojans had defeated College of Pacific (40-0), Ohio State (13-12) and Oregon (34-14), but lost to Washington (7-0), California (20-6) and Stanford (7-6). There were also tie games with Washington State (0-0) and Oregon State (12-12).

USC was all-even at 3-3-2.

Arch Ward of the *Chicago Tribune*, reported, "The 1937 battle between Southern California and Notre Dame possibly lacks the glamor that surrounded their contests a few years back when more than 100,000 packed Soldiers' Field and nearly that many crowded into the Los Angeles

91

Coliseum. Those were the days of huge crowds, huge receipts, huge spectacles.

"The game still might attract that many to Chicago's lake front, but Notre Dame now has a stadium of its own and there is no reason for moving the game from the campus, unless you are among the skeptics who contend intercollegiate football is entirely commercial.

"While some of the luster may be gone from the setting, the competitive fires still burn as high as ever."

Only 28,920 paid their way into the '37 game, played at South Bend on November 27. USC, an underdog by as many as 20 points, scored in the second period when Grenville Landsdell tossed a seven-yard pass to Gene Hibbs. But, once again against the Irish, USC missed the conversion, as Robert Hoffman's kick sailed wide of the goal posts. The touchdown would be the only score of the first half.

During intermission, Notre Dame marked its Golden Anniversary of football with a special ceremony in the presence of many old-time players who had returned to the campus as guests of the school.

Gene Hibbs scores in second quarter on a 7-yard pass from Grenville Lansdell, giving USC a one-touchdown lead. The Irish came back for a 13-6 victory.

It was late in the third quarter and USC was still clinging to its slim 6-0 lead when Notre Dame struck without warning.

"It was Notre Dame's ball, first down on its own 43, when (Andy) Puplis dropped back into punt formation," said Ward. "The ball came back on a direct pass from center and Puplis, who comes off his mark like a sprinter, set sail. He raced wide to the right behind beautiful interference. Observing that Southern California's left end had been swept out of the play, Puplis cut back sharply and blazed through the Trojan secondary so fast there actually seemed to be sparks in his wake. He went past one defender after another like a streamliner passing up a string of box cars. There he was and there he went, with nothing but chalk lines streaming out behind him and nothing but clear, uncluttered sunshine ahead."

It was a run of 58 yards to tie the score. And it remained 6-6 when USC's Charles Williams blocked Puplis' conversion attempt. At this point in the series there had been a total of 42 touchdowns, but only 23 conversions.

Early in the final period USC was first down at Notre Dame's 22, but here was that man Puplis again. He intercepted a Landsdell pass at his 12-yard line.

On third-and-five at the 17, halfback Mario Tonelli broke through the line and raced 70 yards to Troy's 13 before being overhauled by Owen Hansen, a shot putter on the track team. A defensive penalty moved the ball to the eight, and Tonelli went through a huge hole for a touchdown. Puplis converted, and the Irish finally had the lead, 13-6.

Notre Dame threatened again late in the game, reaching USC's 14, but Harold Gottsacker, after driving to the five, fumbled to William Sangster.

In completing its 50th year of football, Notre Dame had posted a 293-65-24 record (.798). Only 65 losses in 50 years.

USC led in first downs 12-9, but the winning Irish were out front in yards rushing 284-136, yards passing 27-19, and total yards by a wide margin of 311-155. Puplis and Tonelli, both from Chicago, were virtually even

Chicago Sunday Tribune

THE **WORLD'S** GREATEST NEWSPAPER

NOVEMBER 28, 1937.

A ★★

ARMY WINS, 6-0; NOTRE DAME BEATS U.S.C., 13-6

AUSTIN HIGH CONQUERS LEO, 26 TO 0, BEFORE RECORD CROWD

A TROJAN SCORING THRUST AND AN IRISH POWER PLAY

with their afternoon's offensive output. Each carried the ball only seven times, with Puplis gaining 90 yards and Tonelli 89. Puplis had attended Harrison Technical High School and Tonelli De Paul Academy.

In the last two series games, even though Notre Dame had outgained the Trojans 717 yards to only 208, the Irish had scored just seven more points— 26-19.

After leaving South Bend, USC faced another game in a week, which resulted in a 19-13 win over UCLA, and a final 4-4-2 season. (The last two seasons had resulted in a strange 8-6-5 record.)

With the addition of the Sun Bowl (two years ago) and the Cotton Bowl (last year), the ever-growing list of post-season games had now reached five. It would be a good year for West Coast teams, as California shut out Alabama 13-0 in the Rose and Santa Clara blanked LSU 6-0 in the Sugar. Other bowl winners were Auburn, Rice and West Virginia.

The AP's final top five teams in '37 were Pittsburgh, California, Fordham, Alabama and Minnesota. Notre Dame and Santa Clara tied for ninth.

94

1938

GAME 13

"A Notre Dame Quarterback Is Always Right. And That Is That."

Elmer Layden was beginning the fifth season as Notre Dame coach, and even though his Irish teams had averaged only 12.7 points per game, he had pieced together a 25-8-3 record. That's winning at a .736 clip but still is not quite what lovers of ND football fully expect.

Finally running up a big number on an opponent, Layden opened with a 52-0 trouncing of Kansas. The Irish then defeated Georgia Tech and Illinois by 14-6 scores, Carnegie Tech 7-0, Army 19-7 and Navy 15-0, which impressed the pollsters enough to push ND to No. 2 behind TCU.

The next Saturday, November 12, the Irish blanked No. 12 Minnesota 19-0 and, despite TCU's 28-6 win over Texas, Notre Dame went atop the poll. Then came a 9-7 edging of 16th-ranked Northwestern.

Southern Cal was next, in two weeks, at Los Angeles.

The Trojans lost a season opener for only the second time in 30 years, dropping a 19-7 decision to Alabama at the Coliseum. But six straight victories followed, including wins over Ohio State, Stanford and California, and Troy had worked its way up to No. 9.

But on November 12, USC journeyed to Seattle to meet a Washington team with only one win. The Huskies, catching their visitors looking ahead to UCLA and Notre Dame, pulled off a 7-6 shocker. Coach Howard Jones regrouped his troops and walloped the Bruins by a 42-7 score.

It would be No. 1 Notre Dame versus No. 8 Southern California. Suddenly the "glamor" had returned to "The

95

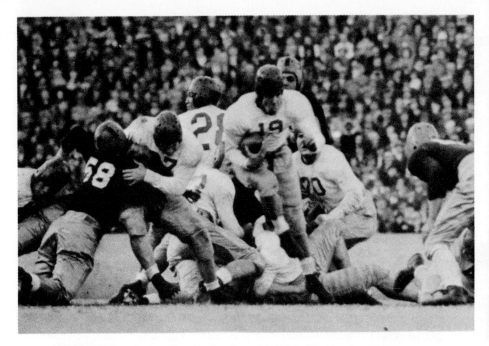

USC's Oliver Day (19) cracks through Irish line in the 1938 game at the Coliseum before a crowd of over 97,000. Other USC players are tackle Ray George (28), guards Harry Smith (70) and Amerigo Tonelli (42) and Notre Dame guard James McGoldrick (58). The Trojans won, 13-0.

Glamor Game," and over 97,000 fans, hopped-up with excitement, poured into the Coliseum that December 3 afternoon for the series' 13th game.

Nothing happened in the first period—except eight punts, one quick-kick and one first down (by ND). And the same type of play continued into the second quarter— four more punts, another quick-kick and a lost fumble by each team.

Finally, late in the period, things began to happen. USC registered its first first down during a 56-yard drive down to Notre Dame's 16, but Phil Gaspar missed a field goal attempt just three minutes before intermission.

That set in motion one of the strangest decisions in series history.

The Irish took possession at their 20 following the missed kick. On first down Mario Tonelli broke off a run of 23 yards out to the 43. Bob Saggau was stopped for no gain. Tonelli, back to pass, was sacked by Gaspar at the

TROJANS vs. IRISH

MICKEY ANDERSON   GRENVILLE LANSDELL   BILL SANGSTER

JACK BANTA

PHIL GASPAR

AL KRUEGER

RAY GEORGE

STEVE SITKO

JOE BEINOR

PAUL KELL

JOE THESING

Los Angeles Times Sports

C   SATURDAY MORNING, DECEMBER 3, 1938.

Roughriders Win, 13 to 12

Roosevelt Capitalizes on Breaks to Trim Fremont in Play-off

BY CARL BLUME

FAVORED FIGHTIN' IRISH TACKLE TROY TODAY

Undefeated Notre Dame Team Due to Lure 100,000 to Coliseum for Grid Classic

Ramblers Set for Trojans

Coach Elmer Layden Says Irish in Top Shape for Game

Big Ten Mum on Rose Bowl Bid Monopoly

CHICAGO, Dec. 2 (P)—

LINE-UPS FOR TODAY'S GAME

Season's Records of Trojans, Ramblers

Past Scores of Trojan, Irish Games

Facts and Figures on Today's Game

97

28, a big loss of 15 yards. Earl Brown gained three, bringing up fourth-and-22.

Less than a minute remained in the first half, and Saggau went back in punt formation. But Saggau, for some unknown reason, decided to run with the ball instead. He did gain eight yards on the surprise play, but it left his team still 14 yards shy of a first down. USC took over at ND's 39.

Quarterback Ollie Day ran for nine. A penalty lost five back to the 36. Day threw long intended for John Stonebraker, but it was too long. Day threw long again, this time to Al "Antelope" Krueger. Antelope caught the ball at the nine and raced in for the touchdown. Only five seconds were left on the clock. Gaspar missed the conversion.

Had the Trojans not scored, Notre Dame's decision not to punt would have forever been forgotten. But the Trojans did score.

Braven Dyer of the *Los Angeles Times* wrote, "It was a costly and utterly inexcusable mistake made by the supposedly invincible lads from South Bend...The Irish took the ball and were guilty of a boner seldom seen in high school competition...It was dumb strategy and Elmer Layden fairly jumped out of his boots on the sidelines."

Saggau, on the ensuing kickoff, sped by 10 Troy defenders and was headed for a touchdown but was tripped up by USC's "last chance"— Ollie Day—at midfield.

Halftime: Trojans 6, Irish 0.

The third quarter settled back into more punts and another Notre Dame first down. Then, early in the final period, USC scored again. Notre Dame's Milton Piepul fumbled, and James Jones recovered at the Irish 35.

Bill Anderson threw to Jones at the 25 for a first down. Anderson carried to the 23, Jack Banta to the 19, Anderson to the 16, then to the 14 and another first down. Banta rammed it down to the 10. On the next play he was stopped for no gain. Anderson hit to the five, where it was fourth-and-one. Banta got it, with a yard to spare. Anderson scored on the next play. Gaspar kicked good.

Notre Dame immediately marched to a first down at USC's 16 but, on fourth down from the 14, Saggau's pass was intercepted by Jones at the goal line and returned to his 30. It was ND's final threat.

Final score: Southern California 13, Notre Dame 0. The No. 8 team had upset the No. 1 team.

The game produced only 11 first downs (6 by USC), 293 total yards of offense (151 by USC), and 24 punts (13 by USC). In fact, the teams kicked the ball over 900 yards for the afternoon.

As for that controversial non-punt decision, it was finally sifted out that Irish quarterback Steve Sitko had called the play. After the game, the press naturally questioned Coach Layden about it, and he simply said, "A Notre Dame quarterback is always right. And that is that."

The defeat cost Notre Dame the 1938 national championship. Two days after the Irish lost to the Trojans the final AP poll came out and TCU was voted No. 1, followed by Tennessee, Duke, Oklahoma, the Irish, Carnegie Tech and then the Trojans, coming in at No. 7.

Southern Cal and California were all even in the Pacific Coast Conference wars, each with 6-1-0 records, with the Rose Bowl nod going to the Trojans. They met a "perfect" Duke team— nine wins, no losses, no ties and no points allowed. Troy smashed all the streaks, but barely. The Blue Devils led 3-0, until 40 seconds from the end, when Doyle Nave, a fourth-string quarterback, threw a 19-yard touchdown pass to Al Krueger, capping a 61-yard drive. USC won 7-3.

On the same day as the 1938 ND-USC game, Glenn "Pop" Warner, 67, was in Gainesville, Fla., ending a 44-year coaching career. His Temple Owls defeated the University of Florida 20-12, giving him 313 all-time victories, which was a record at the time. Amos Alonzo Stagg, 76, was coaching at College of Pacific in Stockton and had completed his 48th year of coaching. Stagg had 284 wins.

After 13 ND-USC battles the Irish led 7-5-1, while the Trojans held a slight advantage in touchdowns, 23-22, and in overall scoring, 150-148.

1939

GAME 14

Troy's Last Hurrah—For Awhile

Each passing month brought more and more dreadful news from Europe. In the spring of 1939, Adolf Hitler rode triumphantly into Prague, Czechoslovakia. By late summer, Hitler and Stalin, strange bedfellows indeed, had signed a nonaggression treaty. On the morning of September 1, the Nazis invaded Poland, prompting England and France to declare war on Germany. Russia invaded Finland a month later. Meanwhile, the British government reported "tortures and atrocities beyond imagination taking place in Nazi concentration camps."

World War II was officially on.

Things on the home front were quiet. Dr. James Naismith, the inventor of basketball, bitterly denounced "his game" as being too rough as it was then being played. "The World of Tomorrow" World's Fair opened in New York. Robert Taylor, 27, and Barbara Stanwyck, 31, were married in San Diego. Lou Gehrig made his famous "I'm the luckest man alive" speech at Yankee Stadium before 62,000 teary-eyed fans.

President Roosevelt changed Thanksgiving Day from the last Thursday in November to the third Thursday. It was said, "While retailers welcome the change, it gives football schedulers a headache. Their big day of games is now a mere Thursday in November." It was the holiday's first change since 1864.

Two classic movies premiered in 1939— Gone with the Wind and Judy Garland's The Wizard of Oz.

The first NCAA Basketball Tournament was held that year, and Oregon of the Pacific Coast Conference defeated

Wet, Cold Field for U. S. C.-Irish

CAN THE ROSE BOWL HEROES • REPEAT AGAINST • NOTRE DAME'S IRISH TODAY

Trojans Rated 5-6 Favorite In Big Game

Bruin-Beaver Game Is Rated Toss-Up

Parting of the Ways
Taylor-Stanwyck Split on Irish, Trojan Game

U. C. L. A. Faces Tough Test On Grid

BARBARA STANWYCK
"Come on you boob"

ROBERT TAYLOR
Rooting for S. C.

"Antelope Al" Krueger, pictured here grabbing one of Nave's passes out of this air...has featured Trojan workouts en route back to Notre Dame. The work of the "touchdown twins" has set accompanying fans to buzzing over what they'll do today.

Big Ten Title Is Goal for Ohio State

Schiechl Named All-American
By Movie News

Doyle Nave, above, hurled four completed passes to Al Krueger, on the opposite end of this pitching picture, and as a result the Trojans beat Duke in the Rose Bowl. Today the Trojan hopes were that he would again pitch the Trojans to victory, this time against Notre Dame at South Bend.

Maryland
Coach Resigns

Duquesne On the Short End

Victorious Trojans Home Tomorrow

AS CAMERA CAUGHT TROJAN WIN OVER IRISH

Iowa Prison Eleven Drops Game to Pros

Injuries Hurt Troy's Chances Against Huskies
By GEORGE T. DAVIS

Work Started On New Race Track

Here's Granny Lansdell, the Trojan quarterback, who electrified some 56,000 people at the Notre Dame Stadium Saturday with his brilliant runs, taking off for a six-yard gain in the first quarter through the Irish line. Identified Trojans are (78) Lansdell with ball; Bob Robertson (28), Al Krueger (42), Bob Winslow (73), Ed Dempsey (80) and Ben Sohn (55). Lansdell was All-American in the game.

FOR SAKE OF SPORT
Sutherland, Layden Hail Troy Eleven

Irish Coach Gives Praise To Phillips

Big Ten Teams Superiority Challenged

Army, Navy 100,000 Witnesses

Gonzaga Trims Portland

Texas at San Francisco, Oklahoma at Philadelphia and Ohio State at Evanston, Ill., to win the championship. In baseball the Yankees won their fourth straight World Series with a sweep of Cincinnait. Also of note, two nights before the '39 ND-USC game, the Los Angeles Bulldogs buried the Dayton Bombers in an American League Football game. The score was 65-0.

Six weeks after collegiate football's opening bell, the season had been good to both Notre Dame and Southern California.

The Irish scratched out close wins over Purdue (3-0), Georgia Tech (17-14), SMU (20-19), Navy (14-7), Carnegie Tech (7-6), and Army (14-0).

The Trojans opened with a 7-7 tie against Oregon but then cracked Washington State, Illinois, California and Oregon State by a score of 98-7.

The top four teams at this point, according to the Associated Press poll, were Tennessee, Texas A&M, the Trojans and the Irish.

The following week, however, ND lost 7-6 to the strong Iowa Hawkeyes, while USC stuffed Stanford by a 33-0 count. Troy moved up to No. 3, the Irish fell to No. 9.

The next Saturday found the Trojans in Los Angeles with nothing to do except think about their next opponent— Notre Dame in a week at South Bend.

At the same time, the Irish were struggling to squeak out another victory, 7-0 over Northwestern.

Notre Dame had scored only 12 touchdowns and was averaging just 11.0 points per game but owned a 7-1-0 record. The reason, of course, was that the Irish had given up a mere eight touchdowns and 6.6 points. Southern Cal, on the other hand, was 5-0-1 by an average score of 23-2.

USC was ranked No. 4, the Irish stood No. 7.

Almost 55,000 crammed Notre Dame Stadium under dreary, wet skies to watch the school's 400th all-time football game. They would also witness still another grand affair which this rivalry had become famous for staging. This one wouldn't be decided until two minutes from the end.

The Trojans scored on their first possession, moving

102

67 yards in 12 plays and gaining five first downs. Grenville Lansdell carried six times for 24 yards, Robert Peoples had 21 yards in three attempts, and Lansdell completed a 10-yard pass to Bill Fisk. Lansdell scored from the two to complete the impressive drive. Phil Gaspar missed the conversion.

USC immediately got the ball back when Robert Hoffman intercepted a pass at Notre Dame's 42. But nothing came of the big break, and the game settled into a punting duel.

Midway through the second quarter Troy had the Irish backed deep and received a punt at Notre Dame's 33. Eight plays had USC in perfect shape with a first down at the one, but Doyle Nave fumbled into the endzone for a touchback.

With only two minutes left in the half, however, it was now USC backed to its one. Ambrose Schindler punted out to his 30. Two straight sacks sent the Irish back to the 41, where it was third-and-21. Harry Stevenson then passed eight yards to Steve Sitko and 13 yards to John Kelleher, just enough for a first down at the 20. A fumble lost five yards, but Stevenson came back with a 20-yard strike to John Kovatch, who stepped out of bounds at the five with only two seconds on the clock. Instead of trying another pass, or a field goal, Kovatch tried to run it in. He was stopped for no gain. Troy had survived the scare.

Halftime: USC 6, ND 0, just like last year and the year before.

Notre Dame returned the second-half kickoff to its 31. On second-and-nine, Bob Saggau got off a tremendous quick-kick all the way to Troy's seven— a 61-yard boot. Following that, Landsell's punt was partially blocked, and Notre Dame started at USC's 30. But the Irish would get only to the 14.

Late in the period ND's John McIntyre intercepted a Lansdell pass and returned 24 yards to USC's 46. An incomplete pass and a reverse which lost nine yards put the Irish in a third-and-19 situation. Benny Sheridan threw complete to Sitko for a gain of 15. Fourth-and-four at Troy's 40. Sitko blasted for six yards and a big first down at the 34. Sheridan connected with Steve Bagarus for 14 more down to the 20. After Sheridan lost a yard, he came back with another completion, this one to John Kelly for 11 yards, and another first down at the 10. Milton Piepul rammed to the four as the third period came to an end.

While the teams swapped ends of the field, the crowd was roaring for their Irish to take it on in, kick the conversion, and grab a 7-6 lead.

Piepul, on a hidden ball reverse, scored. It would also be Piepul kicking the go ahead conversion. But he missed it.

ND 6, USC 6.

The Trojans were soon punting, but Lansdell picked off a Piepul pass at Notre Dame's 42 and then converted the big play into a touchdown. The Irish were penalized 15 yards for holding on first down, moving the chains to the 27. Lansdell ripped off gains of six and eight yards to the 13. Bob Robertson went to the eight. Two Lansdell cracks got it to the five, where it was fourth-and-two.

All 55,000 were on their feet screaming, "Hold That Line!" But the Irish couldn't quite do it. It was Lansdell again, and he went wide right for the score. Robert Jones kicked the conversion to give his team a 13-6 cushion.

The ensuing kickoff went out of bounds at the Notre Dame 35-yard line, and the Irish took it there. On first down, Troy was penalized five yards. Sheridan bucked the line, suddenly broke into the clear, and sped 60 yards for a touchdown— surely the "tying touchdown." John Kelleher was chosen to get it done, but he missed the conversion! Now the series "conversion curse" had gripped the Irish.

USC 13, ND 12.

Notre Dame even botched the ensuing kickoff, squiggling the ball only to Southern Cal's 42-yard line, where tackle Howard Stoecker fell on it. But no damage resulted, and Troy punted to the Irish 28.

Four minutes remained in the game.

Notre Dame ran six plays but faced a fourth-and-11 situation at its 39 and had to gamble. Piepul's pass was incomplete.

After no gain, Schlinder tore straight through the

USC tailback Grenville Lansdell breaks off tackle in 1939 action at South Bend. He scored twice in 20-12 Trojan triumph.

middle of the line and went 39 yards for a touchdown. With just over a minute to go in the game, Jones kicked good.

Sparked by a 37-yard pass from Bernie Crimmins to Saggau, the Irish quickly reached Troy's 11-yard line, but time ran out.

Final score: Southern California 20, Notre Dame 12.

The losing Irish led in first downs 14-12, yards passing 139-56, and total yards 271-247, while USC rushed for more yards 191-132. Notre Dame threw 20 passes and completed 11, both series highs at that time.

Some extremely interesting statistics emerge from the last five games. Even though Notre Dame was way out front in total yards 1398-796, USC had scored more points 65-58, and the five-game series stood 2-2-1.

The Irish finished 7-2-0 and a No. 13 ranking. In the decade of the 1930s, the average attendance in their 43 games at Notre Dame Stadium was only 28,364, whereas the 47 road games averaged 58,545. In all, Notre Dame football drew just under four million fans during the "depression decade."

The Trojans not only had to face their long train ride back to Los Angeles but also Washington the next Saturday, followed by UCLA in another week. Troy edged the Huskies 9-7 but settled for a 0-0 tie with the Bruins.

USC, with a 5-0-2 Pacific Coast Conference record, beat out UCLA's 5-0-3 mark by one-half game and bagged its second straight Rose Bowl invitation.

The Trojans would be facing Tennessee, a team carrying even more awesome figures than last year's opponent, Duke. The Vols were on a 23-0-0 roll (by a 550-16 score) and had not allowed a point in their last 15 games.

USC 14, UT 0. And Coach Howard Jones had won his fifth Rose Bowl in five trips.

Southern Cal finished with an 8-0-2 record. Its final AP ranking, decided before the bowl games, was No. 3, behind Texas A&M and Tennessee.

Other bowl winners that year were the Aggies, Georgia Tech and Clemson.

"The Glamor Game" was close. Notre Dame led 7-6-1 in wins; Southern Cal led 170-160 in points.

Little did Trojan fans realize in 1939, but it would be 11 long years before they would again celebrate a football victory over Notre Dame.

1940

Piepul 10
Peoples 6

Southern California entered the new decade fresh from two seasons of only two losses, two wins over Notre Dame and two Rose Bowl victories over teams which went west unscored upon.

There would be no such fun in 1940. The Trojans started with tie games against Washington State and Oregon State. Then came wins over Illinois and Oregon, followed by losses to Stanford and California.

So, six weeks into the season, Troy was struggling along with two wins, two losses and two ties. USC would also split its next two games, losing to Washington but beating UCLA.

Notre Dame was next in the finale.

The Irish were off and winging, winning their first six games by a 158-34 tally. There was, however, some mighty strange voting in the Associated Press' weekly poll. Notre Dame, at 3-0-0, was No. 2 behind Cornell. But after defeating Illinois, Army and Navy, the Irish tumbled all the way to No. 7. But maybe the pollsters knew something after all, for then Notre Dame stumbled with back-to-back shutout losses to Iowa and Northwestern.

Southern California was next in the finale.

ND was 6-2-0, USC 3-3-2. ND had scored 168 points, USC 82. ND had allowed 61 points, USC 88.

"Notre Dame Rules 2-3 Favorite Over Trojans Today," read the headline atop the *Los Angeles Times'* sports section the morning of the game which in 1940 fell on December 7.

The subhead said, "Flu Does Its Bit Toward Making

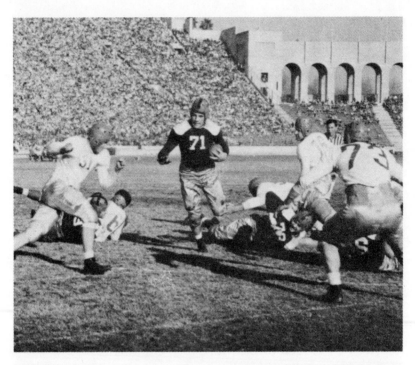

Milt Piepul (71) scores Notre Dame's only touchdown in 10-6 win in 1940. USC's Bob Berryman (31) and Willmar Bledsoe (73) close in, but too late.

Troy Underdogs." The *Times'* Paul Zimmerman reported, "At least half the gridsters who will wear the Maroon and Gold for Troy this afternoon got in little or no practice licks this week due to mild attacks of influenza that sent them to the Good Samaritan Hospital...Those who were not bitten by the bug had little work either, because the coaching staff couldn't find enough able bodies to put on scrimmage practice...In all, 16 of the squad of 32 have been in and out of the hospital ward this week."

Flu or no flu, it didn't scare away any of the cash customers, as 85,808 streamed into the Coliseum for the rivalry's 15th game, bringing the series' total attendance to over one million.

Flu or no flu, it also didn't prevent still another close, exciting game that had become the trademark of this great intersectional rivalry.

Irish captain Milton Piepul registered all ten points in 1940 decision over Troy, 10-6.

Just the opposite of last year's game when 20 of the 26 points were recorded in the last quarter, this one would see all the scoring in the first 17 minutes. But, like last year's game, this one would also have a *wild* ending.

Under a warm winter sun, USC received the opening kickoff, and Bob Robertson's short 18-yard quick-kick enabled Notre Dame to take a quick lead.

Starting from the USC 48, Steve Juzwik skirted right end for 19 yards to the 29. Unable to get any closer than the 12, Milt Piepul then kicked a field goal—only the second of the series, and Notre Dame's first.

The Trojans stormed right back.

Robertson returned the kickoff 32 yards out to his 36. A reverse to Jack Banta gained 11. Bobby Peoples, on some beautiful broken field running, raced for a touchdown of 53 yards. But, incredibly, USC missed still another conversion against Notre Dame, the 16th failure in 27 attempts.

Still, though, Troy had a 6-3 lead.

Getting the ball right back on a punt, the Trojans began bullying their favored opponents again. Starting from the USC 23, runs by Peoples and Robertson moved it 13 yards. Robertson broke free and rambled 45 yards before being hauled down by Steve Juzwik at the 19. Robertson threw to Peoples for 12, and Troy was first down at the seven. But the Fighting Irish then put up a game-saving defensive stand, forcing USC into a fourth-and-goal situation at the five as the quarter ended.

DeLauer came on for a field goal try, but he never got it off. The snap from center was fumbled back at the 15.

It would prove to be the game's turning point, as Notre Dame went 85 yards for its only touchdown of the day—and victory. Dippy Evans got it started with a 12-yard run. Evans followed with a pass to Raymond Ebli which turned into a big gainer of 36 yards to Troy's 37. On third-and-12, Evans then passed to Bob Hargrave for 15 yards to the 24. Evans and Juzwik hoofed it down to the 11, and another first down. Evans shot for eight, and Piepul got the remaining three yards and a touchdown. Piepul also kicked the point-after.

Irish 10, Trojans 6.

There were still 43 minutes left in the game, but that's the way it ended. Neither team came close to scoring—until seven seconds from the finish.

Trojan quarterback Bob Berryman threw a long, desperation pass intended for Joe Davis. Davis and three Irish defenders, including Bernie Crimmins, all went up for the ball at the 32-yard line. It fell harmlessly to the ground. But an official ruled interference!

First down at the Irish 32. Seven seconds left. Berryman went to Davis again, this time in the endzone, but Bill Earley batted the ball away.

Milt Piepul had scored all of Notre Dame's points, Bob Peoples all of USC's.

As the game ended, ND coach Elmer Layden stormed the field and lambasted every official in sight over the interference call only moments earlier. He also had harsh words with Howard Jones, USC coach, and later with Bill Hunter, USC athletic director.

Still fuming, Layden slammed through the doors of the

Irish dressing room and headed straight for Crimmins. After asking him whether he had interfered with Davis, Crimmins admitted that he had.

A suddenly subdued Layden went directly to the USC locker room to see Jones.

Paul Lowry of the *Times* was there and reported, "'I've come to congratulate you on the game played by your team, but particularly to make my peace with you. I was wrong when I yelled bloody murder on the ruling of interference...Bernie Crimmins admitted to me that he pushed your receiver. The ruling was correct, and I want you to know how badly I feel that I was wrong.'"

The two coaches shook hands. They would never see each other again.

Troy had the advantage in the statistics, leading in first downs 11-10, yards rushing 199-154, yards passing 88-69, and total yards 287-223. Robertson led all rushers with 121 yards in 26 carries.

The Irish finished with a 7-2-0 record, the Trojans 3-4-2.

The Pacific Coast Conference's representative won its fourth Rose Bowl in a row, as Stanford, ranked No. 2, topped Nebraska (No. 7) by a 21-13 margin.

Minnesota won the national championship.

The 1940 USC-ND game would be the last for Howard Jones and Elmer Layden as coaches.

Jones died of a heart attack on July 27, 1941, at the age of 55.

Howard Harding Jones. He is one of the great all-time collegiate coaches. He began his career as an assistant at Yale in 1905 and became head coach at Syracuse three

years later at the tender age of 23. After stints at Ohio State, Iowa and Duke, Jones became gridmaster at USC in 1925. He won seven Pacific Coast Conference titles, five Rose Bowls (out of five) and three national championships. His overall 194 wins ranks him 14th among coaches. Jones' record at Troy was 121-36-13 (.750). He was 6-8-1 against Notre Dame.

Layden's five-year contract would expire three months after the 1940 ND-USC game. He approached Father Hugh O'Donnell, president of Notre Dame, about its renewal. Father O'Donnell, however, would offer him only a one-year contract. Layden refused. He resigned on February 4, 1941. A few months later he became the first commissioner of the National Football League.

Undoubtedly, Notre Dame officials thought Layden's .770 winning record (47-13-3) warranted no more than a one-year renewal. A close look at Layden's record reveals that he was defeated by six different teams, and those teams combined for an impressive 88-23-8 record (.773) during the years his Irish lost to them. In fact, Layden

Legendary Howard Jones was the first Southern Cal coach to do battle against Notre Dame.

never lost to a team with a *losing* record.

His stonewalled defenses allowed just 6.6 points per game. That offset his team's conservative offenses which scored only 14.2 points on the average.

Layden was 4-2-1 against Southern Cal.

In the 10 years "Since Rockne," the Irish had been "only" 63-22-5 (.728) on the football field. Notre Dame was still searching for a coach to match Rockne's record.

They were to find him.

Meanwhile, the war raged in Europe. The Nazis had overrun Norway, Denmark, Holland and Belgium. Paris had fallen, the massive evacuation of Dunkirk had been miraculously pulled off, and Luftwaffe crewmen spoke of "an ocean of flames" over London in constant day and night bombing raids.

1941

GAME 16

Ziemba And Kovatch Prevent David From Slaying Goliath

The 1941 game looked like a modern-day version of David versus Goliath— Southern California, with only two wins and four touchdowns, facing Notre Dame, unbeaten and rated as the fourth best team in the country.

David didn't win, but neither was he slain. He was a formidable foe and had Goliath wobbly-kneed and very much concerned.

Goliath won by two points, but only because David failed to make any of his three conversions. He was so disgusted on the third one that he resorted to attempting a pass for the one point. It also failed.

A conversion here and a conversion there, at strategic points in the 16-year rivalry, and USC would hold a 10-5-1 series advantage, instead of a 6-9-1 disadvantage.

Both teams had new coaches: Sam Barry for USC and Frank Leahy for ND. Barry had been an assistant on Howard Jones' staff. Leahy had played for Knute Rockne in 1928-29. Since then he had been an assistant at Georgetown, Michigan State and Fordham. In 1939, Leahy became head coach at Boston College, where he posted a 20-2-0 record, including a win over Tennessee in the Sugar Bowl.

Simply stated, no coach ever wanted a coaching job more than Frank Leahy wanted his new one.

The Irish made victims of Arizona, Indiana, Georgia Tech, Carnegie Tech and Illinois, but a scoreless tie with Army snapped their winning ways. Back on track, ND took care of Navy and Northwestern. It was now time for another Troy visit to South Bend, where they would be

114

Los Angeles Times

JAPS OPEN WAR ON U.S. WITH BOMBING OF HAWAII

City Springs to Attention

Los Angeles, Stunned by Sudden War Start, Turns Wholeheartedly to Defense Task; 'They Started It, We'll Finish It,' Motto

F.D.R. Will Ask Congress Action Today

President to Make Plea Personally on Move to Answer Japan Attacks

WASHINGTON, Dec. 8

Berlin Shy About Aid to Tokyo

BERLIN, Dec. 8 (Monday.) (P)—Obligated under the three-power pact to go to Japan's assistance if Japan is "attacked," Germany referred early today to hostilities in the Pacific as

Toll Feared High in Attack Against Isles

Field Near Honolulu Takes Brunt of Bombing; Naval Battle Reported

HONOLULU, Dec. 7 (P)—

Fleet Speeds Out to Battle Invader

Tokyo Claims Battleship Sunk and Another Set Afire With Hundreds Killed on Island; Singapore Attacked and Thailand Force Landed

---

about a four-touchdown underdog.

The Trojans opened with a 13-7 win over Oregon State and later defeated Washington 7-6, but there were losses to Ohio State, Oregon, California and Stanford by a wide 80-6 margin.

In a note of interest, on Thursday before the big USC-ND clash, the Hollywood Bears defeated the Los Angeles Bulldogs in a Pacific Coast Professional League football game at Gilmore Stadium before 15,000 "shivering fans." The score was 17-2.

A crowd of 54,967 filled Notre Dame Stadium on a dank November 22 for the 16th renewal of this grand gridiron show.

Notre Dame ran three plays after receiving the kickoff, and Owen "Dippy" Evans was in punt formation. Ralph Heywood broke through and blocked his kick, and the Trojans had the ball 33 yards away from a touchdown. Bob Robertson and Mickey Anderson punched out a first down to the 23. On fourth down from the 20, Robertson threw to Heywood in the endzone, where he leaped high and out-fought defender Steve Juzwik for the football. It was a quick 6-0 USC lead, and it stayed that way when Walter Ziemba blocked Bob Jones' conversion try.

The Trojans kicked off and immediately got the ball back when Robertson intercepted Angelo Bertelli's long pass and returned 45 yards to ND's 19. Three plays gained nothing, and kicker Jones came on for a field goal try. The kick was low and wide.

Notre Dame scored early in the second quarter, also from 33 yards away, after receiving a punt from Heywood standing in his own endzone. The Irish struck quickly. Juzwik, on first down, rambled all the way to the seven. Quarterback Bob Hargrave scored three plays later. Juzwik converted, and Irish fans were relieved with their 7-6 lead.

Moments later, ND had the ball and another touchdown. Evans recovered a Robertson fumble at Troy's 46. Bertelli passed to Bob Dove for a 20-yard gain to the 26. On third-and-four, Dove smashed to the four, and a play later, Juzwik drove into the endzone. He missed the conversion, but his team had a 13-6 lead.

Southern Cal answered. The ensuing kickoff sailed out of bounds at the USC 35, and the Trojans started from there. Bill Musick passed 11 yards to Doug Essick, Robertson ran for 10, Robertson hit Paul Taylor for 20, Robertson went back to Essick for 15 more and, just like that, Troy was first down at the Irish nine. After a run netted nothing, Musick floated one into the endzone, and Bill Bledsoe made a sky-catch for the touchdown, pulling USC within one, 13-12. Jones was set to tie it. Back went the snap. Jones kicked it. *Thruumph!* John Kovatch blocked it.

Halftime: Notre Dame 13, Southern California 12.

The Fighting Irish scored again in the third period, starting from their 47 after receiving a punt. Bertelli passes to Dove and Harry Wright, plus two runs by Juzwik, got the ball to USC's 17. Bertelli then pitched a little flat pass out to Evans, and "Dippy" did the rest, evading three Trojan defenders with some fancy footwork and scored just inside the flag. Juzwik's kick made it 20-12.

Sam Barry's gallant Trojans, fighting stacked odds all afternoon, took the ensuing kickoff and drove to Notre Dame's 25, but a major penalty killed the drive.

Later in the final period, Barry's weary boys marched to a first-and-goal at the eight but were stopped at the three.

116

Loyola - 7	Michigan - 20	Minnesota - 41	Oregon - 19
New Mexico - 3	Buckeyes - 20	Badgers - 6	Washington - 16

IRISH SHADE TROJANS, 20-18

Notre Dame punted out to the 37, and here came Troy again. Highlighted by a 23-yard air strike from Paul Taylor to Joe Davis, USC once again had a first down at the eight. Robertson, on first down, zipped in for a touchdown. Totally gun-shy by now of even trying to kick a conversion, Coach Barry ordered up a little trick play. He had kicker Jones throwing for the conversion. His toss was barely out of Essick's reach in the endzone, keeping the score at 20-18.

There was still six minutes, plenty of time left to play, and USC was pumped and primed.

But the rugged Irish took the ensuing kickoff, and Troy's offense never got to play with the football again.

"Much of the six minutes of that closing drive was consumed by the officials, who never quite seemed to get together on what they were doing," reported Paul Zimmerman of the *Los Angeles Times*. "The Irish wisely consumed time to the hilt on every play and the Trojans, who had played all out, didn't have enough strength left to prevent Juzwik and Evans from knocking off consistent yardage....But the sad work of the officials should not take from Bertelli his great passing performance even though the arbiters' deeds did definitely play an important part in the Notre Dame triumph."

Leahy told the press, "The turning point, I believe, came right at the start when Wally Ziemba blocked that try for the extra point."

A dejected Bob Jones said, "If only I could have kicked each point after touchdown."

Jack Gallagher of the *Times* wrote, "The Notre Dame dressing room was comparatively quiet. The regulars were too tired to be talkative."

The real heroes of Notre Dame's 1941 victory over Southern Cal were a center named Walter J. Ziemba and

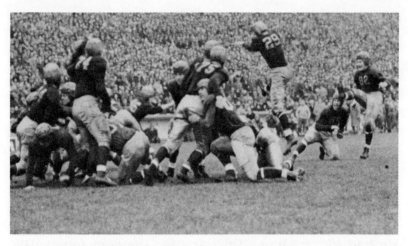

USC failed on all three conversion attempts in 1941 game at South Bend and lost, 20-18. Notre Dame's John Kovatch (29) is shown blocking Bob Jones' kick in the second period. Other Irish players are Angelo Bertelli (48), Walt Ziemba (74) and Paul Lillis (75).

an end named John G. Kovatch, both from their defensive positions. They blocked Troy's first two conversion attempts and kept David from slaying Goliath.

No doubt about it, three successful kicks would have enabled USC to pull off the biggest upset in series history. But it didn't happen, and this one goes down simply as "Game 16" in the overall scheme of things.

The Trojans led in first downs (13-11) and passing yards (163-156), while the Irish were tops in rushing yards (125-45) and total yards (281-208). Bertelli, with 13 completions for 156 yards, set individual series highs in both categories.

It was Notre Dame's final game, and Frank Leahy broke in with an 8-0-1 record and a No. 3 rating behind Minnesota and Duke. Texas and Michigan rounded out the top five.

Barry's Trojans had two games remaining, which resulted in a 14-13 loss to Washington and a 7-7 tie with UCLA. Troy's 2-6-1 season was the worst in 40 years, dating back to an 0-1-0 record in 1901.

There were some unique circumstances surrounding the Pacific Coast Conference's "Run For The Roses."

Oregon State, a charter member (1916), won its first championship, and its nine-game schedule was against all the other nine conference members. The Beavers were *finally* going to the Rose Bowl—but they wouldn't be playing *at* the Rose Bowl. War restrictions did not allow any large gatherings on the West Coast, so the game was moved to Durham, N.C., home of OSU's opponent, Duke, which was 9-0-0 and ranked No. 2. The Beavers were 7-2-0 and rated 12th. But Oregon State carried the PCC flag with honor, upsetting the Blue Devils 20-16.

The war news was grim. Germany had swept through Greece and Yugoslavia in April and made its massive attack on Russia in June. By September, the Axis had encircled Leningrad, prompting Hitler's announcement to the world, "Russia has been struck down and will never rise again." A month later, Moscow was in a state of panic and siege. In November, the *Los Angeles Times* carried a front page headline: "Russia War Casualties Placed at 15,000,000; Soviet Gives Nazi Figures as 5,000,000."

But the most dreaded news of all came just 15 days after the 1941 Notre Dame-Southern California game. Japan sprung its game plan on Pearl Harbor. And nothing would ever be the same again.

1942

GAME 17

A Crazy Day At The Coliseum

America's fighting role in World War II was about to reach its first full year but the pace of mobilization had not, as yet, substantially affected the college football programs around the country. Drastic interruptions would come a year later.

Bold front page headlines screaming the war's horrible news became a daily part of American life throughout all of 1942— cities leveled by devastating bombing raids...huge ships going down in powerful sea battles...entire squadrons of planes shot from the air...invasions...retreats...captured and tortured GI's...death marches...thousands of American fighting men dying in North Africa and on Pacific battlefields such as Bataan, Gaudalcanal and many other "over yonder" places.

But as they say in the business, "The Show Must Go On," and, brother, Notre Dame-USC is show biz. When the Irish come to town, any town, the people flock to see 'em.

Something to do with "star attraction."

Notre Dame, with two losses, was in Los Angeles to play USC, with three losses. But even with five defeats between them, the biggest college football crowd of the season, more than 90,000, was expected for the 17th game of the series.

"Factors contributing to the popularity of tomorrow's game include gas rationing, which is scheduled to take effect December 1," reported the *Chicago Tribune*. "There's the realization that this will be the only coast appearance of Angelo Bertelli, Notre Dame's passing star, and general

120

Notre Dame halfback Creighton Miller scored first touchdown on a 48-yard toss from Angelo Bertelli as father Harry and uncle Don, both former Irish monogram winners, witnessed the feat in 1942 at the Coliseum. The visitors won, 13-0.

agreement that the Trojans need this victory with its resulting national prestige for Rose Bowl consideration."

Speaking of "star attraction", the stars were out in force at movie houses around the country that weekend in '42: Ray Milland and Ginger Rogers in *The Major and The Minor,* Clark Gable and Lana Turner in *Somewhere I'll Find You,* Walter Pidgeon and Hedy Lamaar in *White Cargo,* and Gene Tierney and Preston Foster in *Thunderbirds.*

The Irish started slowly. There was an opening 7-7 tie with Wisconsin, then a 13-6 loss to Georgia Tech. Coach Frank Leahy became ill after the Tech game and was sent to Mayo Clinic in Rochester, Minnesota, for examinations and plenty of bed rest. He missed three weeks and three wins— 27-0 over Stanford, 28-0 over Iowa Pre-Flight and 21-14 over Illinois. Leahy returned for shutouts of Navy 9-0, Army 13-0 and Wisconsin 27-0. But there was also a 32-20 loss to Michigan— Notre Dame's ninth loss in 10 games to the Wolverines. UM's 32 points were also the most scored on an Irish football team since 1904.

With a 6-2-1 record, Notre Dame was ranked No. 8.

Sam Berry, last year's USC coach, had been called to military duty, and Jeff Cravath took the reins. Cravath was a Trojan center in the first ND-USC game in 1926. He was a member of the Troy coaching staff before becoming head coach at the University of San Francisco last season. USC called, and Cravath "went home."

Southern Cal was only 3-3-1, beating Washington State, California and Oregon, but losing to Tulane, Ohio State and Stanford. The tie was a 0-0 struggle with Washington, USC's fourth scoreless tie in the last six years.

ND's average score was 18-10, USC's 17-13.

In terms of on-the-field shenanigans and boisterous fan behavior, the 1942 game was, far and away, the wildest the series had seen up to that time.

Maybe the war had something to do with it.

There were 17 infractions called, resulting in 145 yards. (As a comparison, the series' first 16 games averaged only 52 yards in penalties.) And the 17 didn't include the refused penalties, or the the ones not spotted, or the ones not enforced.

Five players were thrown out of the game.

Los Angeles Times: "Notre Dame was guilty of more illegal tactics than any team we ever saw, and didn't get penalized half enough. Four times the officials warned Irish players for infractions, but none of these warnings was a penalty decreed. That's where the officials made a grave error."

Chicago Tribune: "Apparently the Trojans were not prepared for the sharp blocking and tackling of Notre Dame, and they became embittered as they saw a potential Rose Bowl bid slipping from their grasp."

Times: "They're the Fighting Irish, all right! What was ballyhooed as a football game, turned out to be a free-for-all....Notre Dame players were the most flagrant offenders. Three of them were kicked off the field by harassed officials...Two Trojans also got the old heave-ho."

Tribune "Leahy said that he believed that the fast whistle employed in games on the West Coast led to the

122

charge that Notre Dame was piling on and aroused Trojan feelings."

A crowd of 95,519 showed up, and early in the afternoon they absolutely couldn't believe final scores of two games just finished back in the Eastern time zone of Boston and Athens, Ga. But more on that later.

In the game at Los Angeles, Notre Dame won 13-0 as quarterback Angelo Bertelli passed for both touchdowns.

The Irish scored their first TD late in the second period. Bob Livingstone returned a punt 17 yards to Troy's 49. After a yard gain, Bertelli threw over the middle to Creighton Miller, who was cutting across. Miller turned it into a touchdown of 48 yards. And among the big crowd at the Coliseum that day were Creighton Miller's father, Harry, who was a starting halfback for four years at Notre Dame (1906-09), and Creighton's uncle, Don Miller, one of the Four Horsemen in 1924. What a thrill that touchdown must have been for young Creighton that November afternoon in 1942—not to mention for pop Harry and uncle Don.

"That's *our* boy!" they must have shouted.

The conversion was missed, but that had become a series tradition, and the Irish led by a 6-0 score.

The Trojans roared right back and missed a sure touchdown by inches—literally. On second-and-seven from his 21, Mickey McCardle's 53-yard bomb to Ralph Heywood put the ball at the Irish 26 as the first period came to a close, and a late-hit penalty on the play moved the ball to the 11.

Bob Musick rammed to the seven. After an incomplete pass, Musick took it to the five. Fourth-and-four. McCardle charged into the line and pushed down to the one. First down? Too close to call. Out came the chain. Stretching it out under the watchful eyes of the 22 huddled players, it was short. Two inches short! The Irish were ecstatic, the Trojans dazed and crushed.

After an exchange of punts, Notre Dame began from its 20 and hammered out a 15-play scoring march. Two runs by Livingstone gained seven. Corwin Clatt broke for nine and a first down at the 36. Bertelli passed to Bob Dove for 14 to midfield. Runs by Miller, Livingstone and

123

Clatt took it to USC's 37 and another first down. Bertelli's pass to George Murphy was good for 17 yards to the 20. Livingstone moved to the 17. After an incompletion, Bertelli came back with a six-yard strike to Clatt to the 11, where it was fourth-and-one. Clatt fought for two. First-and-goal at the nine. After two running plays and a penalty on the Irish for "stalling," Bertelli rifled a pass to Livingstone. Touchdown. With just over three minutes left in the half, John Creevey added the conversion.

There was only one serious threat in the second half, and that came when Southern Cal took the kickoff and went from its 33 to Notre Dame's 14, but four plays gained nothing, and the Trojans were finished for the day.

"The second half was devoted so much to foul play that the main objective of advancing the ball across the opponent's goal line was forgotten," reported the *Times*. "When the final gun broke the chill air, players from both benches rushed to the field, followed by a swarm of hot-headed fans, and fists flew fast before the riot was quelled and the mob dispersed...It was a sad commentary on the American game of football."

"The game ended in a free-for-all," said the *Tribune*. "The day's final play touched off the fuse under a powder keg of emotion built up through the third and fourth quarters."

On that same afternoon in Chicago the city prep football title game between Leo and Tilden at Soldier Field attracted 75,000 fans and took in $110,000. All of the $100,000 profit went to three Chicago Military Service Centers. By the way, Leo's Lions beat the Blue Devils 27-14.

The final statistics of the Irish-Trojan "15 rounder" showed ND leading in penalties (11-6), penalty yards (85-60), players tossed out (3-2), yards rushing (180-74), and total yards (292-223). USC led in first downs (13-11) and yards passing (149-112). Troy also set a series record at the time with 30 passes attempted (13 were completed). Bertelli was 6-for-13 for 112 yards, while Clatt was the game's leading rusher with 55 yards in 13 carries (4.2).

Notre Dame had one game remaining, and Southern Cal three.

Georgia - 34 | Cougars-0 | Holy Cross-55 | Irish-13
Georgia Tech-0 | Huskies-0 | Boston Col.-12 | Troy-0

Sport
Postscripts Los Angeles Times
Sports
By PAUL ZIMMERMAN

Georgia Accepts Rose Bowl Bid | Irish Defeat
Troy, 13-0

SUNDAY, NOVEMBER 29, 1942

Bulldogs Roll to 34-0 | Players Vote | Cougars' Postseason | Bertelli Too
Win Over Georgia Tech | to Come Here | Game Hopes in Setback | Much for Troy

Winners Spoil Engineers' Undefeated Slate, | Southern Gridders | Washington Gridders Blast Chances of
Rose Bowl Dreams With Decisive Triumph | Appear in Annual Classic | Rivals to Play in Classic With 0-0 Tie
| for First Time Jan. 1 | SEATTLE, Nov. 28 (P)—Washington State College's Rose

The Irish rallied from a 13-point deficit to tie a strong
Great Lakes Naval Air Station "All-Star" team, 13-13, at
Chicago. It ended a 7-2-2 year, matching the 1921 season
as the most games in one season.

USC later defeated Montana and St. Mary's Pre-Flight
but lost to UCLA 14-7 in the Pacific Coast Conference's
title game, sending the Bruins to the Rose Bowl for the
first time.

Georgia, featuring Charley Trippi and the '42 Heisman
Trophy winner, Frank Sinkwich, defeated UCLA at Pasadena 9-0, breaking the PCC's five-year bowl winning streak.

The 1942 season had an incredible finish to determine
its national champion. On November 28, Boston College,
ranked No. 1, was hammered 55-12 by Holy Cross, while
No. 2 Georgia Tech was battered 34-0 by Georgia. With
the two top teams losing by a combined 89-12 score, No.
3 Ohio State, which already had completed its season,
slipped through the back door and claimed the big prize.

The final AP poll came out two days later. Following
the Buckeyes were Georgia, Wisconsin, Tulsa, Georgia
Tech and the Fighting Irish.

Looking back on that fall of '42, it seems only appropriate that the season should have such a whirlwind

wrapup. It was to be football's "last hurrah" for awhile.

Every boy of age and physically fit, college student or not, in just a few months would be a "million miles" away participating, one way or another, in a war. Football, in a few years, would return to take its normal, crazy place in our society. But first, there was more important business that had to be taken care of.

It was "Time Out."

The Notre Dame-Southern California series would also take a break. Next game: November 30, 1946, at South Bend.

1946

GAME 18

Coy McGee Leads A
Real Bushwackin'

The continuance of wartime football and major league baseball, despite acute manpower shortages and travel difficulties, was encouraged and tolerated for civilian and military morale reasons. There was also the element of a psychological ploy, as President Franklin Roosevelt wanted the enemy to know that America could fight a war on foreign soils and seas and, at the same time, "play games" at home.

It was postwar 1946, and collegiate football had returned to "big time" status. Gone were the fuzzy-cheeked freshmen too young for the draft and players who could not meet military physical standards. Instead, rosters across the nation were well-stocked with returning war veterans and former lettermen—now older, meaner and tougher. (They were also wiser, which imposed new problems. Coaching staffs were now dealing with men instead of boys.)

It was also time for Notre Dame and Southern California to get "The Glamor Game" revved up and back on stage.

During the three-season hiatus, the Irish posted a 24-5-1 record. It included a claim on the national championship in 1943 over the wailing howls of their friends down the road—Purdue. The Boilermakers finished 9-0-0, which included a 23-13 win over Great Lakes Navy. Notre Dame was 9-1-0, its only loss coming to Great Lakes Navy, 19-14. No wonder PU's boiler overheated.

Powerful Army captured the national crown in 1944 and 1945. One of its wins in '44 was a 59-0 rout of the

127

Irish, still Notre Dame's worst defeat on the gridiron. Doc Blanchard, Cadet fullback, said, "If there is anyone to blame for the size of the margin, it was Notre Dame itself, which fired our desire to win after its long humiliation of Army teams."

It was Army's first win over the Irish in 13 years and its first touchdown in six years.

Meanwhile, out West, Southern Cal won three straight Pacific Coast Conference championships and took two-out-of-three Rose Bowl games. The Trojans highest ranking came in 1943, when they were No. 4 with a 6-0-0 record.

USC's 23-6-2 record during the three years came within one win of matching Notre Dame's.

The '46 season was highlighted by one of those "Game Of The Century" clashes, this one between No. 1 Army and No. 2 Notre Dame. It was a game which reportedly could have sold a million tickets. It ended 0-0. And the Irish continued chasing the Cadets for the nation's top spot.

When time came for the Trojans to pack their bags and head east for South Bend, they had won five games but lost to Ohio State, Oregon State and UCLA.

The Irish were 7-0-1 by an average score of 31-3, while USC was 5-3-0 by a more modest 17-8 average.

On game day, Arch Ward of the *Chicago Tribune* wrote, "We may wait a long time to see a season that will match this in attendance, number of competitors, equality of competition, recruiting, subsidizing, and general chaos." Ward also offered his readers these opinions: "Best college team— Notre Dame and Army, no choice. Best professional team— Cleveland Browns and Chicago Bears, no choice. Best team, college or pro— Notre Dame and Army, take your pick."

The *Tribune's* Edward Burns reported, "Notre Dame and Southern California, foes in some of the greatest football thrillers ever held on any gridiron anytime anywhere, will meet here today in the 18th game of the series."

Coach Frank Leahy, in the Navy for the last two years, returned for the 1946 season, but he would not be

USC halfback Don Garlin (29) struggles for yardage in 1946 game at South Bend. Irish defenders are George Strohmeyer (60), Wilmer Russell (61) and George Conner (81). Notre Dame won, 28-6.

present for the USC game because of what was reported to be a "severe cold and nervous exhaustion."

Over 55,000 filled Notre Dame Stadium on November 30 and watched their Irish squeeze a bone-crushing vice around the Trojans all afternoon. Forget the final score of "only" 26-6. Notre Dame overwhelmed Troy in the following categories: 26-9 in first downs, 517-108 in yards rushing, 106-59 in yards passing and 623-167 in total yards of offense. Even with these outlandish numbers, however, USC trailed only 13-6 as late as the third period.

What kept the score respectable? Ten Irish turnovers! Troy can be most thankful that ND lost eight fumbles and threw two interceptions, plus the fact that 90 yards in penalties were stepped off against the home team.

Coy McGee returned the opening kickoff 80 yards for an apparent touchdown, but a penalty killed it, and the game's tone was set.

Notre Dame scored its first touchdown early in the second period. McGee broke off a gain of 50 yards to

Troy's 17, but quarterback Johnny Lujack fumbled on the next play. Verl Lillywhite, on first down, got off a booming quick-kick, with the ball rolling just inches into the endzone. It was a boot of close to 90 yards, from where Lillywhite kicked it.

On second-and-eight, the ball was handed to McGee again, and he raced 78 yards for the touchdown. It also gave Coy 128 yards in back-to-back carries which, interestingly enough, was more than any other player had been able to gain in a series game. The previous high had been 124 yards in 22 attempts by ND's Christie Flannagan in 1927.

Later in the period, John Panelli got off a run of 17 yards, Floyd Simmons rambled for 16 and 12 yards and Bob Livingstone hit for 15 yards, as ND reached Troy's seven-yard line. After a holding penalty set the offense back to the 22, quarterback George Ratterman passed to huge Leon Hart for a touchdown. Earley's kick made it 13-0.

Southern Cal scored in the third quarter to cut its deficit to only seven. Bob Musick recovered a fumble at ND's 25, but four plays later the ball was still at the 25. Moments later, Musick fell on another fumble, this time at ND's 45. Aided by an interference call on a long pass that put the ball at the one, Johnny Naumu scored two plays later. But he missed the conversion.

ND 13, USC 6, and the Trojans were, somehow, still in the game.

It stayed that way until the final period when the Irish scored twice more. A 49-yard pass from Ratterman to Floyd Simmons set up McGee's TD run of eight yards. It remained 19-6 when Early missed another conversion.

At this point in the series, ND and USC had converted only half of their conversions— 32 of 64.

The Irish later finished out the game's scoring when Gerry Cowhig ran in from eight yards. The conversion? Early got it.

After Coy McGee's rocket start, he got the call just four more times in the game (18 yards) and finished with 146 yards in only six attempts for a 24.3 average.

It was the fourth straight win for the Irish over South-

Coy McGee rushed for 146 yards in just six carries in leading Notre Dame to a 26-6 win over Southern Cal in 1946.

ern Cal. It extended their series lead to 11-6-1 and their overall point advantage to 229-200.

While Notre Dame was pounding USC that November 30, Army edged Navy 21-18 at Philadelphia to wrap up its third straight unbeaten season with a 27-0-1 record. The final Associated Press poll would be out Monday also declaring the Cadets as its third straight national champ.

Surprise!

Army was *not* voted No. 1. It was Notre Dame!

The previous week's voting had given Army nearly twice as many (72-38) first place votes as the Irish. But a total of 183 sportswriters cast ballots in the final poll, and it was Notre Dame receiving twice as many as Army (104.5-52.5), with other teams getting 26. Georgia, UCLA and Illinois finished 3-4-5.

The outcome for No. 1 was hotly debated for months.

Also on that November 30, there was a game of truly historic significance in Stockton, California. But, *amazingly,* nobody seemed to know— or care. College of Pacific defeated San Diego State 19-13, giving Amos Alonzo Stagg his 314th (and last) coaching win— one more than Pop Warner— and the all-time record. That fact wasn't even mentioned in press reports of the game. Stagg's record would stand for 35 years, or until Bear Bryant won his 315th in 1981. (Bryant had 13 wins in 1946.)

This was the first year of the Pacific Coast-Big Ten Rose Bowl pact. It was a decision termed "dreadful" by football fandom throughout the East, Southeast and Southwest. Locked-out of the "granddaddy of them all," they pondered, "How could the Rose Bowl do this? Or why?" (More than 40 years later, many are still pondering).

Anyway, Illinois stomped UCLA 45-14.

1947

GAME 19

The Magnificent Dud

What a game this would be! What a buildup! The hype began in earnest on Monday before the big upcoming bash at the Los Angeles Memorial Coliseum. But the collision course had begun taking shape much earlier, as both teams, week after week, clicked off win after win.

It unfolded this way:

	SCORE	AP RANKING FOLLOWING
SEPTEMBER 27		
SC-Washington St.	21−0	WEEK. POLL DIDN'T BEGIN
ND, no game	-	UNTIL OCTOBER 6
OCTOBER 4		
ND-Pittsburgh	40−6	1st
SC-Rice	7−6	20th
OCTOBER 11		
ND-Purdue	22−7	2nd (behind Michigan)
SC-Ohio State	32−0	11th
OCTOBER 18		
ND-Nebraska	31−0	2nd (behind Michigan)
SC-Oregon State	48−6	10th
OCTOBER 25		
ND-Iowa	21−0	1st
SC-California	39-14	5th
NOVEMBER 1		
ND-Navy	27−0	1st
SC-Washington	19−0	5th
NOVEMBER 8		
ND-Army	27−7	1st
SC-Stanford	14−0	5th
NOVEMBER 15		
ND-Northwestern	26-19	2nd (behind Michigan)
SC-UCLA	6−0	4th

Chart continued on next page.

133

	SCORE	AP RANKING FOLLOW-ING WEEK
NOVEMBER 22		
ND-Tulane	59–6	1st
SC, no game	-	
NOVEMBER 29		
ND, no game	-	1st
SC, no game	-	3rd

SMU had been 3rd the previous week, but was tied 19-19 by TCU, moving USC up a notch

That brought the campaign to Saturday, December 6. Notre Dame, ranked No. 1 with an 8-0-0 record, versus Southern California, 7-0-1 and rated No. 3. ND's season scoreboard read 253-45 (32-6 average), while USC's showed 179-27 (22-3).

The pre-game hoopla was staggering. It generated as much frenzied ballyhoo as a heavyweight championship fight, a Kentucky Derby or an Indianapolis 500. Throughout the week, area newspapers were crammed with stories about the teams and their upcoming big battle.

And the biggest crowd ever to see a sports event on the West Coast at the time— 104,953— were there, plus a couple of hundred more who got in illegally.

"Some 200 persons got into yesterday's SC-Notre Dame football game free when a crowd rushed Gate 4 on the south side of the Coliseum just at kickoff time," reported the *Los Angeles Times*. "Two policeman were mauled in the rush...University police said 300 to 400 men and youths joined the first assault on the gate guarded by three officers...Police reinforcements finally ended the rush."

Had the game itself been a 15-round heavyweight bout, one of the combatants would have been slammed to the canvas at the beginning of the eighth round, just past the midway point, and finished.

Notre Dame led 10-7 at intermission and was on the receiving end of the second-half kickoff. Bob Livingstone returned it out to his 24. On first down, *WHAP!* Emil Sitko belted Tommy Trojan with a jarring right, flush to the jaw. Sitko, on first down, streaked 76 yards for a touchdown, making the score 17-7, and the glazed-eyed Trojans were nothing more than a defenseless punching bag the remainder of the way.

Jack Kirby scores from eight yards out in second quarter, bringing USC to within three points (7-10). The Irish dominated from there on, with the final score of 38-7.

Final score: 38-7.

The Chicago Tribune: Arch Ward wrote, "From that moment (Sitko's run) the excitement of close and uncertain combat was missing...This was a battle of a good team against a great team...The Irish substituted one unit after another in an effort to hold down the score, but the reserves moved with the precision of the regulars."

The *Los Angeles Times*: Braven Dyer reported, "Sitko's mad dash so fired Frank Leahy's magnificent squad that nothing the Trojans could do thereafter made any difference...This to me was the greatest Notre Dame team ever to play against Southern California...There was considerable evidence during the first half that the roof might cave in on the Trojans eventually. It was sort of like the executioner's ax hanging heavy overhead."

The game's first score came just after the opening kickoff. USC's Verl Lillywhite fumbled on the first play from scrimmage and Charles Conner recovered for the Irish at Troy's 33. When things stalled at the 12, Fred Earley kicked a field goal for a fast 3-0 lead.

A 17-play, 82-yard drive that began late in the first period and extended into the second, was capped by a one-yard plunge by Sitko. Earley added his first of five conversions for the day and a 10-0 lead.

Southern Cal fought back into the game just before halftime. The drive covered 44 yards in nine plays, after Jimmy Powers intercepted a Johnny Lujack pass. The big gainers came on a 12-yard run by Powers, plus an 18-yard pass from Powers to Jack Kirby. Kirby later scored from the eight, Tom Walker kicked the conversion, and Troy trailed by only 10-7.

After Sitko's brilliant run to open the second half, the Irish quickly scored again. Lujack intercepted a long pass at his 10 and returned 37 yards, setting in motion an eight-play scoring jaunt. John Panelli went over from close range, increasing the difference to 24-7.

Two more touchdowns went on the books in the final period. The Trojans had worked their way to a first down at ND's 11, but it would be the Irish getting the points. It had been that kind of a day for Troy's weary warriors.

Notre Dame stopped the surge at the eight, took possession, and on first down gave the ball to Bob Livingstone. Touchdown! Ninety-two yards. It is still the longest touchdown run from scrimmage in the series.

And, just to add insult to, well, insult, a fourth-string sophomore right tackle by the name of Alfred Zmijewski intercepted a Wilbur Robertson lateral and hoofed it back 28 yards for the final score of the day.

Ball game.

Coach Leahy told the press afterwards, "I have never seen a better college football team than we were today...This was our best game of the year, and not only did we play our best, but we really had the luck of the Irish."

Aided by their long runs, Livingstone and Sitko recorded some impressive rushing totals. Livingstone had 134 yards (8 carries) and Sitko 130 yards (11 attempts). The Irish led in just about everything, first downs (14-10), yards rushing (397-118), yards passing (64-55) and total yards (461-173). ND's passing game was 6-for-9, while USC was only 9-for-29. Notre Dame was also penalized more yards (50-10). In the last two years, the Irish had

Chicago Sunday Tribune

SPORTS · MARKETS

NOTRE DAME BEATS SO. CALIFORNIA, 38--7

Tribune to Stage 2 Day Basket School for Youth

104,953 SEE

| JOE LOUIS NEAR END OF STRING | Coaching Greats Lend Talent to Stadium Clinic | 1,263 TOPS FIRST DAY | As Irish Rolled to All-Victorious Season | IRISH SCORE 9TH IN ROW |
| 'Beaten' Walcott to Claim Title | | PIN SCORES Bomar Ranks 2d To Easterner | | 1st Perfect Year Since Rockne |

blasted USC with 914 rushing yards.

"The luck of the Irish?" There certainly hadn't been any Irish luck in the series' penalty department. In the first 19 ND-USC games, the Irish had been penalized exactly *twice* as many yards as the Trojans— 770-385.

Notre Dame's series lead over Troy also went to twice as many, 12-6-1, and its scoreboard advantage was up to 267-207.

Going into the USC game, Notre Dame's point total in the AP poll was a slim 1184-1178 over Michigan. But when the results of the final balloting came out two days later, it wasn't even close. The Irish received 107 first place votes and 1410 points, to Michigan's 25 first places and 1289 points.

Rounding out the Top Ten that year were SMU, Penn State, Texas, Alabama, Pennsylvania, the Trojans, North Carolina and Georgia Tech.

The Big Ten made it two straight in the Rose Bowl after Michigan's 49-0 blowout of USC— still its worst football defeat.

Troy, after a 7-0-1 record and a No. 3 national ranking, lost their last two games by an 87-7 score.

137

1948

A Guy Named Gay

Mighty Notre Dame was mighty good in 1948, but it wasn't mightier than Michigan. Or maybe the Irish were. We'll never know. The majority of sportswriters who voted in the Associated Press poll, however, thought Michigan was mightiest.

By the time Notre Dame was to play Southern California on December 4, the final AP poll had already been taken.

Looking back on the '48 season, it's difficult to understand how, and why, Michigan replaced Notre Dame at the top.

Notre Dame was 9-0-0 by an average score of 34-9 (a 25-point difference). Michigan was 9-0-0 by a 28-5 score (a 23-point difference).

Notre Dame was two-time defending national champions and hadn't lost in 27 games (26-0-1). Michigan had won 23 in a row.

When the first poll emerged, both teams were 2-0-0. ND was ranked No. 1, while the Wolverines were in seventh place. The next two weeks resulted in the Irish beating Michigan State 26-7 and Nebraska 44-13, while UM topped Purdue 40-0 and 10th-ranked Northwestern 28-0.

That, in the opinion of the pollsters, was strong enough to shoot Michigan from No. 7 all the way to the top and drop Notre Dame to second.

Two weeks later, however, Notre Dame regained the lead. But the next week, November 6, Notre Dame whacked a weak (2-7-0) Indiana team by 36 points (42-6), and

Michigan cracked an even weaker (0-8-2) Navy club by 35 points (35-0).

On the strength of defeating a *winless* team, the pollsters voted the Wolverines back into the lead—and kept them there. Even a 46-0 ND rout of Washington (after Michigan had ended its season) could not "save" the Irish.

Although pollsters seldom take into consideration a particular team's *strength-of-schedule* analysis, maybe they did in 1948. Michigan played a tougher schedule. The Wolverines' nine opponents had compiled a 44-37-3 (.541) record that year. Notre Dame's opposition was 33-48-4 (.411), and only three posted winning records (Pittsburgh, Michigan State and Northwestern).

Still, though, was that a great enough difference to dethrone the two-time defending champions?

A tired Frank Leahy, his staff and their bitterly disappointed and weary-of-it-all squad now had to turn to blackboard *Xs* and *Os*, plus banging practice sessions, in preparation for still another opponent—Southern Cal.

While the Irish and Wolverines were scrapping it out all fall for top honors, the best USC could do was third place—in its own Pacific Coast Conference.

The Trojans were 6-3-0 after beating Utah, Oregon State, Rice, Stanford, Washington and UCLA, and losing to Ohio State, Oregon and California.

But USC would be ready for this one. Last year's haunting 38-7 humiliation was still burning vividly in the minds of "Noble Trojans, all."

A headline in the Saturday edition of the *Los Angeles Times* read, "TROJAN PEP RALLY ROCKS CITY HALL, SC Homecoming Parade Climaxes Week of Preparation for Notre Dame Game."

It was the second year in a row that Los Angeles hosted the game, and it would also attract back-to-back 100,000-plus crowds (100,571). It would, however, be the last ND-USC game to draw a six-figure attendance— at least until the 1990's.

There was also strong talk around town that USC was about to cancel the series.

The *Times'* Braven Dyer reported on game day, "Next year the teams go back to South Bend. After that? Well, there have been recurring rumors that Troy won't renew. But Father (John) Cavanaugh, Notre Dame's able president, is with us this weekend, and I won't be surprised if a new contract is signed before he leaves town."

Father Cavanaugh, speaking at the Jonathan Club's breakfast meeting on Friday said, "It is doubtful whether any football series now in existence ever drew as many spectators. When you add these to the millions who have enjoyed listening to these games on the radio, you must arrive at the conclusion that this series is a fine inspiration to many people."

It was also a huge money-maker for both athletic programs.

Play ball!

Notre Dame was ruled a big four-touchdown favorite. But it didn't quite turn out that way. What it turned out to be was one of the most exciting games in series history.

Troy got an early break when Notre Dame's Terry Brennan fumbled the opening kickoff and Charles Peterson recovered for USC at the Irish 24. But three running plays lost eight yards, and Don Doll, aiming a punt for the coffin corner, kicked it into the endzone instead.

USC halfback Jack Kirby is chased by ND guard Robert Lally in thrilling 14-14 tie at the Coliseum in 1948.

The game remained scoreless until early in the second period when Notre Dame took the lead. Bill Gay returned a punt nine yards to his 39. John Panelli gained nine on two runs, and Emil Sitko rammed for six more and a first down at the USC 46. On third-and-nine, quarterback Frank Tripucka shot a pass over the middle to big Leon Hart, 6-4, 245-pound end. Hart caught the ball at the 39. At least six Trojans had a good shot at bringing him down, but his strength shed them like dolls, and Hart thundered in for the touchdown.

Dyer of the *Times* wrote, "It is doubtful if any end in college, save Hart, has the power to accomplish such a run as he did yesterday— with the Trojans hitting the way they were."

Steve Oracko added the conversion for a 7-0 score.

USC drove down close just before intermission. On fourth down, Art Battle made a great catch at the four of Dean Dill's low throw, and would have scored the tying touchdown, except for Jerry Groom's saving tackle at the one.

Then, with Notre Dame killing the clock, Tripucka was seriously injured and had to be taken from the field on a stretcher.

USC took the second-half kickoff and went 59 yards to

Notre Dame's 23 but once again could do no damage.

Finally, late in the third quarter, Troy got something started and tied the score just after the final period began. Sophomore Bob Williams, who had replaced Tripucka at quarterback, was intercepted by Jack Kirby at the Irish 42. Dill lost five yards on first down but came back with a 31-yard pass to Kirby, who made a spectacular grab at the 18. Dill, back to pass, couldn't spot an open receiver and darted straight ahead to the six. Bill Martin plowed to the three, Art Battle to the two and Martin scored. Dill's conversion made it 7-7.

The big Coliseum crowd was delirious. The place was a madhouse. The Irish were in deep trouble—and they knew it.

With nine minutes left to play, the viciously-hitting Trojans recovered their *sixth* fumble of the game, this one at mid-field. But a team is not undefeated in three years by folding when the going gets tough—and the going was tough at this precise moment—so Notre Dame braced and forced a punt.

Dill kicked it down to the five. More Irish trouble. Unable to move, they punted it out to their 42.

Here came the Trojans.

After a penalty pushed the offense back five yards to the 47, Kirby blasted his way through for 16 yards and a first down at the 31. Dill threw to Ernie Tolman at the 18, as the game clock was down to four minutes. Dill threw incomplete into the endzone. Once again unable to find a receiver, Dill once again shot up the middle, this time to the 12, where it was third-and-four. Martin rammed straight ahead. First down at the six. Battle blasted to the four. And Martin crashed into the endzone for the second time in the game.

Touchdown! Time remaining: Two minutes and 30 seconds. The place was sheer bedlam.

Dill added the point-after, but nobody really noticed. Or even cared. Southern Cal 14, Notre Dame 7.

"SC rooters were hysterically happy," wrote Dyer. "Their underdog Trojans had whipped the mighty Irish, or so they thought, while preparing for a long night of celebration...Strong men grew weak slapping each other

on the back and some even headed for the exits, certain they'd seen a gridiron miracle."

The Trojans, now fired to the heavens, kicked off. Bill Gay, a halfback from Chicago, took it at the one. He veered to the sidelines. He picked up blockers, and speed. Suddenly, Bill Gay was speeding past the USC bench. A Trojan had him at about the 40, but Gay got away. He was headin' for the "land of milk and honey." But here came Troy's speedy halfback, Don Doll, not to be confused with teammate Dean Dill. Doll finally caught Gay and rode him down at the 13-yard line. But Bill Gay had returned the kickoff 86 yards.

The Coliseum's pandemonium quickly turned to shock.

Williams, on a quarterback keeper, gained five yards. Williams threw to Gay streaking in the endzone. Too high! Third-and-five at the eight. Time running out. Williams threw to Gay again in the endzone. Once more too high! Fourth down.

But wait! There was a red penalty flag in the endzone (penalty flags were red then). Field judge Orian Landreth had called pass interference on defender Gene Beck. Even though the rule called for the ball to be placed at the one-yard line, the officials put it on the two. There was that much tumult at the moment.

Panelli hit to the one. Fullback Emil Sitko, a 5-8, 180-pound stump, scored on the next play. The Irish still trailed by a point, but Steve Oracko's pressure-packed point-after tied the score to "win it" for the Irish.

With only 35 seconds left, shock in the Coliseum had now turned to grief.

Final score: Southern Cal 14, Notre Dame 14.

And the Irish still had not been beaten since the final game of the 1945 season— 29 games ago.

Two earthquakes hit the area that December 4. One was the real thing that shook the Southland; the other was a man-made thing that trembled the Coliseum.

"You'd have thought SC had just lost to UCLA— or Vassar even," reported the Times' Al Wolf from the Trojans' dressing room. "They had stunned the nation by achieving a tie with the vaunted South Benders, and by rights should have been reducing the Coliseum to rubble as the first step in a wild celebration. But after being so close to going all the way, the 'moral victory' soured into a 'moral defeat.'"

Dyer wrote, "The penalty for pass interference? I've seen much more vigorous defensive play go uncalled. Maybe the movies will prove something. But they can't change the score, of course. It's mighty rough that the outcome was probably due to an official's decision, but it's happened before."

Through all the gloom, however, the Trojans were given a tremendous roar of gratitude as they left the field.

A big crowd of USC students had gathered outside their team's dressing room, and when Coach Leahy tried to enter to congratulate his opponents, the students hoisted him on their shoulders and even gave him three cheers.

"This is the first time in my coaching career that I have been so highly honored by the student body of an opposing school," said the surprised Leahy.

Notre Dame led in first downs 14-12, yards rushing

230-74 and total yards 304-204. USC completed 16 passes in 31 attempts (both series highs) for 130 yards, while the Irish were 5-for-16 for 74 yards. Once again, ND was penalized more yards (40-21), but the biggest penalty of all was that six-yarder against Troy at the end of the game. Gay was also the game's leading rusher, gaining 71 yards in only seven carries.

Even though Oregon had a better league record (7-0-0) than California (6-0-0), the Pacific Coast Conference was represented in the Rose Bowl by the Bears. Michigan, the national champs, couldn't represent the Big Ten because of the strange "no-repeat" rule. So runner-up Northwestern, with losses to Michigan and Notre Dame, went instead. The Wildcats upset 10-0-0 Cal by a 20-14 score.

1949

USC Was Just Another Game On The Schedule

The twinkle of a collegiate football star is only a few short autumns, but the burnout is forever. Frank Leahy, however, had his wagon hitched to a heaven of stars, and the sport in 1949 was wondering when, if ever, his shiny system would even dim. He hadn't lost since 1945.

Three weeks into the season his Notre Dame was back as the nation's top team and would remain there.

By the last weekend in November when Southern Cal's Trojans were scheduled at South Bend for the series' 21st game, Leahy's forces had hardly broken sweat beads. Falling under the Irish gridroller were Indiana, Washington, Purdue and Tulane, then Navy, Michigan State, North Carolina and Iowa. None came remotely close to pulling off an upset.

Average score: Notre Dame 38, Opposition 7.

Jeff Cravath, in his eighth season at USC, had beaten Navy, Oregon, Washington, Washington State and UCLA, had tied Ohio State and lost to California and Stanford. It added up to a sour 5-2-1 season (any Trojan season is sour that includes losses to Cal and Stanford). But with UCLA's hide already nailed to the wall and, if Cravath could also hammer Notre Dame's beside it, then the season could be called somewhat successful.

Average score: Southern Cal 27, Opposition 17.

In reality, though, it was nothing more than USC's time on the choppin' block. And a crowd of 57,214 filled Notre Dame Stadium on a subfreezing November 26 afternoon to watch, and cheer, the proceedings.

Just like last year, Notre Dame fumbled the ball away

Leon Hart's four-year Irish career against USC was 3-0-1. He caught touchdown passes in three of those games (1946-48-49), made All-America as a sophomore, junior and senior, and in 1949 became the last lineman to win the Heisman Trophy.

in the opening seconds of the game. Also like last year, USC was unable to take advantage. Larry Courte fumbled on first down, and Mercer Barnes recovered at the Irish 26. After knocking out a first down at the 14, quarterback Dean Schneider, back to pass, was smashed by Leon Hart and fumbled. Jim Mutscheller recovered for Notre Dame at the 22.

Later in the quarter, Troy gambled and lost, leading to the game's first score. USC was fourth-and-four at its 40, and Schneider was standing in punt formation. But instead of kicking, Schneider threw a pass to Don Stillwell. He dropped it.

Notre Dame quickly hopped on its unexpected break. Bob Williams passed four yards to Frank Spaniel, then 36 yards to Leon Hart. Touchdown. Just like that. Steve Oracko converted, and it was 7-0.

It became 13-0 moments later when John Petitbon intercepted a pass and returned 43 yards for a touch-

Irish fullback Emil Sitko was the first player to score four touchdowns in the series (1947-48-49).

down. Oracko missed the kick.

The Trojans threatened again early in the second period after Don Rogers picked off a Williams pass at the Irish 27. But on fourth-and-one at the 18, USC failed to get the yard.

The Irish upped their lead to 19-0 when USC's Jay Roundy dropped a punt that Bill Barrett recovered at the Trojans' 24. The TD took only three plays. Barrett burst to the 11. Hart, on an end-around, went to the five. And Emil "Six Yards" Sitko scored from there—becoming the first player to score four touchdowns in the series.

The Irish drove back to USC's eight just before halftime, but Williams misfired on three straight passes.

Spaniel's two-yard plunge in the third quarter, and Barlett's one-yard buck in the fourth period, plus another Oracko conversion, capped the easy win.

Final score: 32-0.

Leahy, in his last 37 games, was now 35-0-2.

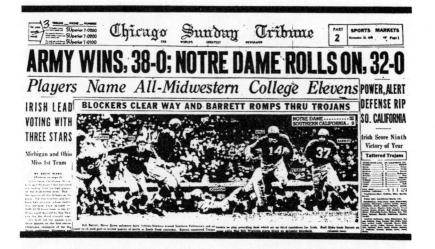

ARMY WINS; 38-0; NOTRE DAME ROLLS ON; 32-0

Players Name All-Midwestern College Elevens

IRISH LEAD VOTING WITH THREE STARS

Michigan and Ohio Miss 1st Team

POWER, ALERT DEFENSE RIP SO. CALIFORNIA

Irish Score Ninth Victory of Year

Tattered Trojans

BLOCKERS CLEAR WAY AND BARRETT ROMPS THRU TROJANS

NOTRE DAME 32
SOUTHERN CALIFORNIA - 0

The game statistics were about what one would expect after a 32-point win. The Irish led in first downs 17-9, and rushed for 316 yards, while holding USC to only 17. Troy threw the ball 36 times, a series high, and completed 16 for 148 yards. Notre Dame's air game was only 7-for-22, but for 112 yards and a touchdown. Total offensive yards: ND 428, USC just 165. The Irish, once again, also led in penalty yards by a wide 50-15 margin. Only three times in the series' 21 games have the Trojans been penalized the most yards.

Southern California finished the season with a 5-3-1 record.

The Irish had a game remaining against SMU in Dallas. The Mustangs were 5-3-1, with losses to Baylor, TCU and Rice, and posed no big threat to "the streak." ND jumped to a 14-0 lead, but by the fourth quarter it was 20-20, and the 75,000 at the Cotton Bowl were howling. The Irish made it 27-20, but Kyle Rote and SMU roared down to the Irish five late in the game. Jerry Groom intercepted a Rote pass.

Notre Dame had posted its fourth straight unbeaten season and 38th game without a defeat. Meanwhile, Frank Leahy's nine-year coaching record at ND swelled to 75-7-6 (.886). Only seven defeats in nine years?

149

Besides the Irish, there were three other major teams with perfect records in '49— No. 2 Oklahoma, No. 3 California and No. 4 Army.

For the second year in a row, California carried a 10-0-0 record into the Rose Bowl, and again had it clipped, this time by Ohio State (6-1-2). The score was 17-14, and the Big Ten had won four straight Rose Bowl games.

Meanwhile, Notre Dame's series lead over USC stood at 13-6-2.

The Pacific Coast Conference experienced its first casualty in history following the 1949 season. Montana, a member since 1924, decided to drop out, and the passing is noteworthy only because of its prolonged futility. Excluding games against league member Idaho, the Grizzlies won only one conference game— and that took 23 years— a 13-12 squeaker over Washington State in 1947. Overall, Montana left behind a 9-79-3 PCC record.

1950

Jim And Paul
Save USC's Day

"The Glamor Game" of 1950 was short on glamor, but long on excitement.

Also that year, the Associated Press published a pre-season poll for the first time. Notre Dame, unbeaten in the last four years and defending national champion, sustained its No. 1 ranking and, obviously, remained there after an opening 14-7 win over North Carolina at South Bend.

The following Saturday, October 7, the Irish were again at home, this time to face Purdue, which had only seven wins in the last two years and was a loser to Texas a week earlier in its opener.

A national sports shocker! Purdue 28, Notre Dame 14.

It was ND's first football defeat since December 1, 1945, and "The Streak" had reached 39 games (37-0-2). During that time, the Irish outscored their opposition 1256-262, an average of 32-7 per game.

Did Purdue emerge as a 1950 grid power after the big upset? It would be the Boilermakers' only win, until a season-ending 13-0 shutout of Indiana.

The Irish rebounded in the school's 500th football game to edge Tulane at New Orleans, 13-9. But the next week resulted in another shocker, a 20-7 loss to an Indiana team able to win only two other games that season.

It had been a swift and mighty tumble for Notre Dame— from No. 1 in the United States all the way to No. 3 in the state of Indiana— in only three weeks' time.

The loss to the Hoosiers also dropped Notre Dame out

Jim Sears' 94-yard kickoff return for a touchdown in the 1950 game sparked a 9-7 USC win, Troy's first over Notre Dame since 1939.

of the Top Ten AP rankings for the first time since November 14, 1944, and out of the Top Twenty for the first time since December 2, 1940— an entire decade.

When the Irish lost again, 36-33 to Michigan State, it became "old news." But ND came back with wins over Navy (19-10) and Pittsburgh (18-7), before butting Iowa to a 20-all draw.

Next: Southern California.

If Irish fans thought they had it bad in 1950, then Trojan faithful had it *horrible*. USC, believe it or not, entered its final game of the season with a grand total of one win. That single victory was against Oregon, and Oregon beat only Montana that year. Troy had tied Washington State and Stanford, and lost to Iowa, California, Navy and Washington, before suffering a 39-0 disaster to crosstown foe UCLA.

Next: Notre Dame.

The Irish were 4-3-1 and a 10-point favorite to take the 1-5-2 Trojans. But even with the teams winning only five of their 16 games, there were still over 70,000 interested enough to show up for the series' 22nd game. On the other hand, it was the smallest ND-USC crowd in Los Angeles since 1934.

Forget the records. The game's outcome wasn't decided until the final minutes, even though ND had piled up huge statistical differences.

It was, in fact, a miracle that USC was even in the game.

With the world now in the Atomic Age, gone forever were the long train treks that Notre Dame and USC had been accustomed to in their past annual battles. In 1950, the Irish flew to Los Angeles.

The Irish would also be without their coach, Frank Leahy. He was confined in Long Beach with the flu. Not Long Beach by the Pacific, but Long Beach by Lake Michigan.

The Irish scored first on the last play of the first

Notre Dame coach Frank Leahy grimaces in pain from his sick bed as the Trojans block a punt to eke out a 9-7 win over the Irish in 1950.

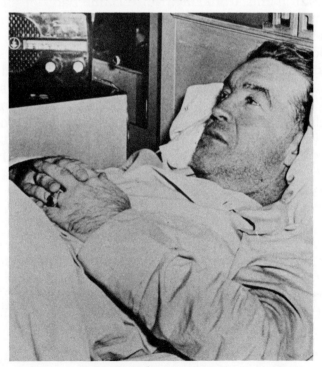

quarter. USC's Bill Jessup pounded a punt from his own endzone all the way to Notre Dame's 46. John Petitbon broke off a 10-yarder and a first down at Troy's 44. Quarterback Bob Williams threw complete to Bill Barrett for five. After an incompletion, Barrett gained only three, bringing up fourth-and-two at the 36. Williams' run gained five and the first down at the 31. John Landry rammed to the 26, then to the 22, and Williams reached the 19 for another first down. Following a yard loss, Williams drilled one to Petitbon down at the one. USC's Lou Welch grabbed Petitbon as he lunged forward trying to get into the endzone, and in charged Jessup with a vicious hit on Petitbon. He was through for the day with a concussion. Williams, on the next play, sneaked it over, Vincent Meschivitz converted, and the Irish had a 7-0 lead.

The lead lasted for only a matter of seconds. Jim Sears received the ensuing kickoff at the six and swoosh! Sears shot 94 yards for a touchdown. After Frank Gifford converted, it was suddenly a 7-7 score.

It was only the second kickoff returned for a touchdown in the series, matching Russell Saunders' feat in the 1929 game. Ironically, Notre Dame had not allowed any opponent such a score in the 21 years between the runs by Saunders and Sears.

Notre Dame continued to hammer USC, but the score remained tied until five minutes into the third period. The Irish faced fourth down from their 20 and Williams was back to punt. In crashed a 31-year-old guard from Rio Hondo, Texas. His name was Paul McMurty. He blocked Williams' kick, and the football bounded into the endzone. USC's Volney Peters dived on it, but the ball squirted from his grasp out of bounds. Safety! Two points! The first one in the series.

Trojans 9, Irish 7. But there was still 25 minutes left to play.

Southern Cal's bogged-down offense never came close to even a threat the rest of the way. But their defense, playing like a pack of wild mad dogs, continued to keep the Irish at bay.

At the game's four-minute mark came a break, and it

154

Jeff Cravath enjoys a victory ride in his last game as USC coach. Entering the game with only one win, his team pulled off a 9-7 upset at the Coliseum. Cravath was USC's team captain in the series' first game in 1926.

went Notre Dame's way. USC's Dean Schneider sliced a nine-yard punt out of bounds at his 36.

"Ohhh, no!" groaned Trojans everywhere, now thinking, even expecting, still another bitter defeat to the Irish.

John Landry gained five to the 31. John Mazur, in at quarterback for Williams who was now in the hospital after taking a lick from Pat Cannamela, threw into the endzone to Meschievitz. The pass was right on target, but the ball, two defenders and Meschievitz all arrived at the same place at the same instant. Meschievitz was stripped of the ball and, at the time, also the ball game.

On the next play, USC was penalized 10 yards, giving ND a first down at the 21. But three plays gained only two yards, bringing on Meschievitz for a field goal try. It wasn't even close.

Southern Cal had held its ground! The Coliseum was going cuckoo screaming its kudos.

Even Tommy Trojan, the bronzed statue a few miles away on the USC campus, did a couple of flips.

Final score: USC 9, ND 7—Troy's first conquest of the Irish since 1939—11 long years ago. Even glitzy L.A. would become just like any other celebrating college town that night. They would also be celebrating their school's

TROJANS SCORE SURPRISE WIN OVER IRISH, 9-7

Inspired Navy Gang Ruins Army Before 103,000, 14-2

Next Move Runs Away With Vanity

Sears Runs 94 Yards to TD Before 70,177

300th all-time football victory.

And the biggest heroes of the day were a 19-year-old sophomore halfback named Jim Sears and a 31-year-old senior guard by the name of Paul McMurty, playing his last collegiate game.

The 1950 game was similar to the 1936 game in that Notre Dame finished with overwhelming statistics but nothing to show for its superiority except a tie and a defeat. The '50 figures saw the Irish way ahead in first downs (13-1), yards rushing (145-70), yards passing (104-4) and total yards (249-74). ND threw the most passes ever against USC (30) and completed 12, while Troy tried just two and completed one after throwing 97 times the last three series games. The Irish also led in turnovers (4-2) and penalty yards (71-56).

But in '36 a 96-yard interception return by USC's Lawrence Langley didn't count as "total yards," just as Jim Sears' 94-yard kickoff return didn't in '50.

Combining the two games, Notre Dame led in first downs (31-2) and total yards rushing and passing (655-127). However, Southern Cal scored more points (22-20) and escaped with a tie and a win. Incredible.

But the series lead still belonged to Notre Dame by a 13-7-2 margin, and their point total was 320-230 (15-11 average).

The Irish finished 4-4-1, their worst season since 1933. Southern Cal was 2-5-2.

Even a big upset of Notre Dame, plus a 19-7-3 (.707) record against the California-Stanford-UCLA trio, could not salvage Jeff Cravath's coaching job at Troy. There had been rumblings and grumblings the last few years, and though his contract still had two years to go, "Mr. Nice

Guy" was cut loose.

Cravath's overall (nine-year) record was 54-28-8 (.644) which included two successful Rose Bowls. But seven wins, eight losses and three ties the last couple of seasons was nowhere near USC's grid standards. He was 1-4-1 versus Notre Dame.

For the third straight year, California took unbeaten credentials (9-0-1) to the Rose Bowl, only to lose again. Michigan, just 5-3-1 and the worst record in the bowl's history, beat the Bears by a 14-6 score, marking the Big Ten's fifth straight victory.

1951

GAME 23

Almost...

One USC faction wanted Illinois' Ray Elliott as its new coach, another wanted Paul Brown of the Cleveland Browns. Unable to land either, the Trojans plucked "one of their own" who was right there on campus as track coach— 44-year-old Jesse T. Hill.

Hill had been a Trojan running back and track stand-out in 1928-29. Upon graduation, he began a professional baseball career that got off to a rousing start. Signing with the Hollywood Stars of the Pacific Coast League, Hill hit a home run in his first pro appearance at bat, against the Los Angeles Angels. He later was an outfielder for the Yankees, Senators and Phillies (1935-37). Hill batted .289 in the majors. After coaching stints at the high school and junior college level and six years in the U.S. Navy, Hill returned to USC in 1947 as track coach.

Jesse Hill was just what the good grid doctor ordered.

After topping Washington State, San Diego Navy, Washington and Oregon State, Hill's hot Trojans went to Palo Alto to meet No. 1-ranked California. The Bears had not lost a regular-season game in four years, since a setback to USC in 1947, and their streak had reached 38 games (37-0-1).

Troy 21, Cal 14, and Hill had USC ranked No. 6 in the nation.

Good things continued to happen, as TCU and Army also fell, and USC was 7-0-0, its best start since 1932.

Crash! Stanford 27, USC 20...UCLA 21, USC 7.

The Irish, meanwhile, opened with a 46-0 drubbing of Indiana and were rated No. 5. The following Friday,

October 5, Notre Dame played its first-ever night game, opposing the University of Detroit at Briggs Stadium (now Tiger Stadium). In the first quarter, John Petitbon scored three touchdowns, which totaled a phenomenal 226 yards, to lead a 40-6 rout before a crowd of 52,231.

Notre Dame then lost its first home game in nine years, a stunning 27-20 upset by SMU, which would win only two other games that year. After drubbing Pittsburgh, Purdue and Navy by a combined 82-9 score, the Irish absorbed a 35-0 road pounding by No. 5-rated Michigan State.

Next came Notre Dame's 400th football victory, 12-7 over North Carolina at Chapel Hill. The following game resulted in a 20-20 knot with Iowa.

The Irish then headed for Los Angeles for the second straight year and the fourth time in five years. The 12 previous ND-USC games played at the Coliseum had averaged just over 82,000 in attendance. But the 1951 encounter attracted only 55,783 on a misty, smoggy December 1 afternoon. The second half was played under the lights, and it was reported that the players could hardly be identified from the press box.

The Trojans were 7-2-0 by an average score of 24-17, Notre Dame 6-2-1 by 25-12. USC, for some reason, was a seven-point favorite. Was it the "home field advantage?" Actually, there wasn't one; Troy had beaten ND only four times at the Coliseum. Or maybe it was because this was the youngest Fighting Irish team in history, averaging only 19.5 years.

This was the 24th game of the series and would be the 12th time the final outcome was settled by one touchdown, or less.

Like so many times in the series, USC got a break early in the game but once more couldn't capitalize. ND's Johnny Lattner fumbled and George Bozanic recovered at the Irish 27. Four plays netted only three yards.

Late in the quarter, Troy started from its 35 and took the lead with a seven-play march. Dean Schneider made a dazzling catch of Frank Gifford's pass, which resulted in a gain of 22 yards to Notre Dame's 43. Harold Han's run gained 16 more to the 27, and Gifford got it to the 23 as

Gracing the Administration Building, the Golden Dome of Our Lady has overlooked the Notre Dame campus for more than 100 years.

the first period ended. After play resumed, Han went to the 19, Gifford to the 14, Han to the eight, and Gifford scored from there. Gifford missed the point-after, but the Trojans led 6-0.

The Irish answered. Coach Frank Leahy pulled senior quarterback John Mazur and sent in Ralph Guglielmi, an 18-year-old freshman sensation from Columbus, Ohio.

Guglielmi immediately went to work.

160

Starting from his 23, he passed to Chet Ostrowski for 16 yards. On third-and-14, he threw to Petitbon for 17 to Troy's 48. Then, facing third-and-nine, he fired another one to Ostrowski, this one good for 31 yards down to the 16. Lattner legged it to the three and scored two plays later. But the score remained 6-6 when Dan Zimmerman blocked Bob Joseph's conversion attempt.

Southern Cal, after taking the kickoff, zipped back down the field. It was second-and-two at the Irish 15, and Gifford was cracked hard by linebacker Becker Shannon. He fumbled, and Lattner recovered at the 14.

The Trojans moved ahead again with a touchdown in the third period, set up by Nick Nunis' interception of a Guglielmi pass at the ND 33. On third-and-16, Schneider's pass to Sears was good for 31 yards down to the five. Sears scored on the next play, but Gifford again missed the conversion. (USC had converted only 15 of its 37 touchdowns against the Irish.)

Notre Dame, also using an interception, fought back to tie it early in the fourth period. USC had driven to the Irish 33, but Eugene Carrabine picked off a Sears pass at the 27. From there Lattner, Neil Worden and Joe Heap, on seven running plays, quickly advanced to Troy's 39. Worden then broke through and scored. But with the "conversion curse" returning to the series, Joseph missed, and the score remained 12-12. (Of the series' 88 touchdowns at this point, just 47 had been converted.)

Once again, the Trojans roared right back, only to blow yet another chance to win the game. They were first-and-goal at the eight and somebody on Troy's side selected a strange play to try to get the job done. Cosimo Cutri was sent into the endzone as a pass receiver. He was covered by Dan Shannon. Cutri was 5-6, 160 pounds. Shannon was 6-0, 190 pounds. Quarterback Sears, the hero of last year's game with a 94-yard kickoff return, threw to Cutri. The throw was intercepted by Shannon in the endzone. It was Sears' second interception of the day.

The frustrated Trojans absolutely couldn't believe it. "All of those lost opportunities..." they lamented.

Notre Dame received a punt at its 39 in the final period and drove to the winning touchdown. Guglielmi, on first down, pitched a short pass out to the speedy, swivel-hipped Johnny Lattner, whose fancy footwork resulted in a big gain of 31 yards before the Trojans could corral him at their 30. Operating seven straight plays inside the USC tackles, Lattner went to the 29, Worden to the 25, then to the 23, Petitbon to the 20, Lattner to the 12, Petitbon to the 11 and Lattner to the seven. The crumbling Troy line, braced for even more inside stuff, then watched as Petitbon sped around end for the touchdown. Joseph finally kicked a successful conversion.

The game clock showed six minutes still left, but this game was over.

"The final Irish score took the heart out of the USC team," reported Arch Ward of the *Chicago Tribune.* "The players were battered, dispirited and done at the end. There was no mistake about what had happened to them."

Final score: 19-12.

The disgusted Trojans could just sadly sit there and mull over their numerous chances that could have put the game away. They had been first down at the 27...second down at the 15...first down at the 33...and first down at the eight. No points resulted.

The Irish were so thrilled to escape with a victory that the players, for the first time, "escorted" a fully-clothed Coach Leahy into the showers for a thorough drenching.

The final statistics were about as close as the game itself. Each team rushed for 183 yards, while ND led in first downs 16-15, yards passing 153-126 and total yards 336-309. It was the first time that Troy had reached the 300-yard plateau against the Irish. Worden led all rushers with 91 yards in 22 carries (4.1). Guglielmi completed eight of 13 passes for 161 yards.

Southern Cal started the season with seven straight wins but finished with a bitter 7-3-0 record in Jesse Hill's break-in campaign. The Irish were 7-2-1. Neither team cracked the final Top Twenty poll. The leading five teams in 1951 were Tennessee, Michigan State, Maryland, Illinois and Georgia Tech.

In the Rose Bowl, the Big Ten made it six straight as Illinois walloped Stanford by a 40-7 score.

1952

GAME 24

Jinxed? Yes

At this stage of the Notre Dame-Southern California football rivalry it's safe, and also sad, to say that the dreaded sports term, "JINX," had become a part of this otherwise-wonderful series.

The Trojans were 9-0-0, ranked No. 2 in the nation and had buried their opposition by an average score of 27-4.

The Irish were 6-2-1, ranked No. 7 and had topped their opposition by a modest 19-12, on the average.

But USC blew still another game to Notre Dame, washing a great season down the drain and giving the Irish a commanding 15-7-2 series lead. In six of the games which Troy failed to win they were outscored by only nine points, 76-67. Eke out four of those and the series would be tied.

One can call it what he may—jinx, voodoo, demon trinkets, monkey dust, or maybe even "the luck of the Irish." Whatever, it raised its head in three of the first four games of the series back in the 1920's and has, for the most part, been spooking the Trojans for a quarter of a century.

Notre Dame pulled off a unique ploy in 1952 by meeting, and beating, four conference champions: Texas of the Southwest Conference 14-3, Oklahoma of the Big Seven 27-21, Purdue, co-champ of the Big Ten 26-14, and then, for a clean sweep, a hard-earned 9-0 victory over Southern Cal of the Pacific Coast.

The Irish were tied 7-7 by Pennsylvania, and their losses were to Pittsburgh (22-19) and national champion Michigan State (21-3).

As the 24th USC-ND game approached, Jesse Hill's Trojans had rolled over nine opponents, which included a 78-19 combined shellacking of California, Stanford and UCLA.

Subfreezing temperatures and snow greeted USC upon its Friday arrival in the Midwest but, instead of holding an afternoon workout out in the elements, the team practiced on the parquet-floored Athenian Ballroom of the Elkhart Hotel in nearby Elkhart, Ind. The speedy Trojan team found more bad news the next day at Notre Dame Stadium—a frozen field.

The visitors were made six-point favorites, and it was reported that "several hundred USC rooters were among the crowd of 58,394."

And they all watched as the Trojans shot themselves in the foot, not once, but repeatedly throughout their frustrating and dismal afternoon of football.

For the fifth year in a row Southern California got a break on the opening kickoff, and for the fifth time it resulted in nothing positive. Joe Heap, trying to field the bouncing kick near the sidelines, fumbled it out of bounds down at the six-yard line. Johnny Lattner punted to his 44. Leon Sellers, on two straight carries, rammed to a first down at the 31, but things fizzled and Troy punted.

The Trojans, on their next possession, faced a fourth-and-three at the Irish 33. No first down.

USC really shot itself early in the second period. Lattner punted to Troy's 40, but a penalty gave him another chance, and this time he kicked to the 25, where Jim Sears caught it, started up field, and suddenly lateraled to Al Carmichael. But Carmichael wasn't there and was not even expecting a lateral. Menil Mavraides recovered for Notre Dame at the 19.

What a gigantic difference that penalty made.

Lattner went to the 17, Ralph Guglielmi to the 12, Lattner to the nine and a first down. Coach Frank Leahy then pulled off his ol' "sucker shift" play, in which the backfield shifts from the T formation into the single wing. It drew USC offsides and moved the ball to the four. It also brought a loud protest from Coach Hill. On fourth down Lattner scored from the one. The conversion was no good

164

Notre Dame running back Joe Heap fights a frozen turf and USC's defense in the 1952 game at South Bend.

because of a fumbled snap from center, but the Irish had a 6-0 lead with 8:35 left in the half.

BAM! USC fired into its foot again to start the third period. Carmichael fielded the kickoff on the goal and slipped down at the five. Des Koch punted from the endzone to his 46, and the Irish turned it into three points. Stalling at the 10, Bob Arrix booted a field goal for a nine-point lead.

The Trojans kept on shooting themselves.

Later in the third quarter, Sears intercepted a Guglielmi pass at the Irish 22. But on fourth down from the 18, Koch missed a field goal try so badly that the ball flew out of bounds at the four-yard line.

This definitely wasn't Southern Cal's day.

More shooting in the final period. Sears completed a 51-yard pass to Jim Hayes at ND's 28. Sears came back with another pass, but Dan Shannon, just like last year, intercepted a Sears pass in the endzone.

The Trojans quickly forced a punt, and Carmichael returned it all the way to the Irish one-yard line, but a clipping penalty retreated the offense back to the 29. Sears threw another interception, this one to Jack Alessandrini at the 18. Notre Dame, however, fumbled it right back, when Bob Hooks recovered Tom Carey's bobble at the 22.

USC drove to a first down at the 11. A pass from Sears to Ron Miller got it to the three. Two smashes by Sellers brought up a fourth-and-one for a first down, fourth-and-two for a touchdown.

Sellers crashed the line again. He came up inches short. USC had run out of bullets.

Final score: Notre Dame 9, Southern Cal 0. The bitter Trojans were more than ready to get out of town.

As for the "sucker shift," Coach Hill told newsmen after the game, "That shift is an evasion of the spirit of the rule. I thought it was definitely uncalled for."

A few months later the Rules Committee legislated against the shift.

Braven Dyer of the *Los Angeles Times* reported, "Our lads took a solid beating statistically and otherwise, yet as late as the fourth quarter they still had a chance to win the game...I hate to be so brutally frank in view of the fine season Jim Sears and his pals gave us, but the boys played a bad ball game and left several hundred rooters with a very sour taste in their mouths. There were repeated penalties on clutch plays and there was also some very doubtful strategy...The dejected squad of Trojan players who saw their undefeated season and hope for national championship honors slip out of their icy grip, showered and dressed slowly under the grandstand of Notre Dame Stadium."

The Irish completed only one pass (for 10 yards) in 15 attempts, while USC was 8-for-17 for 82 yards. But ND led in first downs 12-5, yards rushing 194-67 and total yards 204-149. Eight Trojan turnovers (five interceptions and three lost fumbles) destroyed any chance they had of winning. Once again, however, Notre Dame led in penalty yards, this time, 95-65. Only three times (1928-32-38) had USC been penalized more than the Irish. Total series penalty yards: ND 1081, USC 573.

Neil Worden (73 yards) and Lattner (66 yards) paced ND's ground game. Sellers of USC also gained 66 yards.

Notre Dame, with a 7-2-1 record, finished No. 3

Read 'Em and Weep
Notre Dame, 9, SC, 6
LSU, 30, Tulane, 6
Marquette, 27, COP, 3.

Los Angeles Times

S.P.O.R.T.S

VOL. LXXI   CC *   SUNDAY MORNING, NOVEMBER 30, 1952   PART 7

IRISH RUIN TROY'S 'PERFECT YEAR,' 9 TO 0

behind Michigan State and Georgia Tech. Oklahoma was fourth, followed by Southern Cal.

The Pacific Coast Conference hadn't won a Rose Bowl in seven years, but Southern Cal snapped the slump with a 7-0 victory over 6-2-1 Wisconsin, co-champ with Purdue of the Big Ten.

The Trojans finished with a 10-1-0 record. A good season, no doubt, but....

1953

GAME 25

Color The Series' Silver Game
Blue & Gold And Black & Blue

Before a game had been played in 1953, the Fighting Irish had replaced Michigan State as the nation's No. 1 team.

Eighty-four of the 171 writers making up the Associated Press' pre-season poll voted Notre Dame at the top, followed by the Spartans, Georgia Tech, UCLA and Alabama, with Southern California ranked eighth.

After defeating Oklahoma, Purdue and Pittsburgh, ND hosted Georgia Tech, which hadn't lost in 31 games (29-0-2). The Irish won 27-14, but Coach Frank Leahy became seriously ill in the first half. He passed out in the locker room during intermission and was taken to the hospital, where he remained until Wednesday. It was first thought to be a heart attack but was later diagnosed as acute pancreatitis.

The Irish remained No. 1 with wins over Navy, Pennsylvania and North Carolina, bringing the season to November 21 and a game with Iowa, 5-3-0 and ranked 20th.

With Notre Dame on the Hawkeyes' 12-yard line just seconds before halftime, and with no timeouts left, Leahy signaled for lineman Frank Varrichione to fake an injury. He blatantly pulled it off, fooling nobody, but the officials had no choice except to stop the clock. The manipulation directly led to a touchdown, which eventually led to a 14-14 final score.

The Irish still had their unbeaten season, but the damage had been done. An enraged national press blasted Leahy for such tactics, and it was dramatically reflected in the next AP poll.

Irish quartet (left to right) *John Lattner, Neil Worden, Joe Heap and Ralph Guglielmi combined for 59 points against USC during 1951-52-53 games.*

During the previous week No. 2 Maryland had received only 42 first place votes (less than half the number as Notre Dame), but a week later 154 writers voted the Terps No. 1 (more than three times that of Notre Dame).

The Irish fell to No. 2—and stayed there.

While Notre Dame was experiencing another nail-biting season, Jesse Hill's Southern Cal Trojans were adding up a 6-2-1 ledger, beating Washington State, Minnesota, Indiana, Oregon State, California and Stanford, tying Washington and losing to Oregon and UCLA.

ND's average score was 29-14, USC's 21-13.

It was November 23 and time for the series' Silver Anniversary game. Just under 98,000 filled the Los Angeles Coliseum, but by the fourth quarter's early minutes, the place had almost cleared out—except for those wearing Blue and Gold.

Notre Dame hammered on Troy all afternoon and emerged with a 48-14 triumph, the biggest victory margin in the series. Now, after 25 games, the Irish held a 17-6-2 advantage, and their scoreboard total increased to 396-256 (16-10 average).

Johnny Lattner, the Heisman Trophy winner that

169

USC running back Des Koch tries to escape Notre Dame's Fred Mangialandi in the 1953 game. Trailing the play are Notre Dame's John Mense (51) and Joe Bush (73) and USC's Roger Hooks (16) and Vern Sampson (53).

year, scored four touchdowns and rushed for 157 yards, both series records at the time. Lattner also became the only player in history to score four touchdowns against USC.

Troy took the opening kickoff and put on an impressive drive of 62 yards to the Irish 15, but no more. Following an ND punt, USC kicked it right back, and Joe Heap, taking it at his six, streaked 94 yards for a touchdown. The rout was on.

Notre Dame made it 13-0 on its next possession, moving 61 yards in nine plays, with Lattner scoring from the nine. Ralph Guglielmi added his first of five conversions.

The Trojans got on the boards in the second period. Des Koch returned a punt 43 yards to ND's 31, and he later scored from the five. Sam Tsagalakis added the conversion for a 13-7 difference.

It took only four plays for another Irish score, highlighted by Neil Worden's 55-yard scamper to USC's two. He got the call again and scored to make it 20-7.

Early in the third period ND, on a punt, had USC back on its five. Addison Hawthorne cracked for 10 but fumbled, and Paul Matz recovered for the Irish at the 15. It was Lattner for five, then Lattner for 10. Touchdown. ND 27, USC 7.

Troy fought back. Jim Contratto came on at quarterback and took his team 64 yards in only six plays for a score. Aramis Dandoy got it from 12 yards out, Tsagalakis kicked good, and it was 27-14.

But the relentless Fighting Irish came right back with another touchdown, marching 61 yards in eight plays, capped by Lattner's one-yard run.

Still in the third quarter, the boys from the Midwest made it 41-14, compliments of the host team. USC was backed near its own goal when Dandoy got trapped in the endzone. In desperation he threw a "forward pass" across the field toward Jim Contratto, who was also behind the goal line. It fell incomplete, but Notre Dame's left guard, Pat Bisceglia, pounced on the ball for a touchdown. The officials ruled it a lateral.

The Irish scored again in the final period. Troy's Contratto fumbled, and Matz came up with his second

Notre Dame halfback Johnny Lattner scored six touchdowns in victories over USC in 1951-52-53.

Notre Dame's Neil Worden, escorted by Don Penza (83), runs for 55 yards in second quarter of the 1953 game in Los Angeles. Caught at the two-yard line by USC's Leon Clarke, he scored on the next play en route to a 48-14 rout of Troy.

recovery that led to a touchdown, this one at Notre Dame's 35. Three plays gained 15 yards to mid-field, and that man Johnny Lattner zipped in from there. Jack Lee converted this one.

Mercifully, it ended a little later.

Both teams knocked out 17 first downs, ND led in rushing yards 336-112, USC passed for more yards 143-41, while the winners were out front in total yards by 377-255. Five Trojan turnovers aided in the game's lopsided difference.

Braven Dyer of the *Los Angeles Times*: "The Irish line ripped holes in the Trojan line that the whole Notre Dame band could have marched through, had they been there."

Wilfrid Smith of the *Chicago Tribune*: "Southern California was a determined team. This could be questioned on basis of the final score except that those who watched this battle know that the Trojans refused to quit long after they realized they had no chance for victory."

One game still remained in Leahy's coaching career, SMU at South Bend on December 5. He won it 40-14.

Notre Dame halfback Joe Heap holds distinction of being the only player to return a punt for a touchdown in series history: 94 yards in 1953.

Notre Dame coach Frank Leahy posted a 8-1-1 record against USC. He had six undefeated teams and ranks number 2 in career all-time winning percentage (.864) behind Knute Rockne.

Francis William Leahy, because of health problems, was forced to retire, and it became official on January 31, 1954. He still ranks second behind Knute Rockne in winning percentage among college coaches with at least 10 years of service.

Including his two seasons at Boston College and 11 at Notre Dame, Leahy coached 129 games, compared to Rockne's 122. Leahy was 107-13-9 (.864), Rockne 105-12-5 (.881). Leahy had seven undefeated seasons (six at ND), won four national championships (1943-46-47-49) and finished second twice. In one stretch from 1943 to 1950 (Leahy didn't coach in 1944-45), he lost just once in 51 games (47-1-3). Only one team, Michigan State, beat him more than once.

Leahy was 8-1-1 against Southern California.

1954

Too Much Morse

Southern California had beaten Notre Dame only once since 1939, and there was no hope, really, of any change in 1954.

Terry Brennan, a former Irish halfback (1945-48), became the new coach at Notre Dame. After winning three straight city championships at Mount Carmel High School in Chicago, Brennan returned to Notre Dame in 1953 to coach the freshman squad. His father and brother had also played for the Irish.

The 26-year-old Brennan inherited a team which the Associated Press ranked No. 1 in its pre-season poll. His first game was a 21-0 shutout of Texas at South Bend. But then came a 27-14 loss to Purdue, and Irish boosters would not see their team at the tiptop of the polls for another 10 years.

But Notre Dame football returned to normal with wins over Pittsburgh, Michigan State, Navy, Pennsylvania, North Carolina and Iowa. Next on the list was USC.

Jesse Hill's Trojans, after defeating Washington State, Pittsburgh and Northwestern, were rated No. 9 and awaiting TCU's visit to the Coliseum. The Horned Frogs were only 1-2-0 but pulled the rug, and Troy tumbled 20-7—and all the way out of the Top Twenty.

USC, however, rebounded by beating Oregon, California, Oregon State, Stanford and Washington for a rise to No. 7. But looming straight ahead was a powerful 8-0-0 UCLA bunch, ranked No. 1 earlier in the season and now second behind Ohio State. It wasn't even close. Bruins 34, Troy 0. If that wasn't enough misery for the USC players,

175

they had only a week to pull up their broken and tattered bootstraps and get ready, mentally and physically, for another dreaded trip to South Bend.

Once more, the Trojans had to tolerate wet and cold wintry weather, a slippery and soggy field, plus a noisy Notre Dame Stadium crowd that numbered 56,438.

The Irish were a solid 14-point favorite.

USC received the opening kickoff and knocked out three first downs before punting to the Irish 14. On first down Don Schaefer fumbled, and Marv Grox recovered for Troy at the 16. Jim Contratto, on the fifth play of the drive, scored from the three. Sam Tsagalakis converted, and five minutes into the game it was 7-0. It was also USC's first first-quarter score against ND since 1941.

The Trojans missed a good chance for more points early in the second period. ND faced fourth-and-26 at its four-yard line. Joe Heap was back to punt, and in rushed Mario DaRe. Heap eluded DaRe and managed to get off a

USC coach Jess Hill (left) *and Notre Dame coach Terry Brennan* (right) *meet on a cold, wet South Bend day in 1954.*

Read 'Em and Weep
Nine 25 Auros 20
Vallenova 41 Fordham 6
Vanderbilt 26 Tenn. 6

Los Angeles Times   SPORTS

VOL LXXIII   CC   SUNDAY MORNING, NOVEMBER 28, 1954   PART II 7

IRISH SHADE SC ON LATE 72-YD. RUN, 23-17

short kick out to the 19. Three plays netted only two yards, and Tsagalakis missed a field goal.

Taking possession at the 20, Heap's 40-yard burst highlighted a quick advance to USC's 29. Later from the 12, quarterback Tom Carey lateraled to Heap on what was thought to be an end run, but Heap stopped and passed to Jim Morse for a touchdown. Schaefer's kick was good for a 7-7 tie, and that's the way the first half ended.

The Trojans regained the lead five minutes into the third period. Starting from their 47 USC sent Contratto off on a 39-yard run to ND's 14. It was soon fourth-and-13, however, and Tsagalakis came on and kicked a field goal for a 10-7 advantage.

After an exchange of punts the Irish strung out the most incredible drive in series history. Starting at the 14, they overcame two penalties for 20 yards en route, registered six first downs, and kept the football for 22 plays and just over 10 minutes of playing time. Capping the journey, which actually totaled 106 offensive yards, was a smash from the two by Schaefer. It was the series' 100th touchdown. He also tacked on the conversion, giving him 14 points for the day and giving his team its first lead, 14-10, as the game had moved into the fourth period.

USC, picking itself up, came right back.

Contratto completed five of five passes— 13 yards to Ernie Merk, eight and 13 yards to Leon Clark, eight yards to Gordon Duvall, and 21 yards to Chuck Griffith and a touchdown, sparking a nine-play, 72-yard drive. It was Troy's first TD pass against the Irish in 13 years. Ed Fourch converted.

USC 17, ND 14, 10:30 left to play.

The hopped-up Trojans soon had the ball again when Orlando Ferrante grabbed Heap's fumble at Notre Dame's 40-yard line.

177

The full house sat in stunned silence.

The Irish defense, however, prevented any further damage and forced a punt that went out of bounds at the 21.

Heap picked up three yards. Schaefer got four, bringing up third down. Third-and-three at the 28. Hold here, USC, get the ball back, and...

Quarterback Ralph Guglielmi took the snap from center Dick Szymanski and pitched back to sophomore Jim Morse, who received the ball at full stride around his left end. Speeding to mid-field, he met Contratto, USC's "last chance." Morse ripped through Contratto's desperate tackle and was in the clear. Seventy-two yards. Touchdown!

Jim Morse's sensational play jolted Notre Dame Stadium into an eruption of hysteria topped off by wild screams of ecstasy. They absolutely couldn't believe it. But neither could the grief-stricken Trojans. Total desolation. Total hopelessness.

Schaefer converted. But who gave a hoot? The score now stood: ND 21, USC 17. Time left: 5:57.

Notre Dame scored again just 70 seconds from the end. Well, sort of scored. USC was backed to its 14-yard line when a wild snap from center sailed into the endzone. Halfback Frank Clayton rushed back and frantically tried to pick the ball up. Unable to get a handle on it, he just slapped it out of bounds. Safety and two points for the Irish.

Final score: Irish 23, Trojans 17.

Southern California lost valiantly in the series' 26th game that dreary November afternoon in 1954, but Notre Dame was also valiant in victory. This was the era of "60-minute" football players, and Coach Brennan played only 19 men throughout the grueling game.

With USC winning only one of the last 12 games, Notre Dame's series lead had now ballooned to 17-7-2.

Six Irish turnovers, compared to Troy's one, kept the '54 game as close as it was. Strangely, the series had turned into almost a "turnover bowl," with 72 in the last 10 games. The winners led in first downs 17-8 and total yards 399-181. The Irish completed two of nine passes for

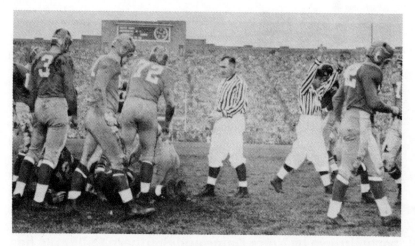

On the ground and barely visible is USC's Jim Contratto (12) after plunging for the game's first touchdown. Notre Dame players looking on are Ralph Guglielmi (3) and Ray Lemek (72).

26 yards, USC seven of 16 for 81 yards.

Jim Morse, the hero of the day, set a new series rushing record with 179 yards (19 carries), 22 yards more than the previous high set by Johnny Lattner in last year's game.

Notre Dame still had a game remaining against SMU in Dallas. The Irish won 26-14 and finished with a 9-1-0 record and a final No. 4 ranking behind Ohio State, UCLA and Oklahoma.

Southern Cal also had one left, in the Rose Bowl. UCLA was the '54 Pacific Coast Conference champ, but the "no-repeat" rule prohibited its return, so the runner-up Trojans went instead. Ohio State 20, USC 7.

Troy, once 8-1-0, finished 8-4-0.

1955

Hornung Wins The Battle, Arnett Wins The War

For almost all of the last 15 years, the annual gala party thrown by Notre Dame and Southern California has seen the Irish in black ties, while Troy was parking the cars and washing the dishes.

The '55 affair appeared to shape up as more of the same.

A harassed Jesse Hill was in his fifth year as coach at USC, and even with a respectable .727 (31-11-2) winning percentage, he had beaten UCLA only once and never defeated Notre Dame. Furthermore, the pre-season reports from the area press piled even more pressure upon Hill by tagging his 1955 team as another Thundering Herd.

Everything began well. The Trojans walloped Washington 50-12 and Oregon 42-15, before topping always-tough Texas 19-7. Then the bottom fell out. Troy won only two of its next six games, which is an extremely unhealthy momentum factor going into the season finale against the Irish.

Notre Dame, meanwhile, acted like Notre Dame. It began as the sixth-ranked team in the nation, blanked the first three opponents, lost 21-7 to Michigan State, then chalked up five straight victories. It was time to pack the tuxedos and head for California.

ND was 8-1-0 and ranked No. 5. USC was 5-4-0.

It didn't seem to matter that the Irish were made the big favorite, nor that the Trojans were a sure-fire cinch to fail for the 12th time in the last 13 series games. Still, nearly 95,000 fans poured into the Coliseum for the 27th

180

USC's Jon Arnett races into the endzone ahead of ND's Paul Hornung in 1955 game. Arnett scored 23 points, Hornung 14; they combined for 546 all-purpose yards in the Troy victory, 42-20.

game between these old intersectional foes.

What a party! They combined for 35 first downs, 919 total yards of offense and 62 points.

The game wasn't billed as a personal duel between Notre Dame's Paul Hornung and Southern Cal's Jon Arnett, but it should have been. The two combined for 37 points and accounted for 546 yards. Hornung scored two touchdowns, kicked two conversions, and rushed and passed for 354 yards. Arnett tallied three TDs, kicked five conversions and totaled 192 yards rushing, receiving and returning kickoffs.

USC took the opening kick and went 68 yards in 11 plays to take an early lead. Facing a fourth-and-six at ND's 39, Coach Hill thought, "What the heck. Go for it!" And the gamble paid off when quarterback Elsworth Kissinger passed complete to Don Hickman for a gain of 18 yards to the 21. From the 15, C. R. "Runaway" Roberts rambled all the way to the one. Kissinger sneaked it over. Arnett's toe made it 7-0.

The Irish retaliated with an almost identical drive, going 67 yards, also in 11 plays, to tie. Facing a fourth-and-seven situation at USC's eight, Coach Terry Brennan thought, "What the heck. Forget the field goal. Go for it!" And the gamble paid off when Hornung broke two tackles and battered his way into the endzone, hauling two more Trojans on his back. Hornung also converted for a 7-all score.

Troy came right back. Arnett returned the kickoff 31 yards to his 43. Ron Brown bashed out an 18-yard gain on first down. After the Trojans worked it to the 15, Kissinger, on the first play of the second period, quickly pitched out to Roberts, and "Runaway" scored for a 14-7 advantage.

It was soon 21-7. Dick Fitzgerald fumbled the ensuing kickoff, and George Galli recovered at ND's 21. On fourth down at the 17, Hill ordered a little trickery this time. He sent in kicker Bob Isaacson for an apparent field goal try. Kissinger, the holder, knelt at the 25. Upon receiving the snap, "Kissy" (as he was called) jumped to his feet and fired a pass to Arnett at the 10 and a first down. A play later from the 11, Arnett scored. Isaacson converted.

Just two minutes before intermission, USC punted to the Irish 22. Hornung, on first down, heaved a long one—right into the hands of Jim Morse. Touchdown. Seventy-eight yards. And remember, this was the same Jim Morse whose 72-yard run beat Troy last year. (The Hornung-to-Morse click is still the longest TD pass in the series.) But Hornung's conversion attempt was wide. Halftime: Southern Cal 21, Notre Dame 13.

Plenty happened in the third quarter, but no points resulted. The Irish recovered a fumbled punt at Troy's 37, only to have Leon Clark intercept a Hornung pass. Later in the period Roberts fumbled at ND's five, ruining a chance for a 28-13 lead. Two plays later from the 13, Hornung skirted end, broke clear and raced 59 yards before being overhauled by Clark at USC's 28, saving a touchdown. Hornung came right back with a burst to the 14, then passed to Dean Struder at the three as the wild period came to a close.

After the break to swap ends of the field, Schaefer crashed the line, was hit hard by a host of Trojans, and

USC's C. R. (Runaway) Roberts picks up yardage in his team's 1955 victory. Other players are USC's Marv Goux (52) and Notre Dame's Pat Bisceglia (62) and Ray Lemek (72).

the ball popped free into the endzone. Ron Brown recovered for USC.

By this time the big crowd was wilting fast from the frenzied, action-packed performances of both teams.

Two plays later from the 12, Ernie Zampese blasted a quick-kick which rolled dead at Notre Dame's 34—a 54-yard boomer.

But here came that Hornung-to-Morse passing combination again. This one went for 60 yards, all the way to Troy's six. Hornung scored from the one, and after his conversion, the Fighting Irish now trailed by only one, 21-20.

The game clock still showed 11:58 to play. Plenty of time for Notre Dame to win...or for Southern Cal to lose.

After the kickoff, quarterback Jim Contratto made his first appearance of the day. Facing a third-and-six at his 36, Contratto, a southpaw, rolled left, jerked free of two Irish tacklers, and hummed a long pass that Arnett took in stride at the 26 and hauled home to complete the 64-yard thriller—the second longest TD pass in the series. Arnett capped it with another conversion, and the Trojans extended their lead to 28-20. Still, however, just over 11 minutes remained.

"Hold on," pleaded Troy rooters everywhere. "Please hold on for 11 more precious minutes..."

On Notre Dame's next possession, USC guard Laird Willott rushed in and deflected a Hornung pass that was intercepted by Bing Bordier at his 49.

The Coliseum was now upside down.

Brown, on first down, burst through the line for 36 yards to the 13, and a play later from the 12, Contratto zipped a pass to Don McFarland streaking across the middle for a touchdown. Following Arnett's conversion, the count was up to 35-20, which was USC's biggest lead over the Irish since 1933.

Time left: 7:26. The Trojans began smelling victory. Moments later, here came that man Willcott again, batting another Hornung pass into the air that enabled McFarland to pick off at the Irish 23. Arnett later scored from the seven, and his conversion gave him his 23rd point of the game.

With the clock down to the 2:58 mark, the Trojans could now begin celebrating.

Running back John Arnett scored three touchdowns, kicked five conversions, and gained 192 all-purpose yards in 1955 as the Trojans thrashed the Irish, 42-20.

Read 'Em and Weep		
SC 42, Notre Dame, 20		
Army, 14; Navy, 6	**Los Angeles Times**	SPORTS
N. Carolina, 21; Virginia, 14		
Tulane, 13; LSU, 13 (tie)		

| VOL. LXXIV | CC | SUNDAY MORNING, NOVEMBER 27, 1955 | Part II 7 |

SC UPSETS IRISH, 42-20, BEFORE 94,892

Final score: USC 42, ND 20. What a thrill! What a victory! What a party!

Not counting the war years of 1944-45, it was the most points run up against a Notre Dame football team since 1900.

Jesse Hill got a victory ride to midfield, his first such joy since New Year's Day of 1953, 31 long games ago.

Here are some observations from reporters of the *Los Angeles Times:* Al Wolf — "The Trojans, making like a pigskin posse, cut Jess Hill down just in the nick of time and triumphantly carried him off into the sunset, with the rope still dangling from his honest neck...Once reaching the privacy of their dressing quarters the Trojans voted by acclamation to give the game ball to the coach...Tears streamed down Jess' face as he gulped through a thank-you speech...And after the press was admitted, it was several minutes before he could compose himself."

Paul Zimmerman— "Last night the alumni wolf cry for Hill was stilled. No effigy of his was found on the campus. Jess was back in the throne room."

Ned Cronin— "Jesse Hill had his scalp sewed back on yesterday afternoon at the Coliseum surgical center. It took 42 stitches...Hill is now in a position to where he can wear his hat without thumbtacks to keep it from sliding off. His scalp had been scaled back until his head looked like a bowling ball."

Dick Hyland— "This was the Trojan attack opposing coaches knew SC could mount. This was the overwhelming speed, power and deftness the team has refrained from putting together in four losing games this season. This was El Trojan at his best."

But even with "El Trojan at his best," Notre Dame still amassed 521 yards of total offense (238 rushing and 283 passing). USC's offense totaled 398 yards (252-146). ND

185

also led in first downs 18-17, and its passing game showed 11 completions in 23 attempts, while Troy completed seven of 11. There were 10 turnovers, seven by the Irish. Penalty yards? For this first time since 1938 and only the fourth time in series history, Southern Cal was penalized more yards (55-46).

The series now stood 17-8-2, Irish.

Notre Dame finished 8-2-0 and a final No. 9 ranking; USC was 6-4-0 and rated 13th. But with a season-ending triumph over the Irish, Troy's four losses were much easier to endure.

This marked the 10th year of the Big Ten-Pacific Coast Conference tie-in with the Rose Bowl, and the Midwesterners made it nine wins when Michigan State edged UCLA 17-14.

1956

2 Straight!

Except for the 1942 wartime game, nothing had upstaged the annual Irish-Trojan clash— until 1956— when it took a real beating by a big controversy between two Notre Dame men. Like most disputes, this one began simply, was fueled by words and egos, then exploded into a full-blown feud that made headlines all over the country.

In reality, however, the fuse leading up to the big fuss had been spewing sparks over the past three months. Irish faithful expected big things from Coach Terry Brennan's third edition when the Associated Press' preseason poll had their team ranked No. 3 behind Oklahoma and Michigan State.

Notre Dame's opener was at Dallas against an SMU team coming off a 4-6-0 record the previous year. The Mustangs pulled off a 19-13 "upset." But a 20-6 win over Indiana got the Irish back in the groove.

Then, like the mighty *Titanic*, Notre Dame football hit its iceberg and was sent to the bottom.

There was a 28-14 home loss to Purdue...a 47-14 home loss to Michigan State...a 40-0 home loss to Oklahoma...a 33-7 loss to Navy at Baltimore...then a 26-13 loss to the Panthers at Pittsburgh. And never before, in its 70 years of playing the game, had Notre Dame lost five in a row.

It was something that had the nation's football fans in disbelief.

The shocking streak, lasting 42 days and 42 nights, was finally snapped with a 21-14 victory over North Caro-

187

PHONE NUMBERS TO SERVE YOU

Chicago Daily Tribune *Sports / Finance* PART 2

Saturday, December 1, 1956

PATTERSON WINS TITLE; KO'S MOORE IN 5

Count Archie Out on 2d Knockdown

Youngest Champ Carries Fight to Aged Foe

THE KNOCKOUT

Archie Moore grimaces under power of right hook landed by Floyd Patterson (right) in first round at heavyweight title bout last night in Stadium.

The strain and ravage of 20 years in the ring are etched on Moore's face as he grovels on the floor with Referee Frank Sikora counting the count of doom.

Brennan Blasts Leahy in Irish Feud

LAYDEN BACKS TERRY; CALLS EX-COACH 'PUBLICITY CRAZY'

'Personal Thing' No Pressure on and Slur Set Coach,' Says Off Row Alumni Head

FRANK LEAHY   TERRY BRENNAN

Ron Delany Wins Record 1,500 Meters

MELBOURNE, Australia, Dec. 1 (Saturday)—The United States won three gold medals on the closing day of track competition in the Olympics today, to total 16 and beat its 1952 performance by two.

In addition, Ron Delany, a Villanova student running for Ireland, beat the world's best milers in the 1,500 meter run to give the United States a record victory.

A capacity crowd of 103,000 sat in a warm, clear weather to see Irish student defeat the world's mile record holder, who Landy of Australia, in 3 minutes 41.2 seconds, breaking the Olympic record of 3:45.1 set by Jozy Barthel of Luxembourg in 1952 and being only 4.10 of a second slower than the world mark held by Istvan Rozsavolgyi of...

In the WAKE of the NEWS
By DAVID CONDON

THE YOUTHFUL CROWN PRINCE lifted himself to separation from the ancien pretenders aha a quickly turned out, was merely the smart prince his reign may be a long one ... Yes, Floyd Patterson, who will not be a big one ... Yes, Floyd Patterson, who will not be 22 until Jan. 14, was magnificent in becoming the youngest ever to enter the heavyweight championship ... Yes, Archie Moore was pathetic in attempting, at 39, to become the oldest ever to ascend to the prize ring's most coveted prize ... Time was on Patterson's side, but so were two stinging fists that sneaked out repeatedly to bruise Moore's face as braised as a man bewildered ... Experience was stopped in he on the sage of Moore, 20 years a gladiator. This experience did not prevent Archie from making the biggest error of his life—stepping into the ring against Patterson. And Archie's experience was a useless weapon against the Patterson thrusts that, even as early as the first round, left most of the Chicago Stadium fans stunned speculating only on how long Moore could last ...

SHORTLY AFTER 9 P. M. Floyd Patterson made a humble entrance into the ring and unceremoniously doffed his blue and orange robe. Almost a half hour later he made a triumphant exit, as suddenly recognized by all America's hero that the thought may be frighten-

Floyd Calm in Ascending Ring Throne

BY ROBERT CROMIE

Heavyweight Champion Floyd Patterson, who less than 10 minutes before had won the most glittering prize boxing has to offer, sat on the edge of his dressing room table facing a crowd packed of approximately equal layers of sports writers and publicists with drag enough to promote press tickets.

His forehead was beaded with sweat and the shine on his face was faint and enigmatic. It was the smile of a poker player who has just raked in the biggest pot of the evening on a fourth ace.

Floyd sat patiently and without any emotion. He obligingly posed with his left fist placed gently against the side of ...

Manager Cus D'Amato was, and waited for the flashing bulbs to stop ...

Floyd Patterson Fight

His left jaw stung just as much as his left hook, and these added to powerful body blows with both hands, made Moore look like the one who had been fighting professionally only four years.

Patterson beat to his jab right off the reel, driving Moore to the ropes at the beginning of the opening round.

He tied the devoted edge on that one, however, for Moore, fighting masterfully from his corner, bobbing and weaving, managed to roll up almost more points for the younger...

The second round was almost like the first. Much of it was tit and tire, and it also could have been scored as even ...

Then in the third, when Patterson got up a head of steam, and the fourth, when, while still a bit tapping, and...

Floyd Almost Judicious

The questions began, and all of ing the running of the old ...

---

lina at South Bend. But the winning ways lasted only a week, until a 48-8 crushing at Iowa City by the Hawkeyes.

And now it was on to Los Angeles, where the 2-7-0 Irish would meet Southern Cal for the seventh time in the last 10 years.

And Southern Cal was lickin' its chops.

At the same time Notre Dame was getting off to its miserable start at Dallas, USC was in nearby Austin taking care of the Longhorns by a big score of 44-20, propelling Troy to No. 6 in the nation. Next came a 21-13 win over Oregon State which was "only good enough" for a fall to No. 10. After defeating Wisconsin 13-6 and Washington 35-7, the pollsters moved the Trojans back to sixth place.

But a trip to Palo Alto turned sour as Stanford fooled the Trojans 27-19, and it was bye-bye Top Ten. Next on USC's mind were UCLA and Notre Dame, but first, Troy was scheduled at Eugene to get 3-4-1 Oregon out of the way. Oops! Ducks 7, Trojans 0.

Now USC could get serious in its thoughts about UCLA and Notre Dame. And it did, starting with a 10-0 shutout of the Bruins.

The big ND-USC buildup took on its normal once-a-year hoopla— until Friday— when the fuse burned into the dynamite.

BOOM!

The controversy hit. Who started it? None other than the ol' coach himself, Frank Leahy.

Leahy hosted a television show and a few days earlier had asked Paul Hornung to appear for an interview. Hornung had to refuse because of a team rule which would not permit a player to go on television the week of a road game. It was, in fact, a rule Leahy had started when he was coach. He kept insisting. Coach Terry Brennan finally had to step in and give him a flat "No!"

Leahy got, well, sort of peeved.

Leahy told the Associated Press in Los Angeles, "It's not the losses that upset me, it's that attitude. What has happened to the old Notre Dame spirit? Those great fourth-quarter finishes. That old try right down to the final whistle even if there was no chance of winning?"

The AP release went on to say, "Many observers close to the scene have felt that key injuries and an inexperienced sophomore line have been main factors contributing to Notre Dame's miserable showing...There were 22 sophomores on the squad of 38 for the Iowa game...But Leahy discounted Notre Dame's greeness when he said, 'You don't stay green forever and these boys, as freshmen, were rated among the greatest prospects ever at Notre Dame.'"

Brennan replied, "This is a personal thing. Something came up between us a couple of days ago. But I won't talk about it now. I think if Leahy's interest in Notre Dame was sincere he wouldn't have said such a thing."

Leahy fired back, "If any Notre Dame man is critical of

what I've said, I can only reply, 'Isn't it true?' Notre Dame can lose games, but in the past they have always gone down swinging...The team just quit last week against Iowa."

Elmer Layden, the former Horseman fullback and Irish coach, came to Brennan's defense. Layden said, "Leahy's statements were in very poor taste. Leahy's publicity crazy, and he's only trying to keep his name in the newspapers. He should remember that his 1950 team lost four and tied one. Sure, Leahy had some great teams, the teams after the war, when he had returning service men. But in 1950 he had boys. Being able to coach men, instead of boys, is damn nice— if you can get it."

Things raged on, but veteran Notre Dame publicist, Charley Callahan, summed it up best when he said, "None of these things happen when you're winning."

How true. One of the easiest things in the world is to be a good sport— when you're on top.

Speaking of controversies, almost half the Pacific Coast Conference was in hot water. Southern Cal, California, UCLA and Washington were on probation for under-the-table payments in excess of what the conference allowed for living expenses. Included among USC's penalties was that players could participate in only half the games in 1956. They could choose. And it seems mighty strange why the coaching staff would allow its All-American running back, Jon Arnett, to miss the Notre Dame game. He had already played out his allotment.

Of the 53 players listed on the roster that year, only eight with previous varsity experience failed to see action against the Irish. But one was Arnett.

This would also be Jesse Hill's last game as coach. He had resigned and accepted the role of athletic director.

Fans don't follow 2-7-0 teams on the road, not even Notre Dame, so the attendance for the series' 28th game on that balmy December 1 was held down to only 64,538.

But it doesn't seem to matter how many people show up, or what the situation might be, these two teams almost always put on a sterling show when they get together.

The 1956 contest was no exception.

In 1955-56 games against Southern Cal, quarterback Paul Hornung amassed 569 all-purpose yards, scored 22 points and punted nine times. USC captured both games in which the 1956 Heisman Trophy winner played.

Just as in last year's game, both clubs scored on their first possession. USC's Don Hickman returned the opening kickoff 14 yards to the 34. Ernie Zampese gained five and Hickman 19 to the Irish 42. Eight plays later from the 10, Jim Conway circled end untouched for the touchdown. Ellsworth Kissinger converted, and it was a quick 7-0 score.

Notre Dame then marched 76 yards, also in 10 snaps. The big play was a 40-yard gain on some zany doings. From the Irish 24 Dick Lynch hit the line for four yards, and the ball suddenly popped into the air, only to have teammate Dick Royer snatch it and gallop 36 more yards to Troy's 36. Quarterback Bob Williams later scored from the six. Hornung, suffering painful injuries to both thumbs and switched from quarterback to halfback for this game, missed the conversion.

The Trojans made it 14-6 on their next series of downs. And it didn't take long. Starting from his 23, R.C. "Runaway" Roberts shot for 18 yards. Runs by Roberts and Zampese gained 17 more to ND's 42. Conway, back to pass, got trapped but was sprung free on a crushing block by Hillard and gained 18 yards to the 24. Tony Ortega took it to the 20, and Zampese to the 15. Conway then pitched out to Roberts, who in turn lobbed a pass into the endzone to Hill. Rex Johnston kicked good.

With 6:36 left in the second period, Notre Dame scored its second touchdown. Hornung returned a punt 35 yards to USC's 49. Overcoming two major penalties, the Irish still advanced to the 10, and Williams threw to Bob Wetoska for the tally. Hornung converted.

Halftime: Trojans 14, Irish 13.

To begin the third quarter a clipping penalty was the major factor in forcing a Hornung punt from deep in his own territory. Zampese returned the kick nine yards to ND's 37. Led by the bruising runs of Zampese, who was the game's leading rusher with 125 yards in 20 carries, Troy reached the 15. Conroy then completed a pass to Don Voyne for a touchdown. Kissinger converted, once again giving his team an eight-point advantage.

It lasted only a few seconds. Hornung took the ensuing kickoff at his five, swung to the sideline, cracked through the first wave of onrushing defenders, stiff-armed a couple more, broke into the clear at his 35, and was off all alone to the finish line. It was a 95-yard run and the fourth longest in the series. Hornung also booted the conversion, and for the third time in the game, the Irish trailed by a point.

And, just like last year, Southern Cal took a 21-20 lead into the final quarter.

Early in the period, USC faced a fourth-and-one at Notre Dame's 38. The ball was handed to Zampese to get the yard and the big first down. Mr. Zampese did much more. He blasted off tackle, kept churning, powered his way into the clear and sped for a touchdown. Kissinger kicked good for another lead of eight points with 14 minutes still remaining in the game. But there was no more scoring.

Final: 28-20, giving USC back-to-back wins over the Irish for the first time since 1938-39.

Chicago Sunday Tribune *Sports / Finance* PART 2
DECEMBER 2, 1956

NAVY, ARMY TIE; FIGHTIN' IRISH LOSE, 28-20

FUMBLE HELPS MIDDIES GAIN 7-7 DEADLOCK

Cadets' Defense
Surprises Foe

Leo Beats Calumet, 12-0, for Prep Title

TRAFFIC HEAVY, BOTH ON FOOT AND IN THE AIR LANES

Ryan and Boyle Lead Victory Before 66,282

BY JOHN LEUSCH

On the Ground

HORNUNG'S 95 YARD GALLOP THRILLS FANS

Trojan's Ground Power Wins

The Trojans led 20-13 in first downs (a first since 1942), 314-112 in rushing yards and 394-254 in total yards (a first since 1940). ND's passing chart showed 11-for-15 for 142 yards, USC's 6-for-12 for 80 yards. The game produced only three turnovers, the fewest since 1940. The Irish, meanwhile, set a series record with 111 yards in penalties.

Hornung, on just 17 "attempts," accounted for 215 all-purpose yards. In the 1955-56 games against Southern Cal, he rushed for 119 yards (18 attempts), passed for 284 yards (11-for-24), caught three passes for 26 yards, returned a kickoff for 95 yards and returned two punts for 45 yards. It all added up to 569 all-purpose yards. He also punted nine times for a 37.1 average and scored 22 points with three touchdowns and four conversions.

Paul Hornung won the Heisman Trophy in 1956.

The *Times'* Frank Finch reported, "Somebody wanted to know if Jess (Hill) agreed with Frank Leahy that Notre Dame had lost its fighting spirit. Without mentioning Leahy's name, Hill snapped, 'The man who made that statement doesn't know those Notre Dame boys. I have long since learned to respect and admire Notre Dame teams'....most of the Trojans agreed that Leahy was off his rocker."

Finch went on to say, "It had been rumored that Hill might be persuaded to stay on during the Trojans' penance to the PCC. It was argued that no coach in his right mind would want the SC job next year, what with nothing but a handful of sophs, frosh and transfers available for action."

193

Asked if he would return as coach, Hill said, "Yes, but I'd want a 50-year contract."

Hill's six-year stay as coach resulted in a 45-17-1 record (.722). But as with any USC coach, the record must be divided into two categories—one against the California-Stanford-UCLA-Notre Dame combination, and one against all the others. Hill was .833 (32-6-1) versus "others," but only .542 (13-11-0) playing the "Big Four." He defeated Cal all six times, split with Stanford, and was 2-4 with UCLA and the Irish. Hill's last team did, however, beat both UCLA and Notre Dame—the first time that the Trojans had done that in one season since the Howard Jones days of 1938.

USC finished 8-2-0, but it was only good enough for a final AP ranking of 18th. Notre Dame's 2-8-0 was, of course, the worst in its history—not counting an 0-1-0 in 1887, the school's first year at the game.

But the Irish still led in their wars with Troy, 17-9-2, and the scoring derby by 459-343, an average of 16-12 per game.

Oregon State won the 1956 PCC title and kept up the league's tradition of losing to the Big Ten in the Rose Bowl. It was Iowa 35, Beavers 19, giving the Midwestern teams a 10-1-0 advantage. The one loss? To Jesse Hill's Trojans following the 1952 season.

1957

GAME 29

Where Had All The
Glamor Gone?

"Turnabout," as they say, "is fair play."

In 1955, Notre Dame lost five straight games for the first time and endured its worst season since an 0-1 record in 1887.

In 1956, USC lost five straight games for the first time and endured its worst season since an 0-1 record in 1902.

The Pacific Coast Conference was reeling from its second year of probation of four members. One imposed sanction was that juniors in '56 lost their eligibility as seniors in '57.

USC's 51-member roster consisted of only 14 returning lettermen, 29 players not on last year's squad, and a rookie coach, Don Clark, who got the job simply because nobody else wanted it.

Clark, captain of the 1947 Trojans, later a lineman for the San Francisco 49ers and an assistant under Jess Hill, was talked into taking on the responsibility.

"When I became coach, we hadn't recruited for two years. They (the PCC) didn't say we couldn't recruit but they put severe restrictions on us. In the spring of 1957, we were down to walk-ons— no quarterbacks or receivers to speak of," he told Mal Florence of the *Los Angeles Times*.

Where had all the glamour gone?

The Trojans, despite playing a surprisingly rough brand of football, still lost their first five games— 20-0 to Oregon State, 16-6 to Michigan, 20-14 to Pittsburgh, 12-0 to California and 13-12 to Washington State. After topping Washington 19-12, it was three more losses— 35-7 to Stanford, 16-7 to Oregon and 20-9 to UCLA.

195

Standing next in the belt line was Notre Dame— with steel-tips.

The Irish, even though coming off a poor 2-8-0 season, were ranked No. 18 in the pre-season poll of the Associated Press and, astonishingly, received two first-place votes.

After blanking Purdue 12-0 and Indiana 26-0, then edging Army 23-21 and Pittsburgh 13-7, Notre Dame football "was back," with a No. 5 rating behind Texas A&M, Oklahoma, Iowa and Auburn.

But consecutive losses to Navy (20-6) and Michigan State (34-6) tumbled the Irish out of the Top Twenty. Not for long, though.

That brought the season to November 16 and a trip to Norman to meet No. 2-rated Oklahoma, with its awesome 47-game unbeaten streak. The Sooners' last loss had been to the Irish "way back" in 1953. But ND pulled off one of the great victories in its storied history, 7-0, and it carried enough influence with the pollsters to zoom the Irish from nowhere all the way back up to No. 9. The "high," however, lasted for only a week, as No. 8 Iowa pulled off a 21-13 triumph. Southern Cal was coming up.

ND was 5-3-0 and rated 12th in the nation. USC was 1-8-0 and rated only ahead of Idaho in the Pacific Coast Conference.

The coldest day in series history welcomed Clark's California sun boys to the frozen Midwest. The 20-degree temperature was made even more bitter by strong winds and swirling snow. The crowd was considerably short of capacity, but still 54,793 braved the icy elements and huddled together like a huge flock of frozen sheep.

Even though it was just as uncomfortable in Chicago, a high school game there attracted over 17,000 *more* than the Irish and Trojans could pull at South Bend.

Where had all the glamor gone?

Taking everything into consideration that November 30, the final score was about what one would expect. ND 40, USC 12.

The Irish took advantage of two turnovers and bunched quick scoring thrusts in the first period to grab a 13-0 lead. The first was set up when Bob Williams intercepted

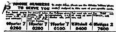  
IRISH OVERPOWER TROJANS IN 40-12 ROUT
Navy Beats Army, 14-0; Accepts Bid to Cotton Bowl

a Tom Mauldin pass and returned 28 yards to Troy's 29. Ron Toth scored six plays later from the three. The conversion was missed.

Three plays after the ensuing kickoff Clark Holden fumbled, and Charles Puntillo recovered at USC's 27. On the fifth play from the 17, Williams passed to Monty Stickles for the touchdown. Stickles converted.

But the Trojans fought back in the second period when Rex Johnston scored from the 10. The score stayed 13-6, however, on a flubbed conversion attempt.

Notre Dame got the six right back. Pat Doyle took the kickoff and raced 92 yards—untouched—for a touchdown. It was the second year in a row for such a play, as Paul Hornung hauled one back 95 yards in the 1956 game. Stickles again missed on the conversion. Maybe the toes just couldn't bear the cold.

Halftime: 19-6.

Notre Dame took the second-half kickoff and marched 66 yards in 10 plays to make it 26-6. Jim Cotty blasted over from the two, and Stickles kicked good this time.

USC cut it to 26-12 late in the third period as Mauldin sneaked in from the one. Once again the conversion was missed.

The Irish recorded two more touchdowns in the final quarter. Williams lobbed a seven-yard pass to Stickles, and Stickles also converted, giving him 15 points for the day. Then sophomore quarterback George Izo came off the bench to lead an 81-yard charge and capped it with an eight-yard toss to Dick Prendergast. Aubrey Lewis got his name in the scoring book with the game's final point, a conversion.

A week later Notre Dame traveled to Dallas and closed out the season with a 54-21 smashing of SMU. It was the most points by the Irish in exactly 100 games, dating back to a 59-6 rout of Tulane in 1947.

The statistics were about as lopsided as the game. The winners smothered the losers in all categories: First downs 23-11, yards rushing 292-127, yards passing 120-59 and total yards 412-186. ND completed 10 of 14 passes, while USC was a woeful six completions in 29 attempts. Toth led all rushers with 73 yards in 18 carries (4.1).

As for the high school game, a crowd of 72,157 watched at Soldiers Field as Mendel edged Calumet, 6-0, to capture the all-Chicago prep championship. The only score came on the game's last play, a 41-yard pass from Jim Brennan to Jim Gallagher.

Notre Dame finished 7-3-0 and a No. 10 national ranking, while Southern Cal was left to stew over a disastrous 1-9-0 campaign.

Howard Jones wouldn't have believed it.

Neither would Jones have believed that the Pacific Coast Conference had been reduced to sending a representative with three defeats to the Rose Bowl. It would be 7-3-0 Oregon versus 8-1-0 Ohio State. But with no West Coast team ranked in the Top Twenty that year, it was the best the PCC had to offer.

The Bucks beat the Ducks 10-7.

1958

GAME 30

The Great Goal Line Stand

The Pacific Coast Conference hit rock bottom in 1958. Washington State's No. 10 ranking the first week of the season would be the only time all season a PCC team would crack the elite club. At season's end, California's 16th position represented the league's only ranked member.

The PCC also posted the worst non-conference record in its 43-year history, winning only 10 of 28 games. And to make the record even more unimpressive, there was only one win against a team (College of Pacific) with a winning record (6-4-0). And the 10 wins were against opposition whose combined record was a lowly 33-65-1.

Southern Cal had played .500 football when time arrived to meet Notre Dame in the finale. There were wins over Oregon State, Washington State, Stanford and Washington; losses to Michigan, North Carolina (both by one point), Oregon and California. Also thrown in was a 15-all tie with UCLA.

The football situation at Notre Dame was hardly any better.

Somebody once said, "When the wolf comes to the door, love goes out the window." Well, the wolf, the howling wolf, was perched at the door of Coach Terry Brennan.

Brennan's once-glowing halo now resembled a disfigured figure eight. It doesn't seem to matter what kind of material Notre Dame might have, or might not have, the pollsters constantly rate it high in the pre-season polls, which is part of the "problem." Notre Dame coaches are

199

fully expected to sustain those lofty positions which, of course, is an *impossible* task on a year-in-and-year-out basis.

It's known as "pressure."

But that's why Notre Dame is the *toughest* coaching job in America. It's also why Notre Dame has the highest winning percentage and has won more national championships than any other collegiate football team.

Before anybody had kicked off in '58, Notre Dame was pegged by the Associated Press behind only Ohio State and Oklahoma. That left the Irish players, the Irish coaching staff and the multitude of Irish fans hardly anywhere to go— except down.

And that's where they went.

Things began as everybody had planned. The Irish defeated Indiana and SMU. Next was No. 3 Army, visiting South Bend for only the second time in its 36-game rivalry with Notre Dame, which had slipped to No. 4. The Cadets won 14-2, marking ND's 100th all-time football defeat (in 579 games).

It was a real see-saw season from that point on. There was a win over Duke and a loss to Purdue...a win over Navy and a loss to Pittsburgh...a win over North Carolina and a loss to Iowa.

Next: ND versus USC at Los Angeles.

On paper, the teams were fairly evenly matched. The Irish were 5-4-0 by an average score of 23-18, the Trojans 4-4-1 by 15-11.

Still, however, the visitors were made a big 11-point favorite. Troy's "home field advantage" in this series had long ago disappeared.

Just under 67,000 showed up at the Coliseum for the series' 30th renewal and they would witness still another head-bashing affair. The first 34 minutes of the game were a whirlwind of offensive action, while the remaining 26 minutes featured the rivalry's greatest goal line stand.

The Irish kicked off, quickly picked off a pass and went for a score. Bob Sholtz intercepted and returned 18 yards to Troy's 42. Nick Pietrosante drove for 10 and a first down. Bill "Red" Mack, in two carries, gained 11 and another first down at the 21. A Pietrosante run and a short pass from George Izo to Pietrosante netted eight more to the 13. After an incompletion, bringing up fourth-and-two, Pietrosante rammed ahead for three and a first down at the 10. Jim Cotty cracked to the six, Pietrosante to the one, and Pietrosante for the touchdown. Monty Stickles missed the conversion.

The Trojans came right back to take the lead. Don Buford, who would have a fantastic game, took the kickoff and sped past 10 defenders, only to be tripped up by the last, Chuck Puntillo, at the USC 48. Five plays later from the Irish 41, Buford, retreating all the way back to his 46, unleashed a long spiral— right into the hands of Hillard Hill as he crossed the goal. Don Zachik kicked

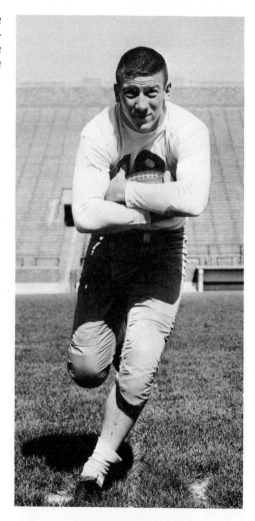

Irish fullback Norm Odyniec caught the winning 21-yard pass from Don Williams in 20-13 win over the Trojans in 1958.

good, and Southern Cal had a 7-6 advantage.

Buford, called the "Bantam Buzzsaw" because of his 5-5, 155-pound frame, intercepted an Izo pass on Notre Dame's next possession and ran it back 21 yards to the 13. But on fourth down from the eight, Tom Maudlin threw incomplete into the endzone.

USC got the ball again moments later when Jerry Traynham intercepted another Izo aerial and raced 31 yards to ND's 35. But the Irish forced a punt.

Notre Dame went to its 43, and on the first play of the second period, Izo threw another interception, again to Buford, and "Buzzsaw" returned 44 yards to the enemy 24. The Trojans scored in three plays as Buford ripped off a 16-yarder to the eight, a penalty moved it to the three, and Traynham took it in from there for a 13-6 lead.

For some weird reason, however, Coach Don Clark, or one of his assistants, or somebody, called for a two-point conversion try, the first year of the new scoring system. A pass failed, and the lead remained at seven instead of a possible eight.

Bob Williams replaced Izo at quarterback on Notre Dame's next possession and he immediately faced a third-and-11 at his 29. Williams came through with a completion to Bob Wetoska for 18 yards and a big first down at the 47. Five running plays advanced it to USC's six, and Williams ran it over for the score. The conversion, however, was flubbed due to a bad snap from center and the Irish still trailed by a point.

Halftime: Southern Cal 13, Notre Dame 12.

The terrific pace continued in the third quarter. The Irish received the kickoff and, staying on the ground, pounded out a drive that reached USC's 21. Williams then went to the air, hitting Norm Odyniec at the 12, and "Ody" refused to be stopped, bulldozing his way into the endzone with two Trojans hanging on.

With an 18-13 lead, obviously, the Irish went for two, and they got it when Williams connected with Cotty. That made the score 20-13 just four minutes into the second half.

Late in the period, USC drove 77 yards and a first down at Notre Dame's *one-foot* line.

202

WILLIAMS RALLIES IRISH TO 20-13 VICTORY

Army Power and Passes Beat Navy, 22 to 6

RELIEVES IZO, LEADS THIRD PERIOD SURGE

CADETS RALLY AFTER SUDDEN MIDDIE SCORE

66,903 Also Cheer Trojans' Buford

CRISP BLOCKING, LONG LUNGE BRING AUSTIN SIX BIG POINTS

Clark Holden hit into the line and fumbled, but teammate Maudlin recovered back at the one-yard line.

On second down, Maudlin swung wide and was stopped for a yard loss by Williams and Scholtz.

On third down, Maudlin kept and was met head-on by Frank Reynolds. No gain.

On fourth down, it was Buford trying for the two yards and the touchdown, but he was stopped short by Myron Pottios.

Braven Dyer of the *Los Angeles Times* wrote, "Sometime, somewhere some football team may have staged a greater goal line stand than the Fighting Irish of Notre Dame did in the fourth quarter of yesterday's heartstopper with the Trojans of Southern California. But I doubt it."

Late in the game Williams intercepted a Maudlin pass at Troy's 22. After reaching the eight, Odyniec fumbled and Dan Ficca recovered for USC at the two.

But it was that goal line stand that saved the game for the Irish.

Final score: Notre Dame 20, USC 13.

The Irish, as usual, were way out front in the statistical battle, leading in first downs 22-15 and total yards 346-256. Troy led in passing with 118 yards (8-for-18) to 58 for ND (4-for-13). The Irish also led in turnovers 4-3 and in penalty yards 49-25.

Buford accounted for 216 all-purpose yards. He rushed for 34 yards, passed for 41 yards, returned two kickoffs for 68 yards, returned two interceptions for 65 yards and one punt for eight yards.

203

Notre Dame's series lead went to 19-9-2.

The passing of the 1958 season brought with it the passing of the University of Idaho as a 37-year member of the Pacific Coast Conference. The Vandals had not won a conference game in four years, only one in eight years and just seven since World War II. In all, UI posted a 31-122-5 record in PCC play. Even though members of the same conference, USC and Idaho hadn't met since 1929.

California won the conference crown in '58, but lost 38-12 to Iowa at Pasadena, the league's 14th loss in its last 16 Rose Bowl appearances.

The nation's football fraternity got a severe jolt a few days before Christmas when Notre Dame announced that Terry Brennan had been fired.

Except for President Harry Truman's firing of General Douglas MacArthur seven years earlier, it's doubtful that any dismissal created so much national attention. And in Brennan's case, so much outrage, if for no other reason than its timing—December 22.

Brennan coached five years at the Golden Dome and left behind a 32-18-0 (.640) record, including a 3-2-0 slate against Southern California.

For the first time since 1951, both Notre Dame and USC failed to make the Top Twenty.

1959

Upset At South Bend

Coach Don Clark's Southern Cal Trojans, overlooked as pre-season Top Twenty timber, racked eight straight opponents and earned a No. 4 national ranking behind Syracuse, Ole Miss and LSU.

Troy's two biggest rivals, UCLA and Notre Dame, were still ahead but neither posed a serious obstacle. The Bruins were 3-3-1, and the Irish even worse off at 3-5-0.

Trojan fans were beginning to visualize a national championship draped in Cardinal and Gold.

For the eighth straight time since 1917, Notre Dame called upon "one of its own" as football coach. His name was Joe Kuharich.

Kuharich grew up in South Bend and as a child hung around Knute Rockne's practice sessions. He attended Riley High School. Upon graduation from Notre Dame, where he lettered as a guard in 1935-36-37, he coached the freshman team, then played two years for the NFL Chicago Cardinal. After serving four years in the U.S. Navy, Kuharich later held head coaching jobs at the University of San Francisco, and with the Cardinals and Washington Redskins.

Kuharich inherited a team which had lost four games the previous season and was returning only 12 lettermen. Still, however, the Associated Press pollsters ranked Notre Dame as the country's 16th best team in its pre-season tally.

After an opening 28-8 win over North Carolina, Kuharich's Irish leaped eight notches up to eighth. Reality took over. Notre Dame then lost to Purdue (28-7) and later

205

to Michigan State (19-0), Northwestern (30-24), Georgia Tech (14-10) and Pittsburgh (28-13). On the better side were wins over California and Navy.

The season had now reached November 21. Unbeaten USC faced UCLA at the Coliseum, and ND was at Iowa City to meet 16th-ranked Iowa.

Upset! Bruins 10, Trojans 3.

Upset! Irish 20, Hawkeyes 19.

USC's great season was all awash. And now the Trojans had to take their devastating defeat to South Bend, where they hadn't won since 1939.

More woe awaited their Midwest arrival—bitter cold weather—for Californians. The thermometer was in the mid-twenties and a 15 mile-per-hour wind was whipping in out of the Northwest.

Troy was 8-1-0 and ranked No. 7, Notre Dame was 4-5-0. USC had scored 34 more points than ND and surrendered 100 less. But despite the wide on-paper differences, the visitors were made only a one-point favorite.

The series' smallest crowd since the depression days of 1937, 48,684, bundled up and shivered through that overcast November 28 afternoon.

The Chicago press blamed the low turnout on the weather, Thanksgiving Weekend and the South Bend transportation strike. But the primary reason, most likely, was the won-lost record of the home team.

Notre Dame won the toss and elected to receive. The Irish worked it to their 44 before George Sefcik punted to USC's eight, leading to the game's first score.

Facing a fourth-and-one at his 17, punter Clark Holden was rushed hard by Monty Stickles and got off a short kick to his 38. Gerry Gray, on first down, broke away for 30 yards but fumbled when hit by Jerry Traynham at the eight. The ball bounded forward another six yards and ND's Nick Buoniconti recovered at the two. Gray slashed into the endzone on the next play. Stickles converted for a quick 7-0 lead.

Later in the period, USC got something going, before a critical clipping penalty killed the surge. Bob Levingston intercepted a George Izo pass and returned 32 yards to Notre Dame's 38. Quarterback Willie Wood tossed a screen pass out to Traynham and, behind beautiful blocking, reached the Irish five-yard line— but there was that clip— and Troy was forced to retreat back to its 29. After getting a first down at the 26, the threat froze on some wild passing by Wood.

The Trojans staged another bluff just before intermission. Levingston picked off another Izo pass and ran it back 26 yards to his own 38. Wood led a drive to ND's 23, where it was fourth-and-two. An incomplete pass stuffed it.

Halftime: 7-0.

The Irish scored again midway through the third period. Starting 49 yards away after taking a punt, Izo passed 15 yards to Stickles to the 34. After a Gray run, a major offensive penalty, and a 20-yard strike from Izo to Jim Crotty, ND faced a third-and-one at Troy's 25. Gray got the first down at the 23. Bob Scarpitto went to the 20, Izo passed to Pat Heenan at the 10, Scarpitto advanced to the six, Izo to the one, and Gray into the endzone for his second touchdown of the game. Stickles kicked good again for a 14-0 advantage.

Eleven seconds later it became 16-0. Stickles kicked off to Angelo Coia, who headed for the sideline, got cornered, headed back for the other sideline, and along the way was forced to retreat just inside his goal. Coia was then nailed by Gray. It was a safety, the series' third.

USC finally got off the mat in the final period with its only touchdown, going 84 yards in 11 plays. From the Irish 13, Ben Charles threw to Coia, who made a leaping catch in the endzone. A two-point conversion pass was unsuccessful.

Final score: Notre Dame 16, Southern Cal 6.

The Irish victory was just as solid on the statistical side as it was on the scoreboard. They led in first downs 17-11, yards rushing 219-97, yards passing 147-118 and total yards 366-215. The Trojans set a series record by throwing 38 passes (only 10 completions), breaking the previous high of 36 (by USC) in the 1949 game.

The Pacific Coast Conference had dissolved over the past year and a new conference was formed called the Athletic Association of Western Universities. Dropping out were Oregon, Oregon State, Washington State and Idaho from the previous year, leaving the five-member AAWU with USC, UCLA, California, Stanford and Washington. (Washington State would rejoin the league in 1962, and the two Oregon schools would return in 1964, forming the Pac-8.)

But of the five AAWU teams in 1959, three tied for the title, as USC, UCLA and Washington all finished 3-1-0.

The Huskies got the Rose Bowl bid and made the most of·it, walloping Wisconsin by a 44-8 score.

Notre Dame, once only 3-5-0, rallied with impressive back-to-back wins over tough Iowa and Southern Cal to finish .500 and a final No. 17 ranking.

USC finished 8-2-0, but it was a miserable 8-2-0, along with its final national rating of 14th.

Don Clark concluded his three-year stay as Troy coach. He was 13-16-1 overall and 0-3-0 against Notre Dame.

John McKay was on his way to LA.

As the series moved into the 1960s, Notre Dame maintained a commanding 20-9-2 lead and a big scoring advantage of 535-372. But USC over the next three decades, would hold its own against the Fighting Irish.

Averaging almost 70,000, "The Glamor Game" had attracted over two million fans.

1960

Duck Day In L.A.

The day of the 32nd clash broke delightful and gorgeous...for ducks. For humans, it was neither delightful nor gorgeous. In fact, it could be said the day was unpleasant. The truth is, it was miserable. Indeed, so wretched it was with raindrops falling on shoulders and every other area of one's anatomy that the fans stayed away from the Coliseum by the thousands.

The brave ones that did come—28,297—constituted the second smallest crowd ever to see a Notre Dame-Southern California football contest. The ones that stayed away by the thousands probably opted for the enclosed comfort of their local flick house where a former USC football player—of sorts—named Duke Morrison was starring in a movie entitled *North to Alaska.* Of course, over at Hollywood and Vine he was known as John Wayne.

But the drenching weather was probably not the sole factor that encouraged fans to seek entertainment elsewhere. Another reason was the records of the two participants: Southern Cal with five losses in nine games, Notre Dame winless in its last eight outings.

That losing streak would change on this dark, rain-soaked day in late November, thanks primarily to an upstart named Daryle Lamonica, himself a native Californian. Passing, running, tackling, intercepting a pass and even punting, the poised sophomore was the guiding light to Notre Dame's convincing, no-fluke victory over Southern California, 17-0.

Lamonica was just another number on the field when

209

Joe Kuharich gathered his lads about him to begin his second term as Notre Dame's head guru. There were 15 lettermen in the group, headed by Norb Roy, George Sefcik, Nick Buoniconti and Myron Pottios, coming off an injury. But conspicuous by their absence were Ken Adamson and Monte Stickles.

The Irish were allotted a No. 17 ranking in pre-season polls and vindicated this judgment by lacing California in their curtain raiser. Then: collapse, total collapse! In its next eight games, Notre Dame was a loser— clobbered by unranked Purdue, shaded by North Carolina, blanked by Michigan State (in Game No. 600 for the Irish), nipped by Northwestern, one touchdown short to Navy, Pittsburgh and Miami (Fla.), shut-out by No. 2 Iowa. Never before had Notre Dame lost eight straight games and, yes, the foreboding possibility existed for the Irish to compose their worst season ever. Only the improbable— a victory over Southern Cal could repudiate this dishonor.

So what was the make-up of this Far-West school that posed such a titanic challenge to Notre Dame? For one thing, the Trojans had fetched themselves a new head coach— John McKay, a shrewed tactician, a dry wit, a born winner. Nineteen lettermen from ex-coach Don Clark's 8-2-0 squad were on hand to greet McKay, including the McKeever boys, Marlin and Mike, as well as George Van Vlick, Jim Maples and Mike Bundra. But eligibility of Ron Mix and Willie Wood had expired.

The presence of a neophyte coach and the absence of a great number of big-time names, however, did not deter the pollsters from placing Southern Cal at the No. 6 spot.

Tommy Trojan quickly disposed of that lofty position, dropping his first three games while scoring a mere six total points. In a rebound of sorts, USC conquered Georgia, California and Stanford, lost to Washington and Baylor, then upset highly-favored UCLA.

A 4-5-0 catalogue was not exactly reminiscent of the Thundering Herd of Trojans past, but it was adequate to persuade the bookies to give a bettor seven points if he/she took Notre Dame.

Rosters from both schools were riddled by injuries. Sefcik, Notre Dame's leading rusher, did not make the trip to California. Mike McKeever, Luther Hayes and Dan Ficca were hobbled for Southern Cal.

"I can't say the injury situation at USC has gotten out of hand," jested McKay, "but I think we're the only team in college football which practices with an ambulance on the sideline and a doctor in the huddle."

But, healthy or infirm, there was a game to be played and there was mud and goo in which to play it.

Taking the opening kickoff and starting from their 29-yard line, the Irish capitalized on a 16-yard rollout by Lamonica and steady gains by Bill Ahern and Angelo Dabiero to achieve SC's 14-yard stripe. When the drive bogged down, Joe Perkowski put three points on the board with a 31-yard field goal.

That was the beginning of Southern Cal's barren day. And it became even more bleak just after the Trojans received the ensuing kickoff. On second down, Bill Nelsen's long pass intended for Jim Bates was deflected by Ahern and fielded by Lamonica, who sped back 18 yards to SC's 45-yard line. Lamonica hurled 18 yards to Dennis Murphy and four smacks through the line by Dabiero advanced the ball to the one, from where Lamonica sneaked into the endzone. Perkowski added the PAT and ND led, 10-0.

Now on a roll, the Irish mounted an 80-yard drive that produced yet another touchdown late in the second period. Lamonica engineered the foray, trotting 19 yards on two carries, and executing fakes and handoffs to Ahern, Bob Scarpitto and Ed Rutkowski. Scarpitto handled the TD chore on a determined, tackle-breaking, churning bolt from nine yards out. Perkowski's kick elevated the score to 17-0, and the scoreboard slumbered the rest of the game.

Southern Cal threatened to score twice, on the last play of the first half and on the last play of the mud battle. First threat: With Nelsen pitching, the Trojans entered enemy territory. Still moving, Nelsen hit Marlin McKeever on ND's 20-yard line, and the All-American streaked for paydirt. He got as far as the 10 where Lamonica dropped him to earth as the gun sounded, preventing a sure touchdown. Second threat: From the Irish 20, sub QB Ben Charles nailed Maples on the numbers, but the

It was a muddy mess in Los Angeles for the 1960 game, played before a mere 28,297 fans, the second smallest crowd in series history. Sophomore quarterback Daryle Lamonica hands off to Angelo Dabiero for a short gain. The Irish won, 17-0.

halfback slipped, dropping the ball as he crossed the goal line, just as the game ended.

Notre Dame had broken its eight-game losing streak, as well as shunned the infamy of creating the poorest record in its long and storied history. And the loss by Southern Cal prevented McKay from breaking even in his first season, winding up at 4-6-0. Needless to say, there were no bowl scouts getting wet in the Coliseum that day.

In addition to controlling the scoreboard, the unheralded visitors from South Bend also dominated the statistics: 306 net yards to only 74 for the home team, 18 first downs to seven.

Despite the exhilarating triumph, Kuharich's job as ND coach, while still afloat, sailed murky waters. After compiling a 7-13-0 two-year ledger, there was speculation that he might not return for his third year.

"What makes you think I won't?" asked Kuharich. "I told you writers a couple of weeks ago I could not understand why there was so much conjecture."

Did he return? Read on.

1961

Notre Dame's Line Of Credit

Southern California's quarterback was thrown for losses totaling **77** net yards. USC's total net rushing for the entire game was MINUS four yards. Total points scored by the Trojans were zero. Notre Dame had sculptured a defensive masterpiece on its visitors from Troy, and its bullish, aggressive line was due most of the credit for the 30-0 drubbing.

Three and four linemen were consistently in the Trojan backfield, sacking the quarterback, breaking up plays before execution could develop, and seeing to it that Southern Cal's offense would get no closer than six yards from the Irish goal line.

"I've never had a team with that much minus yardage," confessed John McKay, Southern Cal's head mentor, "but Notre Dame is big, fast and powerful."

McKay's athletic director, Jesse Hill, joined the admiration society: "Notre Dame is the best team we've seen this year."

Now, considering the fact that SouCal had played only three prior games, Hill's evaluation could have been passed over with a yawn. But one of those three opponents was No. 1 Iowa, which barely nipped the Trojans, 35-34, when McKay, disdaining a kick and a tie, gambled on a double-point conversion and lost.

Southern Cal opened its season with a loss to Georgia Tech, then shaded SMU before facing up to the Hawkeyes. At this point in its schedule the script called for SC to be 2-1-0, not 1-2-0; so its pre-season rank of No. 19 had now fallen by the wayside.

Three starters in the backfield — Bill Nelsen, Hal Tobin and Jim Maples— were among the 19 returning lettermen as McKay prepared for his second autumn at USC. Back also were Mike Bundra and Frank Buncom, but missing were Marlin and Mike McKeever, Jerry Traynham, Dan Ficca and Luther Hayes. Two sophomores — running back Willie Brown and end Hal Bedsole— put a gleam in McKay's roving eyes, however.

Rightfully so, too. In Troy's three games Brown showed a 7.8 average with 293 yards on 36 carries. Bedsole had flagged two touchdown passes and accounted for 127 yards.

Nineteen lettermen were back for Notre Dame, too, including its entire backfield— Daryle Lamonica, Angelo Dabiero, George Sefcik and Mike Lind. A major loss was Myron Pottios, but his departure was offset by the return of Nick Buoniconti, Norb Roy and Joe Carollo.

The Irish were not included in the Top Twenty of pre-season polls, but worked their way up to No. 8 by wheeling past Oklahoma and Purdue. One mainstay behind Notre Dame's vehicle was Dabiero, a 5-7 scatback who had averaged 9.7 yards while gaining 242 yards on 25 carries.

"When Dabiero came here, I don't think anyone else wanted him," said coach Joe Kuharich. "He's a self-made player— the result of effort, work, practice and determination."

Those attributes were evident in the stocky senior, as well as in all of his Irish mates, when the terrors of Troy, a two touchdown underdog, set foot in Notre Dame Stadium on a fall day beset with gray skies and intermittent showers. It was the earliest meeting ever (October 14th) for the two schools, and 50,427 soggy spectators were on hand to see it.

The tone of the affair was struck early. Notre Dame kicked off, held the Trojans, and forced a punt. Fielding the ball at midfield, Dabiero scooted 50 yards into the end zone, but the tally was nullified by a clipping penalty.

Undaunted, ND moved 55 yards in 10 plays to register a legitimate TD. Dabiero, Sefcik and Gerry Gray did leg work down to SC's 12-yard line from where Lamonica skirted his right end and scored without so much as a brush. Joe Perkowski added the PAT.

Still in the first quarter, Dabiero returned a punt 16 yards to launch Notre Dame on a 74-yard scoring trek. Frank Minik contributed the big gainer— a 22-yard dash— but he was assisted by other key runs from Lind, Dabiero and Sefcik. Finally, on the seventh play, Lamonica arched a 19-yard fling to Jim Kelly who made a running snag in the endzone. Perkowski up and over— Notre Dame, 14-0.

Late in the initial period, SC's Nelsen connected on a 50-yard sling to Bedsole, who was knocked out of bounds by Lind at the Irish 15. Nelsen then picked up nine yards on a keeper, but Notre Dame stiffened and denied the Trojans any further progress.

After an exchange of punts, it took ND just seven plays to erase 83 yards— thanks mainly to a 43-yard jaunt down the sideline by Dabiero— and jump into a 20-0 lead. A 15-yard penalty against the visitors spotted the ball on the 12, from which point Joe Rutkowski bolted to the six, and then swept his left end for a marker. Perkowski's kick was wide.

Southern Cal was now playing without its best offensive punches— Brown out for the game and Bedsole sidelined midway of the second stanza with bruised ribs. But the Irish, despite the nearby Golden Dome of Our Lady admonishing benevolence, were not inclined toward mercy...they would, however, accept charity.

Nelsen, trying to pass, fumbled when rocked by Carollo, who then promptly recovered the loose ball on SC's 13-yard stripe. The Trojans were penalized to their one for interfering with a pass intended for Les Traver, and Lamonica plunged across the double stripe. Perkowski swung true to spread the margin to 27 points as the third frame concluded.

The outcome of the contest was settled; only the final score remained for the tale. And that became 30-0 when Perkowski drilled a 49-yard field goal in the fourth quarter. The opportunity was ignited when Minik purloined a pass from Pete Beathard on the Trojan 43, and was sparked by Joe Kantor's 12-yard scamper.

The length of Perkowski's FG didn't take Kuharich by surprise. "He kicked one 61 yards with the wind in practice yesterday," he pointed out.

The Trojans could point to four drives in the second half, none of which, however, reached fruition. In the third period, they reached the Irish 39 and 42-yard lines before stalling, and, in the fourth, advanced to the 29 and 27.

"This was the best defensive effort by Notre Dame this year," exuded Kuharich. "It was a team effort." According to the press, Buoniconti was the leader of the "team effort" charge.

Even though Notre Dame racked up 30 points, it did so under the stress of 15 penalties totaling a whopping 167 yards.

"The penalties were due to over-aggressiveness, particularly by a lot of players who saw action today for the first time," remarked Kuharich.

While taking nothing away from the Gold-and-Blue winners, McKay felt the thumping was not a true measurement of his club. "We really missed Brown—he's far and away our best football player," said McKay. "And our pass receiving really suffered with the loss of Bedsole. We're a better team than we looked today."

The Trojans rang true his words in their next four games, dropping California, Illinois and Stanford while mixing in a scoreless tie with Washington. They then yielded to Pittsburgh by one point and to UCLA by three to draw the curtain on a 4-5-1 season.

Despite its swift start and promises of stardom, Notre Dame waylaid only two opponents the rest of the year—Pittsburgh and Syracuse. The Irish bowed to No. 1 Michigan State, Northwestern, Navy, Iowa and Duke, to etch a 5-5-0 slate.

Disappointing for the year, yes. But the triumph over Southern Cal was an offsetting and glorious memory. No other Notre Dame era had ever defeated Southern California five uninterrupted, straight years, and no other Irish team had ever held the Trojans scoreless two years.

1962

Return Of The Thundering Herd

Put out to graze for moons untold, the Thundering Herd of Southern California stormed from its pasture in Game No. 34, stampeding roughshod over Notre Dame, 25-0, on a hectic way to its first undefeated, untied season since 1932.

The margin of 25 points was the largest spread for USC in the history of this aging and noble gridiron series, and the win also clipped a five-year losing streak to the Irish.

So prolific were the horses of Troy that their fodder from Indiana felt they were at times matched against a legion of warriors, three deep at every position.

"Coach (John) McKay kept running his different units on and off the field," wrote Sid Ziff in the *L.A. Times*. "He's got so many outstanding players it's hard to tell the first team from the third."

But if there existed a solitary stallion among the offensive gladiators, it was fullback Ben Wilson, picked by all but two writers in the packed press box as "back-of-the-game."

At least two Irish players agreed. Center Ed Hoerster: "That Wilson is a helluva fullback. He's the hardest man to stop I've ever seen." Quarterback Daryle Lamonica: "We've faced some good fullbacks but Wilson's the best by far."

Wilson was just one of 15 lettermen who set foot on the sod of Bovard Field as McKay inaugurated his third year, the blot of two losing seasons still mired in his conscience. But ace receiver Hal Bedsole was back, as was running

218

back Willie Brown plus quarterbacks Bill Nelsen and Pete Beathard.

Lost to graduation were such veterans as Jim Maples, Mike Bundra, Ben Rosin, Britt Williams and Frank Buncom. But the overall depth of the Trojans convinced the scribbling seers of the sport to award USC a No. 13 pre-season spot.

Only 14 lettermen greeted Joe Kuharich as he started his fourth— and although it wasn't known at the time, his last— season at Notre Dame. Not yet had he produced a winning season at South Bend, and the members of the Fourth Estate projected no illusions that 1962 would be any different, assigning the Irish a pre-season rank of No. 24.

True, end Jim Kelly and QB Lamonica were back, but pickings thereafter were not extremely noteworthy, excluding Hoerster, Bob Lehmann and a few others. Kuharich would be without such linemen as Nick Buoniconti, Tom Hecomovich, Norb Roy, Bob Bill and Joe Carollo, as well as halfback Angelo Dabiero and specialist Joe Perkowski.

The Irish, however, got off to a good start, traveling to Oklahoma and spanking the Sooners. They then starred in a Dr. Jekyll and Mr. Hyde role, losing their next four games to Purdue, Wisconsin, Michigan State and Northwestern before subsequently winning their next four over Navy, Pittsburgh, North Carolina and Iowa. That figured to a 5-4-0 mark as ND took flight and headed west for

Smogland, riding the wings of a four-game winning streak.

Now, while Notre Dame had wheeled a see-saw, up-and-down season, the direction of Southern Cal had been all up, up and more up. Nine assailants had thrown their best Saturday punches at the Trojans and all were squashed, a la Beetle Bailey. They were Duke, SMU, Iowa, California, Illinois, Washington, Stanford, Navy and UCLA... and all nine pugilists could muster a total of only 57 points against the stout SC defense.

On the comparative scores of two mutual foes—Iowa and Navy—the Irish fared better, inducing the foolhardy to predict an ND win over SC. But the bookies knew better, establishing SouCal a one-touchdown favorite to remain pure and clean.

"We'll settle for a one-point win," McKay told columnist Jim Murray before the battle.

Chances are, the remark was made in jest. For McKay, better than anyone, knew about the plethora of stars that twinkled three deep into his roster. Consider, for example, the quarterback position. Nelsen, Troy's total offensive leader for the past two years, hadn't started a game all season, and was now second string behind Beathard. And Craig Fertig, of the third unit, would be a starter at many schools.

"Naturally, I'd like to be playing more," Nelsen told writer Al Wolf, "but winning the national championship is the big thing. And under our three-unit system, everybody gets to play."

The Trojans had already accepted a bid to meet Wisconsin in the Rose Bowl when they swung into Memorial Coliseum to meet the Irish on a warm winter day in early December. A crowd of 81,676 partisan fans clicked through the turnstiles to witness the event.

They didn't have a very long wait to see what they came to see as USC rolled to a 13-0 lead in the first half, Wilson plunging into the endzone for both touchdowns.

Southern Cal kicked off and immediately forced an Irish punt. On first down from his 40-yard line, Beathard hung a swing pass to Brown for five yards, and Brown added three more on a pitchout. On third down, Brown pulled in a short spiral at midfield, spun off Frank Budka, was impeded by Jim Carroll at the 25 and finally brought to earth at the 18 by Gerry Gray, after a sprightly 34-yard sprint. Wilson smashed for eight yards, then three. ND was penalized for encroachment, Beathard pushed to the one, and Wilson dived over. Tom Lupo looped the PAT.

Seven points do not a victory make, so said the Irish, who struck back with Don Hogan on the ground and Lamonica going airborne to Kelly— advancing the ball to USC's 28-yard line. But ill fortune intervened on first down when Joe Farrell fumbled the handoff and Bedsole enfolded the errant oval on the 22.

Swiftly, Southern Cal erased those 78 yards in nine running plays for its second TD. Big gainers were a 28-yard rollout by Beathard and a 21-yard pitchout by Brown. Wilson devoured the final 14 yards in three plays,

Fullback Ben Wilson is the center of attention after scoring his second touchdown, staking USC to a 13-point lead in 1962. USC went on to a 25-0 shutout to cap a perfect season and a national championship. Sharing the moment is Coach John McKay, Armando Sanchez (54), Ken Del Conte (20), Phil Hoover (83) and Willie Brown (26).

bullying off-tackle from the one for the marker. Lupo's PAT try failed.

Sporting a 13-0 lead late in the first half, McKay displayed his confidence in his Trojans when, instead of punting on fourth-and-six from the SC 48, Brown was handed the ball and was jarred for an eight-yard loss. Arising to the occasion, however, the defenders of Troy broke up three heaves by Lamonica as intermission arrived.

"After that, we knew we could stop Lamonica and their offense," said McKay, whose decision not to punt could have earned him a "goat" title.

Both teams filed point bankruptcy in the third stanza and, although Notre Dame chalked up six first downs, its deepest penetration expired on the USC 45.

Early in the fourth frame Pete Lubisich sacked Lamonica for a 16-yard loss back to the Irish 11, forcing a punt. Ken Del Conte returned the kick to ND's 40-yard stripe, and runs by Rich McMahon, Nelsen and Jay Clark positioned the ball on the ND 14. From there, Nelsen twirled a low pass down the middle to Fred Hill who scooped in the ball at the one-yard line and scored. A pass attempt for two points went asunder.

With reserves mopping up the debris, Southern Cal tallied again in the last minute, receiving its chance when Armando Sanchez intercepted Lamonica's toss on the Irish 20. Fertig, the aforementioned No. 3 QB for Troy, rifled a 13-yard pass to Gary Hill, Ernie Jones gained one, and Fertig rolled out from the six to score, untouched. Again, a double-point pass attempt failed, leaving the final score at 25-0.

"We didn't have a man playing in his right position when Fertig scored," said a gleeful McKay. "We had guards playing halfback, halfbacks playing end, and every which way. We couldn't call time, so we had to let them go."

Then more calmly, McKay added: "This was our best game and this was the best game anyone ever played. We won, 25-0. We went in with a lot of pressure. We were playing a crap game. We had won all the money and all we had to do was hold it."

Notre Dame's quarterback and coach echoed the words of McKay. Lamonica: "The Trojans threw three good clubs against us. They had real great deep coverage. We were outcharged all the way." Kuharich: "They (USC) have great balance with Beathard throwing and running, Brown going to the outside, and Wilson to the inside."

Offensive prowess, to be sure. But chivalry abounded on SC's defense, too— marshaled by Lubisich, trooped by Damon Bame, Ernie Pye, William Fisk, Marvin Marinkovich, Robert Svihus and Sanchez, among others. What did they allow the Irish? Ten first downs and just 152 total net yards.

The shellacking by the Trojans reinforced rumors that Kuharich had coached his last game for Notre Dame, that headmaster for the National Football League Los Angeles Rams would be his next assignment.

"I get a kick out of these tales. There is no credence to the rumor. I'm coaching Notre Dame, and if ever there's a change, you gentlemen of the media will be the first to know," Kuharich told the gentlemen of the media.

The stories were half-truths. Kuharich did leave Notre Dame, and he did go to the NFL...as supervisor of game officials. He left behind unpopular credentials of 17 victories and 23 defeats, but his finger of pride could point to three triumphs in four starts against arch-rival Southern Cal.

The Trojans romped to a 42-37 conquest of Wisconsin in the Rose Bowl to polish off their season at 11-0-0, best record ever for the men of Troy. McKay was named Coach-of-the-Year, Bedsole was honored as a consensus All-American, and Bame was tabbed on two All-America teams.

But not content with the title of national football champions, Southern California also walked away with 1962 conference laurels in seven other sports. The Trojans were tops in tennis, golf, track and field, swimming, water polo and gymnastics, while sharing the crown in baseball.

Too bad the conference didn't have competition in ping-pong.

1963

Something Old, Something New

Winless Notre Dame reached deep into its football cornucopia and fetched a gimpy-legged senior and two green-behind-the-ears sophomores to marshal its assault against Southern California in Game No. 35. The trio, ably assisted by a rugged defensive unit, responded with a brilliant and exciting 17-14 victory, the ninth consecutive triumph for the Irish over the Trojans in South Bend.

One neophyte was Bill Wolski, an untested yet dynamic halfback who had carried the ball a mere three times this season. Against the Trojans, Wolski racked up 87 yards on 16 rushes and scored a touchdown. The other yearling was Ken Ivan, who didn't even make the traveling squad for ND's previous game, but who calmly kicked a late field goal to provide the Irish with their three-point margin of victory.

The veteran of yore was Frank Budka, scuttled from the ranks of the infirm, an involuntary absentee from spring practice, still unsound in Notre Dame's first two games...but the inspirational leader as a signal caller and running quarterback in this rampage against the men of Troy. Budka carried 18 times for 84 yards.

"Wasn't he (Budka) tremendous?" asked Hugh Devore, Notre Dame's interim head coach. "He didn't have any spring practice at all and he's been limping around this fall. But I figured he was ready this time— and it was his day."

Joe Kuharich had departed from the hurrah of college coaching to enter the glitter of the National Football

The sterling quartet from Troy—Damon Bame (64), Pete Beathard (12), Hal Bedsole (19) and Willie Brown (26)—won 18 of 21 games during the 1962-63 seasons, splitting with Notre Dame. All four made All-Conference honors, while Bame and Bedsole also earned All-America honors.

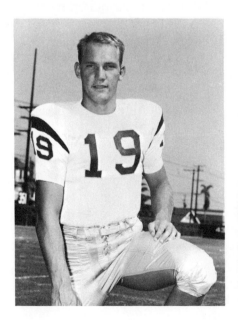

League, and Devore had agreed to handle the reins at Notre Dame for one year. He inherited 17 lettermen, including such men of stature as Jim Kelly, Bob Lehmann, Tom Goberville, Bill Pfeiffer and Jim Carroll, as well as a question mark named Budka. Halfback Don Hogan would have returned but a severe off-season automobile accident decked his season, thus joining Daryle Lamonica and Ed Hoerster among the missing.

Crystal-ball lookers saw nothing rosy in Notre Dame's future and omitted Devore's club from pre-season, Top Ten rankings. This logic was justified when the Irish were bumped, though lightly, by Wisconsin and Purdue in their season-opening games.

But if the prognosticators of gridiron fortunes overlooked Notre Dame, they focused sharply on the elite potential of Southern Cal, placing the defending national champs at the top of the heap.

In so doing, they pointed to the ammunition stacked behind the walls of Troy— 23 returning lettermen, including the famous "B-boys": Pete Beathard, Hal Bedsole, Willie Brown and Damon Bame. Other veterans included Gary Kirner, Pete Lubisich, Bill Fisk and Ernie Pye.

The Trojans broke well by blanking Colorado, but the next week were upset by potent Oklahoma. Knocked from the summit, USC bounced back to nudge Michigan State, thereby bringing a 2-1-0 manifest to the Hoosier state.

But in the process, SouCal unveiled a sensational runner to complement Brown. He was a sophomore named Mike Garrett and his three-game stats showed a gain of 248 yards in 29 rushes for an average of 8.5 yards per carry.

Students from both institutions engaged in pre-game rituals on their respective campuses on the eve of the skirmish. Devore evoked cheers as he kissed a sliver off the Blarney stone at a vociferous pep rally in South Bend. And out West in Los Angeles, USC scholars celebrated "Howard Jones Day" in honor of the legendary coach who guided the last Trojan team to beat Notre Dame in Indiana, way back in 1939.

Edward (Moose) Krause, athletic director at Notre Dame, provided some incentive for his Irish players when

Rescued from the ranks of the infirm, veteran quarterback Frank Budka led Notre Dame to its narrow victory in 1963.

he announced that the university might reverse its long-standing policy against post-season games and accept a bid to a bowl game.

"Notre Dame would certainly consider a post-season offer if such a game meant something concerning a national championship," Krause told sportscaster Mike Walden of *WTMJ-TV*. "Travel now is much easier, players would not miss too many classes and a post-season game would be a wonderful trip, giving our young fellows a liberal education," he concluded.

With that on record, a warm and pleasant day blanketed the environs as Notre Dame, a touchdown underdog, and Southern California prepared for battle on the lush green of Notre Dame Stadium in mid-October. And 59,135 zealots, in light attire, settled in for the festivities.

The first break of the tussle came midway of the first quarter and favored the Trojans when Garrett recovered a fumble by ND's Ron Bliey on the Irish 46-yard line. But the Irish got the second break and turned it into something meaningful. For on second down, Beathard lofted a pass in the direction of Bedsole. It was slightly over-thrown and deflected by Bedsole— right into the bosom of Tom McDonald at his 38-yard line. The Irish cornerback headed for the sideline, followed a downfield block by Pfeiffer, and raced 62 yards to paydirt. Ivan's PAT kick was true.

The soldiers of Troy strutted 74 yards in nine plays to lock the score in the second period, Beathard bolting the last three yards behind a vicious block by Pye. Important plays along the way were keepers of nine and 16 yards by Beathard and an 18-yard thrust through left guard by Garrett. Dick Brownell's boot evened the score at 7-all.

Five plays later, following SC's kickoff, which Wolski returned 30 yards, Notre Dame again grabbed the lead. Starting at the Irish 37, Wolski picked up five yards, Budka connected with Kelly for 14 and Wolski popped up the middle for 36 crackling yards to the SC eight. Budka slanted for two on a keeper, then Wolski zapped through a left guard-center hole for the final six and a six-pointer. Ivan converted that into a seven-pointer.

Now ahead 14-7, Notre Dame threatened to blow out SouCal when Goberville pounced on a bobble by SC's Brown on the Trojan 47. With Budka, Wolski and Joe Kantor hauling the ball, ND rode to the Trojan seven-yard stripe. Three plays resulted in a loss of four yards, so Ivan tried a field goal. It was blocked by Kirner, sustaining the lifeline of hope for USC.

Injected with new vigor, Southern Cal mastered 93 yards in 10 plays, mostly through the air, to again knot the score just 33 seconds before halftime. The Beathard-to-Bedsole combo was accurate on passes of 15, 13 and 42 yards before Beathard rifled a 12-yard scoring toss to Garrett. Brownell split the uprights, and the teams left the field for halftime lectures, locked 14-14.

The score remained unchanged in the third quarter although both clubs threatened. Taking the second-half kickoff, Notre Dame drove to Southern Cal's 12-yard line where Wolski fumbled and Pye claimed the wayward pigskin for Troy. Later, Bedsole cradled a pass on the Irish three-yard line, but a bullish hit by McDonald broke up

Field Goal Gives Irish 17-14 Victory

the completion, a play that turned out to be Southern Cal's last flirtation with points.

"If there was a turning point in the game, that was it— Bedsole dropping the ball," opined John McKay, chief at USC.

Time was now drawing nigh for Ivan to do his toe thing—kick the field goal that would bring mirth to the home folks and misery to their visitors. The stadium clock blared a dwindling 6:28 left to play when an Irish drive that started on their 17 stalled on SC's 15-yard stripe. So, without further ado, Ivan's toe met leather, sending it hurtling over the crossbar for a 32-yard FG. That ended the scoring with Notre Dame atop, 17-14.

USC could not move after receiving the kickoff, and ND ground out the final four and one-half minutes. At the final gun, Budka rushed off the field and awarded the game ball to Hogan, his lame mate who had been side-lined for the year.

"I was glad to see the team give the game ball to Hogan," said Devore. "His spirit has been a great boost for all of us, and played a part in today's outcome."

Krause, the AD who played with Devore on Notre Dame's 1931 team, didn't disagree with Hogan's getting the ball but surmised amid moist eyes that his old buddy was also due an accolade.

"This was the one," he beamed. "This was for you, Hugh, just as much as it was for your team that played such a grand game."

Modestly, Devore diverted the laurels to his fellows on the field, the names of Wolski, Budka, Kantor, Goberville, McDonald and Norm Nicola crossing his lips. "And what a day Pfeiffer (17 tackles) had," he exclaimed, "...and Jim Snowden played a whale of a game at tackle...but I can't go

229

on without mentioning each and every one of the boys out there today."

Devore wrestled no argument from McKay. "With defensive play like Pfeiffer and the rest of the Irish showed us today, there really is no excuse I have to offer. Notre Dame outplayed us. That's it in a nutshell," McKay commented.

Their season now even at 2-2-0, the Trojans sallied forth to bump Ohio State, California, Stanford, Oregon State and UCLA, being curbed only by Washington. Their record of 7-3-0 did not warrant a Top Ten ranking.

While USC was losing only a single game throughout the remainder of the year, Notre Dame could generate only a single victory, that over UCLA one week after nudging the Trojans. The Irish then fell to Stanford, Navy, Pittsburgh, Michigan State and Syracuse to stagger home with 2-7-0 credentials. The contest with Iowa was canceled out of respect for the death of President John Kennedy.

Three performers from the two schools were listed on various All-America teams: Bame for Southern California, Kelly and Lehmann for Notre Dame.

1964

Trojans Puncture Irish Balloon

A grotesque thing happened to the Fighting Irish of Notre Dame on their 1964 way to an untarnished season and, hopefully, their first national championship since 1949. They were side-tracked, 20-17, by the Trojans of Southern California, who unleashed a mother lode of never-say-die spirit in the second half to overcome a 17-point deficit, and, in the process, squash the dual aspirations of the ramblers from Indiana.

Under new head coach Ara Parseghian, Notre Dame had mastered an incredible reversal of form. The Irish closed out the previous year under Hugh Devore with five straight losses, but the era of Ara blasted off with nine consecutive victories, moving the Irish up the poll ladder from a no-rank in pre-season to No. 9, to 6, to 4, to 2 and in November, to No. 1. Visions of eminence pranced across the South Bend campus until the dreams were shattered by a red-haired senior named Craig Fertig and a red-haired sophomore named Rod Sherman, both ably abetted by a host of Cardinal-and-Gold-clad warriors from Troy.

But while the stakes in their 36th clash were high for Notre Dame, they were equally tall for Southern Cal. Though abreast with Oregon State for the AAWU title, it was generally felt around Heritage Hall that if the Trojans could upset high-flying Notre Dame, they would play in the Rose Bowl.

Coach John McKay was faced with filling some gigantic holes in his lineup as he began organizing his fifth program at USC. The "B-boys"—Hal Bedsole, Pete

231

IRISH BID FOR PERFECT SEASON TODAY

MIDDIES AIM TO EVEN 65 YEAR SERIES

Reprisal for '63 Is Cadets' Goal

Pro Football Drafts to Be Held Today

Happy Young Middies

BEARS TO GET 3 OF FIRST 6 SELECTIONS

Leagues Fling Charges

Ara Drills Troops During Pause on March

U. S. C. FINAL HURDLE FOR NOTRE DAME

Trojans Retain Bowl Hopes

Beathard, Willie Brown and Damon Bame— had bid farewell to the land of Troy, as had Gary Kirner, Pete Lubisich, John Ratliff, Loran Hunt and Ernie Jones, among others. But 16 lettermen were back, including Mike Garrett, Bill Fisk, Mac Byrd, Bob Svihus, Gary Hill, John Brownwood and the aforementioned Fertig, now emerging from the quarterback shadow of Beathard.

Few, if any, forecasters offered any great expectations for the Trojans, ignoring them from the elite of Top Ten circles in pre-season polls. This abruptly changed, however, as USC thrashed Colorado and Oklahoma and vaulted all the way to No. 2. In subsequent games leading up to the contest with Notre Dame, the Trojans bowed to Michigan State, pelted Texas A&M, were shut out by Ohio State, shaded California, were tipped by Washington, edged Stanford and ripped UCLA— six wins, three defeats — again, no ranking.

Wallowing through an eight-year doldrum during which it had won only 34 of 79 games, Notre Dame lured Parseghian away from Northwestern, his domicile as head coach during those same eight years.

Parseghian was faced with the task of replacing such stars as Jim Kelly, Bob Lehmann, Frank Budka, Bob Pfeiffer and Tom McDonald, but found a nucleus of 17 returning lettermen on which to build. Among these were

232

Jack Snow, whom Parseghian shifted from halfback to end, Bill Wolski, Jim Carroll, Ken Maglicic, Norm Nicola, Joe Farrell and a quarterback who had been waiting in the wings for stardom—John Huarte. While not prophesied in September, Huarte would become Notre Dame's sixth player to capture the coveted Heisman Trophy.

In compiling its string of nine straight conquests, Notre Dame amassed 270 points while giving up only 57 to its foes. Victims were Wisconsin, Purdue, Air Force, UCLA, Stanford, Navy, Pittsburgh, Michigan State and Iowa.

A mammoth turnout of 83,840 fans, almost equally divided in their allegiance, packed the Coliseum on a late November day to see if Notre Dame could justify its pick as a 12-point favorite to whip Southern Cal and earn for its hallowed halls a niche in football immortality.

The answer appeared to be affirmative when the Irish posted a field goal and a touchdown on their second and third possessions, were thwarted by an interception on their fourth occupancy of the ball, then tallied again on their fifth, commanding a 17-0 lead at halftime.

Sherman fumbled the ball away to Notre Dame to enable Ken Ivan to kick a 25-yard FG in the first quarter. In the second period, ND's 73-yard march ended with Huarte flinging a 22-yard scoring strike to Snow and Ivan converting. The key play in the movement was a 19-yard jaunt by Wolski. Scoring by the Irish was concluded when

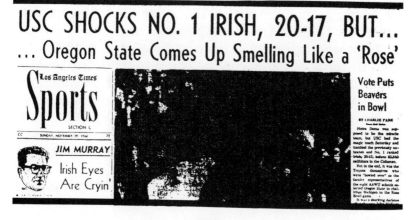

Wolski stepped into the corner of the endzone from five yards out after taking a pitch-back from Huarte on a QB option play. Ivan's foot swung true and Notre Dame's 17-point bulge at halftime seemed insurmountable.

It could have been closer, though...for the Trojans squandered three opportunities to accumulate points in the first half. Thrice they gambled for the distance on fourth down, making none. Once, Fertig missed Dave Moton in the endzone from ND's 16-yard line. Again, shooting for the endzone from ND's 28, Fertig's pass intended for Sherman was broken up by Tom Longo, who followed up by also interrupting in the endzone an eight-yard toss from Fertig to Garrett.

So the Trojans were down...but, in their minds, not out. Garrett: "We never gave up. In the locker room, we still thought we could win." Fertig concurred: "Coach McKay told us we could do it, to go out there and take the second half kickoff to a touchdown and that would be all we needed."

Precisely, that is what SouCal did. Starting from their 34-yard line after taking the second half kickoff, the Trojans scored in 10 plays, Garrett plunging over from the one. Dick Brownell's PAT left USC in arrears at 17-7.

Still in Quarter Three, Notre Dame muffed a chance to widen its lead. After advancing 62 yards to SC's nine, Huarte's pitchout was wide and Southern Cal recovered the loose ball.

The Irish botched another possibility to score early in the final period. Well, actually, Joe Kantor did blast into the endzone from a yard away, but Bob Meeker was cited for holding, nullifying the TD. After three incomplete passes by Huarte, USC took possession.

"The worst penalty a team can suffer is a 15-yarder from the one-foot line, costing you a touchdown," wailed Parseghian, secure in the knowledge that those six or seven points would have ensured victory for his club.

But Notre Dame was still clinging to a 10-point advantage and Father Time was sitting on the Irish bench, each tick of his hands making the purpose of the Trojans more and more difficult.

USC started from its 12-yard stripe after Kantor's

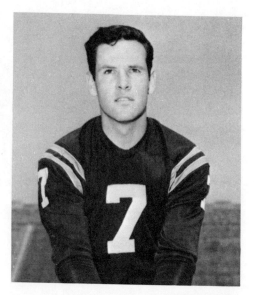

Heisman Trophy winner John Huarte, the first Irish quarterback to complete more than 100 passes in one season and to break the 200-yard passing barrier (114 passes for 2,062 yards) in 1964.

touchdown-that-wasn't, and, in 10 plays, erased those 88 yards. The final 23 evaporated when Fertig faked to Garrett and hurled the ball to Fred Hill, who was wide open in the endzone. Brownell missed the extra point attempt, but ND's lead had been cut to 17-13.

Southern Cal's drive for its winning marker began rather unobtrusively and almost ended before it started. Punting from inside his five-yard line, ND's Snow boomed a low missile past midfield. The ball was fielded by Garrett, who hauled it back 14 yards but fumbled when tackled at the Irish 40-yard stripe. As the officials combed the pile of humanity, trying to determine who had possession, the sole thought running through the fans' minds was clear: if the Irish recovered, they could run out the clock and preserve their lead; if the Trojans recovered, they still had a fighting chance to win. Guess what? Guard Frank Lopez came out of the mass with the prized pigskin for USC.

Now, the home team had just two minutes and 11 seconds to wipe out 40 yards. On second-and-ten, Fertig passed to Fred Hill for 23 yards down to ND's 17-yard line. Garrett smashed to the 15, Fertig threw to Hill in the endzone but the completion was ruled out of bounds, and

On what many call the most electrifying play in the series, Southern California scores on fourth down, with 93 seconds left in the game, against No. 1 Notre Dame. Quarterback Craig Fertig completes the pass to a leaping Rod Sherman (top opposite), *eludes defensive back Tony Carey* (bottom opposite) *and races into the endzone* (top right) *as Notre Dame coach Ara Parseghian grimaces in agony on the sideline* (bottom right). *Final score: Trojans 20, Irish 17.*

Fertig, being rushed, threw wild on third down. The brutal action of 58 minutes and 27 seconds had now reduced itself to one single play. With 93 seconds on the clock, Fertig dropped back, watched Sherman elude safety Tony Carey, then lofted an aerial which the Trojan sophomore gathered in over his shoulder for the touchdown. Brownell's kick elevated the score to 20-17, USC.

Sherman claimed he suggested the TD play, known as 84-Z in the Trojan playbook. "I told coach on the sideline that I thought I could get a step on No. 1 (Carey) and he told me to go ahead and take it into the huddle," explained Sherman.

The honeymoon for Parseghian was over...he had tasted the bitterness of defeat at Notre Dame for the first time. And the dream of splendor shared by his players was mocked with heartache.

"We played a better team today," acknowledged Parseghian, discounting the fact that his team outgained USC, 428 yards to 372. "Southern California is better than any team we faced this year. Their execution was extremely efficient in the second half. It wasn't a case of letting up on our part. They just outplayed us."

His team leader, Huarte, agreed. "The Trojans were up," he stated, "and once they caught fire in the second half, it was Katie bar the door."

Naturally, there were contrasting emotions in the dressing rooms...gloom for the losers, glee for the winners.

"This was the greatest moment in USC's football history," shouted Trojan Athletic Director Jesse Hill. "There's never been a comeback like this."

His opinion was proudly dittoed by Fertig: "It was the greatest comeback of all time!" But McKay's demeanor was more low-key: "I'm just tickled to death," he mumbled.

Stars shone aplenty over the land of Troy...Fertig, of course, with his 15-of-23 passing; the Hill boys, Fred and Gary; Garrett, Ron Heller, Sherman, to name just a few. Garrett was listed on some All-America teams, as was Fisk.

But the brightest light of all glared for the Irish a few days later when Huarte was awarded the Heisman Tro-

Bears Draft Butkus, Sayers, DeLong in First Round

Chicago Tribune | SPORTS **2** A N D BUSINESS **4**
SUNDAY, NOVEMBER 29, 1964

TROJANS SHATTER IRISH DREAM, 20-17

Vocational Keeps Title, 30-7 TURN NOTRE DAME HOPES INTO NIGHTMARE WITH 2 MIN. TO GO

N.F.L. TAKES 14 HOURS FOR TWO ROUNDS!

All Alone and Happy

PREP CHAMPS BLAST LANE EARLY, LATE

Trojans Earn Glory, Beavers Get Rose Bowl

83,840 See U.S.C. Score 3 Times in 2d Half

phy. And Huarte was joined on the consensus All-America team by Snow. Other ND players named to A-A teams were Carroll, Carey and Kevin Hardy.

To the surprise of many and the dismay of others, Oregon State (8-2-0) was picked over Southern California to meet Michigan in the Rose Bowl.

"So far as I am concerned, it is the rankest injustice that ever occurred in the field of intercollegiate athletics," exploded Jesse Hill, USC's AD. (His opinion may have contained some merit— the Beavers were crushed by the Wolverines in the Crown City Classic.)

So, Notre Dame wound up with a 9-1-0 ledger and a No. 3 national rank; Southern Cal at 7-3-0 and No. 10. But their annual clash trudged down an avenue of broken dreams for both.

1965

Irish Torrid, Trojans Horrid

The heavens opened, and downpours of rain ranging from drizzle to torrent descended on Notre Dame Stadium during Game No. 37. So intent on avenging last year's unexpected and devastating knockout by Southern California, the Irish didn't notice. It was as if the elements fell only on the white jerseys of Troy as Notre Dame accomplished its mission by drowning the Trojans, 28-7.

In truth, the soggy encounter was not as close as the score indicated. For Notre Dame, fired with torrid emotion, registered touchdowns on four of its first five possessions to vault into a 28-0 lead, limited Southern Cal to a single first down in the first half and bottled the famed Trojan rushing attack to an embarrassing 74 yards for the entire game.

Mike Garrett, the Trojan workhorse on his path to a Heisman Trophy, was supposed to garner more yardage alone than that. But, for his day's work, the splendid senior, whom his coach, John McKay, described as "...not only the greatest player I have coached, but the greatest college player I have ever seen," could account for just 43 yards.

At this point in his career, Garrett held school records for rushing (2,633) and most carries (495). In five games of the '65 season leading up to the ND clash, Garrett had gained 852 yards and scored eight touchdowns.

But on this wet day of Blarney stones and four-leaf clovers, Garrett was clearly overshadowed by an Irish junior named Larry Conjar, who dodged raindrops and grasping Trojans while racking up 116 yards on 25 carries

240

Fullback Larry Conjar scored all four touchdowns as the Irish swamped USC, 28-7, in 1965.

and scored all four of Notre Dame's touchdowns.

So, with Conjar hauling the mail and a defensive group of Tom Meeker, Dick Arrington, Tom Rhoads, John Horney, Jim Lynch and Pete Duranko putting the stamp of disapproval on every Trojan effort, Notre Dame posted its tenth straight victory over hapless Southern Cal at South Bend.

Most of the above Irish players were among a mob of 23 experienced veterans that also included Nick Rassas, Tom Regner, Phil Sheridan, Bill Wolski, Nick Eddy, Alan Page, Tom Longo and Tony Carey, who met coach Ara Parseghian as he began his second tour of duty under the Golden Dome. Gone were All-American Jack Snow and Heisman winner John Huarte, as well as such competitors as Jim Carroll, Ken Maglicic and Norm Nicola, but soothsayers of the media saw enough talent to peg Notre Dame at No. 3 in pre-season national polls.

Southern Cal was not far behind, coming in at No. 7. This, despite a mass exodus of seniors...Craig Fertig, Bill Fisk, Ron Heller, Ernie Pye, Fred and Gary Hill, Mac Byrd, Robert Svihus, John Brownwood, etc. But Garrett was back, and Rod Sherman was back and David Moton, Frank Lopez, John Thomas, Charles Arrobio, etc.

There was some searching at quarterback for both institutions as the season got underway. Notre Dame would settle on Bill Zloch, a converted end, while SouCal gave the nod to Troy Winslow, a junior of shallow experience.

After decimating California in its curtain-raiser, Notre Dame moved up to No. 1 in national polls, but a loss the following week to Purdue dropped the Irish to No. 8. Northwestern was then trampled, and Army was blanked as Notre Dame opened its stadium gates to Southern Cal with a 3-1-0 record and a No. 7 rank.

The Trojans arrived with a slightly better slate...4-0-1, and a higher rank—No. 4. Minnesota got the draw, while Wisconsin, Oregon State, Washington and Stanford got the boot, the latter two failing to score.

Based on records and ratings, SouCal should have been the favorite to win, but 13 of 15 writers for an Indianapolis newspaper selected Notre Dame to repel the invaders from the West Coast. Handicapper Joe Harris agreed with the majority and put his pick on paper: ND 24, SC 14.

Naturally, though, Parseghian offered words to counterbalance his position as the favorite. "I think all of us should recognize that Southern Cal is a very dangerous team," he cautioned columnist Jim Murray.

Pros and cons notwithstanding, down came the rain and in to the stadium filed 59,235 soon-to-be-drenched fans on this not-to-be-forgotten late October day in South Bend. Thrice they saw Notre Dame score in the first half on drives of 45, 32 and 68 yards to carry a handsome 21-0 halftime lead into the steamy room of blackboards, *Xs* and *Os*.

The initial escapade required 10 plays, all on the ground. Conjar jarred opposing defenders for most of the yardage, including a crucial gain of 13 and a touchdown smash of two. Ken Ivan added his first of four extra points.

Still in the first quarter, the Trojans punted, then were penalized for interfering with Longo, who had signaled for a fair catch. With the SC goal only 32 yards away, Zloch wiped out nine on a quarterback delay, eight more on a pass to Wolski and nine more on a pitch to Sheridan,

Tailback Mike Garrett scored touchdowns against Notre Dame in 1963-64. He was the first player from USC to win the Heisman Trophy (1965), rushing for 3,221 yards during his career.

down to USC's three-yard line. (Actually, the Sheridan completion materialized when Phil Lee tangled with the Irish captain and was called for pass interference.) Conjar lost two, Wolski retrieved them, and Conjar on the eighth play of the drive, sailed across for his second TD. Ivan nailed his second PAT, ND 14-0.

The quarter changed, but the tempo of the Irish didn't and Touchdown No. 3 was just around the corner. Starting from their 31-yard line, the Irish reached pointland in 13 plays, overcoming 20 yards in penalties along the way. Eddy raced 34 yards up the middle on a trap, Zloch kept for six and Conjar ripped up the middle behind Arrington, Regner and George Goeddeke for the final yard...21-0 after Ivan's kick.

The Trojans were staked to one scoring opportunity in the first half when Lopez recovered a fumble by Rassas (off a punt) at ND's 24-yard line. But on third down, Carey filched a flip by Winslow to snuff out the trip.

Yes, the Irish enjoyed a three-touchdown advantage at the recess. But didn't they bask in the light of a 17-0 margin at halftime last year...and lose? Did Parseghian remind his gladiators about that in the dressing room?

243

Running backs Nick Eddy (left) *and Bill Wolski* (right) *of Notre Dame.*

"You bet I did," he chortled. "But it really didn't take much reminding. Revenge is motivation."

Apparently so. For the ramblers from South Bend sloshed onto the gridiron and quickly imprinted another touchdown on the muddy uniforms from University Park.

Rassas returned the second-half kickoff 31 yards, and the Irish set sail from their 33. Wolski, Eddy and Conjar rammed Troy's line for 37 yards before Sheridan snagged an 11-yard heave by Zloch, giving ND a first down on SC's 19-yard stripe. Zloch zapped to the 16, Wolski to the eight, Eddy to the one and Conjar to paydirt. Ivan's boot was accurate.

Now in the fourth period and trailing by 28 points, the Trojans ignored a heavy downpour and pounded out 76 yards to avoid a shut-out. The much-maligned Winslow was the engineer, passing 16 yards to Thomas, 20 to Sherman, keeping the ball five times himself for 25 yards, then hitting Thomas in the endzone corner for an eight-yard scoring toss. Tim Rossovich's PAT etched the final score at 28-7, ND.

But not before the hungry Trojans came back for more. Their appetites whetted by the taste of points, McKay's club reached Notre Dame's nine-yard line, at which point it shifted into reverse gear. Winslow bumped into Garrett and lost six yards...Winslow slipped and fell for a 10-yard setback...Sherman, trying a halfback pass, was decked for a 13-yard loss...'nuff said.

Parseghian credited the play of his defensive line as a major factor in the outcome of the game. "Our line handled them well," he said.

"I'll say they did," pitched in McKay. "There were a hell of a lot of people running up through there."

Both coaches downplayed the weather. Parseghian: "Both teams are basically running clubs, and the footing was good through the first half. It didn't get slippery until the third quarter." McKay: "You can't play every game on an 85-degree day in the sunshine. But, what the heck? We gave Notre Dame our best shot and it wasn't good enough. But we didn't quit. That about covers it."

Cover it, it did, and very little else could be said about that dreary day that beamed a rainbow for the folks in Indiana. But five battles remained on the Irish fight card and the first three— Navy, Pittsburgh and North Carolina — were vanquished. Then came a setback at the hands of No. 1 Michigan State, a scoreless lock with Miami (Fla.), a final mark of 7-2-1, and a final rank of No. 9. Incidentally, while collecting 69 points against Pitt, Notre Dame passed the 15,000 milestone in points scored since its inception of football.

Southern Cal finished with an identical 7-2-1 record...and a No. 10 ranking. California and Pittsburgh were both blanked, UCLA eked out a narrow win and Wyoming was crushed. For the third straight autumn, there were no roses for the Trojans on New Year's Day.

But there was glorious recognition for one of their stellar performers. Garrett was awarded the prized Heisman Trophy, the first Trojan to wear the crown.

Several Irish stalwarts received accolades, too. Arrington, an offensive and defensive lineman, was a consensus All-American, while Rassas, Regner and Lynch were named to various A-A squads.

1966

GAME 38

Blowout In Troy

Perhaps it was an Irish lullaby that lulled the Trojans of Southern California into slumberland where they suffered a hideous nightmare. Maybe it was just an old-fashioned behind-the-barn whipping that scorched the land of Troy and sent its inhabitants reeling into humiliation. Or perhaps there was just no rhyme, reason or logic that could explain Notre Dame's awesome blowout of the Trojans in Game No. 38. Sure, the undefeated visitors from Hoosierland were supposed to win...but 51 to zero? Fifty-one to nothing? Five-one to nought?

That's what it was. Notre Dame 51, Southern California 0, the most points ever scored on the Trojans by any team and the widest margin of defeat inflicted on USC since the school first pumped up a pigskin in 1888.

"I couldn't imagine or dream of a score like that," uttered Ara Parseghian, Notre Dame's head taskmaster.

Neither did the hucksters along Wilshire Boulevard, who installed Notre Dame as only a 10-point favorite. Anyone with fortitude enough to give Southern Cal and 50 points could have earned enough money to purchase Indiana, California and Louisiana.

The outlook at South Bend glistened with cheer as Parseghian laid out plans for his third edition, prompting the wire services to award his club a pre-season slot of No. 6. Lettermen returning numbered 23, and 10 others who saw considerable service were back. Topping the list were Jim Lynch, Nick Eddy, Alan Page and Tom Regner, ably fortified by Pete Duranko, George Goeddeke, Larry Conjar, John Horney, Rocky Bleier and Kevin Hardy, back after a

246

USC running back Rod Sherman (12) is "all dressed up with no place to go" as over 1,100 pounds of Irish beef—Alan Page (81), Mike Heaton (84), John Pergine (50), Tom Rhoades (87) and Kevin Hardy (74)—close in. Notre Dame won, 51-0.

year-long injury.

These and other returning veterans would weigh heavily against the loss of several standouts...Nick Rassas, Tony Carey and Tom Longo...Bob Meeker, Dick Arrington and Tom Talaga...Bill Wolski, Bill Zloch and Tom Sullivan.

The departure of Zloch left a void at quarterback, but Parseghian had a pair of nifty sophomores— Terry Hanratty and Coley O'Brien— from which to choose. "They're better (than Zloch)," stated Parseghian, "so we'll be a much better passing and receiving team."

Out West in the City of Angels, Coach John McKay gathered his troops, searching in vain for someone to fill the big shoes of Heisman winner Mike Garrett, who established a collegiate rushing record of 4,876 yards in his three years at USC.

"Maybe we will interchange two or three players at his halfback spot," McKay told analyst Paul Zimmerman. "With Mike gone, our quarterback will run more and the fullbacks definitely will carry the ball more."

The QB so designated for additional duties would be

247

veteran Troy Winslow, and the FBs with new burdens shaped up as Mike Hull and Homer Williams, returning after a year's absence. These three were among 21 lettermen, and other top-notchers included Nate Shaw, Rod Sherman, Jim Homan and Ron Yary.

And, of course, Garrett was not McKay's only departing senior. Farewell deeds were also on file from Dave Moton, Frank Lopez, John Thomas, Charles Arrobio, Paul Johnson, to list a few. Their absence, however, did not deter forecasters from spotting Southern Cal at No. 9 in pre-season polls.

The Trojans banished their first six opponents—Texas, Wisconsin (victory No. 400 in USC history), Oregon State, Washington, Stanford and Clemson—before yielding to Miami (Fla.) by three points. USC then thrashed California but fell a touchdown shy of matching UCLA, bringing its record to 7-2-0 on the eve of its skirmish with Notre Dame. That slate gave SC a No. 10 rating.

Meanwhile, the Irish were rolling roughshod over eight foes...and engaging in a historic tie with the ninth. After dropping Purdue, Northwestern, Army and North Carolina, Notre Dame moved into the nation's No. 1 slot. The Irish then justified this perch with lopsided wins over Oklahoma, Navy, Pittsburgh and Duke before participating in a 10-10 draw with No. 2 Michigan State. In creating an 8-0-1 slate, the potent Irish defense had allowed only 38 points, an average of just over four per game. (After the USC shut-out, the average dropped to less than four.)

Yes, as might be expected, the Irish were on target to bulls-eye in on another national championship, and only Southern California could sway the direction of their arrow.

Zimmerman was half right when he wrote in the *Los Angeles Times* "...the game could be a low-scoring contest." His logic was based on the fact that the affair would "...bring together two of the top-rated defensive units in the land," and on the fact that Notre Dame's high-scoring offense would be impaired by injuries. Quarterback Hanratty, runners Bleier and Bob Gladieux, as well as center Goeddeke did not make the trip to the West Coast. Also, Zimmerman was aware that Troy's starting QB, Troy

Replacing injured Terry Hanratty, quarterback Coley O'Brien connected on 21 of 31 passes for 255 yards and three touchdowns. He led Notre Dame to its most lopsided triumph over USC: 51-0.

Winslow, would witness the struggle from the bench, compliments of a severe thigh bruise.

Players from each school were obsessed with a notion they wanted to prove as they met before 88,520 avid fans in the Coliseum in late November. The Irish wanted the world to know they were indeed No. 1, despite their previous-week's tie with the Spartans. Tommy Trojan had already been named to host the Rose Bowl, and he wanted the world to know he did indeed deserve the honor, despite a loss to Joe Bruin seven days ago.

Apparently, Notre Dame's intensity was greater, as the visitors wasted no time getting on the scoreboard and posting as many points in the first quarter alone as SouCal had allowed any opponent during a full game.

Taking the opening kickoff and starting from their 20-yard line, the Irish stalked methodically downfield and scored on the 16th play, Conjar smashing over center for the final two. And the concert of points had just begun. For, in staccato fashion, the Irish trumpeted out digits to the following merry tune:

NOTRE DAME ROMPS OVER U.S.C., 51-0

— Still in the first quarter, USC's reserve QB Toby Page underthrew a fling intended for Bob Klein. It was picked off by Tom Schoen who followed blocks by Hardy and Page, then laid down a 66-yard ribbon of fancy footsteps into the endzone, out-distancing Don McCall in the process. Joe Azzaro's second PAT brought the score to 14-0.

— Azzaro added three more points to that lead in the second period with a 38-yard field goal, after Mike Burgener had returned a SC punt 17 yards to put the drive in motion.

— Next, Notre Dame called upon its airborne division to deliver another strike. Flying 64 yards on eight passes, O'Brien connected with Seymour, who evaded Mike Battle and Pat Cashman, for the final 13 yards. The score became 24-0 after Azzaro's kick.

— There was still time for more airborne music before intermission, and the O'Brien-Seymour duet was again on center stage. SC's Dick Hough presented the overture with a 19-yard punt that left ND only 39 yards from paydirt. Subsequently, O'Brien lofted a missile into the end zone which Seymour took away from Battle and Shaw. The home folks went into a mild shock when Azzaro lifted the halftime score to 31-0.

— That shock became a coma when third quarter action saw Notre Dame pick up where it left off before the break. On the second play after the kickoff, Dave Martin recovered Hull's fumble on USC's 41, and ND wiped out those yards in six plays. The clincher was a 23-yard pass from O'Brien to Dan Harshman, who victimized Bill Jaroncyk.

The saga of the Notre Dame onslaught is interrupted at this point to acquaint one and all with a breath of oxygen that was pumped into the fans of Southern California, now sprawling in anguish. After Harshman's TD, USC's Young intercepted an O'Brien heave and scampered 43 yards to

ND's 47-yard stripe on the runback. Toby Page clicked with passes to Ron Drake, Klein and Ray Cahill, moving the Trojans to the Irish nine-yard line. Jim Smithberger batted down a pass in the endzone, and Drake muffed a sure-fire TD in the endzone, and USC frittered away its golden opportunity to avoid a goose egg. Now, back to the rampage:

— Having stymied Troy's best shot and with the end of the third frame drawing nigh, Notre Dame trudged 72 yards in 11 plays to raise the score to 44-0 (after Azzaro's PAT kick). Eddy put on the finishing touch by circling right end for the last nine yards.

— With reserves now on the field in the fourth stanza, Notre Dame marched 46 yards to SC's 14-yard line, only to be stopped by a fumble. But four plays later, Martin plucked off a pass by Steve Sogge and lumbered 33 yards into pointland. Azzaro's extra-point boot finalized the score at 51-0, and the walls of Troy lay in ashes.

"This is by far the best football team I've ever coached," exclaimed Parseghian. "Not only that— it is the best-balanced college team, offensively and defensively, I've ever seen in my life. And this was our most important win."

The Irish boss got no argument from USC's McKay. "I guess I've never seen a better team than Notre Dame was today," he acknowledged. But McKay also felt his squad had contributed to ND's mastery. "Our defensive unit just didn't do the job," he said in an understatement. "It just didn't turn the ball over at all. And our offense did a good job of moving the ball nowhere."

Parseghian could count stars by the dozen, but his initial thoughts dwelt on O'Brien, his diabetic second-string QB whose 21-of-31 passing for 255 yards and three touchdowns earned back-of-the-game honors, and on Seymour, who grabbed 11 passes for 150 yards and two TDs and was named lineman-of-the-game. But others, such as Page, Duranko, Hardy, John Pergine and Tom Rhoads came in for well-deserved plaudits.

Rather than seeing individual glitz, USC's former head coach and current athletic director, Jesse Hill, saw the unity of teamwork. "This is the best Notre Dame football team I've ever seen," he said. "They have absolutely no weaknesses. Well, maybe one. Their kickoffs were a little short."

USC's Sherman arose from the dumps to find an incentive from "...the worst beating we've ever had. But," he added, "now I think we'll come back and play a real good game in the Rose Bowl."

The Trojans did make a strong effort, but it wasn't quite strong enough, as Purdue prevailed, 14-13. So Southern Cal finished its season with seven wins and four defeats. The school boasted two consensus All-Americans — Shaw and Yary.

The names of Notre Dame players that spiced All-America rosters were plentiful. And four— Eddy, Lynch, Regner and Page— were consensus picks. Eight others— Duranko, Hardy, Seymour, Goeddeke, Schoen, Conjar, Hanratty and Paul Seiler— were choices on one or more selections.

After the blowout in Troy, and with a 9-0-1 mark, pollsters had little choice other than to vote Notre Dame at the top of the heap. It was the fifth national championship for the Irish since formal polls were started in 1936.

1967

After Ten, A Win In South Bend

The last time Southern California beat Notre Dame in South Bend, the colossal movie *Gone With the Wind* was two months away from its stirring premiere in Atlanta. The year was 1939. Autumns came and autumns went, but the Indiana Story for the Trojans never changed— come to Notre Dame Stadium, get beat.

But finally, after 10 chapters of futility, the script did change— and the Hollywood Story was written.

Perhaps it was an atonement for that dreadful drubbing of '66. Perhaps Tommy Trojan simply reared back on his haunches and bellowed, "Ten is enough!" Or perhaps the men of Troy sensed the smell of a championship aroma in their future and refused to allow a band of leprechauns or an arena monitored by a Golden Dome or novels of any plot block the purpose of their visit, which was to win, and which they did by a 24-7 count.

Discount the improbable fact that the Irish endured nine— count'em, nine— turnovers. Count the pure fact that the Trojans took advantage of these errors to construct their 16-point triumph.

A win by Southern Cal over Notre Dame was not foreseen before the season started, as wire service polls pegged the Irish as the No. 1 team in the land and the Trojans as the No. 7 club.

Notre Dame's top billing was somewhat of a puzzle, since Coach Ara Parseghian would begin his fourth fall minus 10 starters, major contributors such as Jim Lynch, Nick Eddy, Larry Conjar, Alan Page, Pete Duranko, John Horney and Tom Regner. But, on the other hand, a

253

All-America linebacker Adrian Young helped Southern Cal preserve its No. 1 ranking en route to a national championship in 1967 by intercepting four Notre Dame passes.

plethora of gifted performers were on hand to fill every void, and then some...Kevin Hardy, Tom Schoen, Jim Seymour, John Pergine, Dick Swatland, Jim Smithberger, Rocky Bleier, among others.

And then there was quarterback. Not one, but two quality veterans graced this position—Terry Hanratty, who threw for 1,248 yards as a sophomore, and Coley O'Brien, aptly described by Parseghian as "...the best No. 2 QB on any college team."

But if Notre Dame was well-stocked at quarterback, question marks engulfed the same position at Southern Cal, where Troy Winslow had disappeared into the sunset. Coach John McKay would have to decide between a senior—Toby Page—or two sophomores—Mike Holmgren and Steve Sogge.

Otherwise, prospects were bright around University Park, the return of 22 lettermen lending its strength. Six starters on defense were back, including guys such as Adrian Young, Tim Rossovich, Gary Magner and Mike Battle. And, despite the loss of Rod Sherman and Jim Homan, offensive returnees were equally impressive...Ron Yary, Mike Hull, Mike Scarpace and Ron Drake, whose 52 receptions in '66 set a school season record.

254

But poised for admission to the galaxy of football stardom was a junior college transfer named Orenthal James Simpson, better known simply as "O.J." In USC's four victories leading up to the ND skirmish (Washington State, Texas, Michigan State and Stanford), Simpson had averaged 151 yards per game and was the nation's leading rusher.

"This guy is fantastic," said Parseghian. "He has great speed and size, but he's also durable. He carries at least 30 times a game and never gets hurt."

Now on a fast track of 4-0-0 and a No. 1 rating, Southern Cal blew into South Bend to face a 2-1-0 Notre Dame squad whose rank had dropped to No. 6. The Irish had clobbered California and Iowa, were curbed by Purdue...and were now braced for the Trojans on a mid-October day before 59,075 ticket holders.

Neither school scored in the first quarter, but Notre

Offensive tackle Ron Yary lettered three years at USC, was All-America two years (1966-67) and was the Outland Trophy winner in 1967.

Dame unraveled the knot in the second when Smith-berger intercepted a pass by Sogge on USC's 19-yard line and sped to the three. On first down, Hanratty circled right end and pranced into the endzone, untouched. Joe Azzaro kicked true as the Irish toted a 7-0 lead into the intermission.

Up to this point, Notre Dame had limited Simpson to 41 yards, a stat that dictated a halftime change in strategy by McKay. Simpson would do more running to the out-side.

"We discovered early we couldn't pass very well against Notre Dame's defense," explained McKay, "and we hadn't done well running inside. So we felt our wide running game had to work."

The strategy worked— after an Irish miscue set it on course. ND's Chuck Landolfi fumbled the second-half kickoff, and Steve Swanson sheltered the ball for USC on ND's 18-yard line. After a short Sogge gain, Simpson carried the ball on the next six plays, crossing the goal line from 36 inches out on the last. Rikki Aldridge drilled the tying point.

After clicking on a 17-yard heave to Jeff Zimmerman, Hanratty went to the well again and was picked off by SC's Bill Jaroncyk on the Irish 42-yard line. Simpson raced for seven on first down, then tore around his left end on a pitchout for 35 whopping yards and six points. Aldridge's PAT lifted SC to a 14-7 lead.

Taking advantage of Bleier's tiny 13-yard punt, Sou-Cal was at the Irish 41 and panting for more points. Behind Simpson's runs, the Trojans moved to ND's six, but stalled, whereupon Aldridge hoisted a 22-yard field goal. The third quarter ended with Southern Cal on top, 17-7.

Another pass theft off Hanratty led to Troy's last touchdown, and this time the robber was Battle, who scampered 35 yards to ND's 17-yard stripe. Simpson,

showing a never-to-be-squelched penchant for touchdowns, clipped those 17 yards with a trio of runs, the last
being a three-yarder. Aldridge added the extra point,
bringing the final score to 24-7 and bringing the Irish to
their knees.

Both coaches offered comments about Notre Dame's
defense, although there was some contrast in the nature.
McKay: "Notre Dame's defense doesn't give you a thing. It

*O. J. Simpson carried 38 times in the 1967 contest at South Bend.
"The Juice" scored three touchdowns and rushed for 150 yards in the
24-7 USC victory. Following the play are USC quarterback Steve
Sogge (12) and Notre Dame's Kevin Hardy (74).*

USC quarterback Steve Sogge directs his teammates en route to a 24-7 win. USC's right guard is Mike Scarpace, the center is Dick Almon and the left guard is Steve Lehmer. Mike McGill (60) defends for Notre Dame.

held us twice for less than a yard for first down and you have to give them credit." Parseghian: "Our defense had just too much pressure on it with all our turnovers."

Parseghian was referring to two lost fumbles and seven pass interceptions, four of which were pilfered by linebacker Young.

Simpson maintained his per-game average by netting 159 yards on 38 carries. The pulsating junior, who finished the season with a Trojan high of 1,543 yards, went on to become a consensus All-America, as did mates Yary, Rossovich and Young. Yary also was awarded the Outland Trophy as the nation's outstanding interior lineman, the first Trojan ever to receive this prestigious honor.

Notre Dame also put on display a consensus All-

America— defensive back Schoen. Hardy, Seymour and Mike McGill made one or more first-team rosters while Swatland, Smithberger and Pergine were picked on certain second teams.

After bowing to Southern Cal, Notre Dame proceeded to mow down its six remaining opponents— Illinois, Michigan State, Navy, Pittsburgh, Georgia Tech and Miami (Fla.). The win over the Yellow Jackets was Notre Dame's 500th career victory. That, however, didn't impress the poll voters, who tapped the Irish at No. 6, based on their final slate of eight triumphs and a deuce of defeats.

The bottle of despair at South Bend now uncorked, the Trojans romped to methodical decisions over Washington, Oregon and California. Then, while riding the crest of 8-0-0 credentials— boom— Oregon State spoiled the fun with a 3-0 upset in the mud at Corvallis. But the Trojans bounced back to nip UCLA, then thump Indiana in the Rose Bowl. Their record of 10-1-0 earned the crown of national champion, as well as the ancillary honors of conference, state and city champs.

1968

The Tie That Binds

Some sports wag once proclaimed that playing a game to a tie was like kissing your sister. And, while probably not acquainted with the philosopher, Southern California Coach John McKay concurred.

"I'd rather play out there 'till midnight," he muttered. "I just don't like a tie."

But a 21-21 deadlock was what McKay and his Trojans got in their annual brawl with Notre Dame in Game No. 40.

Southern Cal entered the clash undefeated and untied through nine games, boasting a No. 1 rank by UPI and No. 2 by AP. So, with a national championship in the balance, maybe the West Coast entry had more on the line than did Notre Dame, ranked No. 9 with a 7-2-0 ledger. Maybe so, but Notre Dame Coach Ara Parseghian still harbored his own thoughts about the limbo finish.

"Of course, we were disappointed we didn't win," said he. "But, by the same token, we weren't defeated by No. 1."

Statistically, the Irish overshadowed the Trojans, leading in first downs, 24 to 14, and in total yardage, 442 to 239. Also, the Irish had the Trojans in their hip pocket at halftime, leading 21-7.

The Notre Dame vault was loaded with jewels as Parseghian opened practice drills in late August. Nineteen regulars on offense and 11 on defense were back to vie for starting positions. Offensive gems included George Kunz, Jim Seymour, Jim Reilly, Terry Hanratty and Bob Gladieux. Also on the scene was Joe Theismann, a talented sophomore quarterback, and his presence enabled Parseghian to shift Coley O'Brien to halfback. On defense, the roster included Bob Olson, Bob Kuechenberg, Eric Norri and Chick Lauck.

Graduation claimed a ton of Irish stars, though...Rocky Bleier, Dan Harshman and Dick Swatland from the offense; Kevin Hardy, Tom Schoen, Jim Smithberger, Mike McGill, John Pergine, Dave Martin, Tom O'Leary from the defense. Despite the loss of these and other veterans, Notre Dame, nevertheless, was pegged as the No. 3 club in the nation by pre-season wire polls.

But if the cupboard was well-stocked at Notre Dame, it certainly wasn't bare at Southern California. Twenty-three lettermen answered McKay's call to arms, including the grandest runner on the planet, O.J. Simpson, a viable Heisman Trophy candidate. Mike Battle and Steve Sogge fell in line, too...as did Jim Lawrence, Bob Klein, Bob Miller and Jim Snow.

So overflowing with wealth was the land of Troy that only one team—Purdue—outranked USC in pre-season polls. Apparently, forecasters felt departing seniors such as Ron Yary, Adrain Young, Tim Rossovich, Ron Drake, Mike Hull, Steve Grady and Gary Magner could be replaced.

To be sure, those were leaky losses, but if any holes existed in the USC dike, they were adequately plugged, to which nine victims of the Trojan might would attest. Minnesota, Northwestern, Miami (Fla.), Stanford, Washington, Oregon, California, Oregon State and UCLA all took their heftiest swings at the Trojans, and all sulked

IRISH TIE UP O.J. AND TROJANS, 21-21
Sogge Passes Bring USC Back

CC   SECTION D   41
SUNDAY, DECEMBER 1, 1968

back to the dugout, hitless.

Notre Dame fared well during those same weeks, too...whipping Oklahoma, Iowa, Northwestern, Illinois, Navy, Pittsburgh and Georgia Tech, while being cuffed only by Purdue and Michigan State.

The Irish were on a three-game winning string when the USC conflict appeared on the horizon. For the year, their offense was averaging more than 500 yards per game, but their defense against rushing was equally impressive...a stingy 82.3 yards per game, fourth best in the nation.

Of course, with Simpson hauling leather (1,654 yards in nine games), rushing was Southern Cal's forte. So the contest was pitted as Trojan rushing versus Irish defense as the two teams faced off in Memorial Coliseum on the last day of November. Few, if any, of the 82,659 fans expected to see a stalemate.

The troops of Troy drew first blood, piercing the Irish fortress for seven points just 40 seconds into the fray. ND's Theismann hurled the ball in the direction of Seymour, but SC's Sandy Durko stepped in front, gathered in the ball and stepped 21 yards for a touchdown. The PAT by Vic Ayala was good.

But the quarter was still in its infancy, and the Irish stormed back to tally twice before it died. With Gladieux reeling off a 14-yard run, Ron Dushney an 11-yarder and Theismann a nine-yarder plus Seymour pulling in a 13-yard fling from Theismann, Notre Dame harvested 86 yards in 18 plays, Dushney scoring from the three. Scott Hempel added the extra point.

Notre Dame struck more quickly for its second TD, gobbling up 77 yards in four plays. Theismann started it by keeping for 11 yards, then two plays later pitched out to Gladieux, who picked up blocks by O'Brien and Dushney, broke past Tony Terry and Bob Jensen, and set sail for the SC goal, 57 yards downfield. That put Notre Dame up by six points, and Hempel's kick increased the lead to seven.

The visitors resorted to some trickery to notch their third marker, which came in the second period. SC's John Young punted from his endzone, giving ND good field

O. J. Simpson scores in third period from one yard out to cut Notre Dame's lead to 21-14. The 1968 game ended a 21-21 tie.

position on Southern Cal's 45. On the sixth play of the abbreviated drive, Theismann connected with Seymour for 21 yards to the Trojan nine-yard line. Gladieux swept to the seven, but Theismann was sacked back to the 13. On the ninth play of the movement, Theismann pitched out to O'Brien, who faked a run to his right, stopped and threw back to the left side to Theismann, who eluded Terry, caught the ball in stride and waltzed into the corner of the endzone with 30 ticks on the clock. Hempel hammered the PAT and Notre Dame led at halftime, 21-7.

"We tried that play earlier in the game when I tried to throw to Jim (Seymour)," said O'Brien, "but it was intercepted. They were in a zone (defense) then, so we waited until they went into a man-to-man."

The 14-point bulge enjoyed by the Irish was indicative of their first half dominance: 324 yards and 16 first downs. Meanwhile, USC had generated only three first downs and its galloping horse— Simpson— had been tamed to a trot with just 23 yards for 30 minutes on the track. During halftime deliberations, USC coaches decided to abandon the infantry attack and call upon its air squadron.

Taking the second-half kickoff USC started its comeback trail from its 35-yard line. Fourteen plays later it was in the ND endzone, Simpson sweeping in for the final yard. In between, Sogge passed 11 yards to Sam Dickerson, 18 to Terry DeKraai, 10 to Bob Chandler, Simpson ran for seven, and ND was penalized for pass interference. Ayala's PAT closed the gap to 21-14, ND.

The Trojans tied the score with 10 minutes and 14 seconds to play in the fourth frame. It came to fruition on a 40-yard touchdown strike from Sogge to Dickerson, the sixth play of a 54-yard invasion that was born of a Theismann interception by SC's Gerald Shaw, who scampered 22 yards after his theft. With two-thirds of a quarter still to be played, Southern Cal's brain trust overruled a two-point try and opted for the tie, which Ayala delivered.

As it turned out, the scoreboard would reflect no further change, although Notre Dame had a chance to revise it. Hempel, however, was wide on a 33-yard field goal attempt with 33 seconds to play.

"Down deep in my heart, I really think we should have won," wailed Theismann, who won back-of-the-game honors. "We had 'em on the run."

Certainly the strategy of Parseghian, which basically was to prevent Simpson from getting outside, or the execution of this plan by his defense, could not be faulted. Kuechenberg, Olson, Lauck, Norri and Mike McCoy (voted lineman-of-the-game) restricted Simpson to a mere 55 yards, lowest output of his career, and also kept constant pressure on Sogge.

"When you are conditioned to winning, it's tough to take anything but a win," remarked Simpson, who praised Danny Scott, the man who blocked for him. "Sure, I'm a little disappointed. I had wanted an undefeated, untied season. I didn't need a tie to get me up for the Rose Bowl."

But the remorse of Simpson was exchanged for rapture a short while later when he received the esteemed Heisman Trophy, the second Trojan so honored in the past four years. He was USC's sole consensus All-America, although Battle was listed on first, second or third teams on six selections.

Two standouts from Notre Dame earned consensus All-America laurels—Kunz and Hanratty—and Seymour was recognized on some squads. The Irish finished their season with a 7-2-1 record, sufficient for a No. 5 rating.

But for Southern Cal, there was still the Rose Bowl and robust Ohio State with which to be reckoned. And if the Trojans were dampened by a tie with Notre Dame, they were drenched by a loss to the Buckeyes. Still, nine victories, one defeat and one tie was not a mark of which to be ashamed. Neither was a national rank of No. 4. And neither were Simpson's stats for the year: 1,880 net yards rushing and 23 touchdowns.

With the 1968 encounter taking its place in the annals of time, the Notre Dame-Southern California series was now 40 games old. With the exception of 1933, at which point eight games had been evenly divided, the Irish have led in the series every year, and their lead now stands at 25 to 12 with three draws. Notre Dame also leads in total points scored, 723 to 485—an advantage it has maintained since 1942.

1969

GAME 41

The Tie That Binds, Part 2

Breezing down the track toward national laurels, the Trojan horse was ambushed by a fiesty clan of Irish spoilsports, tied into a 14-14 knot, and left to ponder — "what, again?" Indeed, it was the second year in a row that Notre Dame had scarred with a draw the unflawed record of Southern California, once again detouring its imperial aspirations.

As it was the previous year, the two institutions met under similiar conditions: Southern Cal undefeated and untied, Notre Dame already removed from the ranks of the perfect. And once again, the result was the same— a dead heat, which may not have fully pleased the Irish, but most assuredly did torment the Trojans.

The course of the game afforded armchair quarterbacks to again question the strategy of Notre Dame coach Ara Parseghian, who opted for a tie rather than gamble for a victory with 6:51 to play in the fourth quarter.

The Irish skipper retorted that he was "...not even tempted" to go for two points when his club trailed by one. "I noticed that teams in the Big 10 (conference) are 91 per cent successful in kicking conversions," Ara pointed out, "but they have made just three of 17 tries for two points."

There was good news and bad news for Parseghian as he charted the path of his sixth season under the Golden Dome. The bright side was the return of 15 lettermen plus seven other performers who saw regular service. Joe Theismann, Denny Allan, Mike Oriard, Jim Reilly and Larry DiNardo were among banner returnees on offense; Mike McCoy, Bob Olson, Tim Kelly, Larry Schumacher

266

and John Gasser were their counterparts on defense. Now the bad news: Terry Hanratty, Jim Seymour, George Kunz, Coley O'Brien, Ron Dushney and Bob Gladieux had waved goodbye from the offense; Bob Kuechenberg, Eric Norri and Chick Lauck from the defense.

Looking at the good and the bad, wire service votes pegged Notre Dame at No. 11 in pre-season polls. And after four games, the Irish were still at No. 11, having captured three while letting one escape. The Irish clubbed Northwestern, were upset by Purdue, thumped Michigan State and swamped Army before gearing up for Southern Cal.

A decade had passed underfoot for Coach John McKay at Southern California and the aluminum jubilee shaped up as a good one...so good, in fact, that a No. 5 rating was accorded his troops. Eighteen lettermen cavorted on the practice field...Clarence Davis, Bob Chandler, Sid Smith, Sam Dickerson, Harry Khasigian and Steve Lehmer topping the offensive veterans; Jimmy Gunn, Al Cowlings, Bubba Scott and Gerald Shaw assuming similiar roles for the defense.

McKay's prime challenge, though, was to replace the fabulous O.J. Simpson, two-time All-America, Heisman Trophy winner and holder of Troy's rushing record. And Simpson's departure wasn't the only void, because such denizens as Mike Battle, Steve Sogge and Jim Snow had fled the fold, as well as Jim Lawrence, Bob Miller, Bob Klein and Dan Scott.

But the gaps were plugged, and the Trojans sallied forth with decisions over Nebraska, Northwestern, Oregon State and Stanford. Their 4-0-0 ledger had lifted them to a No. 3 ranking as Notre Dame extended its welcome mat to them.

As usual, the students of the Blue and Gold held their pre-game pep rally on Friday. But to incite the scholars was an unusual guest— Rocky Bleier, 1967 team captain and now a veteran of the Vietnam police action, wounded in combat.

"I left behind bodies of men in Vietnam, some in fields, some in hospitals," Bleier expounded. "All I can say is...let's win tomorrow's game for THEM!"

The student body was charged and ready to shred the invaders from the Golden State, but Parseghian was more cautious. "Without question, USC is a much better team offensively than it was with O.J. (Simpson)," he suggested. "They've got a fourth dimension in the backfield with (Jimmy) Jones."

Of course, McKay envisioned trouble ahead for his club, too. "Our basic problem against Notre Dame is obvious," he warned. "They've got the biggest defense we've faced, we'll have trouble seeing over them and running through them, but we'll just have to prove we can still block when we're smaller than they are."

Apparently, the wager-makers along Chicago's State Street agreed with McKay, establishing Notre Dame, despite its inferior record, as a three-point favorite to win.

"How can we be favored?" asked a bewildered Parseghian who answered his question with the same question. "How can we be favored? Why, they'd probably pick us to beat the Minnesota Vikings."

Well, 59,075 lovers of sport wanted that answer, too. So each and every one of them meandered into Notre Dame Stadium, now covered overhead with a gathering overcast and pierced inside with an autumn chill.

The first half was a washout with neither team able to score, though SouCal initiated three motions in that direction. Taking the opening kickoff, the Trojans marched 75 yards, only to be halted when Charlie Evans dropped a handoff from Jones and ND's Schumacher recovered on his seven-yard line. Then, Ron Ayala's 35-yard field goal attempt fell short. Finally, Davis, who entered the contest as the nation's No. 2 rusher, shed defenders and raced 15 yards into the Irish endzone, only to have the play nullified by a holding penalty on Bill Redding.

Meanwhile, Troy's defense, spearheaded by Cowlings, Scott, Tody Smith, Tony Terry and Greg Slough, was limiting Notre Dame to an anemic 35 total net yards and just two first downs during the first half.

But the tempo picked up after intermission. And it was the home fellows who supplied the drama, traveling 74 yards in 11 plays to break the monotony of the scoreless tie. Theismann passed 16 yards to Ed Ziegler, plus 12 and

All-America defensive end Jimmy Gunn played in only two losing games during his three-year career at USC (1967-68-69).

11 to Dewey Poskon before Bill Barz dived the last yard for a touchdown. Along the way, USC's Bob Jensen drew a 12-yard penalty for pass interference against Tom Gatewood, creating momentum for the Irish and ire for McKay.

"It's the same thing every week," he wailed as Scott Hempel added the PAT. "A lousy pass interference play."

Before the third quarter expired, however, Southern Cal knotted the score. The payoff was a 19-yard scoring strike from Jones to Terry DeKraai, the 11th play of a 75-yard trek. Key plays were jaunts of nine, five and four yards by Davis and 13 by Jones. Ayala tacked on the tying point.

The combatants divided a brace of markers in the fourth period, with both TDs set up by defensive heroics. First, SC's Tyrone Hudson filched a Theismann toss on ND's 40-yard stripe and ran it down to the 15. Moments later, from the 14, Jones rifled a TD bullet to Dickerson,

Ayala kicked true and USC was out front, 14-7.

With eight minutes to play, ND's McCoy blocked John Young's punt and Walt Patulski surrounded the ball for the Irish on SC's seven-yard line. On fourth down, Allan slipped through the right side of his line for the final yard. Playing percentages, Parseghian called on Hempel, whose kick locked the score at 14-all.

"I lined up over their center and right guard," said McCoy, "and managed to crack through one of them. Either the ball or the kicker's foot caught me on the jaw. I can still feel it."

The Irish had two chances to win the game in the fourth period, and success from either would have branded Parseghian's "no gamble" decision as a stroke of genius.

Marching 75 yards, mostly on passes from Theismann to Barz, Notre Dame found its forces perched on Southern Cal's three-yard line. But no closer did they get as Gunn and Terry slammed Theismann to earth 15 yards behind the line of scrimmage. Later, in the ebbing moments of the tussle, the Irish paraded from their 44-yard line to Troy's 14 but found themselves back on the 32 after a clipping penalty. On fourth down Hempel lined up for a 39-yard field goal try. The thrust was straight, the power was weak...the ball hit the crossbar dead-center and bounced backwards. And that was that.

"I'm really proud of our team," remarked Parseghian. "And I'm sure John McKay feels the same way about his boys."

Well, yes and no. "We thought we could move the ball against them and we blew some opportunities," replied McKay. "We didn't catch the ball very well. In fact, we didn't play well offensively, but much of that was Notre Dame's fault."

And much of the credit for Notre Dame's effectiveness could be traced to the defensive antics of Clarence Ellis, a sophomore cornerback who constantly harassed punter Young, Dickerson and Jones.

Holding powerful Southern California to a tie proved to be a shot in the arm for Notre Dame, which proceeded to vanquish the five remaining antagonists on its schedule—Tulane, Navy, Pittsburgh, Georgia Tech and Air Force.

Sporting 8-1-1 credentials, Notre Dame contracted bowl fever and agreed to tangle with No. 1 Texas in Dallas' Cotton Bowl. It was only the second bowl game in Notre Dame's history, the Fighting Irish having dumped Stanford in the Rose Bowl on January 1, 1925. This time around, fate was not so generous as the Longhorns prevailed to keep their No. 1 rating and position the Irish at No. 5.

Shutting out the limbo aspects of the Notre Dame draw, Southern Cal also wiped out the five remaining foes on its schedule—Georgia Tech, California, Washington State, Washington and UCLA. But the Trojans did the Irish one better: they clipped Michigan in the Rose Bowl to construct a 10-0-1 ledger. Texas and Penn State, however, both finished 11-0-0 and both outranked the Trojans in final wire service polls.

Both schools vaunted a consensus All-American: McCoy for Notre Dame; Gunn for Southern Cal. And both had other players who were named on certain rosters: Cowlings, Sid Smith and Davis for the Trojans; Reilly, DiNardo, Oriard and Olson, who was credited with 142 tackles throughout the season, for the Irish.

1970

Irish Win Battle, Lose War

How does a football team run up a staggering total of 557 yards and collect 28 first downs while holding its opponent to 359 yards and 17 first downs...and still lose by 10 points? One way— and a good one, too— is to fashion eight turnovers MORE than said opponent. And, indeed, those were the strange curriculums of Notre Dame's 38-28 loss to Southern California in Game No. 42. (Well, at least it wasn't another trifling tie.)

But it was the third consecutive year that one of the two schools had come into the fracas with a clean and perfect figure, only to depart with a gash across its hide. In 1968 and '69, USC's unscathed slates were marred by a tie; this year, it was Notre Dame's unblemished watermark that met its Waterloo.

It was an ironic twist for the Irish, too. For, on this rain-splattered day at Exposition Park, Joe Theismann set ND records of 33 pass completions and 526 passing yards. Conversely, those figures also were all-time high marks of yield against the defense of Southern California.

It must be mentioned, however, that Theismann's counterpart across the field— Jimmy Jones— was also polishing bright statistics on this dark day. In throwing 15 completions for 226 yards, the junior quarterback raised his career completion total to 209 and his passing yardage to 1,877— both new USC records.

Both institutions were awarded high grades by pre-season wire polls; Southern Cal pre-judged at No. 3, Notre Dame at No. 6.

The Trojan plateau was based on the return of 23

272

FOR SPORTS RESULTS
BETWEEN 3:30 A. M.
AND MIDNIGHT
CALL
222-1234
Chicago Tribune
SUNDAY, NOVEMBER 29, 1970
SPORTS **2**
SECTION A
BUSINESS **4**
SECTION B

Theismann Brilliant in 38-28 Loss

U.S.C. DASHES IRISH UNBEATEN HOPES

lettermen, including such defensive demons as Charles Weaver, Mike Haluchak and Greg Slough, labeled by Coach John McKay as "...the premier linebacker in the college game." But take a gander at some of the offensive threats that brought goosebumps to McKay: Sam Dickerson, John Vella, Marv Montgomery, plus 1969's starting backfield intact— Jones, Charles Evans, Clarence Davis and Bob Chandler. Yes, it was generally acceded that the land of Troy could survive the loss of departing seniors such as Jim Gunn and Sid Smith, Harry Khasigian and Steve Lehmer, Willard Scott and Gerald Shaw.

Not to be outdone by its arch rival, Notre Dame brought back its entire starting backfield, too— Theismann, Denny Allan, Andy Huff and Bill Barz— and these were just four of the 13 regulars (10 lettermen) back on offense. Others included Tom Gatewood, Larry DiNardo and Gary Kos. Fifteen regulars, including 11 lettermen, beefed up defensive returnees for Coach Ara Parseghian, headed by Clarence Ellis, Tim Kelly, Ralph Stepaniak, Walt Patulski and Mike Kadish. Big losses for the Irish consisted of Mike McCoy, Bob Olson, John Gasser, Jim Reilly and Larry Schumacher, among others.

Place-kickers returned for both clubs— Scott Hempel for Notre Dame, Ron Ayala for Southern Cal.

As previously stated, the Irish waded through their first nine foes without so much as a scratch, although the last two— Georgia Tech and LSU— each submitted by a scant three points. The others— Northwestern, Purdue, Michigan State, Army, Missouri, Navy and Pitt— were no match for the ramblers from Indiana. But even a 9-0-0 mark could entice a rating of no better than No. 4 by AP as the Irish honed their sights on USC.

Looking back at them in defiance were the Trojans,

shielding an unimpressive accomplishment of five victories and a tie in ten games. USC took the blue ribbon against Alabama, Iowa, Oregon State, Washington and Washington State, fought to a draw with Nebraska, and went home to University Park empty-handed against Stanford, Oregon, California and hated-enemy UCLA.

After the loss by 25 points to a mediocre Bruin outfit, McKay told Doug Krikorian of the *Los Angeles Herald-Express* that 1970 to that point had been his most disappointing season. "The second one (season) isn't even close," he emphasized.

But the post-UCLA mood of the Trojans was one of somber determination, as expressed by Weaver: "It was quiet until about Thursday," he stated. "Nobody said anything about being worried we might lose to Notre Dame. Then you could see it in everybody's eyes— we just seemed to be saying to each other, 'we've gotta win— or else.'"

And, despite being the big boy on the block, Parseghian was well aware of the challenge the Trojans would offer. "Dickerson and Chandler are real threats every time they go downfield," he commented. "Once a team forces you to defense it in length, you weaken your defense in width. Southern Cal is a perfect example of this kind of test."

So, with caution in the wind and precipitation hovering in the clouds above, 64,694 bold patrons with umbrellas on alert ambled through the gates of the Coliseum on an overcast day in late November.

The *Chicago Tribune* had branded Notre Dame as "...a clear-cut favorite," and that seemed to be an accurate assessment when the Irish scored early in the first quarter. Theismann threw for 19 yards to Gatewood, 12 to John Cieszkowski, then trotted 25 yards into the end zone on the 12th play of an 80-yard drive. Hempel passed his first toe test and ND led, 7-0.

The joy of that lead was short lived as the Trojans marched 70, 51 and 57 yards to register three touchdowns within the next eight minutes, exhibiting a 21-7 advantage at the end of the first period. Jones was seven-for-seven in passing during the maneuvers, which unfolded as follows:

— Jones rolled out and hurled a hummer of 19 yards to Evans, duplicated this yardage on a play-action toss to Chandler, then pitched out to Evans, who scored from the three on the seventh play. Ayala's kick locked the score, and ND never came closer.

— Another pitchout to Davis from ND's five-yard line resulted in SC's second TD, after Jones had moved the Trojans downfield with passes of 31 yards to Davis and 10 to Chandler. Ayala's kick was wide, but not to worry.

— In four plays, Troy had struck again. Jones threw 10 yards to Davis, nine to Evans, then 45 to Dickerson, who out-battled Ellis for the ball and scored. To re-coup the missed PAT, Jones hit Chandler for a deuce.

Some reporters viewed Dickerson's catch as first ricocheting off Ellis' arms. "I had gone downfield, made a move and went by him (Ellis)," declared Dickerson. "He looked at me, but I had my eyes on the ball. I jumped— then he jumped— and I came down with the ball. That's all I remember."

Quarterback Joe Theismann completed 33 passes for 526 yards—a single game record for Notre Dame—in the 1970 loss to USC. His single-season statistics—155 completions for 2,429 yards—set Notre Dame records.

The Irish had not trailed by 14 points all season, so it was proper that they take steps to mend the situation, which they did with a tally midway the second stanza, even though raindrops were beginning to fall.

It was a 60-yard journey which featured a 28-yard aerial from Theismann to Gatewood (who caught 10 during the game), a 14-yarder to Darryll Dewan and a nine-yard heave to Cieszkowski, who carried SC's Kent Carter with him into the endzone. Hempel's boot brought ND to within seven points at 21-14.

But once again, USC stretched the margin as Ayala rammed a 19-yard field goal. He was afforded this opportunity when Weaver tipped a Theismann pass into the eager hands of Bruce Dyer. Jones then aided the cause with flings of 19 and nine yards to Chandler. The half ended with USC atop a 24-14 score. And intermittent raindrops turned to sheets.

The Trojans didn't mind. Within five minutes of the third period, they scored twice, thanks to alert ball-seekers and to Irish athletes who ran with vim but neglected to carry the ball with them.

First, Dewan fumbled when hit by Willie Hall, and SC's Carter fell on the loose ball on ND's 17-yard stripe. Jones flipped to Dickerson for 13 yards. On third down, Mike Berry smashed for the endzone and hit an Irish wall, causing the ball to squirt from his grasp. Johnny-on-the-spot was tackle Pete Adams, who wrapped himself around the pigskin for a Trojan touchdown.

Next, following SC's kickoff, Theismann was dislodged from the ball by Hall but recovered after an 11-yard loss back to his seven-yard line. Now becoming enamored with his frolics, Hall sacked Theismann again, separating the Irish QB from the ball in the endzone where it was pounced upon by Vella...two Trojan touchdowns in 42 seconds. After each, Ayala made good the conversions, and Southern Cal was out front, 38-14.

"I thought we could beat them when we went in for halftime," declared Parseghian. "But those two quick TDs were too much to overcome."

To their credit, though, the lads from South Bend flexed their collective muscles and notched the game's

276

last two touchdowns, changing a rout into respectability.

The first, coming in the third quarter, was the result of a 72-yard trek which Notre Dame eradicated in five plays. Naturally, the last was the best, a 46-yard TD bomb from Theismann to Larry Parker, who also snagged a 12-yarder to complement Ed Gulyar's l0-yard run along the way. Hempel converted.

Then, very early in the final frame, the Irish tallied again, Theismann going over from the one to cap a 69-yard drive that needed 17 plays. Three heaves from Theismann figured prominently...12 and 13 yards to Cieszowski, 16 to Gulyas. After Hempel's kick brought the Irish to within 10 points, the clock still showed 13:52 to play, time enough to find an opening in the victory door. Time enough, maybe...but the Trojans saw to it that every crack was tightly sealed, allowing the Irish no way to escape defeat.

"Maybe we proved something today," said SC's Vella, a junior who was jubilant after scoring his first career touchdown. "These seniors were all too good to go out with a defeat."

Bob Oates of the *LA Times* asked McKay how it felt to conquer the previously unbeaten Fighting Irish. "They are one of the classic teams in the country," he answered, "and 50 years from now, our seniors can sit around the fireplace and say they never lost to Notre Dame."

Although the Irish dented the Trojans for 28 points and rolled for almost one-third of a mile, McKay found words of praise for his defenders, players such as Vella, Weaver, Slough, Carter and Hall, who turned in five sacks, instigated two critical fumbles and was voted defensive-star-of-the-game. But McKay did not overlook his fellows who were charged with moving the ball, singling out Jones, Chandler, Dickerson, Davis, Montgomery and Greg Mullins.

For the first time in five years, Southern California would not be the host in Rose Bowl festivities. So the Notre Dame affair, dubbed by Assistant Coach Marv Goux "...as great a victory as I've ever been associated with," ended its season with six Ws, four Ls and one T— and a national rank of No. 15. Weaver was a consensus All-American, and Montgomery was listed on some selections.

Notre Dame spawned a consensus All-American, too—offensive guard DiNardo. Three others— Gatewood, Ellis and Theismann— were named on various teams.

But its season did not end in the California mud. For the Irish, now caught in the swing of post-season mania, had a re-match with Texas in the Cotton Bowl. The Longhorns were rated No. 1 by both AP and UPI and were riding the crest of a 30-game winning streak. But the Irish broke that string with a 24-11 victory, and their 10-1-0 record earned a No. 2 rank behind Nebraska in the year's final polls.

1971

Same Song, Fourth Verse

Knock the perfect team off its regal pedestal. That, apparently, had become the theme song of Notre Dame and Southern California. And, in Game No. 43, it was the underdog Trojans' turn to warble the tune of prankster, which they performed with gusto in a 28-14 march over the previously undefeated and untied Irish.

With an update of facts, the second paragraph in the chapter describing Game No. 42 can be repeated: "It was the fourth consecutive year in which one of the two schools had come into the fracas with a clean and perfect figure, only to depart with a gash across its hide. In 1968 and '69, USC's unscathed slates were marred by a tie; last year and this year, it was Notre Dame's unblemished watermarks that met their Waterloo."

All fudging aside, be reminded that prior to the scuffle, the Fighting Irish had laced Northwestern, Purdue, Michigan State, Miami (Fla.) and North Carolina...had yielded a bare 16 points in all of those games and none in the last 10 quarters...boasted the nation's third best rushing defense and fourth best total defense...was ranked No. 6 in the land...and was favored to win by 13 points on Friday and 21 at kickoff.

And what counteroffer did the men of Troy present for inspection? Two sparse wins and four unwelcome losses, three of these coming in the last three games. That's all.

Expectations in early September were much brighter along the corridors of Heritage Hall than the realities of subsequent weeks revealed. Coach John McKay told Dwight Chapin "...Our 1971 offense should be improved", so, since the '70 offense was USC's highest production (343 points) in 40 years, Chapin (writing for *Street and Smith* magazine), felt justified in picking Southern Cal to capture top honors in the PAC-8 Conference.

At the time, the Trojans were not an unlikely choice, as evidenced by a national pre-season rank of No. 5. Twenty-one lettermen responded to McKay's drills, defensive hulks such as Willie Hall, John Grant, Bruce Dyer and John Papadakis; offensive operators such as John Vella, Pete Adams, Lou Harris, Mike Ryan, Allan Graf and Sam Cunningham, as well as a tandem of neat quarterbacks—senior Jimmy Jones and junior Mike Rae.

These and other veterans, along with a sterling crop of sophomores, painted a vivid forecast that obscured the brushes of darkness etched from departed seniors such as Charles Weaver, Sam Dickerson and Clarence Davis, Bob Chandler, Mike Haluchak and Greg Slough.

So, the season started and right out of the gate Southern Cal was tripped by Alabama. The Tide didn't know it was supposed to lose, but Rice and Illinois did, and both were shut out by the Trojans in the following two weeks. Next, thud! And the walls of Troy came tumbling down as Oklahoma, Oregon and Stanford all measured Tommy Trojan for a coffin and buried him.

But if the season had turned sour for the Trojans, it had started and remained sweet for the Irish...until, that is, Southern Cal came to town.

Coach Ara Parseghian was in his eighth autumn at the Dome, and 24 lettermen plus eight other performers of active status graced the mass of humanity before him. In an understatement of grandeur, Parseghian envisioned "...a fairly decent defensive unit," but endless were the number of titans on hand to staff his "fairly decent" brigade— Walt Patulski and Clarence Ellis, Greg Marx and Mike Kadish, Fred Swendsen, Mike Crotty and Ralph Stepaniak.

"Our offensive team will be inconsistent, at least at the start," opined Ara. And it wasn't that the coach was overlooking the return of such veterans as Tom Gatewood, Dan Novakov and John Dampeer, or Mike Creaney, Ed Gulyas and Andy Huff, back after a year-long injury.

Tempers flair in the second quarter of the 1971 game.

Nay—his apprehension centered around quarterback, where a quadruple of unknowns would essay to replace Joe Theismann. And, besides Theismann, offensive holes were left by Larry DiNardo, Gary Kos, Denny Allan and Bill Barz, while defensive departures included Tim Kelly, Jim Wright and Bob Neidert.

When practice sessions were replaced with the call of competition, there was an instant jell of Parseghian's "fairly decent" defense and his "inconsistent" offense. For, as already pointed out, five victims fell in rapid order to the Irish wrath. And Southern Cal was earmarked to be the sixth.

But the Trojans brought an intimidating factor of nary a loss at South Bend since 1965. And the weatherman brought a promise of overcast skies and scattered showers. And 59,075 partisan spectators brought umbrellas and a vote of confidence for their home town shamrocks.

Early on, their faith was slightly smirched when Southern Cal rambled out front midway the first quarter. Dyer set the scenario in motion by intercepting a pass

281

from ND's Cliff Brown on SC's 24-yard line. He scurried back 28 yards to the Irish 48, from which point Troy crossed the double stripe in three plays. The first was a 13-yard pitch from Jones to Charles Young, and the third was a 31-yard fling from Jones to Edesel Garrison, who swept past a sprawling Ellis, to score. The point-after by Rae was good.

Perhaps at this point, the fans recalled the pre-game warning issued by Parseghian. "Southern Cal will be the biggest club we've looked at in quite a while," Ara had cautioned, "and they appear to have tremendous offensive capability."

Southern Cal kicked off. Gary Diminick fielded the ball on his goal line, zoomed up the middle, darted to the sideline and raced 66 yards to SC's 34-yard line. Seven plays later, Notre Dame knotted the score as Huff plunged across from the one, and Robert Thomas arched the PAT.

Notre Dame's three-year defensive starter Walt Patulski was a consensus All-America in 1971.

Huge play along the way was a 15-yard dart by Larry Parker.

Notre Dame kicked off. Charles Hinton fielded the ball on his goal line and zoomed 65 yards to ND's 35-yard line. Four plays later, Southern Cal unraveled the knot as Garrison, a carbonated sophomore with fizz in his legs, outran Crotty and cradled a 24-yard TD toss from Rae, who then booted the PAT as the first quarter ended. USC, 14-7.

"I love to see man-to-man coverage," said Garrison. "I don't think there is a defensive back in football who can cover me one-on-one."

The Trojans had now discovered an unfamilier but pleasant pastime— putting points on the board. So in the second period, they did it again and again. And though he didn't post SC's third marker, it was that speedster Garrison who again proved to be the Irish thorn. From the Irish 46-yard line, Jones connected with Garrison for a 42-yard pickup, down to ND's four. Cunningham challenged the Irish line four times before finally cracking the last yard. Now it was 21-7 after Rae's conversion.

The quarter was still young when SouCal lengthened its lead to 28-7. It was that larcenist Dyer again, and this time he made his theft of a Brown aerial pay off by streaking 53 yards to paydirt. Rae converted.

Well, Notre Dame couldn't score in the second stanza, but it did live up to its name of Fighting Irish...along with some cooperation from the Trojans. The brawl was started by a medley of blows exchanged between Marx and Vella but soon exploded into an all-out, bench-clearing melee that extended over several minutes and required intervention by state police.

"There had been a fumble on the play," stated Vella, "and I was on the ground and the next thing I know Marx is swinging and hitting me. So I hit back."

McKay found himself pushing Marx, a 250-pounder. "If he had hit me, he would have killed me," wailed McKay. "If I had really wanted to fight someone, I'd have found Parseghian, not Marx."

But the fisticuffs ceased, and shortly thereafter the

teams took the halftime recess, there to let their tempers cool.

Not a great deal can be reported about the second half. Southern Cal was held scoreless. Also, the home folks were treated to one Notre Dame touchdown, and almost to another, but it was a matter of too little, too late.

The Notre Dame TD was triggered when Mike Zikas separated Rae from the ball, which was then claimed by Jim Musuraca on the Irish 46-yard stripe. Notre Dame erased those 54 yards in four plays, the major one being a 41-yard heave from Brown to Creaney. Three plays later, John Cieszkowski slashed four yards into the endzone, after which Thomas drilled the PAT.

The final score of 28-14 was inscribed, but the Irish made one last spurt to revise it. With less than three minutes on the clock, Notre Dame reached Troy's five-yard line, but Brown fumbled and a Trojan whose name is unknown, recovered the ball.

His dream shattered, his brow unflinching, Parseghian remained gracious in defeat. "Southern Cal was an excellent football team. It did not show us anything new, but executed well. Just say that we needed the big play several times and did not get it."

Finally triumphant after three straight setbacks, McKay was kind in victory, too. "When you beat Notre Dame, you beat one hell of a team," he commented. "There's always a special feeling in this game. It's USC's biggest of every year."

Continuing, McKay pointed to the reason behind USC's victory. "Humiliation," he said. "Humiliation turned us around. We're just too good a team to lose four straight."

The number of players that piloted Troy to its upset victory would fill a fleet of chariots: Garrison...Jones...Rae...Dyer...Hall...Cunningham...Grant...Young...Harris...Vella...Papadakis...Bob Eriksen...Chuck Anthony...just list the roster.

McKay took leave of South Bend on an optimistic note. "I've felt all along that we are a pretty good team," he remarked. And his opinion was justified as Southern California played out its schedule with verdicts over California, Washington State and Washington plus a tie

284

HOW SWEET IT IS!
TROJANS 28, IRISH 14
McKay: 'Humiliation Made Difference'

BY JOHN HALL, Times Staff Writer

with UCLA. So, from an unpretentious first half, the Trojans finished the year at 6-4-1; not great, but sufficient for a final rating of No. 20.

Notre Dame's loss to Southern Cal was a disappointment but not a disaster. Regrouping, the Irish trounced Navy, Pittsburgh and Tulane before bowing to LSU. Their final rank was No. 13, based on a record of eight wins and two defeats.

And the Irish boasted two honors the Trojans could not—Patulski and Ellis, both named consensus All-Americans. Gatewood and Kadish also appeared on some A-A teams, as did Vella and Hall for USC.

Now 43 games deep into history, Notre Dame maintained a 25-14-4 advantage over Southern California...and led in total points scored, 779 to 565.

1972

A.D. KOs N.D.

National champions. MacArthur Bowl Trophy. PAC-8 champions. Rose Bowl winners. State champions. City champions. Coach-of-the-Year award.

Those are some of the legacies of the 1972 Southern California squad, whose bequeath of 12 victories, zero defeats and zero ties was the best performance ever carved into the walls of Troy. (Yes, there had been six other unblemished seasons, but none with 12 triumphs.)

And what role did Notre Dame play in this dramatic saga? Victim No. 11, on a crisp December afternoon in Memorial Coliseum by a score of 45-23.

"This is probably the best balanced football team that Southern California has ever had," conceded ND coach Ara Parseghian.

"This is the best football team I've ever coached at Southern California," said SC coach John McKay, conceding nothing.

But if the Trojan team stacked a fire of greatness, it was a blazing sophomore from San Fernando who sparked the flame in this particular conflict against the Irish.

His name was Anthony Davis, also know as "A.D". And his heroics against the visitors from South Bend could hardly be described as hospitable.

Had anyone ever scored six touchdowns in a single game against Notre Dame? Davis did. Had anyone ever returned two kickoffs totaling 193 yards for two touchdowns against Notre Dame? Davis did. Had anyone ever scored 36 points in one contest against Notre Dame? Davis did.

DAVIS! DAVIS! DAVIS! DAVIS! DAVIS! DAVIS!

THE BEGINNING—USC sophomore Anthony Davis shakes Notre Dame and 75,243 Coliseum fans with this 97-yard touchdown run with opening kickoff Saturday. He scored five more TDs in USC's 45-23 rout of the Irish.

Anthony Scores Six TDs; Trojans Rout Irish, 45-23

BY BOB OATES
Times Staff Writer

To overcome the Irish, John McKay's big moving machine needed a 6-touchdown performance from Anthony Davis and got it Saturday as the undefeated Trojans won their 11th straight, 45-23.

Notre Dame supplied the racing's No. 1 team but on its defense Davis, USC's sophomore sensation, who broke the backs of the Irish with touchdown runs of 97, 1, 5, 4, 8 and 8 yards.

A 185-pound plus standing 5-9, Davis won it with two long kickoff returns to put McKay on the doorstep of his third national championship. USC romps Monday. The final AP poll will be taken after USC's last game against Ohio State in the Rose Bowl.

It was in the first 11 seconds that Davis brought 75,243 to their feet as the Coliseum with his explosive 97-yard trip with the opening kickoff to key a 19-3 first quarter lead that was cut to 19-10 at the half.

Los Angeles Times

Sports

CC   SECTION D   2t

SUNDAY, DECEMBER 3, 1972

Clements hit his third touchdown pass to pare USC's lead to 25-23.

That was a moment of uncertainty, trouble for the Trojans and their fans and the nervousness was hardly reduced when Notre Dame's coach Ara Parseghian gambled and lost on a 2-point shot at 25-23.

The Irish, as of that moment survived damaging fumbles and interceptions to seize the momentum, on the accurate arm of a 15-year-old quarterback.

Then Davis killed them.

He put the Notre Dame kickoff in the end zone, 96 yards distant, and the Irish at long last were done, 32-23.

The sag was immaterial's noticeable. The famous Irish spirit which had sustained them for three quarters had been beaten out of them by Davis' second big run. And in the confusion, the Trojans made it a rout with two touchdowns in the fourth quarter, pouring it on with a 13-yard pass in the last 5 minutes to set up their last six points.

McKay's best team—and quite possibly USC's best of all time—spent a hard afternoon turning back one of the most spirited challenges ever made by an underdog in this long series.

Notre Dame led in yards, 360-320; first downs, 19-18, and by a significant margin in total plays, 75-61.

Another sobre was clearly in the making in the third quarter. The measure of the Trojans at this high point in McKay's career is their 11th straight.

Please Turn to Page 6, Col 1

AGAIN—Davis drives into the end zone from one yard away for his second touchdown, climaxing a 63-yard drive in the first quarter. Victory made it a perfect, 11-0, regular season for USC.

JIM MURRAY

'Ouch!'--Ara the Coach

"Well," says I to Kinsella, "what's so grand about football? The only a game, after all."

"Ya may be right," says Kinsella, "Let's go have a pint."

—From the Collected Post-Game Sayings of Gonigle the Poet.

"Heathen!"

—Culligan the Theologian as Richard Wood ran down an ND halfback.

"Do ye think the man has any idea in the world what the game is all about?"

—Fogarty the Undertaker as Parseghian the Coach, third period.

"Well, let's put it this way, he's no Rockne, now, is he?"

—Clancy the Scholar in the third period.

"Ryan downed the punt for the Trojans?! Why, the man's little better than an Informer to turn on his own that way! He'd be afraid to leave his bed in the old days after a brick like that!"

—Casey the Used-Car Salesman on Mike Ryan, the punt-downer.

"D'ye think prayers help a'tall when officials are crooked?"

—Halloran, the Unemployed Carpenter on a penalty was called against ND.

"Well, I wish they would stop calling them 'Irish.' I shouldn't be surprised there's an Ulsterman among 'them. A pity some people can't tell an Irishman from an Orangeman?

—Costello the Streetcar Conductor as the score mounted.

"Well, it's a good thing they teach them something, now, isn't it? You could scarcely call that algebra now, could you?"

—Kelly the Laundromat Operator of the USC halftime card stunts.

"What'd ye expect when they stopped saying the Mass in Latin?

and you could eat on your way to Communion and they let guitars in church and not bingo?"

—Hannigan the Unpublished Author and Part-Time Bartender.

"Is he as good as George Gipp?"

—Fagan the Pants-Presser as Anthony Davis scored 6th touchdown.

"The ball was heavier in Gipp's day."

—Kerrigan the Expert on Everything.

"The saddest thing is, there's no part for Paddy O'Brien, the fifllum actor, in the whole lot. He can't play that Parsahoogan, he's some kind of an atheist, now, isn't he?"

—Duffy the Movie-Goer.

"We've got them now."

—Cassidy the Optimist as Notre Dame drove to 1-yard line.

"Well, the Lord does work in mysterious ways. They say everything always works for the Best."

—Cassidy the Optimist a minute later as the Irish's Art Best fumbled.

"God must be sitting on a rock some place today and weeping."

—Boyle the Altar Boy as the score went to 45-23.

"It's a cinch he can't feel too good about it."

—Kinsella the Judge.

"How would a man write about a terrible thing like this?"

—Hennessy the Dry Cleaner in the fourth quarter.

"Outlined against a blue-grey December sky, the One Horseman rode again.' His name in dramatic here is 'Anthony Pestilence.'"

—Gogarty the Publican.

"D'ye think if we all said a good Act of Contrition before the Orange Bowl?"

—Conway the Cop.

"Well, we can sure put away the beads today."

Please Turn to Page 12, Col. 1

3

TOUCHDOWNS CONTINUED ON PAGE 5

... AND AGAIN—As Trojan blockers clear his path to the goal line, Davis streaks around right

and for his third TD on 3-yard sweep. Fumble recovery set up USC score that made it 19-3.

Times photos by Larry Sharkey and Rick Browne

NO. 2 'BAMA BOWS AS AUBURN BLOCKS TWO PUNTS, 17-16

BIRMINGHAM, Ala. (P) — Bill Newton blocked two punts in the final quarter and David Langner ran the ball for touchdowns both times as ninth-ranked Auburn upset second-ranked Alabama, 17-16, Saturday.

Langner sealed Alabama's doom in the incredible upset shortly after his second touchdown by intercepting a pass at the Auburn 41.

It was the first regular season loss for Alabama in 22 games, and virtually ruined the Tide's chances for a national title.

Alabama will take its 10-1 record into the Cotton Bowl against Texas.

Please Turn to Page 6, Col. 2

Bruins Win 48th Straight With 81-48 Romp Over Pacific

BY RON RAPOPORT
Times Staff Writer

University of the Pacific, helpful to a fault, has outfitted its basketball players this season in uniforms bearing their names on the back. Considering what happened to the Tigers at Pauley Pavilion Saturday night, however, they might have preferred anonymity.

Belted about virtually at will in an 81-48 defeat by UCLA, Pacific found itself helping to establish several milestones. Had it not been for the honor, the visitors probably would have wished it had happened to someone else.

The victory was not only UCLA's

48th in a row—its longest streak ever and the second most extensive in the history of college basketball. It also was the 804th win in 1,000 games for coach John Wooden, including his 11 years as a high school coach and 1 at Indiana State.

Although Pacific didn't try to stall at Bradley had on Friday night, it took the Tigers even longer than the 6 minutes the Braves needed to get on the scoreboard. The game was 5 minutes and 14 seconds old before forward Jim McCargo scored Pacific's first points on the 10th shot of

Please Turn to Page 10, Col. 2

RECORDS TUMBLE

Davis Predicted Breakaway Plays Two Weeks Ago

BY JEFF PRUGH
Times Staff Writer

The toughest run Anthony Davis had to make all afternoon was from the USC dressing room to the showers.

Newsmen swarmed around him like mosquitoes. The crush was as heavy as a New York subway ride at 5 p.m.—certainly more suffocating than anything the Notre Dame defense threw at him while getting trampled Saturday by the Trojans, 45-23.

As Davis fielded questions again and again like a courtroom witness, teammate Glenn Byrd shouted a holler cry for this season—or maybe 1973 and 1974.

"Anthony Davis for the Heisman Trophy?"

Characteristically, Davis stood there poker-faced and gave answers more predictable than his moves with the football.

Huskies Hit Harder

No, he doesn't "worry about records." Yes, he thinks this is the best college football team ever assembled, to which a teammate yells, "You tell 'em, A.D.!" No, Notre Dame wasn't the hardest-hitting team he's faced —the Washington Huskies were. And, no, he had never scored 6 touchdowns in one game "I scored 5 in one game in high school," said the sophomore from San Fernando. "It was a Valley record."

If just about everybody was left spellbound by Davis' performance, Anthony himself seemed nonchalant about it. Two weeks ago, he had sat quietly with a writer in the USC dining room and pondered the game with the Fighting Irish.

"They're big and strong," he had said, "but if I can get outside—get into the open—I think I can go all the way a few times."

As it was, Davis probably could have run forever.

When it was over, Davis took a deep breath and expressed a sentiment that typified the Times under-

Please Turn to Page 6, Col 5

Perhaps the banner headline in the *Los Angeles Times* proclaimed it best: "Davis! Davis! Davis! Davis! Davis! Davis!"

But harken a moment. Before it may be assumed the confrontation was a blowout for Davis and Tommy Trojan, kindly be assured it wasn't. With less than 17 minutes remaining in the game, the Fighting Irish trailed by just two points, and only the failure of a two-point conversion prevented the skirmish from being tied at that point.

To be sure, Notre Dame was nothing less than a formidable opponent for Southern Cal. Ranked No.10 in the nation, the Irish brought 8-1-0 credentials and a four-game winning streak to Troyland. Only a four-point upset loss to Missouri marred an otherwise perfect slate that included wins over Northwestern, Purdue, Michigan State, Pittsburgh, TCU, Navy, Air Force and Miami (Fla.).

A fine record, yes. But not equal to that of No. 1— Southern Cal, 10-0-0. In procuring the pinnacle, the Trojans had banished Arkansas by 21 points, Oregon State by 45, Illinois by 35, Michigan State by 45, Stanford by nine, California by 28, Washington by 27, Oregon by 18, Washington State by 41 and crosstown rival UCLA by 17. In so doing, USC had racked up 401 points, (and for the entire season the figure would grow to 467, the most since Howard Jones' 1929 juggernaut).

In a pre-season statement, Trojan coach McKay had predicted, "We'll be very good by the end of the season." He could have replaced "...by the end of the" with one word— "all".

So, as expected, Southern Cal entered the affair as the favorite to win, which it did, for the third consecutive year.

And if some of the 75,243 fans missed the opening fireworks, it's because they were more than 13 seconds late reaching their seats. For that's all it took for Davis to grab the opening kickoff on his three-yard line, follow an opening wedge to his left, watch Charles Hinton and Ed Powell throw key blocks, and sprint 97 yards for a touchdown. It was the longest kickoff return in Troy history.

"Notre Dame is big and strong," Davis had remarked before the game, "but if I can get outside— get into the open— I think I can go all the way a few times."

Anthony Davis celebrates one of his six touchdowns against Notre Dame in the 1972 game at the Coliseum. USC won, 45-23.

The Irish were unruffled. As the fans settled down following Davis' electrifying dash, Notre Dame calmly launched an 82-yard drive that ended with a 45-yard field goal by Bob Thomas on the ninth play. Andy Huff and speedster Eric Penick each bolted for 12 yards to spice the drive.

But USC quickly retaliated with a brace of markers to claim a 19-3 advantage at the end of the first quarter as two conversions failed.

After Thomas' FG, Southern Cal went 53 yards in six plays, aided somewhat by a 12-yard pass from Mike Rae to Davis, but more importantly, by a 40-yard pass interference call against ND's Reggie Barnett, which placed the ball on the one-yard line. From there, Davis crashed into the endzone, and Rae booted the extra point.

As the quarter neared its end, Penick fumbled on his nine-yard stripe, Dale Mitchell recovered, and the Trojans scored in three plays, Davis sweeping in from the five.

The second period was mostly defensive, although the Irish did manage to close the gap to nine points, thanks mainly to QB Tom Clements. Firing a 17-yard pass to Mike Creaney, a 36-yard screen toss to Gary Diminick and a five-yard TD aerial to Willie Townsend, the six-foot sophomore led the 73-yard campaign, which, after Thomas' PAT, put ND back into contention at 10-19.

The two assailants matched points in the third frame, 13 apiece. But it was after Notre Dame's final TD that its two-point conversion failed and its hopes for victory faded.

Before that, though, Davis posted his fourth touchdown on a four-yard run which capped a 41-yard SC journey in seven plays, ignited when Hinton intercepted a Clements pass and rumbled nine yards. Then, to set up Davis' TD scamper, Rae passed 26 yards to Lynn Swann.

That gave SC a 25-10 lead, but the Trojan players were still cautious. They knew the Irish were moving the ball well and "...we weren't getting a good pass rush on them," said middle guard George Follett, filling in for the injured Monte Doris, "and they were throwing well off play-action."

The concern of the host team proved justifiable as an aroused Mike Townsend stole two Rae passes and Clements capitalized on both with touchdowns. The cheers of the Trojan boosters were suddenly silenced.

After M.Townsend's first theft, Clements stroked W. Townsend with a 15-yard completion. Then Diminick gathered in a Clements' flip from 11 yards out to terminate a 47-yard, seven-play jaunt. Thomas was true on the conversion.

Next, with Art Best running nine, five and ten yards, Notre Dame erased 42 yards in seven executions, the last an 11-yard pass from Clements to Creaney. SC 25, ND 23.

Enter now the moment of decision, the two-point attempt, the possible tie. Clements dropped back and fired at his target, W. Townsend. Straight as an arrow the ball headed for Townsend, but so did Trojan defender Steve Fate, who batted away the ball...as well as the hopes of the Notre Dame rooters.

Now, if that failure didn't deflate the Irish balloon, the

next play did. And once again it was that nemesis, Davis.

Duplicating his opening kickoff TD return, Davis took Cliff Brown's airborne kickoff on his four-yard line, raced to the right sideline, and cruised 96 yards to paydirt, giving the last Irish defender, Tim Rudnick, a nifty fake. Rae's PAT put the Trojans up by nine points, leaving only the final score in doubt.

"I wanted to keep him inside," stated Rudnick, who met Davis on the sideline near the 25-yard stripe, "but he made a quick move and I went with it."

With the outcome of the game practically moot, Davis still had to add his sixth tally, and this he did on an eight-yard blast after Artimus Parker pilfered a Clements heave and returned it 19 yards to ND's 26-yard stripe. PAT by Rae was accurate.

Then, to finalize the day's activities, Sam Cunningham dived one yard to climax a 69-yard trek that was

All-America tight end Charles Young was the leading receiver as Southern Cal's 1972 Thundering Herd roared to a 12-0-0 season and another national championship.

highlighted by a 16-yard pass from Rae to Jake McKay, son of the coach.

"Beating Notre Dame three years in a row!" exclaimed tackle Pete Adams. "There's no other feeling like it."

To which linebacker Richard Wood, whose 13 tackles paced the Trojans, added, "They were physical, but we knew we'd be tougher in the second half."

While heaping accolades on Davis, the Irish were not as lavish in judging the lads of Troy as a team.

"The Trojans have a great offense," opined All-American tackle Greg Marx, who blocked SC's PAT effort after its first TD, "but we've faced better defensive teams." Marx may have had a point. Notre Dame amassed 360 yards and made 19 first downs, eclipsing USC in both catagories.

With two interceptions, Mike Townsend set a Notre Dame school record of ten, and earned for himself a tie with USC's James Sims as defensive-player-of-the-game. Sims was credited with a pair of crucial sacks on Clements.

Offensively, of course, the game laurels went to Davis, despite Clements' passing for 199 yards and three touchdowns. In addition to his long kickoff returns, Davis rushed for 99 yards from scrimmage, giving him 1,034 yards for the regular season. Only Morley Drury, Mike Garrett, O.J. Simpson and Clarence Davis had preceded him as 1,000-plus yard gainers at Tailback U.

"I guess I've never seen a greater day by an individual than Anthony Davis' performance today," McKay, who was named Coach-of-the-Year for the second time, told Mal Florence of the *LA Times*.

Davis, however, was not named to any first-team All-America rosters, although five of his mates were. Tight end Charles Young was a consensus choice, while Wood, fullback Cunningham, defensive tackle John Grant and offensive tackle Adams were selected on one or more A-A teams.

The stigma of defeat continued to wave over the Gold and Blue of Notre Dame in the Orange Bowl as No. 9 Nebraska, led by Heisman winner Johnny Rodgers and Outland winner Rich Glover, clobbered Ara's boys, 40-6.

But for Southern California, the Rose Bowl was just more icing on the cake— a sweet 42-17 frosting of Ohio State, ranked No. 5 going into the match.

Yes, 1972 was also the year that Don Shula's Miami Dolphins constructed the best record in National Football League history: 17-0-0. But, who knows? If Southern California had played five more games...

1973

Turnaround Is Fair Play

There's a little ditty that vocalizes, "Anything you can do, I can do better."

Those words may have harped strong on the minds of Notre Dame coach Ara Parseghian and his warriors throughout the torturous months leading up to the start of the 1973 season. After all, their chief rival, Southern California, was the reigning national champion, and, hurt of hurts, the Irish had helped put them there.

So, with the advent of a new season, Notre Dame was ready to take out its frustrations, ready to reach for the summit of college football, just as it had in many seasons past.

Street and Smith magazine's pre-season issue read: "This is no rebuilding year for Notre Dame. The tipoff may be that the usually ultra-conservative Ara (Parseghian) complains only of lack of depth."

As it turned out, Parseghian had nothing of which to complain. Riding the All-America deeds of tight end Dave Casper and defensive back Mike Townsend, the Fighting Irish rolled up, over and through 11 opponents, including Southern Cal, with nary a blemish thereon.

The final conquest was top-rated Alabama in the Sugar Bowl, and once again Notre Dame wore the tiara of football supremacy.

Southern California, national champion, 1972; Notre Dame, national champion, 1973. Could there be a college rivalry of greater intensity?

No, if you believe the opinion of David Condon of the *Chicago Tribune.* "Since college men first began agitating

294

bags of wind on autumn Saturdays, no intersectional football rivalry has produced the drama attendant Notre Dame's annual showdown with Southern California," he wrote.

This, the 45th meeting of the two schools, upheld his view, as the Irish kicked the Trojans, 23-14, on a misty, overcast and sometimes wet day in late October. It was the first loss for the men of Troy in 24 consecutive games. And their first loss to their Indiana foe since 1966.

So, certainly there was no relaxation on the part of the Irish as they prepared for the battle. If anything, it may have been the Trojans who may have bordered on over-confidence.

Returning a veteran nucleus from his previous squad, Coach John McKay had indicated his main worry for the upcoming season was complacency. And this concern did not subside when USC was ranked No. 1 in all pre-season polls.

Number 28 represents Anthony Davis, who hangs in effigy on the Notre Dame campus in 1973. The previous year he had scorched the Irish with six touchdowns.

295

This is it! Notre Dame vs. Southern Cal

"I hope we're not silly enough to worry about national rankings," McKay countered.

Later, honing in on Notre Dame, the USC mentor extended his fretfulness. "You must make the big plays against Notre Dame—you can't beat them with ball control. You just can't slug it out physically. They're bigger than we are defensively," he uttered.

"Notre Dame throws you off when you look at their films," McKay continued. "They'll roll up more than 500 yards a game, but not many points, excepting Army."

Of course, Parseghian had accolades for the Trojans, too, and the memory of Anthony Davis bashing six touchdowns on his 1972 team had lingered for eleven anguishing months.

"But you can't key on Davis alone," cautioned the coach. "Concentrate on Davis, and Southern Cal will murder you with Pat Haden's passes to Lynn Swann and J.K. McKay. Key on passes and Davis will run you wild. But fortunately, our defense is quicker and better than last year."

The encounter was termed a toss-up. Notre Dame was 5-0-0 and ranked No. 7; Southern Cal was 5-0-1 and ranked No. 6.

Northwestern, Purdue, Michigan State, Rice and Army had felt the sting of the Irish whip, while Arkansas, Georgia Tech, Oregon State, Washington State and Oregon had fallen to the Trojans. Their solitary scratch was a draw with third-ranked Oklahoma.

So, while some folks lined up at the Loop Theatre in Chicago to see *Last Tango in Paris* and others out West watched on television as California Governor Ronald Reagan assailed those persons who wanted to impeach President Nixon, more than 59,000 other citizens crammed the corners of Notre Dame Stadium to see their Saturday heroes in action.

Perhaps the partisan crowd wondered, this time around, did Ara have a game plan that would work against SC.

"Unfortunately, in our last three games we've had to junk our game plan and go to catch-up football because Southern California has taken the early lead," responded Parseghian. "So our plan today is to choke off their early lead."

Did it work? Yes. Even though USC overcame ND's early 3-0 lead, the Irish fought back and went into the half-time break with a 13-7 lead, an advantage they never relinquished. Here's how the scoring developed:

Midway through the initial quarter, Bob Thomas popped a 32-yard field goal to stake Notre Dame to a 3-0 lead. The Irish had gotten excellent field position when Tim Rudnick partially blocked Jim Lucas' punt, which then carried only 15 yards and did not reach midfield. Six plays later, including a 16-yard pass from Tom Clements

Notre Dame's Eric Penick dashes away on an 85-yard touchdown in the 1973 game at South Bend. Also in the photo are Notre Dame's Mike Fanning (88), Gerry DiNardo (72) and Art Best (23) and USC's Dale Mitchell (85), Ray Rodriguez (52) and Art Riley (70). The Irish won, 23-14.

to Pete Demmerle, ND put the first points on the scoreboard.

Before the period ended, however, the visitors from Troy stormed back, erasing 65 yards in nine plays and snatching the lead when Davis swept the final yard for six points. It was his sixth carry of the drive as he consumed 22 of the 65 yards. But the big gainer was a 26-yard aerial from Haden to Swann.

"Lynn (Swann) is as valuable to us as Johnny Rodgers was to Nebraska," McKay had declared, who then labeled Swann as the best Z back he had ever coached.

Chris Limahelu converted, the Trojans led, 7-3, and a sprig of doubt permeated the Irish faithful.

It was short-lived, for soon their fears vanished as Ara's boys dominated the second period with a field goal, a touchdown and the point-after.

The three-pointer (33 yards by Thomas) culminated a 59-yard drive that survived 14 plays on runs by Art Best, Eric Penick and Wayne Bullock, plus a 14-yard pass from Clements to Demmerle.

The six-pointer (one yard sneak by Clements) dotted a 47-yard campaign that survived 11 plays on runs by Best and Russ Kornman plus a nine-yard sling from— you got it— Clements to Demmerle. The short trek needed by the Irish to score was set up by a diminutive 22-yard punt by Lucas. After Thomas added the PAT, the clubs broke for intermission with Notre Dame on top by six points.

Things were going good for the Irish. But the best was yet to come.

With less than four minutes gone in the third frame, Penick, Notre Dame's swift junior, burst off tackle, picked up early blocks by guards Gerry DiNardo and Frank Pomarico, dodged USC linebacker Ray Rodriguez (subbing for the injured James Sims) and artfully raced 85 yards to glory land. Thomas' extra point gave the Gold and Blue a 13-point margin and gave SC supporters the blues.

The scintillating call was a mis-direction play off a wing-T formation, As the flow went right with a fake to fullback Bullock, Penick and his guards went left.

"Tell us about the 85 yard run, Ara," asked Cooper

Chicago Tribune
Sunday, October 28, 1973

Sports

Section 3
CLASSIFIED ADS

Irish power ends U.S.C. streak 23-14

*Jubilant Ara celebrates
most satisfying victory*

By David Condon
Chicago Tribune Press Service

NOTRE DAME, Ind., Oct. 27—All
good things must come to an end. In
football, it's most often the Fighting
Irish of Notre Dame who bring them to
an end.
The Irish did it again today, shaking
down the Thunder thru a nasty overcast.

Rollow, *Chicago Tribune* sports editor.

"Well, it started on the 15," responded the jubilant Ara, who was more concerned with the end result than its ramifications.

Trojan Richard Wood was a bit more precise. "Perfect play," he said. "Their guards led him around and he was gone."

And Penick? "I don't remember anything about the play," he stated.

But if the Irish zealots were getting out their pencils to mark the game in the "W" column, the Trojans were not yet ready to accept the "L".

Just 65 seconds after the Penick dash, SC scored a touchdown, putting once more the outcome of the struggle in question.

The retaliatory marker came on a 27-yard fling from Haden to Swann, who executed an aerobatic catch in the end zone while fending off defender Tom Lopienski. It was the fifth play of a 70-yard trek that also included two other receptions by Swann totaling 28 yards. The second snag resulted in Notre Dame being penalized for a personal foul on Reggie Barnett and his subsequent ejection from the game.

"Barnett stuck an elbow into somebody (McKay) and they kicked him out without even warning him," complained Parseghian, who exchanged heated words with an official about the incident.

Limahelu was true with his swing, cutting ND's lead to six, with still a bundle of time on the clock.

299

As champions do, however, Notre Dame did what it had to do—fight back and put some insurance points on the board.

It was just a field goal which came as the third quarter was winding down, but it put more pressure on the Trojans as they headed down the stretch.

Calling on the legs of Best, Bullock and Penick, Notre Dame eradicated 59 yards in 13 plays, ending in another 33-yard FG by Thomas. ND, 23-14.

As an omen of what was to come in the fourth period, Southern Cal had seemingly stopped the Irish short of midfield, but George Stewart was called for offsides, giving ND a first down and sustenance to its FG drive. Then Clements fumbled, but his fullback, Kornman, caught the ball in mid-air and proceeded to gain five yards.

In playing catch-up, USC was its own worst enemy. First, Davis fumbled away the ball to Lopienski on Notre Dame's 20 with still nine minutes to play.

"I just got hit and I didn't have a good hold on the ball," he explained.

Then Jake McKay lost a fumble to Luther Bradley after catching a pass on ND's 40. But the coach's son disagreed with the call.

"I never really had the ball," he said.

Finally, Haden threw an interception—freshman Bradley was the culprit—and the Trojans had nothing left but a trip of woe back to Vermont and Jefferson streets.

The Irish victors gave the game ball to their coach. "I'm delighted to have the game ball," said Ara, "because Southern California's long streak began here at Notre Dame and it's appropriate that it end here."

The Trojans felt they beat themselves, and McKay endorsed their opinion by citing poor field position, poor punting and crucial turnovers as huge detractions to the performance of his team.

After the game of glamor against USC, Notre Dame went on to clobber Navy, Pittsburgh, Air Force and Miami (Fla.). Then, as previously mentioned, edged Alabama in the Sugar Bowl to finish with an 11-0-0 record and another national crown.

Southern Cal wrapped up its regular season with

All America flanker Lynn Swan paced the 1973 Southern Cal team with 42 receptions.

victories over California, Stanford, Washington and UCLA, but was crushed by Ohio State in the Rose Bowl. Its final slate was 9-2-1, adequate for an eighth place ranking.

Oh, back to the USC-ND melee for a flash. For the first time in the history of the series, Southern Cal brought along its marching band to South Bend. Alas, at game's end, it had little of which to toot.

But, as McKay the Trojan receiver, put it: "It's no disgrace to lose to Notre Dame."

That's right, Jake. Especially when they're the national champion.

1974

A Rare Rally

If ever a football game tendered two faces, it was the bizarre 46th clash of the Notre Dame-Southern California series.

Picture this. The clock is ticking down to its dying seconds in the first half...just 11 seconds remain. It has been ALL Notre Dame, verified by the scoreboard—Notre Dame 24, Southern California 0. The picture changes. Now it is 104 seconds into the fourth quarter and it has been ALL Southern Cal, verified by the scoreboard—Southern California 55, Notre Dame 24.

Amazing. In the brief span of less than 17 minutes, the Trojans amassed eight touchdowns—55 points—against the No. 1 defensive team in the nation, one that had surrendered just nine touchdowns against ten previous opponents. And all this after trailing by 24 points!

"You wouldn't think a team could score 55 points in that time even if Notre Dame stayed in the locker room," wrote Jim Murray in the *LA Times*.

"It was two football games," said ND coach Ara Parseghian, still in shock. "We won the first and they won the second."

"Yes, it's fair to say this is probably one of the wildest things that ever happened on a football field," added SC coach John McKay.

Once again, it was tailback Anthony Davis who drove the nails of destruction into the Irish coffin. Indeed, Davis' ardent devotion to the cause of scoring points prevailed again as the nimble senior tallied four touchdowns and a two-point conversion—26 points. His three-year output

USC coach John McKay (left) *and Notre Dame coach Ara Parseghian* (right) *faced each other 11 times. McKay won six, lost three, and tied two.*

against Notre Dame reached 68 points, a plateau unscaled by any other player.

And it was Davis' second TD, a splendid kickoff return of 102 yards to open the second half, that sparked the Trojans to their come-from-behind, lopsided verdict.

"His (Davis) kickoff return sparked us, it turned the game around for us," observed QB Pat Haden of Davis' record-breaking run.

Both squads brought fine records to the site of battle; ND was 9-1-0 and ranked fifth, SC was 8-1-1 and notched at sixth. And, of course, the visitors from the Golden Dome were the defending national champion.

Although ranked third in pre-season polls, many writers and armchair quarterbacks envisioned the Irish as repeat champions. And why not? Sure, such stars as Dave Casper, Frank Pomarico, Willie Townsend and Gary Dominick were missing from an offensive unit that set a ND rushing record of 3,502 yards. And gone from the frugal defensive corps was, well, Mike Townsend, but very few others.

What's more, the entire starting backfield was back — Art Best, Eric Penick,Wayne Bullock and Tom Clements.

"Clements is now throwing with more authority and accuracy," Parseghian told *Street and Smith* magazine in a pre-season interview. "His arm is stronger— added maturity has helped him."

Notre Dame started strong by thrashing Georgia Tech and Northwestern, but were then shocked by unranked Purdue. Rebounding, the Irish conquered Michigan State, Rice, Army, Miami (Fla.), Navy, Pittsburgh and Air Force.

Southern California had lost such stalwarts as Booker Brown, Artimus Parker, Lynn Swann and James Sims but was returning 14 starters, seven from each unit.

"I see no reason why we shouldn't be better this year than last," predicted USC coach McKay in a pre-season publication. "Our offense should be stronger, while our defense should be quicker and more experienced."

Knowing both Haden and Davis were serious Heisman Trophy candidates may have spurred McKay's optimism. "No team has a better quarterback than Haden," remarked McKay.

The rosy outlook of the outspoken tutor quickly paled, however, as Arkansas stunned his Trojans in the season opener. Aroused, SC played out its schedule leading up to ND with wins over Pittsburgh, Iowa, Washington State, Oregon, Oregon State, Stanford, Washington and UCLA, plus a draw with California.

So, despite a dank, overcast afternoon, a crowd of 83,552 fans poured into Memorial Coliseum, certainly unaware of the quake that awaited them.

Festivities commenced early as Notre Dame registered a pair of touchdowns in the first quarter. Drew Mahalic served up the initial marker by intercepting Haden's pass

USC's Anthony Davis plays havoc with Notre Dame's defense, firing the Trojans to a remarkable 55-24 comeback triumph in 1974. He scored the most points in series history (68 during 1972-73-74 games); his 11 touchdowns totaled 331 yards.

intended for Jim O'Bradovich, and Bullock finished the opportunity with a two-yard plunge into the end zone. In between, Clements hit Ron Goodman with a 21-yard strike. Later, Notre Dame regained possession when Mahalic stopped Haden on a fourth-and-inches sneak, and, on the next play, Clements rifled a 29-yard TD toss to Pete Demmerle.

Dave Reeve drilled both PATs, then added a 20-yard field goal to start the second period. His kick completed an 80-yard, 15-play drive that thrived on runs by Bullock, Al Samuel, Tony Parise and Penick, as well as a 15-yard bullet from Clements to Ken MacAfee.

This gave ND a 17-0 lead, but the Irish wanted

more...and got it. Down the field they came— 79 yards— on the arm of Clements who threw 15 yards to Mark McLane, 14 to Goodman, then 20 and 14 to MacAfee. McLane did the TD honors with a nine-yard scamper, Reeve added the extra point and, with less than a minute of the first half remaining, it was a 24-0 rout-in-the-making for Notre Dame. Surely, Irish eyes were smiling.

So what if Southern Cal bounced back with a desperate touchdown with ten seconds on the first-half clock? So what if Haden passed 29 and 20 yards to Shelton Diggs, then seven to Davis in the end zone? Look, Kevin Nosbusch even blocked Chris Limahelu's PAT effort. Okay — 24-6 was not quite as great as 24-0, so...

But if Irish tears were needless in the first half, Davis brought at least moisture to their eyes as the second half opened.

Fielding the kickoff two yards into his end zone, Davis veered to his left, broke a tackle and made a beeline for the sideline. Deftly cutting behind blocks by Mosi Tatupu and Mario Celotto, Davis broke into the open and outraced Ted Burgmeier to the double stripe— a dazzling TD dart of 102 yards.

"I found the lane, wedged my way through, then I found the opening," Davis exclaimed. "Yes, this was more of a thrill than the kickoff returns of 1972," he added.

The run provided the lift needed by the Trojans. "It was the turning point," acknowledged Parseghian.

Even though Haden was halted on a two-point conversion try, Tommy Trojan was unstoppable for the next 16 minutes. Traveler, the white horse of Troy, reached a state of exhaustion from galloping around the stadium as USC rolled up an additional 43 points in staccato fashion.

The next two touchdowns were also scored by Davis, and he converted his second with a two-point play that staked USC to a permanent lead at 27-24. Davis entered paydirt on a six-yard burst, then on a four-yard pitchout. Haden passed 31 yards to split end Johnny McKay to sustain the first TD drive (38 yards, five plays), and Kevin Bruce enfolded Demmerle's bobble (forced by Danny Reece) to seed the second (36 yards, five plays— two of which were Haden passes to Diggs and McKay totaling 30 yards).

A.D. Turns Irish Around, Upside-Down, 55-24

Behind 24-0, USC Hurries Back

From This...

...to This!

JIM MURRAY
The Divil, They Say

OK, put away the beads. Never mind lighting any more candles. It's... Would you believe anything that didn't have cannons could score 55...

Trojans Ecstatic, Call Comeback Win Wild and Fantastic

BY TED GREEN

They were more shocked that anguished, more philosophical than demoralized when it was over. Ara Parseghian, the head coach, unfathomably had difficulty ex...

Ara Feared Second-Half Collapse

BY JEFF PRUGH

These were Notre Dame's Parthing Irish late Saturday afternoon in the wake of one of their darkest hours.

The shock of their 55-24 defeat by USC's Trojans hadn't yet worn off as they dressed hastily amid speedy...

Now the flood gates were open wide, and now, most surely, Irish eyes were not smiling.

— Trojan Marvin Cobb returned Tony Brantley's punt 56 yards to ND's 19-yard line, and one play later, Haden found McKay for an 18-yard touchdown.

— Trojan Charles Phillips pilfered Clements' pass aimed for MacAfee and rambled 19 yards to midfield, then Haden connected with McKay again, this time a 45-yard marker. As he did after McKay's first TD, Limahelu added the extra point, the 35th in the third quarter alone. As may be suspected, that was the most points ever posted in a single quarter against Notre Dame and, forsooth, it was more than the scoreboard could handle, which, in surrender, became temporarily inoperative.

307

Before taps could play for the now-frustrated Irish, however, turnovers gave birth to 14 more Trojan points, all before two minutes had expired in the fourth period.

— Bruce pounced on a Penick fumble and, on the next play, Diggs cradled a 16-yard TD aerial from Haden, Limahelu converted.

— Finally, Phillips filched an errant toss and raced 58 taunting yards for six salt-on-the-wound points. So, after Limahelu tacked on the 55th point, McKay mercifully pulled his front-line troops from the fray.

"Ten years from now, I'll be watching a USC-Notre Dame game and saying 'Do you remember 1974? I was in that crazy game,'" exalted Phillips.

Parseghian was a mite more sober. "They got good field position throughout the second half— didn't have to drive very far," he commented. "We just didn't play like we are capable of in the second half— made too many mistakes."

"You can't let a loss like this affect you," lamented Clements. "You just gotta forget it."

But if Phillips was ecstatic and Parseghian was objective and Clements was philosophical, Irish linebacker Greg Collins was simply baffled by the incredible turn of events. "What was the final score, anyway?" he asked.

An oddity that added to the complexity of the blowout was the fact that ND, while obliterated on the scoreboard, actually accumulated more first downs than did its conqueror, 24 to 20. So, perhaps no one said it, but the thought must have hung heavy over Irish heads: where was the Gipper when we needed him?

Both schools had bowl engagements, and both were victorious. Southern Cal shaded Ohio State by a point in the Rose to complete a 10-1-1 season and a runner-up slot to Oklahoma in the final rankings. Notre Dame clipped Alabama by two digits in the Orange Bowl to complete a 10-2-0 season and a sixth place slot in the rankings.

For his heroics, SC's Davis earned consensus All-America honors, as did mate Richard Wood. Phillips, Bill Bain and O'Bradovich were named to some A-A rosters.

Notre Dame had a couple of consensus All-Americans, too— Demmerle and Gerry DiNardo. Others making one

Linebacker Richard Wood was the first Southern Cal player to be named All-America in three consecutive years (1972-73-74).

or more A-A teams were Mike Fanning, Steve Niehaus and Clements, while Collins and Steve Sylvester were listed on some second and third teams.

It wasn't known at the time, but this was the last time that Southern Cal would face a Notre Dame team coached by Parseghian. After 11 years at the helm, the personable headmaster resigned at the end of the season, etching a ledger of 95 victories, 17 defeats and four ties. Not once did he endure a losing season, but his mark against USC was not as impressive— three wins, six losses, two draws.

Parseghian's stint at Notre Dame brought three national championships and three bowl triumphs. He was named Coach-of-the-Year in 1964.

By the way, Southern Cal's third game of the season (versus Iowa) was the 700th played by the Trojans, known originally as the Methodists or Wesleyans, since a varsity program started in 1888. Few, if any, could compare with the explosiveness of the 708th battle with Notre Dame.

1975

GAME 47

Clang!

When an unsuppressed force wearing Cardinal and Gold and bearing the harmonic name of Ricky Bell wreaked havoc on Notre Dame's defense, the media had a field day with puns and quibbles.

"Trojans— for whom the Bell toils"

"The bells are ringing for SC"

"Bell rings Irish Dome"

"SC's victory Bell"

"Trojans saved by the Bell," et cetera, et cetera, et cetera.

To be sure, the phrases were so many plays on words, but there was no frivolity by Bell on the turf of Notre Dame Stadium. His tone was pure labor.

Encompassing the chromatic scale with 40 carries for 165 yards, Bell was the catalyst that enabled Southern California to thrice come from behind and finally subdue Notre Dame, 24-17, on a radiant October afternoon in Indiana. His 165 yards was the most any Trojan had ever collected against Notre Dame.

"There's no doubt in my mind Bell could be starting in the NFL right now," flatly stated ND's new coach, Dan Devine, fresh from a four-year coaching stint at Green Bay.

"Yes, Ricky Bell is a Heisman Trophy running-back," agreed SC coach John McKay, who was making his final visit to South Bend.

All of the semantics about Bell may have started at an emotional pep rally on the Irish campus the evening before the game.

"Ring Ricky's Bell, ring Ricky's Bell," the chant emitted from thousands of young men and women. The students cried out for revenge, too...revenge from last year's humiliating disaster.

But, alas, they got neither. Ricky's bell was not rung, and the previous year's loss was not avenged.

The 47th meeting of Notre Dame and Southern California presented an interesting scenario: Devine would be coaching his first game against the Trojans; McKay his last against the Irish.

Devine inherited 35 lettermen from his predecessor, Ara Parseghian, but only eight were starters.

In pre-season comments, Devine indicated he would not drastically change things. "Basically, I have used the wing-T" he said. "But I do prefer an offense that is quarterback oriented."

Fine, thought the Irish supporters, but who is the quarterback? Tom Clements had been running the QB show for three years, and now he had run out of eligibility.

The pollsters must have seen some talent dressed in Gold and Blue, however, as they pegged Notre Dame No.

John McKay was the sixth USC coach to match wits with Notre Dame and the first to post a winning record (8-6-2). Of the 20 coaches who have participated in the series, his 16 games are the most.

10 in pre-season listings.

By the date of the Southern Cal contest, though, the Irish had slipped to No. 14 in the polls, despite decisions over Boston College, Purdue, Northwestern, North Carolina and Air Force weighing heavily over a solitary loss to Michigan State.

McKay had just eight starters returning to University Park, but he was optimistic. "Don't worry about the Trojans," he said. "We'll survive in seventy-five. We'll be a solid team with a good chance to become a very good team. We should mature tremendously as the season goes on."

Actually, the maturity must have been present from the beginning as Southern Cal found easy pickings in Duke, Oregon State, Purdue, Iowa, Washington State and Oregon, improving its pre-season rank of No. 5 to No. 3 as it approached the slugfest with Notre Dame.

At the pep rally, Devine and split end Ted Burgmeier had promised the students, "We'll be ready," and those words were vividly recalled when Notre Dame punched across a touchdown before the game was three minutes old.

Southern Cal received the opening kickoff, was stopped and Glen Walker's short 31-yard punt spotted the Irish just 57 yards away from pointland. They arrived there in two plays, Al Hunter bolting the last 52 yards on a reverse. The extra point failed when Kevin Bruce deflected Dave Reeve's kick.

Both teams tallied in the second period, Southern Cal first to snatch the lead, then Notre Dame to reclaim a 14-7 margin at intermission.

The visitors from Troy lit the scoreboard when Shelton Diggs pulled in a 21-yard pass from QB Vince Evans to cap a 55-yard, eight-play drive and Walker added the PAT. Southern Cal gained possession when David Lewis recovered Jerome Heavens' fumble. Bell contributed two crucial first-down runs, but the invasion pivoted on an Irish penalty (holding) after they had presumably stopped the Trojans and forced a punt. SC 7, ND 6.

Showing their grit, the Fighting Irish scored their go-ahead touchdown— twice. First, Luther Bradley slammed

312

through and blocked Trojan Walker's punt which was recovered in the endzone by Tom Lopienski. Touchdown? No. Notre Dame was inflicted with an offside penalty, a call which infuriated Devine.

"They (SC) moved, drawing us offsides," he stormed out. "I'm not blind."

No matter. The Bradley-Lopienski show was on stage for the second act. High snap to Walker, another Bradley block and this time Lopienski picked up the ball on the 13-yard line and, with steps of joy, pranced into the endzone for a touchdown that did count. Then, on a halfback pass, Hunter hit Kris Haines for a two-pointer.

As the half drew to a close, Notre Dame came within a

tackle of adding to its 14-7 lead when Lopienski intercepted an Evans pass and headed for the goal line, only to be denied at the 27 by the last Trojan in sight. That Trojan was Ricky Bell.

The same Bell moved Southern Cal ahead early in the third stanza after Doug Hogan had committed larceny on a Joe Montana pass. Employing an infantry attack, Mosi Tatupu, Bell and Evans combined to advance the ball 35 yards, and Bell popped over from two yards out. The score was knotted after Walker's conversion.

But not for long. Moving 60 yards in 14 plays, Reeve booted a 27-yard field goal and the Irish pushed ahead with a scant three-point advantage. Big play in the push was an 18-yard connection from Montana to Ken Mac-Afee.

It had been surmised that if the game reduced itself to the final period with the teams battling on even or close terms, Southern Cal would prevail. And it may be that the Trojans, the more physical squad, did in fact wear its courageous adversary into fatigue.

"You can't ask 17-and-18-year-old kids to stay out there on defense that long and expect them to last," said one of Devine's assistant coaches.

Starting at their 29-yard stripe, the Trojans unleashed an assault that featured slashing runs of 19, 12 and 11 yards by Bell and a 13-yarder by Tatupu, as well as other single digit gains by both. Of his 19-yard burst on which he broke sharply to the sideline and eluded four defenders, Bell explained, "I'm on my own on that play."

"He simply outran our players," said Devine. "That's not a lack of effort on our part."

But success almost eluded the fury of Southern Cal' s attack. From the one-yard line, Bell tried to dive over the goal line but was separated from the ball when hit by a bevy of determined blue jerseys. The luck of the Irish, however, was somewhere other than South Bend as Trojan Melvin Jackson wrapped his 253-pound frame around the loose pigskin, and SC had a reprieve.

"I was blocking down on (Steve) Niehaus and I saw the ball out of the corner of my eye," related Jackson. "Believe me, I was lucky."

Not one to snub fate, Evans faked to Bell and sneaked into the end zone on third-and-two. Walker's PAT gave USC a 21-17 lead and even the most staunch Irish supporter could see dark handwriting on the wall.

Just to embellish their vision and to imprint the seal of victory, the Trojans augmented their lead with a final field goal, a 35-yarder by Walker. The opportunity was born when Danny Reece intercepted a Montana fling, and the embryo was nourished by the legs of Bell and Tatupu.

It was McKay's farewell gesture to the Dome, and who could blame his troops for wanting to send him away as a winner?

"All I want to say is I really appreciate the way the guys played today," responded the panjandrum of Troy. "They did it all." McKay then flipped the game ball to Bell, shouting, "And the game ball to Ricky Bell!"

No one disputed that gesture, but assistant coach Marv Goux thought someone else was due recognition, too — McKay.

"Wait a minute," Goux called out. "We can't let it go just like that. This may be John McKay's last Bend, but whatever, we give another game ball to the coach of the year— this year and every year!"

McKay accepted the oval, but would not elaborate on his future plans, diverting instead his remarks to praise the talents of his hosts.

"Notre Dame's defense is outstanding," he began, "and they are very strong, as always. They are even stronger than they were last year. But we were ready. You've got to be great any time you win in Notre Dame Stadium."

Across the field, Devine, from the gloom of the Notre Dame dressing room, found words of applause for his visitors. "Southern Cal was well-prepared, well-coached, played hard and did everything they had to to win," he said, graciously.

The Irish went on to defeat Navy, Georgia Tech and Miami (Fla.), but lost to Pittsburgh, thereby presenting Devine with an 8-3-0 record for his first season. He produced one consensus All-American— Niehaus— as well as two others— MacAfee and Bradley— whose names appeared on some selections.

315

The Trojans departed South Bend riding a crest of seven straight wins. But a strange twist awaited, as they were surprisingly lashed by California, Stanford, Washington and bitter rival UCLA—four consecutive losses. Only a blanking of Texas A&M in the Liberty Bowl sent McKay out on a winning note.

He would carry away a USC ledger of 127 victories, 40 losses and eight ties. Eight of those victories were over Notre Dame, while six of the losses and two of the ties were to the Irish. McKay brought four national championships to University Park. And his last uncontested All-American was...Ricky Bell.

1976

GAME 48

A Luckless Shamrock

Some days you can't win for losing. Ask Notre Dame's Dan Devine.

"We took it to them, kicked the bleep out of them, but we sure didn't have any luck today," moaned the Irish coach after his young team had blown six scoring opportunities, suffered five turnovers and finished on the short end of a 17-13 stick to powerful Southern California in the 48th renewal of these gridiron giants.

And Devine wasn't through. "We were in field goal range three times in the first half alone and the fumbles and interceptions really hurt us," he added.

With or without Lady Luck, John Robinson, Southern Cal's yearling coach figured—like a rose—a four-point win is a four-point win is a four-point win.

"I'm really proud of our guys," he commented. "We were down after a very emotional game last week with UCLA. But that's not taking anything away from the Irish. Notre Dame is Notre Dame. If you come out with a half-point win, you've accomplished a lot."

Before delving into the crossfire between blunder and brilliance, plus all of the other elements that found niches in this affair of strangeness, inspect the paths of the Irish and the Trojans that led to the Coliseum.

Both were rather free of stones, although the Trojans did get off to a rocky start. Ranked No. 8, nobody expected them to lose to unranked Missouri, but they did. Wasn't close, either. Robinson's troops from Troy, however, pulled themselves up by their collective bootstraps and marched on to lace Oregon, Purdue, Iowa, Washington State, Ore-

317

gon State, California, Stanford, Washington and their Westwood antagonist, UCLA. Only Pittsburgh and Michigan outranked SC as ND appeared on the kickoff horizon.

The Irish, pegged No. 11 in pre-season polls, lost their season opener, too— to Pittsburgh— but rebounded with triumphs over Purdue, Northwestern, Michigan State, Oregon, South Carolina, Navy, Alabama and Miami (Fla.), absorbing along the way a loss to Georgia Tech. But despite an 8-2-0 mark entering the USC confab, ND was omitted from the Top Ten.

Notre Dame greeted the season with few seniors, mostly a junior-sophomore squad...but brandishing a freshman crop of blue-chippers. "On paper, an unusually good bunch," Devine rated his rookies. Seven regulars returned on offense and eight on defense, and solid strength abounded for the seven vacant spots.

"I put emphasis on defense," Devine was quoted. "I want the defense to be super first." This emphasis was prevalent in early games— if the Pitt loss can be discounted. For in the next five games, the Irish yielded a total of just 12 skimpy points.

But if ND would depend largely on underclassmen, the land of Troy would find its streets paved with a nucleus of veteran seniors, including elusive Ricky Bell, fresh off a 1,957-yard rushing season and now a stout candidate for the Heisman Trophy.

When new coaches assume command, there is often a tendancy to change things. Not Robinson, whose philosophy was: if it ain't broke, don't fix it. And certainly, the Trojan machine that purred under the wrench of John McKay for 16 years did not sputter.

"We do hope to throw a little more— just try to get a little more variety in the offense," said Robinson. "But our goal is to be a champion again."

With its 9-1-1 record, Southern Cal was tagged an eight-point favorite to whip Notre Dame, and 76,561 folks brushed through the turnstiles on a beautiful afternoon in late November to see how accurate the handicappers would be. Notre Dame started two seniors, Southern Cal 14.

As two boxers might do, the combatants came out

USC's Shelton Diggs, (top) outraces Notre Dame's Ted Burgmeier for a 6-yard touchdown pass from Rob Hertel. USC's Randy Simmrin (bottom) snags a 63-yard scoring aerial from Vince Evans as Joe Restic defends. The Trojans went on to post a 17-13 win over the Irish at the Coliseum.

Al Hunter was the first Notre Dame runner to rush for more than 1,000 yards in a single season (1,058 in 1976).

sparring with each other and the first quarter ended with both end zones untarnished, thanks in part to a couple of pass interceptions. First, Ted Burgmeier filched a long throw by Vince Evans, trotting up to his 38-yard line. Later, cornerback Ron Bush snuffed out the Irish threat 32 yards shy of the goal by picking off a toss by Rick Slager.

That was just a sample of the frustration that suited up in an Irish jersey in the second quarter. Count the futilities:

— Notre Dame moves to SC's 14-yard stripe, Al Hunter fumbles, Bush recovers for SC.

— Notre Dame advances to the SC 23, Rusty Lisch loses the handle, Clay Matthews finds it for SC.

— Notre Dame again reaches the 32. On fourth-and-one, Hunter tries to sweep end and is dropped for a yard loss by Mike Burns.

Sensing fate had found a seat on his bench, Robinson removed his starting quarterback and dispatched Rob Hertel into the fray.

"Vince (Evans) was just a little unsettled," explained Robinson, who, however, did reinstate his senior QB in the second half.

Seizing his opportunity, Hertel completed six-of-seven passes during a 67-yard invasion that terminated ten seconds before intermission with a six-yard TD fling to Shelton Diggs. Other than Diggs, William Gay and Randy Simmrin snagged key passes in the drive, which officially ended when Glen Walker added the seventh point.

The Trojans struck quickly in the third frame, cruising 80 yards in just four plays. After hitting Simmrin for 12 yards, Evans fired a bomb that Simmrin tucked in on ND's 28-yard line and streaked into the end zone.

"Diggs was my primary receiver," related Evans, "but my protection broke down and I had to scramble away from (Ross) Browner." Walker's PAT stretched SC's lead to 14-0.

The Irish closed the gap to seven points with only 50

USC quarterback Vince Evans directed the powerful offensive line against Notre Dame. The Trojans beat the Irish and finished the season at 11-1-0, ranking second in the national polls behind Pittsburgh.

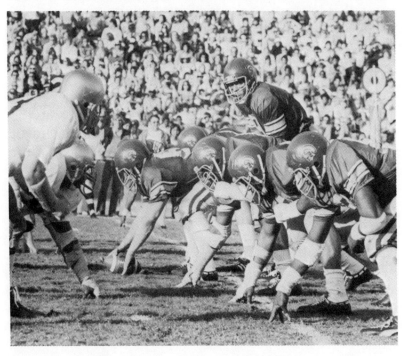

seconds gone in the final period, obliterating 68 yards in a scant three plays, all passes. It was Lisch to Kris Haines for 35, to Dan Kelleher for 16 and lastly, to freshman Vagas Ferguson for 17. Dave Reeve added the PAT, and the visitors from Indiana figured they had found, at long last, a door to victory.

It was subsequently closed as, once again, the Irish proved to be their own worst enemy. Advancing steadily, ND finally stalled on SC's 10-yard line. Chip-shot field goal? Sure, on any other day. But on this luckless day, Reeve missed it.

The Trojans took over on their 20 and moved into field goal range on the impetus of Charles White's 14-yard dash and a 26-yard pass interference call on ND's Luther Bradley. Walker obliged with a 46-yard field goal.

Pass interference was also a factor as Notre Dame tallied with four seconds remaining on the clock. The penalty (Ricky Odom on Haines) netted the Irish 35 yards and a first down on the one-yard line. Lisch carried in the ball to climax a 76-yard journey in 11 plays, the most important being a 17-yard aerial from Lisch to Kelleher. A run failed to produce the two-point effort.

"Our defense was outstanding again," lauded Robinson, "and they were out there an awfully long time." Robinson alluded to the play of Rod Martin, who had 17 tackles, plus Bush, Burns, Matthews, Lewis and Clint Strozier.

These stalwarts, however, did not outperform the activities of Browner or Lisch or Hunter, in the judgment of Devine. Hunter, in fact, became the first Notre Dame player ever to exceed 1,000 yards in one season. His 115 yards brought his season total to 1,058 yards.

Bell's quest for the Heisman Trophy was weakened with his game output of only 75 yards, but it should be pointed out that the senior star switched from his natural tailback position to fullback when David Farmer was injured in the second quarter and Mosi Tatupu was already crippled.

"In many ways, this was Bell's finest hour as a Trojan," said Robinson. "This was his last chance to go out in a blaze of glory—yet, he switched to fullback and played with enthusiasm."

Tony Dorsett of Pittsburgh was selected over Bell for the big "H", but the Trojan speedster, along with Dennis Thurman, Gary Jeter and Marvin Powell were named All-Americans.

Defensive end Browner of Notre Dame captured one of football's highest honors— the Outland Trophy. He, along with Ken MacAfee, were consensus All-Americans, while the names of Bradley and Willie Fry appeared on some ballots

As usual, both institutions had bowl dates to fulfill, and both were winners. Notre Dame nudged Penn State in the Gator to finish the year at 9-3-0. Southern Cal overcame Michigan in the Rose Bowl to complete an 11-1-0 sojourn, earning the runner-up slot in the national polls.

So, in the 50th anniversary year of the ND-SC series, the Irish won the battle (23 first downs to SC's 15 and 352 net yards to SC's 273) but lost the war, 17-13. There was some consolation, though. Notre Dame still led in the series, 26 to 18 with four ties, and in total points scored, 879 to 720.

But who is counting?

1977

The Devine Ploy

Three straight losses. Merely one victory in the past ten years. Those were the stark items of travail that plagued Notre Dame as it prepared for the 49th face-off with its master of late, Southern California.

It was time for a change. It was time for the wearing of the green.

A sell-out crowd of 59,075 avid fans watched casually on a warm, pleasant day as the Irish warriors went through their pre-game warmups on the turf of Notre Dame Stadium— dressed in customary blue. On the same field, the Trojans were going through their preparatory paces, and saw nothing unusual about the blue jerseys that occasionally darted in and around them. After all, Notre Dame had been wearing blue since 1963.

But coach Dan Devine had an inspiration. When his blue-clad athletes returned to their dressing room for pre-kickoff instructions, they discovered in their lockers fresh green jerseys.

"I ordered them three months ago," revealed Devine, "but only our four captains knew about them— not even the coaches. I wanted to illustrate just why Notre Dame is the Fighting Irish."

The reaction among the players was explosive, as if they had suddenly been deeded the sword with which to pierce the walls of Troy.

"We totally went crazy," exuded senior Ted Burgmeier. "It was as emotional as I've ever seen us. What a super idea it was." To which tight end Ken MacAfee added: "This was just the motivating factor we needed."

Receiver Ken MacAfee scored two touchdowns in Notre Dame's 1977 win over USC. He was a consensus All-America in 1976-77.

It must have been. For with fire on their breath, shamrock-colored fabric across their breasts and helmets as gold as the hovering Dome that guarded their campus, the Irish stormed into combat. The result was a 49-19 decimation of highly-touted Southern California...and a breaking of the dreaded drought.

Did the surprise of changing jersey colors startle Southern Cal? "I was indifferent to them," shrugged Coach John Robinson. "We just got the hell beat out of us."

They weren't supposed to, either. The Trojans were a six-point favorite to once again handle Notre Dame. But the odds-makers didn't know St. Patrick would endow the Irish with his fiery green.

Veterans galore spiked the squad that greeted Devine's third term at South Bend. Eleven regulars on defense and eight on offense were on hand, prompting pre-season prognosticators to peg Notre Dame as potentially the third best team in the land.

"This is the first veteran team I've had since I've been here," Devine observed, "and I'd rather have a veteran team."

Smiles also crossed the brow of Devine when it was noted that All-Americans Ross Browner and MacAfee were back, plus Bob Golic who set an ND season record of 146 tackles last year, along with Jerome Heavens, now recovered from surgery.

"Heavens is so important to us," stated Devine. "He's a great one—best sophomore fullback I've ever seen."

Out West at Heritage Hall, the situation was not quite as rosy, although there was hardly any wilting on the stem. The Trojans had lost 12 starters, including the elegant Ricky Bell.

But Robinson looked on the bright side. "We have a chance to be very good again, he told *Street and Smith* magazine. "Graduation took a lot of key players and we have the most difficult schedule USC has had in many years. But we feel we've got good replacements at most positions. The key to our season is how quickly the new people become accomplished players."

Two Trojans who did not have to prove themselves were Randy Simmrin, a split end of smallish stature, and

Ross Browner, consensus All-America on defense in 1976-77, was the third Irish player to win the Outland Trophy (1976).

Wearin' of the Green Leaves Trojans Blue, 49-19

William Gay, a tight end of larger dimensions. Of Simmrin, Robinson appraised, "He may be the greatest receiver in USC history." And of Gay: "He might be the best blocking tight end in college football."

Apparently, the optimism of Robinson and the superlatives he spewed rubbed off on poll voters, who placed SC right behind ND in pre-season guesses—No. 4.

As usual, the students at Notre Dame staged a pulsating pep rally the night before the Glamor Game. And they didn't quite understand the request of the football captains who asked them to "...back the Irish with green tomorrow," then led them in a continuous chant of "Green Machine, Green Machine, Green Machine!"

Of course they learned the answer to all of those "green" requests on the next afternoon, a balmy October day that blossomed with the temperature flirting around the 60-degree mark.

If not exactly balmy, Notre Dame had been better than lukewarm in its previous games. The Irish boasted verdicts over Pittsburgh, Purdue, Michigan State and Army but lost a decision to Mississippi.

Southern Cal was a tad better, recordwise, having kicked Missouri, Oregon State, TCU, Washington State and Oregon, but having been kicked by Alabama by a point. (By the way, the win over the Cougars was No. 500 in the dramatic football history of the Trojans.)

First quarter action saw Notre Dame jump to a 7-0 lead as Southern Cal muffed scoring opportunities that were disrupted by Luther Bradley, an All American-to-be, and Burgmeier. Notre Dame's touchdown was the result of an 80-yard drive that ended on the 11th play when Dave Mitchell pounded across from four yards out. Dave Reeve converted. Other than a face mask penalty, Joe Montana threw key passes to MacAfee and Mitchell and scrambled for a 12-yard gain to sustain the movement.

327

Notre Dame submitted to a tie in the second period, then blasted ahead at 22-7 before the squads left the field for half-time lectures.

Turnovers led to both teams' points. First, Trojan Tyrone Sperling dislodged the ball from Terry Eurick, and linebacker Mario Celotto grabbed it in mid-air and stepped into the end zone. Frank Jordan's extra point locked the score. Then Charles White fumbled for SC, Bobby Leopold recovered on the Trojan 14, and Montana plunged the last yard on the sixth play. Two more points were earned when Burgmeier scooped up a wobbly snap from the center and passed to Tom Domin in the end zone. For the record, Burgmeier played quarterback in high school.

Then arrived the knockout blow to the Trojans, perhaps the turning point of the battle. Bradley purloined a toss from Rob Hertel, setting up the Irish on the SC 37. After three plays failed to produce a first down, placekicker Reeve positioned himself for an apparent 50-yard field goal attempt. It was a fake. Burgmeier, the holder, took the snap and sped around end to SC's 13-yard stripe, from which point Montana rifled a TD strike to MacAfee. Reeve added to the loot with a PAT boot.

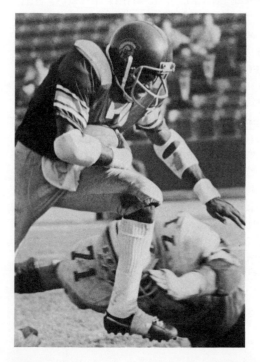

Trojan defensive back Dennis Thurman makes a runback after one of his eight interceptions in 1976. He was All-America in 1976-77.

"That fake field goal run gave us an emotional lift," said Montana.

The third stanza was more downhill for the Trojans as ND inflated its lead to 35-7 on a blocked punt and a 70-yard invasion. Bob Golic slammed his massive frame into Marty King's punt, and Jay Case ran it back for a 30-yard tally. Then Heavens raced a dozen yards, Montana passed 27 to Kris Haines, 24 to MacAfee and to MacAfee again for a one-yard TD. Reeve's toe was true after Case's marker but untrue after MacAfee's.

Southern Cal's best chance to gather points was thwarted when Lynn Cain was divorced from the ball a bare three yards shy of ND's goal. It skidded out of the end zone for a touchback.

Both schools scored twice in the fourth frame, but the outcome had long before been settled.

Southern Cal: Walter Underwood recovered Mitchell's bobble on ND's 22-yard line, and Cain raced in from the four after pass interference was called against Burgmeier; Hertel passed 14 yards to Calvin Sweeney to culminate a 75-yard trek featured by a 25-yard completion by the same twosome. Two-point attempts after both touchdowns failed.

Notre Dame: Montana scored on a short sneak after the Irish took over on SC's 13, the Trojans having run out of downs; Rusty Lisch passed nine and 14 yards to Steve Orsini, then four to Speedy Hart as the Irish wrapped up a 45-yard drive and the game. Reeve made both extra points.

"Oh, yes, this is a sweet victory," Devine told David Condon of the *Chicago Tribune*. "To be honest, this one is the best of all."

"We have no excuses," countered Robinson. "We seemed to be making an unbelievable amount of mental errors. But we lost to an inspired opponent. They outplayed us and outcoached us."

After the skirmish, USC split its four remaining regular season games, beating Stanford and UCLA, losing to California and Washington. A walloping of Texas A&M in the Cotton Bowl wound up the Trojans' year at 8-4-0, a mediocre ledger for the men of Troy.

Notre Dame placekicker Dave Reeve was the only player in series history to score in four games (1974-75-76-77).

But from the scintillating victory over USC came wings of greatness for the Irish as, in rapid-fire succession, they smashed Navy, Georgia Tech, Clemson, Air Force and Miami (Fla.) in regular season events, then crumpled top-rated Texas in the Cotton Bowl to finish with 11-1-0 credentials.

Even though Alabama, Arkansas, Penn State and Texas displayed a similar record, Notre Dame was crowned the national champion, an honor to which the Irish, unlike their green jerseys, were accustomed.

But, reflect back to the tussle at South Bend a moment. Maybe, just maybe, the odds were too great for All-American Dennis Thurman and his Trojan mates to overcome. After all, there was a 90-foot mural of Christ overlooking Notre Dame Stadium and the Golden Dome of Our Lady standing guard and a coach named Devine and a fullback named Heavens and St. Patrick's green all over the place. Face it—just how much can a bunch of guys from Hollywood handle?

330

1978

For ND: A Toe Of Woe

A scant six seconds flashed on the stadium clock as Southern California broke its huddle and lined up in field goal formation, the line of scrimmage at the Notre Dame 20-yard stripe. The Irish, sheltering with desperation a one-point lead, wiped their brows, clawed the turf, and tensed every muscle for a collective charge.

More than 84,000 people jammed Memorial Coliseum and all eyes were fixed on holder Marty King and placekicker Frank Jordan. Earlier, the little Trojan had missed an extra point and a chip-shot FG, much closer than this attempt. Breathlessly, the partisan crowd wondered: goat or hero, win or lose. Yes, 59 minutes and 54 seconds of bashing and gnashing, of plunder and wonder had reduced the contest to this one final play.

The snap. The spot. The rush. The swing. Straight as an arrow, catapulted the ball, splitting dead-center the uprights. And jubilant Southern Cal was a narrow winner — 27 to 25— over an intrepid Notre Dame team in the 50th anniversary game of this historic, magnificent series.

"I was praying the offense would get me in position to redeem myself," Jordan confided, alluding to his earlier miss which enabled ND to eventually forge into the lead.

The curtain-dropping death blow was enlarged in drama by a latent assault of the Irish, who trailed 24-6 entering the fourth quarter, and, behind the wizardry of QB Joe Montana, blitzed their way into a 25-24 lead with 46 seconds to play.

"It was one of the most remarkable comebacks in the history of sport," said ND Coach Dan Devine. But spirited exertion notwithstanding, fate looked with disfavor toward the Irish on this cool, overcast day, instead casting her fickle charms on a stocky lad from San Francisco named Jordan.

For the 1978 season, Coach John Robinson faced a major task of rebuilding the troops of Troy, but with Jordan returning, placekicking was not one of his problems. Experience was, as Robinson could locate only 11 starters and 11 seniors among his top 44 prospects.

"We're extremely young," he pointed out. "We have more open positions than I can remember at USC in years. But we have potential."

The potential would be built around the return of such All-American candidates as Charles White, Pat Howell and Anthony Munoz, with some assistance from an outstanding group of freshmen. Pre-season polls listed the Trojans at No. 8.

As it turned out, SC was underrated as the Trojans tore through Texas Tech, Oregon, Alabama and Michigan before hitting a snag with Arizona State, a new conference member of the newly formed Pacific-10. Oregon State, California, Stanford, Washington and UCLA were

Quarterback Joe Montana led furious Notre Dame comeback in 1978, only to lose on a last-second field goal by Southern Cal.

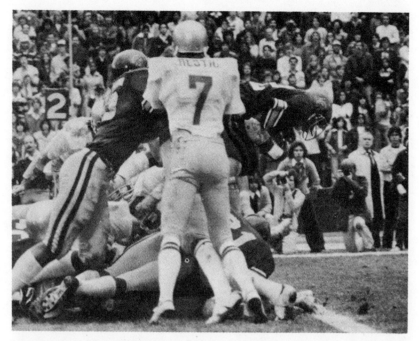

Charles White dives for a third quarter touchdown, giving USC a 24-6 lead in 1978. The Irish fought back for a one-point lead before bowing 27-25. Number 7 is Notre Dame's Joe Restic.

next and all yielded to the USC machine. This slate of 9-1-0 earned a national rank of No. 3 going into the Notre Dame conflict.

Similar to Southern Cal, Notre Dame would construct its team around a trio of proven veterans, too— All-American Bob Golic plus A-A hopefuls Dave Huffman and Montana. It would also look for strength toward eight returning regulars on offense and five on defense, as well as a potent freshman flock.

"Our biggest problem is a lack of numbers," predicted Devine. "We're not physically strong or as deep as last year. On paper, we've got a good freshman class coming in. So, if we can stay healthy, I think we're going to be pretty good."

Although the Irish were the defending national champs, pollsters placed five teams ahead of them in pre-season rankings, which, as the season progressed, proved a rather accurate judgment.

Notre Dame lost its first two games: Missouri and Michigan. Then plowed through the next eight: Purdue, Michigan State, Pittsburgh, Air Force, Miami (Fla.), Navy, Tennessee and Georgia Tech. That calculated to eight wins and two losses and a rating of No. 8.

So even though the fellows from South Bend brought an eight-game winning streak to the Golden State, they entered the melee with Southern Cal as six-point underdogs. But Notre Dame also brought an incentive, possibly undetected by the Las Vegas line. The Irish would be shooting for their 600th victory since the institution began playing football in 1887.

But maybe the bookies did consider that intangible. And maybe the role of underdog was on track as the Trojans jumped to a 6-0 lead, then stretched that to 17-3 by the half.

First quarter. The host team drove 55 yards in five plays as Paul McDonald threw left-handed strikes of 15 yards to White, five to Lynn Cain and 30 to Kevin Williams for a touchdown. Jordan's PAT essay was wide.

"McDonald is the coolest quarterback I've been around and he has developed into a team leader," cited Robinson.

As the quarter drew to a close, ND's Joe Unis drilled a 47-yard field goal to cut SC's lead in half. It was the fifth play of a 56-yard journey sparked by a Montana-to-Kris Haines aerial of 22 yards.

Second quarter, all Southern California. Relying on the legs of White, who contributed key runs of four, 12 and six yards, plus the arm of McDonald, who connected with Calvin Sweeney for 12 yards and with Dan Garcia for 35 and a TD, the Trojans covered 75 yards in six plays. Two points were added when McDonald passed faultlessly to James Hunter.

Calling again on the same two executioners—White and McDonald—but adding for spice a 12-yard dash by Cain, the pride of Troy traveled 71 yards to enable Jordan to hammer a 39-yard field goal.

Down 14 points at the half (and the stats indicated it could have been worse), were the Irish also down in spirits?

"We had to realize we weren't out of the ball game,"

answered Montana.

"I asked the players not to quit," responded Devine, "and they didn't. We were a different team in the second half."

Witness this: With five possessions in the second half, Notre Dame kicked a field goal, drove to SC's one-yard line where Montana lost a fumble, scored a touchdown, scored a touchdown, scored a touchdown.

Third quarter. Notre Dame wiped out 80 yards in 12 plays to set up Unis for a 26-yard field goal. The movement was inspired by passes of 16 and 12 yards from Montana to Haines and a 27-yard penalty when Dennis Smith interfered with Haines.

But USC answered that invasion with seven points, widening its advantage to 24-6. White bucked over from the two to put the finishing touch to a ground and air attack of 87 yards. Previously, White had sprinted for 14 and 13 yards, Dwight Ford had scampered for 16, and McDonald had passed for 14 to White and 22 to Sweeney. Jordan's kick was good.

Fourth quarter, frantic and all Notre Dame...well, almost. Montana, who completed 17 passes in the second half, connected with freshman Dean Masztak for 23 yards, then to Haines for 57 and a touchdown. Haines had eluded defenders Herb Ward and Smith to catch Montana's bomb on SC's 15. A two-point conversion pass was broken up.

His arm now limber and his confidence sky-high, Montana came back throwing— 17 yards to Masztak, 20, 19 and 18 to Haines— as the Fighting Irish eradicated 98 yards in 14 plays. And when a boggle appeared in the spurt, Montana scrambled for 15 yards to the Trojan three-yard stripe. Pete Buchanan crashed over from the one, Unis tacked on the PAT, and Notre Dame was in arrears by just five points with 3:01 left to play.

Now the hometown fans were getting alarmed, but Montana had not yet stated his case. His opportunity came when the Irish defense stopped the Trojans, and King's punt went out of bounds on ND's 43-yard line. The Irish ground out a first down, then Montana hit Vagas Ferguson for 24 yards. Trojan Carter Hartwig was penalized for pass interference, Montana connected with Masztak to the two-yard line, then to Pete Holohan for a touchdown. Notre Dame had overcome the odds to take a 25-24 lead with only 46 seconds on the clock. Naturally, the Irish opted for a two point conversion, but Montana's pass intended for Haines failed.

"On the two-point play, Kris (Haines) thought he could run a maneuver off a play we'd run before," explained Devine. "But we didn't hit it and they came back." While not seeming vital at the moment, the loss of the two points assumed beastly proportions in the final analysis.

The stage was now assembled for Jordan's hair-raising field goal. Notre Dame tried a squib kickoff, and Paul

Coliseum fans are on their feet as USC's Frank Jordan slams a 37-yard field goal with two seconds left in the game. Final score: Trojans 27, Irish 25. Holding for the kick is Marty King (4).

DiLulo was tackled on the SC 30-yard line. Playing on a sprained ankle, McDonald and Vic Rakhshani teamed up for a 10-yard sideline pass. McDonald was then trapped 10 yards behind the line of scrimmage, and the ball squirted from his grasp into the arms of a Notre Dame player. The Irish thought it was a fumble, the Trojans viewed it as an incomplete pass, and the officials concurred with the opinion of the home team.

SC's McDonald: "I knew it was an incomplete pass."

ND's Devine: "That was a crucial call. I won't be happy with it if it was a bad call."

Nevertheless, USC kept possession. With 19 seconds to play, McDonald passed 35 yards to Sweeney. White bolted off tackle for the last four of his 205 rushing yards, and the Trojans stopped the clock at six ticks to get Jordan into the game. You know the rest.

"White's run was designed to put the ball in the middle of the field," noted Jordan. "But it went too far left and I had to kick from the hash mark."

The spot didn't matter to a joyous Robinson. "It was the greatest football game I've ever seen," he expressed. "But maybe every USC-Notre Dame game is."

"I'm going to keep my head up," uttered ND's Haines, who grabbed eight passes in the second half alone. "I really don't think we lost. It was more—I won't say bad luck—just more misfortune."

But if the thousands upon thousands of spectators who jammed the stadium had to wait until the final two seconds to learn the outcome of the struggle, they should have checked with Trojan Sweeney.

"We never had any doubts that we would win," pronounced the senior split end. "Everyone was saying it was far-fetched to expect us to win (after losing the lead in the final minute), but I knew we would beat 'em."

Despite numerous defensive feats of greatness, the melee was primarily a show of offense. The Trojans made 30 first downs and gained 538 yards; the Irish made 23 first downs and netted 411 yards.

Notre Dame met Houston in the Cotton Bowl and eked out a 35-34 decision. Its season ended with nine wins and three losses, good enough for a final ranking of No. 7.

Southern California still had one regular season contest to play against Hawaii and that was a 16-point conquest. Finally, a victory over Michigan in the Rose Bowl formulated a season slate of 12 triumphs and one loss. Ironically, Alabama, an early-season victim of the Trojans, was crowned national champion...with USC the runner-up.

In the department of All-America honors, both schools contributed two consensus choices—Howell and White for SouCal, Golic and Huffman for Notre Dame. And, as he did as a sophomore, senior Steve Heimkreiter paced the Irish defense in tackles, this year accumulating 160.

1979

Earthquake In South Bend

Writing in the *Los Angeles Times*, Jim Murray branded the 51st brawl between Notre Dame and Southern California as maybe the best game he had ever watched...on television. Those armchair quarterbacks who delight in the fireworks of explosive offense would probably agree with his label.

Points scored: 65, with the Trojans claiming 42 and the Irish 23. Total yardage: 1,130, with USC getting 591 yards and ND 535. Series record: SC's Charles White carried the ball 44 times, the most rushing attempts ever made by any ND opponent.

Maybe the volcanic offense of the Trojans was a reaction from an unexpected tie with Stanford the previous week. Not so, according to QB Paul McDonald, who threw for 311 yards against the Irish. "We would have been up for Notre Dame if we'd won, 50-2, last week," he stated.

Okay, then perhaps it was a hangover from that sham of two years ago when Notre Dame switched from blue to green jerseys at kickoff and proceeded to slaughter the soldiers of Troy.

"I figure they're up to something," observed SC coach John Robinson, waxing caution on the eve of the game. "I don't think it will be the jerseys again, that's been done. But I wouldn't be surprised to see the Irish team land in helicopters."

Brad Budde chimed in: "They (ND) embarrassed us and I'll never forget it. That wasn't us out there that day (1977 game)."

Whatever incited Southern Cal, there existed a counter-

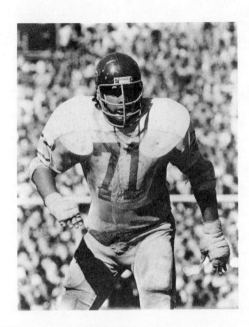

USC's four-year starting center Brad Budde was All-America and winner of the Lombardi Trophy in 1979.

part for aggression on the part of the Irish. Perhaps it was the archives of scores, which imprinted Notre Dame with a higher mark than USC only twice in the past dozen years. Perhaps it was the chance to derail the Southern Cal express, which was steaming toward the depot of national championships. Or, maybe the Irish just wanted to raise the spirits of their coach, Dan Devine, whose wife was recovering from an automobile accident.

Regardless of reasons, motivation was uppermost for both squads when they assembled in South Bend on a warm, overcast day in late October. And the official statistician paid the price.

Notre Dame started the season minus 12 of its starters from a year ago, including such rocks as Bob Golic, Jerome Heavens, Dave Huffman, Joe Montana and Steve Heimkreiter.

The conservative Devine was both hopeful and dubious. "If we can stay healthy," he opined, "we'll be a pretty good football team. But we're not deep, not deep at all."

Of course, replacing the exciting Montana at quarterback posed a major task, and Rusty Lisch seemed the most likely heir. "He's had experience," said Devine, "and he's played well."

There were jewels in the ranks of incoming freshmen, too, prompting Devine to admit, "...when they rate how schools did (in recruiting), I predict we're in the top three."

Starting the season ranked No. 9, Notre Dame upset Michigan, were, in turn, shocked by Purdue, then devoured Michigan State, Georgia Tech and Air Force as appetizers for the main course with USC.

Southern Cal had a solitary blot on its record, too, that aforementioned draw with unheralded Stanford. But the Trojans were attired as victors in all other affairs - Texas Tech, Oregon State, Minnesota, LSU and Washington State. Going into the Glamor Game, USC was ranked No. 4, a drop from its pre-season spot as No. 1.

That lofty position, as seen by scribes across the country, was based on the return of eight starters on offense (including such names as White, McDonald, Budde and Anthony Munoz) and seven on defense (including such names as Dennis Johnson and Ronnie Lott).

So how did Robinson envision his Trojans? "We have the potential to be very successful," he told a *Street & Smith* reporter, "but we've got to overcome the loss of several outstanding players, a difficult road schedule,

Another in the long line of splendid Trojan tailbacks, Charles White racked up five touchdowns against the Irish in 1978-79. He won All-America honors and the Heisman Trophy in 1979.

injuries to eight key players, most of them starters. We'll be exposed to a lot of adulation, people saying we're obviously going to win and all that nonsense. That's inaccurate and premature."

Maybe so, but rankings and records being what they were, Southern Cal entered the battle against Notre Dame as the favorite to win, according to media experts. Linebaker Johnson believed what he read, too. "In my dreams, I'd see us stuffing them," he related.

The first quarter— even the first half— was not indicative of the action that would take center stage in the last half of the game. The scorekeeper slept through the first period with a pair of zeroes, and was only mildly disturbed in the second with a brace of sevens.

The most exciting item in the initial stanza was a darting zig-zag of 79 yards by vigorous Vagas Ferguson, all the way to SC's nine-yard line. But it was no dice for the Irish as the Trojans rose to the threat and repelled it.

Southern Cal slipped out to a 7-0 lead in the second frame on a 12-yard hook-up from McDonald to Dan Garcia, who also enfolded passes of 11 and 12 yards as the Trojans drove 99 yards in 13 plays. White consumed considerable real estate, his longest run being 28 yards. Eric Hipp converted.

Notre Dame replied and entered the intermission locked at seven. Ferguson got the marker with a one-yard dive, the eighth play of a 56-yard trek. Sustaining ingredients were a 27-yard toss from Lisch to Dean Masztak and a 14-yard sweep by Ferguson. Chuck Male added the tying point.

Out from the dressing rooms to start the second half charged the teams, and both appeared ready to make the scoreboard operator start earning his keep.

"Both teams just broke open," said Robinson. "The first half was just very physical, with each team trying to dominate that way. But after the half, it was as if everybody said, the hell with it, let's see what we can do now."

Southern Cal moved out to a 21-7 advantage before Notre Dame closed the spread to 21-14 as the third frame ended.

White tallied both Trojan touchdowns, three yards for

Vagas Ferguson scored twice against USC in 1979. During the year, the All-America running back carried 301 times for 1,437 yards; both were Notre Dame records.

the first, one for the second. The first was the result of an 80-yard drive that featured runs of 13 and 18 yards by White and a 26-yard completion from McDonald to Garcia; the second was the end result of a 65-yard onslaught born of a fumble (loser Lisch, finder Ty Sperling) and nourished by aerials of 33 and 21 yards from McDonald to Garcia and a 12-yard burst by White. Hipp was true on both extra points.

Notre Dame's third-quarter touchdown was again scored by Ferguson, this time a 22-yard gallop that completed a 75-yard attack which was spurred by Lisch flings of 30 yards to Pete Holohan and 12 to Ty Barber. Male nailed the PAT, and the Irish trailed by seven.

But in the final quarter, SC racked up as many points (21) as it had mustered in the first three, at the same time limiting ND to only nine points. Hence— 42-23, USC.

Southern Cal's touchdowns were credited to Kevin Williams on a 12-yard toss from McDonald, to White on a one-yard run and again to White on another one-yard run. Totals for White: 44 carries, 261 yards, four touchdowns.

"He does some amazing things out there," McDonald said in praise of White. "He takes so much pressure off me, the defense can't key on me."

The Trojans' trilogy of TD drives carried 78, 66 and 50 yards and were sustained by McDonald passes of 41 and 47 yards to Williams plus runs of 12 yards by Raymond Butler, 23 by White and 10 by Marcus Allen. Hipp's foot swung pure after each six-pointer.

Notre Dame kept burning its flame of hope when Jim Stone stepped across the double stripe from two yards out to cap a 72-yard journey and Male slammed a 42-yard field goal to cap a 63-yard drive. Lisch threw for 22 and 42 yards to James Hunter to aid the touchdown drive, then for 22 to Ty Dickerson after Stone returned a kickoff 39 yards to ignite the field goal drive. Male failed to convert after Stone's touchdown.

The Trojans sparkled with several defensive gems, such as Jeff Fisher twice intercepting Lisch passes, but it was the massive offensive line that eventually tilted the cup of victory to their lips.

McDonald: "The offensive line is the key to whatever we do."

White: "I can't even get no words out, they're so good."

But despite his offensive spree, White on several occasions found his path abruptly closed by a brick wall collision with ND's sophomore Bob Crable, who would finish the year with 187 tackles, most ever by an Irish player.

"I'll be sore (physically) tomorrow," noted White.

Using the Notre Dame drama as a stepping stone, the gifted senior went on to win the Heisman Trophy in 1979. It fulfilled his prediction of four years ago, as told in a book titled "Best Little Rivalry in Town":

"The aura of confidence was a trademark of White. When he was a green-behind-the-ears freshman, he strode into Heritage Hall, pointed to the Heisman Trophies won by Mike Garrett and O.J. Simpson, and blurted 'I'm gonna' win me one or two of those'. Brashness, you can overlook. Talent, you cannot. White did win himself a

White's Biggest Day Makes It a Very Big Day for USC

**Tailback Pummels Notre Dame
44 Times in a 42-23 Victory**

BY RICHARD HOFFER, Times Staff Writer

SOUTH BEND, Ind.—USC and Notre Dame added several chapters to their storied rivalry Saturday, a rivalry that can no longer be condensed in anything briefer than the Encyclopedia Britanica. In addition to the usual elements of the series—perfect fall weather, an enthusiastic crowd, and enough drama to fill all of prime-time television—the 51st game in America's most famous intersectional rivalry included an enormous amount of scoring. Saturday's scoring summary alone amounts to a separate volume.

The Trojans, maintaining their recent domination of the Irish in a series that has had more swings than an out-of-whack pendulum, scored first, last and quite a few times in between to win, 42-23. Yet the 19-point spread hardly suggests the excitement these two teams—both ranked in the top 10 nationally and each a preseason candidate for the national championship —created among a Notre Dame sellout crowd of 59,075.

About all that the score can be said to represent is that two powerful, breakaway offenses were at work. Unrolling not only a campus full of green-clad football fans but a national TV audience as well.

The offenses slumbered in the first half, settling for a 7-7 tie at intermission.

But more than halfway through the third quarter, the two offenses came alive, scoring eight times between them in the final 31 minutes. Suddenly the two teams were marching up and down the field with more quickness and precision than either of the two bands had employed at the half. USC, behind the magnificent run-

Sports

CC PART ■ †
SUNDAY, OCTOBER 21, 1979

WHITE? IRISH RARELY HAVE A CLOSE LOOK

**Defense Keys on Trojan Tailback and McDonald
Says, 'He Takes So Much Pressure Off Me'**

BY ALAN GREENBERG

Heisman Trophy, which is now on display alongside those of Garrett and Simpson."

White, who became the first Trojan to exceed 2,000 net rushing yards (2,050), was joined in the winners circle by offensive guard Budde, who was meeded the Lombardi Award, and of course, both were consensus All-Americans. McDonald and Johnson were named to some A-A squads.

Honors gazed on the Irish, too, with Ferguson a consensus All-American, plus Bob Crable and Tim Foley listed on some selections.

The remainder of the season was not particularly kind to Notre Dame. There came victories over South Carolina, Navy and Miami (Fla.), but they were offset by losses to Tennessee and Clemson. A 7-4-0 ledger was not adequate for a Top Twenty spot.

But, as does the Mighty Mississippi River, the Trojans just kept rolling along. California, Arizona, Washington, UCLA and Ohio State (in the Rose Bowl) felt the wrath of Troy as a record of 11-0-1 materialized. The only problem was Alabama gleaned a 12-0-0 slate. And, as it was in 1978, so it was in 1979: Alabama No. 1, Southern California No. 2.

1980

GAME 52

Defense (And Hex) Block Irish

Just when the Notre Dame cannonball was on track rolling headlong toward a national championship, that old contentious hex known as Memorial Coliseum— acting on behalf of an army of Trojans— threw up a roadblock that changed its course from hope to despair.

Not since 1966 had the Irish won a football game at the Coliseum. So was the grand old edifice impressed with Notre Dame's record of nine wins and a tie? Or a national ranking of No. 2? Or the fact that Southern Cal was a three-point underdog? Answers: no, no, no. Play the game and the jinx will handle the outcome: Southern California 20, Notre Dame 3.

"I've never felt any lower in my life," mourned Irish coach Dan Devine, who was going up against USC for the last time. "I'm frustrated, embarrassed and disappointed. Because this is the best team by far I've ever coached."

To be sure, Devine's team failed to capitalize on several golden opportunities, but the general conception was that his team was pushed over the brink by the hard-hitting, heads-up, very physical defensive performance of the Trojans.

USC Coach John Robinson labeled it, "— the greatest defensive exhibition I've ever seen."

In justification of his appraisal, let it be known that: Notre Dame's first of only nine total first downs came just 10 seconds before halftime; Notre Dame was limited to a total of 95 total yards rushing; Notre Dame completed just three passes for a net gain of a bare 25 yards.

Prospects for the 1980 season at South Bend were

A consensus All-America player, defensive back Ronnie Lott led USC's 1980 team with eight interceptions for 166 yards.

bright. More than three dozen lettermen, including six starters on offense and eight on defense, were back for encores. What's more, seven players had earned monograms as freshmen, prompting Devine to comment: "I describe this squad as both young and experienced."

And the return of top-notch athletes such as Bob Crable, John Scully and Scott Zettek brought waves of optimism to Devine's lips. Of Zettek, Devine called him, "...as good an end as we've had here— he has to be as good as there is in the country."

Devine's major problem spot was quarterback, left vacant by Rusty Lisch. The leading candidates were senior Mike Courey and true freshman Blair Kiel.

"I've started a freshman at quarterback," said Devine, "but not often. I'm going to keep an open mind."

If QB was Devine's mystery, he did not possess a stranglehold on the riddle. For out West near the San Gabriel mountains, Robinson had lost ace Paul McDonald.

347

So he, too, was vexed with the same puzzle, the solution of which loomed in the person of Gordon Adams, a walk-on senior.

McDonald was not Robinson's only loss, either. Gone, too, were Charles White, Brad Budde and Anthony Munoz, to name just a few.

But not to worry. As always, depth abounded in the House of Troy, and Robinson could count 14 starters among his returnees, seven on each unit. All-Star prospects, too—Keith Van Horne, Ronnie Lott, Roy Foster, Dennis Smith, to name just a few.

Ranked No. 4 in pre-season polls, Southern Cal waded through its first five opponents: Tennessee, South Carolina, Minnesota, Arizona State and Arizona. After a surprising draw with Oregon, the Trojans lashed California and Stanford before suffering setbacks at the hands of Washington and UCLA. The loss to the Huskies snapped a 28-game streak during which USC had not tasted defeat.

Ranked No. 11 in pre-season polls, Notre Dame broke from the gate and sped down the track with seven straight triumphs: Purdue, Michigan, Michigan State, Miami (Fla.), Army, Arizona and Navy. Then, having achieved the No. 1 spot in the nation, behold—lowly Georgia Tech, winner of only one game, tied the Fighting Irish. The next test was against No. 5 Alabama, and ND subdued the Tide, as well as Air Force the following week. Now ranked No. 2, the Irish brought a splendid 9-0-1 ledger to the Coliseum, needing only decisions over USC and Georgia (in the Sugar Bowl) to claim yet another national title.

Both schools would be raw at quarterback as they lined up for the kickoff on an early December afternoon. The freshman, Kiel, would start for the Irish; sophomore Scott Tinsley would replace the injured Adams for USC.

Not surprisingly, defense was predicted as the name of the game. Nationwise, Notre Dame was ranked fourth in total defense and also in scoring defense; SouCal was ninth in total defense.

If anything noteworthy happened in the first quarter, other than feats of defense, scribes on the scene did not report it. Life entered the stalemate in the second period,

348

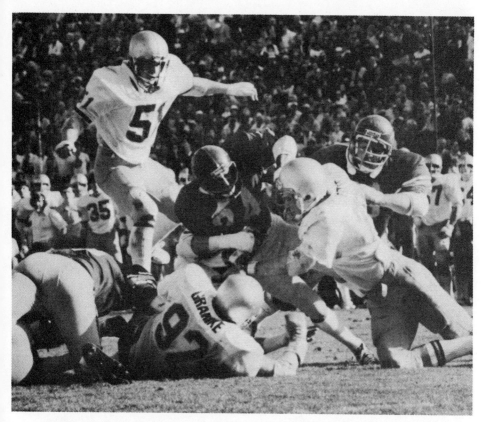

Notre Dame's Scott Zettek (70), Joe Rudzinski (51) and Joe Gramke (92) dig in to stop the Southern Cal attack in 1980. The Trojans won, 20-3.

however, as the Trojans registered 10 points, compliments in part to errors by the Irish.

ND's Phil Carter was jarred loose from the ball and Smith claimed it for SC just 31 yards shy of pointland. Michael Harper picked up yardage in seven, nine and nine gulps, then crossed the goal line from six yards out on the sixth play.

Eric Hipp kicked the PAT, then later added a 22-yard field goal to end a 61-yard drive made 29 yards shorter by penalties of roughing the kicker (by Tony Belden) and pass interference (by Stacey Toran) against Notre Dame. Best contribution by the Trojans was a 15-yard completion from Tinsley to Kevin Williams.

With zero points on the scoreboard at halftime, Devine replaced Kiel with Courey at quarterback. "We were being out-quicked," he explained. "I thought I had to get my quick people in there."

Down by 10, Notre Dame took advantage of a Trojan miscue in the third stanza to post three points, and only sterling defensive play by the host team denied them more. The trio of points materialized when Zettek recovered Harper's fumble in the shadow of SC's goal territory. Six points seemed imminent, but Courey was dropped for a 12-yard loss by Chip Banks and Dennis Edwards, so ND had to settle for Harry Oliver's 30-yard field goal.

Prior to that, the Irish failed to cash another scoring opportunity. Relying on rollouts, Courey moved Notre Dame to a first-and-goal on the three. Carter and John Sweeney each made a yard, but Courey hit a stone wall for no gain on third down. From the one, Carter took a pitch-out...but was stopped inches from the goal by Lott and Charles Ussery.

"If I had it to do all over again, I would send Carter over the top," said Devine, "but I figured USC would be expecting that."

Entering the final frame in arrears at 10-3, Notre Dame was presented another chance by Southern Cal to lock the score. But this one backfired.

Soph Tom Jefferson fumbled away the ball to the Irish on SC's 26-yard stripe. On third down, Courey, under a heavy rush, attempted a screen pass. Linebacker Banks, a 6-5 junior, leaped high in the air, brought down the ball to his chest, bumped over Carter, and raced 49 yards to ND's one-yard line. A ruffled Irish defense, aided by a delay-of-game penalty, prohibited a Trojan touchdown, so Hipp hopped in and chipped a 17-yard field goal, the shortest in series history.

"It was a great athletic play," commented Courey in describing Banks' interception. "But I threw the ball too early."

That rearranged the score to 13-3, but Southern Cal wanted to add a layer of veneer. This it did with a sustained 79-yard drive that required 11 plays, all on the ground. Harper, Anthony Gibson and Bob McClanahan were the workhorses, with Harper doing the TD honors on a 10-yard jaunt. Hipp's extra point finalized the score at 20-3.

The victory was Robinson's 50th since becoming Troy's King Priam in 1976. "That's not important," he said. "Let's talk about the players."

And talk he did, the names spilling out in rapid delivery—Banks, Lott, Smith, Ussery, Edwards, Byron Darby, Riki Gray, Harper, Tinsley—was anyone overlooked?

The Irish lads had praise for their adversaries, too. "USC is definitely the strongest, quickest, best defensive team we've played all year," mulled Courey. To which Carter added: "Even if we're in trouble, we should be able to run. This was the first time we weren't able to."

As stated, this was Devine's swan song season at Notre Dame. Against rival Southern California, his record was not impressive: one victory, five defeats. But, overall, he had won 53 games against 15 losses and a tie, had won three bowl games and a national championship. His farewell game at Notre Dame was his 16th loss and his first in post-season as top-ranked Georgia, behind a fabulous freshman named Herschel Walker, was the Sugar Bowl victor.

Southern Cal was ineligible for post-season activity and finished the season at 8-2-1.

Both institutions placed a pair of players on consensus All-America rosters: Crable and Scully for ND, Lott and Van Horne for SC. And both had a couple on an All-Seventies team picked by Paul Hornung, in which he identified, in his opinion, the finest players of the decade. For the Trojans, it was Lynn Swann and Brad Budde; for the Irish, Dave Casper and Ross Browner.

But it remained for young Kiel to sum up the awe of the stadium in the 1980 skirmish. Mused the freshman, who was five years old the last time Notre Dame beat USC in the Coliseum: "There's something strange about playing them out here. They've got some kind of hex on us."

1981

GAME 53

Trojans Bedevil Faust

To start the 1981 season, Notre Dame brought in a new head coach and his name was Faust— Gerry Faust. Unlike his operatic counterpart, Faust did not sell his soul to the Devil. That wasn't necessary. For a legion of Trojans brought the misery of Hades to him.

It happened on a brisk and cold day in late October in South Bend in the form of an unholy football game: Southern California 14, Notre Dame 7.

The loss was a solid pillow in the construction of Notre Dame's first losing season since 1963, a development foreseen by few, if indeed any, seers in September. Only Michigan and Oklahoma would have better teams than would the Irish, they penned for one and all to fathom.

And why not? The new coach, Faust, was highly acclaimed. Granted, he came from a high school (Moeller in Ohio), but in nine years there he had lost only eight of 90 games, with one tie.

"It was the only place I ever would have left Moeller for," said Faust, a devout Catholic, as he accepted the Notre Dame position.

He inherited a wealth of talent from departing coach Dan Devine, too: a total of 39 lettermen, including eight regulars on offense and an equal number on defense. All-American Bob Crable was back. So were Phil Carter, John Krimm, Tony Hunter, Dave Duerson, Blair Kiel and Harry Oliver.

So of course there appeared yawns and a few "Ho-hums" when, in its opener, Notre Dame stashed away LSU and moved up to No. 1. The glory was short-lived,

352

The fourth Trojan tailback to win the Heisman Trophy (1981), in four years Marcus Allen never tasted defeat at the hands of Notre Dame.

however, as the gavel of defeat fell heavily at the hands of Michigan and Purdue, knocking the Irish from the elite circle of the Top Twenty. The Irish fought back to subdue Michigan State but Florida State was a spoilsport, so ND approached its 53rd encounter with Southern Cal with a losing record (2-3) for the first time in 18 years.

"Sure, I'd like to be 5-0," stammered Faust, "but I've found in college football that there is such a balance of athletes that it is hard to get through a season and win them all."

Notre Dame's fall from grace was not matched by SouCal but neither did the Trojans quite ascend the summit to which they were deemed. Ranked No. 5 by preseason soothsayers, the Trojans climbed into the No. 1 spot, then slipped to No. 14 at season's end.

Proven veterans on both units greeted coach John Robinson as he assembled his troops on Bovard Field. Marcus Allen, Don Mosebar and Roy Foster headed a contingent of six returning starters on offense; George

Achica, Chip Banks and Dennis Edwards headed the six returnees on defense.

So some folks thought it somewhat strange when Robinson declared: "We have a lot of problems at the finesse positions." They were quite sure, however, he did not include Allen, who amassed 1,567 yards last season, in his "problem" category.

USC conquered five of its six opponents prior to the ND scuffle. Broken were Tennessee, Indiana, No. 2 Oklahoma, Oregon State and Stanford; unbroken was Arizona, which jolted the Trojans by three points.

Southern California entered the battle at Notre Dame Stadium as a four-point favorite. And on hand to witness the affair were ten members of the 1931 USC squad that eked out a slim 16-14 astonishing verdict, as well as some members of Knute Rockne's unbeaten 1929 and '30 teams. The grizzled and bent old-timers were there to pay homage to Rockne on the 50th anniversary of his death.

When the teams broke for recess, neither had put a point on the scoreboard, albeit both muffed chances to do so. The Irish produced the deepest penetration, reaching SC's two-yard line after a 54-yard drive. A 20-yard chip-shot field goal would unravel a scoreless knot, but Oliver's left-footed kick sailed wide left.

"The snap, the hold were fine," admitted Oliver. "I just didn't execute right. I picked my head up."

Other futile excursions by Notre Dame reached USC's 39, 44 and 49-yard stripes, while the Trojans penetrated mid-field three times, to ND's 44, 28 and 38, all to no avail.

In practices during the week, Robinson had repeatedly told his warriors that playing Notre Dame was similar to a heavyweight fight, and at halftime, he again brought forth the comparison.

"We've gone through nine rounds," he reminded them. "We've got the final rounds coming up. We've got to take it to them."

It took almost half of the third quarter for the Trojans to convert Robinson's words into points, but break the tie they did. Quarterback John Mazur scrambled 24 yards on a pivotal third-down play, Todd Spencer rambled 27

354

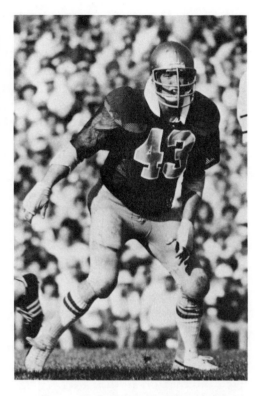

Linebacker Bob Crable, two-time consensus All-America, was credited with 508 tackes during the 1979-80-81 seasons. His 187 tackles in 1979 remains a Notre Dame single-season record.

off a trap and Allen zipped the final 14 of a 69-yard campaign that needed only five plays. Freshman Steve Jordan raised the score to 7-0.

Before the third period ended, though, Notre Dame evened the score, consuming 80 yards in eight plays. Carter entered the end zone from five yards out after having gained 30 yards on four previous carries. Important to the drive, too, was a 14-yard aerial from Kiel to Hunter and a 17-yard personal foul penalty against USC.

Now sniffing victory, the Irish recovered a bobble by Allen and moved 26 yards to Troy's seven-yard line before sputtering. In came Oliver for a short-range field goal effort. But the snap from freshman center Kevin Kelly was high, holder Tim Koegel had difficulty placing down the ball and Oliver's kick drifted wide right.

"If we had made that field goal, it would have switched the momentum," opined Irish tackle Phil Pozdrac. "It was crucial."

355

So now the confrontation was reaching the point of no return— do something or call it a wash.

Trojan David Pryor did something. His high 33-yard punt was downed by John Kamana on ND's three-yard line. The SC defense joined in and forced their hosts to punt from the five. Joey Browner returned the punt six yards to the ND 44, and in three plays USC scored. Allen slithered down the left sideline for 21 yards, then was dumped three yards behind the line of scrimmage by Crable. On second-and-13, Spencer burst through on a counter play, escaped cornerback Stacey Toran, and raced 26 yards for the winning score. Jordan's PAT was insurance.

"The hole was wide open," said Spencer. "Bruce Matthews got his man (Crable), and I keyed off his block."

Spencer's net gain of 74 yards was his most productive game at this point in the season, but his elation at beating Notre Dame was naturally shared by other Trojans.

"Of all our games, nothing compares with this one," remarked linebacker Banks. "It's very special to us. It goes back such a long way."

The intensity of the contest caught the attention of Robinson. "It was like a 2-1 baseball game," he noted. "I told our players that this was a heavyweight championship bout and it wouldn't be won until the 12th or 13th round."

Somehow, through the Cimmerian cloud of defeat, Faust saw a silver lining. "We're on our way," he said, proudly.

In the duel of tailbacks, ND's Carter outgained SC's Allen, 161 yards to 147. "He (Carter) is a quick back," praised Edwards, a Trojan senior. "He's like an Oklahoma back."

But, while no one questioned Edwards' adoration of Carter, it was Allen who garnered the Heisman Trophy for 1981, the fourth in a long line of illustrious tailbacks for Southern California to have been so honored. The inimitable senior finished the year with 2,427 yards, the first college rusher ever to exceed the exalted 2,400-yard mark. Allen carried the ball 433 times and scored 23 touchdowns. His number of carries set a new PAC-10 Conference record and only O.J. Simpson had scored as many touchdowns in a single season.

Naturally, Allen was a consensus All-American, as was his mate, Roy Foster. And, once again, Crable made the honor group for Notre Dame. Krimm and Duerson for the Irish, and Banks for Troy were tapped on various A-A squads.

After leaving South Bend, Southern Cal defeated Washington State, California and UCLA, but lost to Washington (all-time 200th loss) and then in the Fiesta Bowl was upended by Penn State— nine victories, three defeats. Perhaps great for Appalachian State, not great for Southern California.

With five games remaining after USC, Notre Dame needed four wins to avoid a sub-500 season. The Irish won three— Navy, Georgia Tech and Air Force. They fell short to Penn State and Miami (Fla.), and thus was entombed a 5-6-0 season. The Irish faithful moaned.

1982

GAME 54

Trojans Get Fat On Lean Irish

As the 1982 game got underway, Southern California hoped to "...win one for the Fat Man" and Notre Dame hoped to win one to break the jinx at Memorial Coliseum. As the game unfolded at its end, the officials hoped they had made the correct decision on a controversial, last-minute play that solidified the aspirations of the Trojans and dashed the dreams of the Irish.

The "Fat Man" was John Robinson, who three days before the clash, announced his resignation as head coach at USC. The hex was seven consecutive games in the Coliseum without an ND victory. The call of uncertainty was: did or did not SC's Michael Harper, blasting over a mass of humanity, break the plane of the goal line before he fumbled?

"The two side officials (Bob Zelinka and William Fette) said the runner (Harper) was across the plane of the goal line and he lost the ball on the (defensive) throwback," explained referee Charles Moffet.

Case closed. Southern Cal 17, Notre Dame 13.

Earlier in the week, folks around Heritage Hall were numbed when Robinson pegged the Notre Dame game as his last as Southern Cal's taskmaster.

"I'm surprised," stated offensive tackle Don Mosebar. "I didn't think he would be going. He's a class individual, always stressing that you treat people with respect."

So up went the battle cry at USC: "Win one for the Fat Man."

And this they did, though the gem of achievement was, in the eyes of the Irish, tarnished by Harper's disputed

358

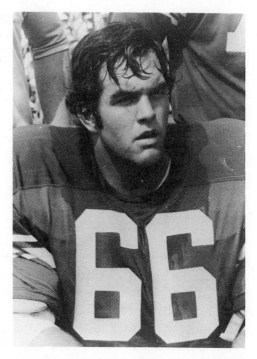

Offensive Guard Bruce Matthews earned All-America honors for Troy in 1982. His class never lost to Notre Dame.

dive that may or may not have been a touchdown.

Get the picture: 48 seconds to play, Notre Dame on top 13-10 but backed up to its one-yard line, fraught with determination not to let the surging Trojans score. Harper goes airborne over a wall of straining bodies...and fumbles. But where? Before or after he broke the plane? Even Harper wasn't sure.

"Nobody hit me when I went over," he said. "But the ball popped out. Maybe a helmet or a shoulder pad hit it. I think I crossed the plane...but I'm not sure. It's not up to me to make the judgment. It's up to the officials and they called it a touchdown."

Kevin Griffin recovered the loose ball for Notre Dame. "The ball came out," he related, "and one official signaled it was a touchdown. Another one said it was our ball. So they had a conference and that was it."

Indeed, that was it. And the gutsy Irish, whose statistics belittled those of Tommy Trojan, trudged off the gridiron of their Coliseum nemesis, once again devoid of victory.

Coach Gerry Faust was in his sophomore term as headmaster at the Golden Dome, and, despite the disappointing showing of his freshman season, his demeanor was one of optimism.

"I think it (previous year) is going to make me a better coach," remarked Faust. "I know more of what has to be done."

In pre-season polls, Notre Dame flagged no better than the No. 18 spot, despite a fine crop of 10 starters returning on offense and eight on defense...solid performers such as Phil Carter, Tony Hunter, Dave Duerson, Blair Kiel and Mark Zavagnin.

While beating Michigan in its opening game, Notre Dame passed the 20,000 mark in all-time points scored. Decisions over Purdue, Michigan State and Miami (Fla.) preceded a loss to Arizona and a tie with Oregon. The next four games were split— victors over Navy and No. 1 Pittsburgh, victims to Penn State and Air Force. So Notre Dame, now unranked, brought a 6-3-1 slate to LAX.

Prospects at USC were not ablaze with opulence, though seven starters on offense and seven on defense were back, a core firm enough to earn the Trojans a No. 10 rank in pre-season polls. It was predicted that the destiny of USC would revolve around such stalwarts as Bruce Matthews, Mosebar, George Achica, Tony Slaton and Todd Spencer.

SC opened its season with a jolt— bowing to Florida. The rest of the schedule leading up to ND shaped up with victories over Indiana, Oklahoma, Oregon, Stanford and Oregon State, a loss to Arizona State, wins over California and Arizona, and, finally, a one-point loss to Joe Bruin of UCLA. The collision with Arizona State was USC's all-time 800th game of football.

So, entering the contest against Notre Dame with 7-3-0 credentials, Southern Cal was installed as a nine-point favorite to win. Apparently unimpressed by the Irish, *Chicago Tribune* sports writer Bill Jauss picked the Trojans to win by 20 points.

Writers figured the battle would be a defensive tussle as Notre Dame's offense had been inconsistent and Southern Cal had lacked continuity in its offense.

In the first quarter, Notre Dame stepped out to a 7-0 lead, extended that to 10-0 in the second period, and took a 10-3 advantage into the halftime break. The margin could have been larger, save for two interceptions thrown by Kiel and a fumble by Carter at the SC 12.

ND's first touchdown was the result of a 74-yard, 11-play drive, polished off by Larry Moriarty's two-yard run. Mike Johnston converted.

It was a miracle of sorts that Moriarty was even on the field on this late October day, playing before 76,459 spectators. As a high school freshman, the senior full-back survived a serious automobile accident, then six months later, contracted spinal meningitis and lay near death.

Notre Dame's field goal of 40 yards by Johnston climaxed a 50-yard movement in 12 plays. The pulse of the drive beat on bolts of 10 yards by Joe Howard, 16 by Moriarty, a pass of 19 yards from Kiel to freshman Allen Pinkett and a roughing-the-kicker penalty.

Until Southern Cal lit the scoreboard with three points just five seconds before the half, its most glowing sparkle came in the initial quarter on a 41-yard slashing dart by Anthony Gibson. But following Notre Dame's three-pointer, Joey Browner returned the ensuing kickoff 30 yards, Scott Tinsley threw stirkes of 15, 14 and 11 yards to Jeff Simmons and Steve Jordan laced a 35-yard field goal. Notre Dame, 10-3.

With its rushing game almost totally stymied by the Irish, SouCal discarded its infantry and switched to an air attack in the second half. The tactic resulted in touchdowns in each of the last two quarters, though not before ND had expanded its lead to 13-3 by virtue of Johnston's 47-yard FG. Heart of this drive was a 17-yard hookup from Kiel to Hunter.

Pass interference on ND's Chris Brown figured prominently in both of SC's touchdown drives. The first, a third-period 70-yard, seven-play journey, was scored by Harper from five yards out after Tinsley's bullets had found a haven in the arms of Tim White for 11 yards, Mark Boyer for seven, Gibson for 10 and Simmons for 24. Notre Dame, 13-10.

The elements were now in place for USC's last-minute, game-winning, controversial touchdown. Ahead by three points with less than three minutes on the clock, ND's Kiel punted 48 yards, and Browner returned nine to his 40-yard line. Tinsley threw strikes of nine yards to John Kamana, 10 to Harper and 17 to White. Then Brown's second interference penalty, which also met with heated controversy, spotted the ball just one yard away from the double stripe. Right or wrong, the officials ruled Harper scored before he fumbled, and Jordan, as did he on SC's previous marker, added the extra point to give USC a 17-13 lead.

Well, was it a touchdown, Coach Faust? "I don't comment on that stuff," he commented.

Time was running out, but the Irish weren't through, and Kiel's passes positioned them on SC's 32-yard line with time for one play. Kiel's target in the end zone was Hunter, but Browner and Darrel Hopper aggressively broke up the pass...too aggressively, according to Hunter.

"When the ball came down, I was on my back," he said. "I don't usually fall down unless somebody hits me."

Capturing six victories in seven games, John Robinson compiled the best percentage record of any Southern Cal coach against the Fighting Irish.

362

So Hunter was down, Faust was down, Notre Dame was down, Southern Cal was up and Robinson was gone...first, carried off the field by gleeful Trojans; next, to a new profession.

"It was a magnificent win for USC— in the USC tradition," exclaimed Robinson. "This exemplifies what USC football is more than anything else."

The Trojan combo of Simmons and Tinsley was outstanding. The senior QB connected on 24-of-37 passes, 11 of which were directed to Simmons.

"Simmons is one of the great players in USC's history," blandished Robinson, "and he has been magnificent this season— but he went beyond that today." This Robinson exuded without knowing Simmons had set school records for most career receptions (106), most catches in a season (56) and most yardage in a season (973).

But if USC carried off individual records, it was Notre Dame that captured team statistics. The visitors from Indiana accumulated 24 first downs to SC's 18 and outgained the home team, 392 yards to 297.

For the first time since 1974, Notre Dame failed to place legitimate All-American, though Duerson, Hunter, Zavagnin and Johnston were not completely overlooked in the process of various selections. And for the second year in a row, the Irish, with a 6-4-1 record, did not qualify for a bowl.

Southern Cal's record of 8-3-0 was adequate for a bowl invitation, but the Cardinal and Gold was still on probation. So All-Americans Matthews, Mosebar and Achica had made their college exit against Notre Dame.

Robinson, who would eventually wind up as head coach of the Los Angeles Rams, left a huge pair of shoes for Ted Tollner, his successor, to fill: 67 victories, 15 defeats, two ties— a national championship— four wins in five bowl appearances— three PAC-10 titles— six triumphs in seven games against Notre Dame.

So the men of Troy once again basked in the joy and the bliss and the rapture that was spawned from a licking of Notre Dame. Little did they know the worm was about to turn.

1983

Green Song, Second Verse

There must be something magical about October 22, provided it is mixed with a smattering of emerald green. Remember October 22, 1977 when Notre Dame, a seven-point underdog, switched from blue to green jerseys just before the kickoff and then clobbered Southern California? Remember?

Well, October 22, 1983, the Irish did it again— changed from blue to green and smashed Southern Cal for the first time since the last time they wore green. The score was 27-6.

Granted, shock waves were not as dramatic as before. And granted, a smidgen of blue graced the green jerseys this time around. But if anyone in Indiana was complaining about the end result of the dress code, they were nowhere to be found.

While in accord for the green jerseys, Coach Gerry Faust insisted on the slight trim of blue. "We'll always wear our school color (blue)," he said. "I'm not opposed to the green jerseys because they represent the Fighting Irish. But our jerseys will always have some blue because that's the color of the Blessed Mother."

Sophomore Allen Pinkett's reaction to the wearing of the green was: "Elation. But we were convinced we could beat USC in blue jerseys, or even in T-shirts."

The color green was not the only incentive afforded the Irish, either. Actor Pat O'Brien, who portrayed the title role in the movie, *Knute Rockne: All-American*, cut an audio tape which was played at the Friday night pep rally for students and players.

"Tonight is the big night, the big rally, and tomorrow is a bigger day," transmitted an emotionally-charged voice, "because it is Victory Day. So as Rock would say 'I want you to go, go, go for Notre Dame'...and bring back that football." O'Brien had made the tape just a few days before his death.

Faust was in his third season at the helm of Notre Dame's fortunes, and his record to date of 15-12-1 did not exactly incite cartwheels from Irish alumni accustomed to a more majestic plateau.

But if the goddess of victory had been lukewarm to Faust, the fickle lady was downright frigid to Ted Tollner, in his first year at the reins for Southern California. After six games, Tollner could point to only two wins and a tie, and would now brace his foundering Trojans against the Irish with a losing record for the first time since 1971. And this from a team picked No. 8 in pre-season polls.

California fans were not at a loss for words as they flooded the media with unkind verbiage about Tollner and Tommy Trojan. But Faust could empathize.

"I've been through it myself, and we're not completely through it," he said. "People just assume there's no adjustment period at USC or at Notre Dame. I sympathize with Ted and I hope USC fans will be patient like people have been here with me."

The stable that Tollner inherited was not brimmed with stakes horses, though in the fold were 11 starters from the previous year. These included Tony Slaton, Jack Del Rio, Keith Browner and Todd Spencer. But put out to pasture were the likes of Bruce Matthews, Don Mosbar, George Achica...All-Americans, three...as well as Joey Browner, Riki Gray and Jeff Simmons.

"I think we're very talented," Tollner told Street and Smith magazine, "but we're also very inexperienced. Our big question is— how fast will our young people mature?"

The fledgling coach was still looking for that answer when he brought his troops to South Bend. First, there was a draw with Florida, followed by a win over Oregon State, losses to Kansas and South Carolina, a victory over Washington State and a loss to Arizona State.

Expectations were high at Notre Dame (pre-season

pick No. 6) with the return of seven starters on defense, including linebacker Mike Larkin, tackle Mike Gann and cornerback Stacey Toran, as well as six on offense, including tackle Larry Williams, tailback Pinkett and QB Blair Kiel.

Faust felt his program was maturing and that upset wins the previous year over Michigan and Pittsburgh were important steps in the process. "We needed to go out and beat some teams people didn't think we could beat," he pointed out.

It was a damp and dreary day when the two schools confronted each other with 59,075 zealots looking on at Notre Dame Stadium. The Irish, having won four of six contests—Purdue, Colorado, South Carolina and Army on the plus side, Michigan State and Miami (Fla.) on the minus—were picked to win by 10 points.

Apparently, the forces of Faust thought the spread was too small. Late in the first quarter, ND took possession of its 20-yard line. On first down, Pinkett took a pitch-out, drifted to his right, and threw to Mark Bavaro, who had gotten behind safety Tony Brewer. The completion covered 59 yards to SC's 21. Pinkett swallowed nine yards, then on the fourth play of the drive, raced across the goal line from 11 yards out. Mike Johnston upped the score to 7-0.

"Notre Dame showed that halfback pass this season and we reminded our players about it before the game," said Tollner. "But Brewer made a mistake and came up for run support."

Pinkett tallied again in the second period, and Johnston added a field goal as Notre Dame escorted a 17-0 lead into the halftime break.

After a short punt by Troy's Troy Richardson, the Irish set goalward from their 45. On the 13th play, Pinkett scored from the nine, after having donated runs of 11 and seven yards, plus a six-yard pass gain from Steve Beuerlein, a freshman from California. To aid their cause, the Irish also accepted face mask and defensive holding penalties, compliments of USC.

Johnston tacked on the PAT, then nailed a 30-yard FG after Rick Naylor pilfered a Sean Salisbury pass, and fled

USC tailback Michael Harper scored both touchdowns in the 20-3 win over Notre Dame in 1980. In 1982 he scored both touchdowns in the 17-13 win, including a controversial last-minute play; and in 1983 he scored USC's only touchdown in the 27-6 loss.

back 22 yards. Despite an 11-yard pickup by Pinkett, the invasion stalled on SC's 13, so Faust called upon the foot of Johnston.

With zero points on the board, Tollner's dressing room strategy dictated a change of quarterbacks for the second half— Salisbury out, Tim Green in.

"I've always felt capable of leading this team," said Green, a junior transfer from El Camino college. "I've never sat on the bench in my life."

Green did supply some spark to the Trojan attack but his third quarter interception— again by Naylor— led to another Notre Dame TD. For the third time, Pinkett gathered the laurels, sprinting into paydirt from 11 yards out, the fifth play of a 42-yard trek. Other plays were gains of nine and five yards by Pinkett, eight and nine by Mark Brooks. The PAT by Johnston was true.

"When I see daylight, it's like I shift gears," Pinkett said, explaining his endearment for the end zone. "My eyes get as big as golf balls."

After sputtering for two-and-a-half quarters, the Trojan machine finally tuned its engine, traveling 80 yards in just six plays. Michael Harper scampered for five and eight yards, Green threw strikes fo 11 yards to Hank Norman and 16 to Timmie Ware, and Pat Ballage was penalized for pass interference on Norman before Harper popped across the goal line from the one. A running play for two points was unsuccessful. Notre Dame 24, Southern Cal 6— that was as near to ND as SC would get.

The dreary afternoon had turned cheery for the Irish, but there was still more than a quarter to play, and everyone on the home side of the gridiron knew of and respected the never-say-die spirit of the Trojans.

So, for insurance, Notre Dame upped its margin as Johnston riveted a 39-yard field goal. The FG followed USC's touchdown and was ignited by Alvin Miller's 29-yard kickoff return. Pinkett sparked the drive with a dart of 21 yards and Beuerlein found Joe Howard for a 12-yard gainer.

Neither team scored in the final frame, so Notre Dame's 27-6 conquest had broken a five-game losing drought against Southern Cal.

Although Pinkett rushed for 122 yards and Beuerlein showed poise with his passes, it was probably the defense which tilted the tide toward Notre Dame's favor. The Trojan touchdown was the only one yielded by ND's robust defense in the last 16 quarters.

The Fighting Irish played out their schedule by slapping Navy but then being slapped by Pittsburgh, Penn State and Air Force. Despite a mediocre slate of 6-5-0, the Irish were invited to the Liberty Bowl, where they shaded Boston College by a point. The names of Pinkett and Williams appeared on some All-American selections.

Southern Cal divided its remaining battles, overcoming California and Stanford but yielding to Washington and UCLA. At 4-6-1, the Trojans suffered their first losing season since 1961. And to make matters worse, they did not score against Washington, the first time they had been shut out in 187 games. One consolation: Slaton was a consensus All-American.

1984

ND To Hex: "Farewell"

Well, so much for the Coliseum hex. It died. For after eight grasping, disastrous stabs at victory dating back to 1966, the Irish of Notre Dame finally declawed the mystical fangs of that ol' Coliseum bug-a-boo and pierced the Trojans of Southern California into a 19-7 submission. Back home in Indiana, 'twas said the Golden Dome ne'er glowed more luminous.

Sure, the weather was miserable that November afternoon in California, a cold, drenching, soaking rain that splattered mud and goo and grime across the gridiron. But the Irish saw only radiance and warmth and a brighter path in their future.

"The rain helped us," said Notre Dame's Mike Gann. "It slowed USC's sweep down and made it easier to contain them. I loved it."

The Trojans hated it. Witness: eight fumbles, six of which were claimed by the Irish, and a pass interception— seven turnovers.

"The difference was that they played more efficiently under the conditions than we did," said USC's coach, Ted Tollner. "In ball movement, we broke about even." Tollner was alluding to the facts that Notre Dame brooked only one turnover and that his Troy troops outgained the winners, 346 yards to 242.

Both Tollner in his second year and Gerry Faust in his fourth at South Bend were under heavy fire from alumni and fans to "shape up or ship out," so to speak. Notre Dame supporters were simply not enamored with Faust's records of 5-6, 6-4-1 and 7-5 and were puzzled by his consistent ability to recruit blue-chip high school seniors but not develop, teamwise, their talents. There were rumors that Faust's contract, which had one year to run, would not be renewed, and that even his strength at recruiting would be affected by the tales.

"I don't think the rumors will hurt recruiting at all," stated Faust. "All of this negative press has actually helped us because they (prep seniors) are rallying behind the cause now."

Indeed, there was a twinkle of sheen for the 1984 Notre Dame fall as eight offensive starters and seven defensive regulars returned for duty. There was tailback Allen Pinkett, whose 18 touchdowns and 110 points in '83 snapped school records. There was sophomore Steve Beuerlein, who took command of quarterback in his fourth game as a freshman. There was All-America candidate Larry Williams, as well as Mark Bavaro, Gann and Mike Kelley.

Although chosen No. 6 in pre-season polls, Faust's gridders were upset by Purdue in their curtain raiser. Then, playing in streaks of three, Notre Dame dropped Michigan State, Colorado and Missouri, were bumped by Miami (Fla.), Air Force and South Carolina, then roped LSU, Navy and Penn State.

Still wrapped in the enigma of Southern Cal's first losing season since 1960, Tollner faced his sophomore annum with confidence.

"I was as disappointed as everyone else about last fall," he told a leading sports magazine. "But we're coming back with a vengeance."

Tollner would rely on veterans Duane Bickett, Fred Crutcher, Jerome Tyler, Tom Hallock and Jack Del Rio to lead Tommy Trojan from his doldrums. Del Rio was of All-America calibre, and Tollner called him "...the most aggressive, intense player I've ever been around".

In the vision of the media, SouCal was a question mark and, consequently, started the season unranked. To refute this, the Trojans disposed of Utah State and Arizona State, fell to LSU, then handled Washington State, Oregon, Arizona, Stanford and No. 1 Washington before kneeling to UCLA.

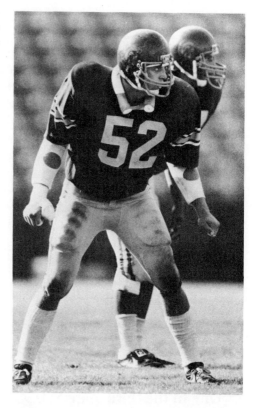

Described by USC coach Ted Tollner as "the most aggressive, intense player I've ever been around," linebacker Jack Del Rio was All-America in 1984.

Now rated No. 14 with its 8-2-0 ledger, Southern Cal entered the quagmire festival with Notre Dame as a two and one-half point favorite. Hearty souls totaling 66,432 waded into the Coliseum, though their number dwindled to about 20,000 by halftime.

Neither school splashed the scoreboard in the first quarter, but midway of the second, the Trojans waddled 67 yards to take a 7-0 lead. Along the way, Tim Green passed 15 yards to Mark Boyer, 19 to Hank Norman and 17 to Kennedy Pola, enabling freshman Ryan Knight to slosh over the goal line from three yards out. Steve Jordan added the extra point.

But before intermission, Notre Dame opened the flood gates and stormed to a 13-7 lead. The first touchdown resulted from a long 76-yard excursion, the second from a short 44-yarder. Three key passes from Beuerlein fueled the first— 20 yards to Bavaro, 37 to Milt Jackson and 11 to Tim Brown on a shovel pass for the TD. John Carney's PAT locked the score.

Referring to Jackson's big 37-yard gain, SC's Tollner said,"That play is a wide receiver delay designed to gain 10 or 12 yards, but our linebackers overran the play."

Notre Dame's go-ahead marker came when Rick DiBarbardo picked off Crutcher's fumble in mid-air, and Pinkett went to work— 12 yards, 11 and three for the touchdown. A big play, too, was Beuerlein's 18-yard heave to Ricky Gray. On the conversion attempt, the snap from center was high and Carney tried to salvage the play with a pass but it fell incomplete. ND, 13-7.

"I really wasn't that concerned at halftime," said Tollner. "Even though it was extremely sloppy, I felt we could throw the ball."

But fumbles by Green in the third period paved the way for two Irish field goals. Wally Kleine recovered the first bobble, and Carney kicked a 45-yard FG; Gann embraced the second, and Carney booted another 45-yarder. Now the Irish were perched atop a 19-7 score, and additional errors by the Trojans put a damper on their efforts to stage a comeback.

Late in the third stanza, USC drove to ND's 29 where Crutcher coughed up the ball. In the fourth, the Trojans reached Notre Dame's 37 and 25, but fumbles by Green, plus an illegal procedure penalty, aborted those aspirations. Another penalty— roughing-the-kicker by Rex Moore— doomed Tommy Trojan to a wet defeat.

"We're over the hill now," exclaimed a jovial Faust. "I think we've got the program going now. We're on a roll now."

"The biggest win we've had," echoed Beuerlein.

Naturally, the atmosphere was more somber in the USC dressing room. "Any loss hurts," uttered Tollner, "but we're the PAC-10 champion and this team has too much character not to come back and play hard."

The coach was referring to Southern Cal's date with Ohio State in the Pasadena Classic, an obligation to be filled despite season-ending setbacks to UCLA and Notre Dame.

"There will be a lot of skepticism about us now," ven-

Irish Say Aloha to Jinx at Coliseum, 19-7

Jim Murray

Next Stop, Honolulu;
USC Falls in the Rain

tured tackle Ken Ruettgers. "People are going to say we don't deserve to represent the PAC-10 in the Rose Bowl."

If some uninformed people did hang such a label on USC, they were forced to swallow their words. The Trojans hung one on the Buckeyes to finish their season at 9-3-0. They boasted a consensus All-American, too— linebacker Del Rio. And Bickett made first team on four A-A selections.

The "roll" that Notre Dame was on (according to Faust) came to an abrupt halt in the Aloha Bowl where SMU wore the lei of victory. So, as the Irish skidded to a 7-5-0 mark, the future of Faust at South Bend was once again in jeopardy.

ND's Bavaro made AP's first-team All-America cast, while the names of Williams, Gann and Kelly appeared on various second-team clubs.

Notre Dame and Southern California had now faced each other 56 times in the Glamor Game series. The Irish have won 29 of the events, the Trojans 23, and there have been four ties. In total points scored, Notre Dame has amassed 1,045, Southern Cal 872.

1985

Game 57

Weather Hot, ND Hotter

The turning point in Game No. 57 occurred before 11 seconds had transpired. Notre Dame kicked off, Randy Tanner received the ball five yards deep in his end zone and, instead of taking a touchback, attempted to run. His effort was abruptly halted at his 15-yard line when he collided with defender George Streeter. The collision dislodged the pigskin and Troy Wilson recovered for the Irish on the two. On first down, Allen Pinkett swept into the end zone, and the rest of the scuffle was downhill for the shocked Trojans.

The final score— Notre Dame 37, Southern California 3 — was the widest margin of victory for the Irish over the Trojans since 1966.

The devastating loss was yet another scar on the battered torso of Tommy Trojan in what was expected to be his season of excellence. Selected by one and all to run away with the PAC-10 title, the gladiators of Troy were also adjudged by a horde of soothsayers to be the finest college team in the land.

The offense, which had sputtered in '84, was returning seven starters. In this fold were James Fitzpatrick, Fred Crutcher, Tom Hallock and Jeff Bregel, whom coach Ted Tollner described as "...strong, fast and nasty."

Only four starters were back from a defense that ranked 12th nationally but two of those were Tony Colorito and Tim McDonald.

As did the defense in '84, Tollner surmised his offense would carry the load in '85. And, buoyed by last autumn's Top Ten ranking, Tollner viewed the upcoming season

After playing fullback in 1985, Notre Dame's Frank Stams made All-America on defense in 1988. Here he gains yardage in the 1984 game as USC's Matt Johnson closes for the tackle.

through rose-colored glasses.

"We re-established our credibility last year," said Tollner. "Now we have to continue to improve."

As the season unfolded, it appeared Tollner should have worn dark-hued spectacles. First came a conquest of Illinois, but Baylor stunned the Trojans and Arizona blanked them, 24-0. Bouncing back, USC crushed Oregon State and Stanford, yet a 3-2-0 slate on the eve of the Notre Dame conflict was a far cry from earlier expectations.

In four years as head coach at South Bend, Gerry Faust had not joined that select coterie of legends that had embellished the hallowed name of Notre Dame football...Knute Rockne, Ara Parseghian, Frank Leahy. And this, the last year of his contract, had reduced itself to a do-or-die situation— restore Notre Dame to its powerhouse plateau, or...sorry, Gerry, no renewal.

"Reality," observed tailback Pinkett, "can be a cold

smack in the face." But, noted Faust, "We were a dominating football team at the end of the year," and the reality he faced seemed encouraging—seven offensive and nine defensive regulars returning from that squad.

One returnee was Pinkett, who rushed for 1,105 yards in '84, and, in so doing, inscribed his name as record holder in several school rushing categories. Another was quarterback Steve Beuerlein, coming off shoulder surgery; also Tim Scannell, Wally Kleine and placekicker John Carney, perfect on 25 PATs last fall.

Pollsters did not view the Irish in the howitzer class, but did concede they had enough rifles to assign them a No. 13 ranking.

That grade disappeared when Notre Dame bowed to Michigan in its season opener. And the best the Irish could manage in their next four games was a split—cuffing Michigan State and Army, being cuffed by Purdue and Air Force. That was it with Southern Cal on the horizon—three losses and a paltry twosome in victories.

Even so, the invaders from Troy were established as only a one-point favorite. The South Bend Chamber of Commerce arranged a glorious autumn day for football, clear and a balmy 72 degrees. So, drawn by the rays of Ol' Sol and by the terrorists of Troyland, a capacity crowd of 59,075 avid fans jammed the crevices of Notre Dame Stadium.

Many of them missed Pinkett's instant touchdown, it happened so quickly. But all were witnesses to Notre Dame's 71-yard spree that ended in the end zone on the ninth play when Beuerlein rolled out from the six. Three weighty plays kept the trek alive—flings from Beuerlein of 14 yards to Frank Stams and 13 to Reggie Ward, along with a 23-yard run by Stams. Carney added the PAT to both touchdowns.

Carney then extended Notre Dame's lead to 17-0 by booting a 26-yard field goal early in the second quarter. To position Carney, the Irish moved 73 yards, punctuated by a 12-yard bolt by Pinkett, plus tosses of 28 and nine yards from Beuerlein to Tom Rehder, and spiced by two penalties on the Trojans—face mask (against Louis Brock) and personal foul.

Fullback Allen Pinkett scored 284 points during the 1983-84-85 seasons, including the thousandth point against USC. In 1987 he scored 110 points, a single-season Irish record.

Southern Cal's Aaron Emanuel failed to make a first down on fourth-and-one, giving Notre Dame the ball just 55 yards away from pointland. Terry Andrysiak hurled 22 yards to Andy Heck, Hiawatha Francisco dashed for 17 and, on the seventh play, Stams broke two tackles and crashed over from the five. Carney's kick escalated ND to a 24-0 lead.

Now the Irish had a comfortable spread, but Pat Ballage wanted more. So the strong safety filched a pass thrown by Sean Salisbury and raced 35 yards with ball in hand. That presented Carney with an opportunity to drill a 33-yard FG, which he did.

Sporting a 27-0 lead at halftime, one would think there was no cause for any theatrics by the host team. But when the Irish came out for the third period— surprise, surprise, surprise...they had changed from blue to emerald jerseys. And Faust had assured one and all that Notre Dame would not be attired in green. Closer scrutiny, however, revealed he had added "...at kickoff."

It was, perhaps, a gimmick not needed by the ravaging Irish, and some scribes felt Faust was "...rubbing it in."

377

"I didn't take it that way," commented Tollner. "I think they had planned to wear the green jerseys no matter what the score was. We were responsible for our embarrassment. If we had taken care of our own program, we wouldn't have been so far behind."

Some of Tollner's players were not so tolerant. "It really bugs me," stated cornerback Matt Johnson. "Pulling something like that was unnecessary. You could call it bush." And Bregel called the ploy "...childish."

Yet maybe the sham served as a pump for the Trojans...momentarily, at least. Momentarily, because the Trojans filed from their dressing room and proceeded to put three points on the scoreboard. But, alas, it was merely a fleeting flirtation with lets-get-back-in-the-game-fellows, for, with those sparse trio of points, the Trojans had fired the iron from their cannon.

It was a 39-yard field goal hoisted from the foot of Don Shafer, and it was made possible by Salisbury's heaves of 14 yards to Crutcher and 11 to Erik McKee as the Trojans moved 43 yards in eight plays. But 27-3 was as close as SC would get to the cavorting Irish.

ND then matched SC's FG with one of their own. Carney did the honors and his swing carried 43 yards. The opportunity came after Marv Spence gobbled up a fumble by Crutcher, and Pinkett spun off runs of 10 and nine yards. Notre Dame 30, USC 3.

There's always an after-dinner mint to every feast, and the Irish wanted to leave this banquet with a sweet taste. So the fighting guys of Faust utilized the legs of Francisco and Tom Monahan and a face mask penalty against USC to maneuver 56 yards to the Trojan eight-yard stripe. From there, Andrysiak hooked up with Joel Williams for six points, and Carney made it seven, and the final score of 37-3 was recorded in the annals of Blue and Gold history.

Oh, yes— Southern Cal did engineer one last-ditch endeavor to dignify the score, reaching the ND four-yard line. But Crutcher lost the ball, Notre Dame found it, and the Trojans began preparations for a long and dismal flight back to Los Angeles.

"There are no excuses for us losing like we did today,"

lamented Tollner. "We were ready mentally and physically, but Notre Dame came out and just pounded us. The opening-kickoff fumble set the stage for the whole game."

For nose tackle Eric Dorsey of Notre Dame, it was a "...to the victor go the spoils" philosophy. "As for me, I don't like USC," he said. "The way I looked at it, we could have rubbed it in their faces."

Though demolished on the scoreboard, Southern Cal actually outgained Notre Dame, 346 yards to 335, and matched the winners in first downs at 18.

Both teams displayed fine offensive performances by individuals. For the Irish, Pinkett piled up 110 yards on 28 carries. For the Trojans, Salisbury threw successfully 21 times, and became USC's all-time leader in pass completions at 318. But it was a record not cherished, for his number of attempts (34) was uncharacteristic of SC's normal method of attack, which is based on a running game and long drives.

"We're not a Boston College-Doug Flutie-type team," acknowledged Salisbury. "And when we got so far behind, we had to get out of our game plan."

At the time, Notre Dame's resounding thumping of USC seemed to secure Faust's shaky grip on his job. And this was further enhanced with subsequent wins over Navy and Mississippi. But then followed a 30-point loss to Penn State, a narrow setback by LSU and a baneful 51-point decimation by Miami (Fla.). Faust's contract was not renewed.

During his five years in South Bend, Faust won 30 games, lost 26 and tied one. His record against Southern California was 3-2-0.

For the fourth consecutive fall, Notre Dame failed to place a consensus All-American, though Pinkett and Scannell were listed on some teams. Tony Furjanic's 147 tackles were the most in a single season since Bob Crable's 167 in 1981.

After their wipe-out by Notre Dame, the Trojans rebounded to beat Washington State, lost to California and Washington, repelled UCLA and Oregon, then lastly, succumbed to Alabama in the Aloha Bowl. That computed to a 6-6-0 read-out, which programmed an uncer-

379

tain future for Tollner.

As anticipated, SC's Bregel was a consensus All-American and McDonald was selected on one team.

Notre Dame had now captured three games in a row over big rival Southern California, a startling turnaround from the dominance of USC in the seventies and early eighties. And, while the Trojans had no crystal ball in which to view the future, well...perhaps it's better they didn't.

1986

GAME 58

Pluck Of The Irish

The way John Carney, Notre Dame's placekicker deluxe, figured it was that if Johnny Baker and Frank Jordan, Southern California's premier placekickers of yore, could do it...well, by golly, so could he.

Flashbacks: 1931, Baker's field goal in the final minute beats Notre Dame, 16-14; 1978, Jordan's last-play FG stuns Notre Dame, 27-25.

Those heroics of yesteryear may or may not have crossed Carney's mind as he planted himself in the shadow of the Trojan goalpost, his team in arrears by two points and a similar number of seconds on the clock.

Holder Steve Beuerlein looked up at his senior teammate. "Johnny, this is the game that's going to make it (the season) all worthwhile," he said. Carney nodded: "I know it."

The snap was true. The ball was spotted on the nine, then drilled arch-wise through the uprights by Carney's patented swing. Time had expired and Notre Dame had plucked a dramatic, improbable, come-from-behind 38-37 win.

"I knew it would be my last collegiate kick," exulted Carney, whose 21st field goal set a school season record, "and I didn't want to have any regrets."

It was a rewarding finish to a season of frustrations, near-misses and disappointments for the Fighting Irish whose 4-6-0 slate on the eve of the Southern Cal melee belied a level of performance that, with a touch of luck here and there, could have been 9-1-0.

The year brought a new head coach to the Blue and

381

Gold of the Notre Dame campus, one charged with the task of steering a misguided locomotive back on track. His name was Lou Holtz, the mastermind who had infused with vigor ailing programs at North Carolina State, Arkansas and Minnesota.

"Notre Dame is the job I've dreamed of since I was a kid," Holtz told a *Street and Smith* reporter.

He would have been in a distinct minority if he had not entertained such a vision, but the array of athletes who greeted him did not induce him into flips of ecstasy. Among the group, however, Holtz could count five returning starters on offense, six on defense...such veterans as Wally Kleine, Cedric Figaro, Mike Kovaleski, Beuerlein and Tim Brown. Holtz's number one priority, though, was to move players into what he believed were their proper playing positions. Flanker Mark Green went to running back, linebacker Robert Banks to defensive line, inside linebacker Mark Nigro and tight end Tom Gorman to defensive line, and tight end Tom Rehder to offensive tackle.

Those people who tell the public in advance which teams are loaded and which are not were not impressed with the antics of Holtz, and ignored his club when it came time to identify the powers-to-be.

The Irish lost to No. 3 Michigan by a single point, bowed to Michigan State by five, then crushed Purdue. No.2 Alabama was a convincing victor, but Pittsburgh slipped by ND by only one point. Then followed one-sided verdicts over Air Force, Navy and SMU before No. 3 Penn State shaded the Irish by five points and No. 8 LSU did the same by two.

While the folks at South Bend had taken steps to solve their coaching dilemma, an air of uncertainty clouded the tenure of USC coach Ted Tollner, now starting his fourth season draped in rumblings and grumblings from disgruntled fans and alumni.

Wrote a citizen from Orange County: "Keep Ted. Keep Ted. Keep Ted. But don't mind me. I'm a UCLA fan."

That was part of the disenchantment for Tollner: his inability to beat UCLA. The other part was his inability to beat Notre Dame. And, overall, an anemic 19 victories

Two-time All-America for Southern Cal in 1985-86, Jeff Bregel's efforts were futile as the Trojans lost to the Irish in both years.

and a draw in 37 games was shy of Trojan standards.

For his showdown session, Tollner welcomed back four starters on offense and six on defense, not a deep well from which to draw. Of these veterans, however, there were some aces, spearheaded by All-American guard Jeff Bregel and supported by David Cadigan, Tim McDonald, Marcus Cotton and Ryan Knight. Much would depend on QB Rodney Peete's recovery from a torn Achilles tendon.

The Trojans broke quickly from the gate and racked up four straight triumphs—Illinois, Baylor, Washington and Oregon. But, while basking in the sunlight of contentment, rain drops suddenly appeared in the form of reversals at the hands of Washington State and Arizona State. Stanford, Arizona and California returned brightness to the Trojan scene, but UCLA again cast a veil of darkness, summing up USC's record at 7-3-0 as the encounter with ND loomed next up.

As the kickoff neared, Holtz singled out individuals from both teams upon whom he deemed praise could be heaped. First, it was his own Brown, a flanker of renown.

"Tim (Brown) is the most gifted, talented player that I've ever been around," lauded Holtz. "He's an instinctive

Irish Give USC, Maybe Tollner, the Boot

Jim Murray

This Merits Call to Colors for the Irish

"OK, Hennessy, it's OK to tootle the flute. Go ahead, McCarthy, thump the old bassoon, while I the pipes do play. Give MacNamara a drink and ask him does he know Galway Bay.

"It's OK to wear green. It's OK to be Irish that day.

"Things are just fine in Glocca Morra. Tell Danny Boy, the pipes, the pipes are playing, all right.

"Give us a chorus of Where the River Shannon Flows, sauce player, get around the keyboard, we'll have a chorus of Mother Machree. I'll Take You Back, Kathleen, to where your heart has ever been. Get your shawl, Macushla, we'll be after having a jig this night.

"Up ... ed Up Clancy Up Rooooo-man! ... hear it for dear old Dono

"Was ... 'e ever a grander game? Co... you write one for Hollywood ... would sell out the Music Hall ... ver?

"Is ther ... part here for the President? Would Paddy O'Brien win an O...?

"In the lilt of Irish laughter, can you hear the angels sing?

"Was there ever a happier ending—38–37 with the clock running out and the lads all running to the line of scrimmage in their gold helmets with the grace of God purring in their hearts?

"Break out the potcheen. Light a candle. Pass the stew. Put a bit of corned beef in the cabbage. Who cares if there's overheads in the chowder?

USC's Tim McDonald can't face it as Notre Dame's players celebrate after a field goal on the last play gave them their comeback win.

Notre Dame Wins on Last Play, 38-37

By MAL FLORENCE
Times Staff Writer

The USC-Notre Dame series is a historic one, and thrilling games, improbable endings and controversy have been part of the package over the years.

Place Saturday's game at the Coliseum in all of those categories.

Notre Dame won, 38–37, on John Carney's 19-yard field goal as time ran out, capping a surging comeback from a 37-point deficit in the fourth quarter before a crowd of 70,614 and a national television audience.

The Irish have lost a lot of close games to some of the nation's best teams this season. Now it was their turn to be the beneficiary.

USC's players flopped on the turf in obvious dejection after Carney's game-winning field goal. The kicker was mobbed by his teammates.

Carney might not have been in a position to make the kick if All-American flanker Tim Brown hadn't returned a punt 56 yards in the final minutes.

This was also a game that some USC players thought was taken away from them by an official's call when the Trojans led, 37–27, and were on the verge of putting the

Please see USC, Page 9

CBS Misses the Winning Field Goal

In an embarrassing mistake, CBS was showing its national audience a commercial Saturday while Notre Dame's John Carney was kicking

---

athlete and he makes things happen."

Of SC's Peete, Holtz extolled: "We don't get a particularly good pass rush, and I don't think there is any way in the world we can get to Rodney (Peete)."

But Beuerlein, Notre Dame's team leader, was more concerned about the game proper than the characters in its cast. "We're looking at USC as our bowl game," he said. "Traditionally, it's the biggest game of the year for us. I can't think of a better way to end my career than with a fourth consecutive victory over the Trojans."

Well, Brown was on the field and Beuerlein was on the field and Peete was on the field and all their cohorts were on the field and 70,614 patrons were in the Coliseum stands to watch them on a pleasant, warm day in late November.

Southern Cal received the opening kickoff and marched 40 yards in eight plays, sputtered, and Don Shafer kicked a 48-yard field goal. The biggest gain along the way was a 12-yard aerial from Peete to Ken Henry.

The 3-0 lead was short-lived as ND's Steve Lawrence pilfered a Peete pass on his 37-yard line. After moving on the ground for nine straight plays, Beuerlein rifled a 12-yard bullet to Brown, then, after a holding penalty, connected with Andy Heck over the middle for six points. Carney's attempt for a seventh digit was blocked by McDonald.

The Trojans regained the lead in the second quarter when Lou Brock, son of the former St. Louis Cardinal baseballer, intercepted a wayward toss by Beuerlein and raced 58 yards to happyville. Shafer's PAT put the Trojans atop a 10-6 score.

After the interception, Holtz yanked Beuerlein, which didn't surprise the senior quarterback. "I knew that if I threw one away, I was out," he remarked. "Coach didn't want any turnovers."

Terry Andrysiak replaced the starter, but ND's drive was stopped by the Trojans on the SC 36-yard stripe, and SC took over. Peete promptly burned the ND defense with a 53-yard bomb to Lonnie White, and Leroy Holt plunged through the right side of his line for a three-yard TD. Shafer lifted the score to 17-6.

Steve Beuerlein is the only Irish quarterback to play in four victories over USC (1983-84-85-86). During his career, he completed 473 of 850 passes for 6,527 yards, both school records.

385

After receiving the ensuing kickoff, Holtz interrupted his sideline pacing long enough to ask Beuerlein: "Are you ready now to play football?"

"Yes, sir," replied the eager Beuerlein, whose parents were in the stands. "You won't regret it."

Starting at their 18-yard line, the Irish erased 76 yards in 11 plays, spotlighted by completions of 22 and 20 yards from Beuerlein to Milt Jackson. From the six, Beuerlein was sacked for a nine-yard loss, so Carney popped in and popped a 33-yard field goal.

Notre Dame kicked off and Peete threw a 22-yard strike to Randy Tanner. With time running out in the first half, Shafer lined up for a 60-yard field goal effort. To the chagrin of the visitors, astoundingly, he made it— clearing the crossbar with about five yards to spare. It was a school and PAC-10 record, and boosted USC to a 20-9 advantage.

"When I went to the locker room, I was feeling there was no way we would be denied this victory," said Shafer.

Shafer was gleeful, but Holtz was fuming at halftime and his anger was compounded when Pernell Taylor fumbled on the first play of the third frame and Keith Davis claimed the errant ball for the Trojans. This led to a 23-yard FG by Shafer. USC, 23-9.

But the Irish retrieved those three points with Carney's 32-yard field goal following a 66-yard drive. A 17-yard fling from Beuerlein to Tony Eason was the impetus for the movement.

Now it was USC's turn to score and Skip Holtz, son of the ND coach, assisted the achievement. His roughing-the-kicker penalty kept alive a 70-yard spree that sent Todd Steele over the goal line from a yard away on the 15th play. Shafer's PAT was up and over, and USC was up, 30-12.

"Jeez, my own son," chuckled Holtz, the coach.

Holtz's chortle turned to a grin when Brown slashed his way for 57 pulsating yards on the ensuing kickoff and Beuerlein hooked up with freshman Braxston Banks for a 22-yard marker. The Irish were back in the game, trailing 30-20, after Beuerlein teamed with Jackson for a two-point conversion.

USC's Don Shafer kicked the longest field goal in series' history, a 60-yarder in 1986.

Notre Dame tallied 18 points in the final period, but not until SouCal extended its lead to 37-20 on a one-yard keeper by Peete and a PAT by Shafer. It was a 67-yard journey in 11 plays, sparked by a 17-yard pass from Peete to Paul Green.

Down 17 points with 12:26 on the clock, it was buckle-up or hit-the-road time for the Irish. So, drawing in their collective breaths, the Irish swept 69 yards in just three plays, the last being a 42-yard TD heave from Beuerlein to Jackson, who outfought defender Junior Thurman. On the first play, the same twosome had connived for a 27-yarder. Notre Dame went for two, made it but was penalized, then settled for Carney's extra point. SC, 37-27.

Striving to protect their dwindling lead, the battlers from Troy swarmed through the Irish defense all the way to the five-yard line. On third down, fullback Todd Steele was stopped by an aroused Irish defense. Now fourth-

and-inches, the Trojans snubbed an FG chip-shot, opting instead for a first down. Keeping the ball, Peete slammed over a mass of bodies but, according to the officials, did not advance the ball sufficiently for a first down.

Peete was livid in his disagreement with the decision and his loss of poise cost the Trojans 15 yards for unsportsmanlike conduct.

"I really don't get mad at officials' calls," Peete said, "but when you only have two inches to go, you only have to fall forward. I not only thought I had made the first down, I thought I made it by over a yard. Then an official marked it as a losing yardage. It was a very bad call, the worst I've ever seen. They didn't even measure it. Then I lost my cool."

Tollner didn't criticize the officials, but did agree with his quarterback. "I can't imagine needing two inches when a pile goes forward like that, we didn't make it. But the head linesman had a better view than I did."

Rejuvenated by the chivalry of their defense who may or may not have gotten an assist from the officials, Notre Dame's offense maneuvered 80 yards in eight plays for a touchdown. Beuerlein swallowed 49 yards with an aerial to Brown, then topped off the excursion with a five-yard TD toss to Banks. At this stage, ND needed two more points and Beuerlein made them materialize when he spotted Heck on the goal line.

The Irish had crept to within two points of SC, but time was their enemy. After the kickoff, the defensive unit again did its job and forced the home team to punt. Cradling the ball on his 28-yard stripe, Brown sped 56 yards to Troy's 16-yard line.

"From the time the ball came off the punter's foot, I knew we were going to have a good return," exclaimed Brown. "I headed to the right and saw no one over there. It was just a matter of getting behind the wall of blockers."

Playing safe, Notre Dame executed five rushing plays, moving to the one-yard line. With one tick and one tock on the clock, the Irish called a timeout, injected Carney into the game and his last-play field goal sent the Irish leaping into the air and the Trojans sprawling on the turf. The 38-37 setback was USC's fourth straight to the Irish.

"It was a classic game in a classic series," said a joyful
Holtz. "I can't think of a finer way to end the season. Our
players fought their hearts out. I'm just so proud of this
team."

Tollner was shaken by the emotional impact of the
game, especially its stirring finish. "We played as well as
we can," he said, "but that's a kind of game that hurts
deep."

Shedding his grief, Tollner still found a spot of admiration for Notre Dame's All-American flanker, Brown. "Tim
Brown is an excellent football player," he stated. "It's

*Placekicker John Carney's last-second field goal
nipped USC by a point in 1986, capping a sensational
Notre Dame rally. It was his eighth field goal against
the Trojans, the most in the series.*

almost impossible to stop him. He does so many things so well."

Defensively, the Irish were paced by Kovaleski, Kleine and Banks. Offensively, Green rushed for 119 yards and Beuerlein was true on 18-of-27 passes for 285 yards and four touchdowns, a school record.

"Steve has played well all year," said Holtz. "He's a fine quarterback. He's had his troubles, but he deserved to go out a winner."

While Peete completed only 10 passes for Southern Cal, his total offense for the season reached 2,262 yards, second all-time high in school history.

But his performance, along with those of All-Americans Bregel and McDonald and all their mates, could not save Tollner from dismissal as SC's head coach. His last game, a 16-7 setback by Florida in the Citrus Bowl, firmed his season at 7-5-0. In four autumns, Tollner won 26 games, lost 20 and tied one. In eight games against chief rivals UCLA and Notre Dame, Tollner was one-and-seven.

In short, that was simply not acceptable to the people of Troy or to the standards of Heritage Hall.

1987

GAME 59

Easy Come, Easy Go

Sometimes when something comes too easy—it escapes just as easily. Case in point: Game 59. Southern California took the opening kickoff and swept 70 uncontested yards in a mere six plays to send Notre Dame reeling under a 7-0 deficit before two-and-a-half minutes had expired.

But the offensive blockbuster of the Trojans and the pseudo defense of the Irish were farces. For, abruptly, the game turned to Notre Dame, which by the end of the third quarter, had posted 26 unanswered points on its way to a 26-15 victory.

"I told our players that we had to make things happen right off the bat," mused ND coach Lou Holtz. "That shows you how much I know."

Holtz may have been amused at his backfired strategy, but USC quarterback Rodney Peete was puzzled. "I thought we would dominate the whole game after that drive," he said. "Maybe we relaxed, thinking it was a piece of cake."

If there was any cake on the field, it was Southern Cal's defense which was mitigated to crumbs by a Notre Dame battering ram that aggregated 439 total yards, all but 88 on the ground.

It was an unpropitious beginning for new Southern California coach Larry Smith, fresh from the arid land of Arizona, against prime opponent Notre Dame.

Smith replaced Ted Tollner, now with refuge in the NFL, courtesy of frigid Buffalo. Upon opening practice, Smith was hailed by 13 starters from Tollner's 7-5-0 outfit. Versatile QB Peete was back to head the offense, as were Ryan Knight, John Katnik and Dave Cadigan, an All-America prospect. Tough Marcus Cotton was back to lead the defense, as were Keith Davis and Rex Moore, whose 206 tackles were tops for the '86 squad. A preseason ranking of No. 14 gave rise to the hope that the Trojans were on their way back to prosperity.

Meanwhile, back at the Golden Dome, Holtz was laying the framework for his second season, one that he felt had possibilities. "We aren't as talented as we were a year ago," he stated, "but I think we may have a better team."

Only 11 starters returned, four on defense and seven on offense. But one of those was flanker Tim Brown, a bona fide, indisputable game-breaker and legitimate Heisman Trophy candidate who held Notre Dame's single-season record of 1,937 all-purpose yards.

"Tim may be the best football player I've ever seen," opined Holtz. "He has good work habits, a lot of personal pride, and he does things you can't teach or coach."

Tailback Mark Green, fullback Braxston Banks and center Chuck Lanza were on hand to assist Brown, as were such defensive stalwarts as Ned Bolcar, Cedric Figaro and Frank Stams, coming off an injury and shifted from fullback. The quarterback position was tinged with uncertainty. Backup Terry Andrysiak would get the nod, but waiting in the wings was exciting Tony Rice, a Proposition 48 casualty in '86. This shaky situation may have been one reason Notre Dame was omitted when the Top Twenty teams were predicted for 1987.

No matter, retorted the Irish, who stepped out and captured four of their first five games prior to the SouCal debacle. Michigan, Michigan State, Purdue and Air Force were the victims, with Pittsburgh the topper.

USC had participated in six battles prior to "The Glamor Game," beheading Boston College, California, Oregon State and Washington, but being scalped by Michigan State and Oregon.

So, while there was no national championship at stake when the two schools paired off in South Bend on a chilly, gloomy day in late October, it was still the incomparable rivalry of a Southern California-Notre Dame confrontation, and this was sufficient to attract a capacity crowd of 59,075 people.

"Southern Cal," said ND's Green. "It's in the air. The game is a big deal for all of us."

And Holtz remained in awe about the magic of this cross-country rivalry. "I didn't realize the magnitude of the game until I got here," he said.

Being a freshman coach at USC, Smith could be forgiven if his sentiments were not centered as much on the aura of "the game" as they were on the exploits of Brown and how to stop him.

"They move him (Brown) all around, throw the ball to him, toss the ball to him on sweeps and reverses, put him in the slot on I-formations," said Smith. "Our offense is the key to our success. We've got to keep Brown off the field."

And, as previously pointed out, SC's offense did indeed start out handsomely, spurting right down the field for a quick touchdown. Steve Webster scooted for seven and nine yards, Peete threw to Webster for 19, to Paul Green for 27, then to John Jackson for nine yards and six points. Quin Rodriguez's kick made it 7-0, USC.

The Southern Cal machine had spurted and then it sputtered as Notre Dame scored two touchdowns, sand-

Flanker Tim Brown's 56-yard punt return set up the winning Irish field goal in 1986. Peter Rausch (64) and Linc Coleman (23) urge him on from the sideline. In 1987 Brown became Notre Dame's seventh Heisman trophy winner.

wiched in between a couple of field goals to enter the halftime recess with a 20-7 lead.

Ted Gradel manipulated both field goals: one from 26 yards to cap a 56-yard drive, the other from 32 yards just two seconds before halftime to seal another 56-yard thrust. The first was an infantry movement churned from the legs of Green, Rice and Banks; the second went airborne as Kent Graham, filling in briefly for an injured Rice, connected with Ricky Watters for 12 yards and to Brown for 11 and 16.

In between, Rice sped 26 yards on an option keeper for a touchdown to culminate an 88-yard, 12-play expedition, and Brown scored from five yards out to end a 90-yard, 11-play drive. Key plays leading to the first TD were a 12-yard sprint by Banks and a 14-yard pass from Rice to Brown. To sustain the second TD drive, Brown raced 17 yards on a reverse, Anthony Johnson picked up 12, and a Rice-to-Watters fling netted 19. Gredel's foot twice swung true and the Irish sat comfortably on a 13-point lead.

"They were just basically knocking us off the ball with dive plays," remarked Tim Ryan, USC's defensive tackle.

The Trojans muffed an opportunity to close the gap early in the third quarter. After recovering an Irish fumble, Peete's pass was intercepted by Bolcar on ND's 27-yard stripe.

That was incentive enough to set the Irish off on another scoring spree. Following an abbreviated 27-yard punt by Chris Sperles, Rice scrambled for nine yards, Green rumbled for 13, then crossed the double stripe from 11 yards away. A run for two points was scuttled, but Notre Dame had built a healthy 26-7 lead.

Acting on instructions from Smith, Sperles was sacrificing distance for hang-time on his punts—a device to prevent long runbacks by Brown.

"We don't have a kicker who can get it out 40 to 45 yards," explained Smith. "I'm not going to kick line drives and have him (Brown) run it back on us. I'll give him the 10 yards. I'm not a dummy."

Southern Cal's deepest threat in the third period ended when Jackson, hounded by cornerback Marv

Spence, dropped Peete's pass at the Irish four-line line. It was Jackson's second miscue, having failed to hold on to an aerial at the Irish 22 in the second frame.

"I'll take responsibility when I can't make the big play," commented Jackson. "It gave Notre Dame an advantage."

But "surrender" is not taught inside the gates of Troy, so the Trojans, not knowing they were beaten, pushed and shoved their way to a last-minute touchdown. It was an 89-yard journey in 10 plays, climaxed by a five-yard jaunt by Scott Lockwood. Most of the yardage was consumed by Peete's passes— 15 and 14 yards to Erik Affholter, plus 18 to Randy Tanner. Peete also hit Tanner for a two-point conversion, which etched the final score at 26-15, favor of Notre Dame for the fifth straight year. It was the longest winning streak enjoyed by the Irish over the Trojans since 1957-61.

"Notre Dame deserved to win," conceded Smith. "They beat us with the basics. They ran the ball down our throats. Our defense played badly and our offense didn't help us at all."

As expected, Brown did go to New York, where he was awarded the Heisman Trophy for 1987, the seventh player wearing the Blue and Gold to be so honored. For the year, Brown averaged 14 yards every time he handled the ball, accounting for 1,843 all-purpose yards.

"Stopping Brown is like trying to grab hold of a piece of electricity," observed Purdue Coach Fred Akers.

Naturally, Brown was a consensus All-American, as was USC's Cadigan. Lanza and Bolcar were second team selections for Notre Dame.

Believe it or not, there is reality after the ND-SC encounter, so each club went its separate ways. The herd of Holtz knocked off Navy, Boston College and Alabama, then was floored by Penn State, Miami (Fla.) and, in the Cotton Bowl, by Texas A&M. The Irish finished 8-4-0 with a final rank of No. 17.

Out West, the students of Smith spun off four consecutive wins, smiting Washington State, Stanford, Arizona and UCLA before yielding to Michigan State in the Rose Bowl. The Trojans' mark matched the Irish: 8-4-0, adequate for a final rank of No. 18.

1988

No. 1 Upsets No. 2

For the first time in the long and fabled history of the Notre Dame-Southern California series, both teams would enter their annual duel with unscathed records of 10 victories, zero defeats and zero ties. For the first time, the schools would meet holding the top two ranks in the nation—Irish No. 1, Trojans No. 2. Not surprisingly, just about every one agreed the national championship was on the line.

But there was no agreement by the two head coaches in their perspective of the game.

Notre Dame's Lou Holtz: "It's just like any week in the season. At least, I'm trying to keep it that way."

Southern Cal's Larry Smith: "The winner will be the odds-on favorite to win it all. It's truly America's game."

With his direct approach, Smith may have fingered the potential of the affair more accurately. For the winner, as Smith forecast, did indeed become, in time, the nation's standard bearer. Unfortunately for Smith, it was not his Trojans, who fell to the mighty Irish, 27-10. Later, in the Fiesta Bowl, Notre Dame methodically subdued No. 4 West Virginia and, ignoring the outcry of Coach Jimmy Johnson of Miami, wore the crown of national champion for the eighth time since the polls were initiated in 1936. To the credit of the Irish mystique, that's more times than any other college.

A wealth of talent roamed the halls of Troy as Smith prepared for his second autumn. Eight regulars on offense were back from his 8-4-0 rookie year...stellar stars such as QB Rodney Peete, who as a junior set a dozen

396

They Take Case to Polls Today
USC-Notre Dame Game Could Settle Score for No. 1

By MAL FLORENCE,
Times Staff Writer

Seldom has there been a regular
season-ending college football
game of more magnitude than the
USC-Notre Dame matchup today

●Matchups Worth Watching: Shav Glick's story, Page 10.

However, considering that USC
and Notre Dame are traditional
rivals with prestigious football programs dating to the 1920s, today's

national championship aspect of
the game, saying that the Irish will
have to play unbeaten West Virginia in the Jan. 2 Fiesta Bowl. He

though he's mindful that his team
still must play Michigan in the Jan.
2 Rose Bowl.
"The winner will be the odds-on
favorite to win it all," he said. "It's
truly America's game."
That Notre Dame and USC have

school career, season and game records in passing and total offense; running back Steven Webster, the PAC-10 rushing champ; leading receiver Erik Affholter; and tight ends Paul Green and Scott Galbraith.

But "...defense could be our rock," predicted Smith, casting a hopeful eye on seven returnees, including such veterans as Tim Ryan, Dan Owens, Mark Carrier and Cleveland Colter.

Pre-season polls tabbed Southern Cal at No. 6. "I knew we'd be picked high," said Smith. "But if we get everybody back that we have on paper, we could be quite a bit better than last year. And that, quite frankly, is our goal."

Notre Dame did not fare as prominently in the late August polls, coming in at No. 13. One magazine, perhaps influenced by the departure of Heisman winner Tim Brown, predicted the Irish seemed destined to lose two games, possibly three or four.

Though his native talent had been, for the most part, dormant, Tony Rice was expected to surface his abilities at quarterback in '88. Six other offensive starters would join him, including running backs Mark Green and Braxston Banks; Ricky Watters, shifted from tailback to flanker; Andy Heck, moved from tight end to tackle; and guard Jeff Pearson.

Holtz's defense appeared solid, especially the linebacking corps anchored by Wes Pritchard, Frank Stams and Ned Bolcar. Other defensive mainstays included George Streeter and Stan Smagala.

As previously mentioned, both institutions ripped through the 10 opponents on their respective schedules, free of tarnish.

Notre Dame had to survive two narrow verdicts, Michigan by two points and Miami by one as the Hurricanes staged a late rally but fell short when a last-minute try for a two-point conversion failed. Other victims were Michigan State, Purdue, Stanford, Pittsburgh, Air Force, Navy, Rice and Penn State.

Southern California escaped a squeaker, too...a 28-27 decision over Washington in the sixth contest. The margin of victory in the other games ranged from four to 50 points, the losers being Boston College, Stanford, Oklahoma, Arizona, Oregon, Oregon State, California, Arizona State and the huge crosstown rival up Westwood way, UCLA.

Despite riding the crest of the polls for five weeks, Notre Dame arrived in the land of Troy as four-and-one-half-point underdogs.

"I think we're the most underrated No. 1 team that ever lived," said guard Tim Grunhard. "For the No. 1 team to play the No. 2 team and be four-and-one-half-point underdogs..."

Holtz concurred. "I think this team is underrated, even though we're No. 1," he added."I've read articles that people sent to me all year saying we were lucky against this team or that team."

Fans throughout the country focused their attention on Los Angeles as these two Goliaths squared off against each other on a breezy, late November day. Television cameras would beam the action back to them, and 93,829 fans were in the Coliseum to witness first hand this classic imbroglio.

Well, it was billed as a classic— 10-0-0 for both clubs, Irish No. 1, Trojans No. 2, you know. But someone forgot to tell the SouCal players. A fumble here, an interception there, another fumble, costly penalties, crippling QB sacks, another interception— it all added up to a 20-7 lead for Notre Dame by halftime. And even 20x70 eyesight could see that oval called a football just wasn't bouncing the Trojan way.

Perhaps the tone of the day was rooted very early in the game— on ND's very first play, in fact. With his team pushed back to the two-yard line, Rice faked, dropped

Irish cornerback Stan Smagala's 64-yard interception return in the third quarter may have been the turning point in Notre Dame's 27-10 thumping of Southern Cal in 1988.

deep into his end zone and let fly a 55-yard bomb to "Rocket" Raghib Ismail, who, by the way, had returned two kickoffs for touchdowns in the Rice game, the first such ND feat since 1922.

Rice had suggested the surprise play to Holtz, maybe as a shock to offset the loss of key offensive players Watters and Tony Brooks, whom Holtz had dispatched back to Indiana for rule infractions. Holtz went along with the call — "I thought it would be a good chance for us to get out of a hole," he acknowledged.

The explosive tactic served only to do just that, but on Notre Dame's next possession, Rice rolled out on an option, cut inside safety Carrier, turned upfield, evaded Tracy Butts and dashed 65 yards to notch six points, and stake Notre Dame to a lead it would not relinquish.

"We felt strongly that they would run the option, and we'd planned for it," said Smith. "But they ran some of our defenders out of there, and Rice made a great cut. That just goes to show you, it can be feast or famine." Diminutive Reggie Ho hammered the extra point.

Late in the first quarter, USC's Aaron Emanuel fumbled a swing pass, and Stams recovered for ND a scant 19 yards away from SC's citadel. Staying on the ground behind Green, Rice and Anthony Johnson, the Irish scored in five plays, Green bursting over from the two. Ho hummed the PAT. Notre Dame, 14-0.

In the second period, Southern Cal squandered a scoring chance when Ricky Ervins lost a fumble on the

Notre Dame Delivers Its 1-2 Punch

Jim Murray

A Wee Bit O' the Irish This Day

USC Turns Contest Into a Bobble for No. 1 Rather Than Classic

By MAL FLORENCE, *Times Staff Writer*

In the most important game of the season and, for that matter, one of the most significant in any season, USC made just enough errors to help Notre Dame retain its No. 1 college football ranking.

Clearly, though, Notre Dame was the better team Saturday at the Coliseum, winning 27-10 before a

Irish 19-yard line. But the Trojans forced a punt, and now, tired of playing the role of benefactor, decided to do something for themselves. So, rolling 66 yards in 11 plays, USC registered a touchdown and provided their supporters a glimmer of hope. A 26-yard pass from Peete to Affholter, short runs by Emanuel, and a personal foul penalty against Jeff Alm on Galbraith moved the ball to the one-yard stripe from where Scott Lockwood took a pitch-out and scored. Quin Rodriguez's PAT pulled USC to within seven points.

But not for long. As the bands readied themselves for the halftime show, Peete pitched a pass intended for John Jackson. The fleet flanker slipped and fell, and the ball whizzed past him and into the waiting arms of Smagala, who waltzed past massive Derrell Marshall and Lockwood on his way to an untouched, 64-yard touchdown sprint. The PAT kick failed, but Smagala's theft may have been the blow of crush to the home team.

"It was a post-corner pattern, and he (Jackson) was open when he cut and fell down," remarked Peete, who was playing with a banged-up shoulder, courtesy of a vicious hit by Stams. "I'm not blaming John— it was my interception— but a team just can't afford to make mistakes like that against the No. 1 team."

In addition to the hampered shoulder, Peete had just recovered from an attack of measles and, leading up to the game, from a bout with laryngitis.

"Rodney wasn't in very good physical shape at the end of the first half," said Smith. "It was questionable about his playing the second half." But he did, rallying his forces to a field goal that came within an eyelash of being a touchdown.

400

Starting at their 44-yard line, the Trojans, by virtue of a 16-yard toss from Peete to Jackson and a 10-yard pickup by Emanuel, moved to ND's four-yard stripe, first down. The Irish stopped cold two dives by Emanuel, then watched the Trojans move backwards five yards when Marshall was cited for a false start. Peete overthrew Galbraith on third down, and USC settled for a 26-yard FG by Rodriguez. At the end of the third quarter, Notre Dame led, 20-10.

Since the weapons of Troy had been dulled, Notre Dame could emerge victorious with no further scoring, but the Irish did emblazon the scoreboard one more time. It was a 70-yard, 10-play drive built on a 23-yard screen pass from Rice to Johnson and runs of 13, six and seven yards by Rice. Green scored from one yard away and Ho converted, finalizing the score at 27-10.

Lou Holtz, Notre Dame's astute coach, stops his sideline pacing long enough to question a controversial call.

The valiant Trojans executed one last-ditch effort to produce points in the ebbing moments, but the drive perished at the Irish 10-yard line. The triumph was the sixth straight for Notre Dame over Southern Cal, the longest streak by either school since the series started in 1926. And that bore hard on the USC seniors, who never enjoyed the sweet smell of success over the Irish.

"The loss was tough to take today, because it means the seniors will never be able to say 'I beat Notre Dame,'" lamented Peete. "It's something we'll have to live with the rest of our lives."

Naturally, Holtz had a comment. "Our football team is prettier than I am, but that's about it," he threw in. "They don't play pretty all the time, but they sure play together as a team."

Holtz may have been alluding to the fact that his warriors, though victors, were outgained, 356 yards to 253, and made only eight first downs to USC's 21.

"Whenever you play a big game like this, you can't afford a lot of big mistakes, and that's what we did," said Smith. "Notre Dame has a fine team and they played an excellent game, and that's why they won. We didn't do anything to help ourselves win."

Southern Cal did not regroup for the Rose Bowl, and was cut down by Michigan. Its record of 10-2-0 earned a rating of No. 7. No Trojan made All-America, although Peete and Affholter were second team choices. During his college career, Peete completed 630 passes in 1,081 attempts for 8,225 yards, all USC school records. He also was runner-up in the Heisman Trophy voting, and was named PAC-10 offensive player-of-the-year.

As stated earlier, Notre Dame rapped the Mountaineers in the Fiesta Bowl to claim national championship laurels. And its 12-0-0 slate was the best ever for the Blue and Gold. The Irish could point to three All-America selectees, too—Heck, Stams and Mike Stonebreaker.

So now "The Glamor Game" had passed its 60th milestone of furious combat. Notre Dame had won 33 games, Southern California 23, and four had ended all-even. In total points scored, the Irish were out front, 1173 to 937.

Appendix

Notre Dame-Southern California Football Series
1926-1988

G	YEAR	DATE	AT	WON	ND-USC SCORE	ND-USC SERIES
1	1926	Dec 4	LA	ND	13-12	1-0-0
2	1927	Nov 26	CHI	ND	7-6	2-0-0
3	1928	Dec 1	LA	USC	14-27	2-1-0
4	1929	Nov 16	CHI	ND	13-12	3-1-0
5	1930	Dec 6	LA	ND	27-0	4-1-0
6	1931	Nov 21	SB	USC	14-16	4-2-0
7	1932	Dec 10	LA	USC	0-13	4-3-0
8	1933	Nov 25	SB	USC	0-19	4-4-0
9	1934	Dec 8	LA	ND	14-0	5-4-0
10	1935	Nov 23	SB	ND	20-13	6-4-0
11	1936	Dec 5	LA	tie	13-13	6-4-1
12	1937	Nov 27	SB	ND	13-6	7-4-1
13	1938	Dec 3	LA	USC	0-13	7-5-1
14	1939	Nov 25	SB	USC	12-20	7-6-1
15	1940	Dec 7	LA	ND	10-6	8-6-1
16	1941	Nov 22	SB	ND	20-18	9-6-1
17	1942	Nov 28	LA	ND	13-0	10-6-1
	1943	No game				
	1944	No game				
	1945	No game				
18	1946	Nov 30	SB	ND	26-6	11-6-1
19	1947	Dec 6	LA	ND	38-7	12-6-1
20	1948	Dec 4	LA	tie	14-14	12-6-2
21	1949	Nov 26	SB	ND	32-0	13-6-2
22	1950	Dec 2	LA	USC	7-9	13-7-2
23	1951	Dec 1	LA	ND	19-12	14-7-2
24	1952	Nov 29	SB	ND	9-0	15-7-2
25	1953	Nov 28	LA	ND	48-14	16-7-2
26	1954	Nov 27	SB	ND	23-17	17-7-2
27	1955	Nov 26	LA	USC	20-42	17-8-2
28	1956	Dec 1	LA	USC	20-28	17-9-2
29	1957	Nov 30	SB	ND	40-12	18-9-2
30	1958	Nov 29	LA	ND	20-13	19-9-2
31	1959	Nov 28	SB	ND	16-6	20-9-2
32	1960	Nov 26	LA	ND	17-0	21-9-2
33	1961	Oct 14	SB	ND	30-0	22-9-2
34	1962	Dec 1	LA	USC	0-25	22-10-2
35	1963	Oct 12	SB	ND	17-14	23-10-2
36	1964	Nov 28	LA	USC	17-20	23-11-2
37	1965	Oct 23	SB	ND	28-7	24-11-2
38	1966	Nov 26	LA	ND	51-0	25-11-2

39	1967	Oct 14	SB	USC	7-24	25-12-2
40	1968	Nov 30	LA	tie	21-21	25-12-3
41	1969	Oct 18	SB	tie	14-14	25-12-4
42	1970	Nov 28	LA	USC	28-38	25-13-4
43	1971	Oct 23	SB	USC	14-28	25-14-4
44	1972	Dec 2	LA	USC	23-45	25-15-4
45	1973	Oct 27	SB	ND	23-14	26-15-4
46	1974	Nov 30	LA	USC	24-55	26-16-4
47	1975	Oct 25	SB	USC	17-24	26-17-4
48	1976	Nov 27	LA	USC	13-17	26-18-4
49	1977	Oct 22	SB	ND	49-19	27-18-4
50	1978	Nov 25	LA	USC	25-27	27-19-4
51	1979	Oct 20	SB	USC	23-42	27-20-4
52	1980	Dec 6	LA	USC	3-20	27-21-4
53	1981	Oct 24	SB	USC	7-14	27-22-4
54	1982	Nov 27	LA	USC	13-17	27-23-4
55	1983	Oct 22	SB	ND	27-6	28-23-4
56	1984	Nov 24	LA	ND	19-7	29-23-4
57	1985	Oct 26	SB	ND	37-3	30-23-4
58	1986	Nov 29	LA	ND	38-37	31-23-4
59	1987	Oct 24	SB	ND	26-15	32-23-4
60	1988	Nov 26	LA	ND	27-10	33-23-4

Notre Dame's Record Vs. Southern California At:

	G	W	L	T	POINTS	AVERAGE
Chicago	2	2	0	0	20-18	10.0— 9.0
South Bend	26	17	8	1	544-357	20.9—13.7
Los Angeles	32	14	15	3	609-562	19.0—17.6
TOTALS	60	33	23	4	1173-937	19.6—15.6

Series Scoring, 1926-1988

SCORING	ND	USC
Touchdowns	158 for 948 pts.	132 for 792 pts.
1-point conversions	115 for 115 pts.	87 for 87 pts.
2-point conversions	5 for 10 pts.	4 for 8 pts.
Field goals	32 for 96 pts.	16 for 48 pts.
Safeties	2 for 4 pts.	1 for 2 pts.

Score By Quarters

	1	2	3	4	TOTAL
Notre Dame	287	353	279	254	1173
Southern California	168	244	233	292	937

ND has scored 640 points in the first half and 533 in the second half. USC is 412-525. Of the series' 2110 points, 1052 have been scored in the first half and 1058 in the second half.

How They Scored

	ND	USC	SERIES TOTALS
Total Touchdowns	158	132	290
TDs by rushing	101 (64%)	76 (57%)	177 (61%)
TDs by passing	45 (28%)	42 (32%)	87 (30%)
TDs by other means	12 (08%)	14 (11%)	26 (09%)

Conversions: ND has converted 120 of its 158 touchdowns (76%), USC 91 of its 132 touchdowns (76%). In the first 23 games of the series, USC converted only 41% (15-for-37).

"Other" scoring: ND, 6 interceptions, 2 kickoff returns, 2 blocked punts, 1 punt return and 1 fumble recovery in endzone. USC, 6 kickoff returns, 5 interceptions and 3 fumble recoveries in endzone.

"20 Pointers"

Players who have scored 20 or more points in the series, 1926-1988

PLAYER-TEAM	TD	PAT	FG	TOTAL	YEARS
Anthony Davis, USC	11	1*	0	68	1972-73-74
Johnny Lattner, ND	6	0	0	36	1951-52-53
Larry Conjar, ND	5	0	0	30	1965-66
Charles White, USC	5	0	0	30	1978-79
Michael Harper, USC	5	0	0	30	1980-82-83
Allen Pinkett, ND	5	0	0	30	1983-84-85
John Carney, ND	0	6	8	30	1984-85-86
Emil Sitko, ND	4	0	0	24	1947-48-49
O.J. Simpson	4	0	0	24	1967-68
Jon Arnett, USC	3	5	0	23	1955
Paul Hornung	3	4	0	22	1955-56

Long Scoring Plays (50 Yards Or More)

RK	YDS	PLAYER-TEAM	YR	TYPE OF PLAY
1	102	Anthony Davis, USC	1974	Kickoff return
2	97	Anthony Davis, USC	1972	Kickoff return
3t	96	Russell Saunders, USC	1929	Kickoff return
3t	96	Laurence Langley, USC	1936	Interception return
3t	96	Bob Livingstone, ND	1947	Run from scrimmage
3t	96	Anthony Davis, USC	1972	Kickoff return
7	95	Paul Hornung, ND	1956	Kickoff return
8t	94	Jim Sears, USC	1950	Kickoff return
8t	94	Joe Heap, ND	1953	Punt return
10	92	Pat Doyle, ND	1957	Kickoff return
11	85	Eric Penick, ND	1973	Run from scrimmage
12	80	Paul O'Conner, ND	1930	Run from scrimmage
13t	78	Coy McGee, ND	1946	Run from scrimmage
13t	78	Jim Morse, ND	1955	Pass from Paul Hornung
15t	76	*Schindler/Berryman, USC	1936	Run/lateral from scrimmage
15t	76	Emil Sitko, ND	1947	Run from scrimmage
17	72	Jim Morse, ND	1954	Run from scrimmage
18	65	Tony Rice, ND	1988	Run from scrimmage
19t	64	Jon Arnett, USC	1955	Pass from Jim Contratto
19t	64	Stan Smagala, ND	1988	Interception return
21	63	Randy Simmrin, USC	1976	Pass from Vince Evans
22	62	Tom McDonald, ND	1963	Interception return
23	60	Benny Sheridan, ND	1959	Run from scrimmage
24t	58	Andy Puplis, ND	1937	Run from scrimmage
24t	58	Charles Phillips, USC	1974	Interception return
24t	58	Lou Brock, USC	1986	Interception return
27t	57	Bob Gladieux, ND	1968	Run from scrimmage
27t	57	Kris Haines, ND	1978	Pass from Joe Montana
29t	53	Frank Carideo, ND	1929	Pass from John Elder
29t	53	Bobby Peoples, USC	1940	Run from scrimmage
29t	53	Bruce Dyer, USC	1971	Interception return
32	52	Al Hunter, ND	1975	Run from scrimmage
33t	51	John Chevigny, ND	1928	Run from scrimmage
33t	51	Mike Layden, ND	1934	Pass from Bill Shakespeare
35	50	Johnny Lattner, ND	1953	Run from scrimmage

*Ambrose Schindler ran 11 yards and lateraled to Dick Berryman who ran 65 yards. Note that Anthony Davis has the two longest runs in the series and is tied for the third longest.

Series Touchdown Passes

NO.	YR	PASSER-RECEIVER	TEAM	YDS
1	1926	Art Parisian— John Niemiec	ND	23
2	1927	Morley Drury— Russell Saunders	USC	7
3	"	Charles Riley— Ray Dahman	ND	28
4	1928	Don Williams— Marger Apsit	USC	19
5	"	Don Williams— Lowrey McCaslin	USC	5
6	1929	Marshall Duffield— Marger Apsit	USC	48
7	"	John Elder— Frank Carideo	ND	53
8	1930	Marchmont Schwartz— Frank Carideo	ND	7
9	"	Marchmont Schwartz— Paul O'Conner	ND	7
10	1932	Homer Griffith— Bob McNeish	USC	21
11	1933	Bob McNeish— Homer Griffith	USC	3
12	1934	Bill Shakespeare— Mike Layden	ND	51
13	1935	Bill Shakespeare— Wally Fromhart	ND	25
14	"	Wally Fromhart— Wayne Millner	ND	43
15	1936	Nevin McCormick— Larry Danbom	ND	17
16	1937	Grenville Landsdell— Gene Hibbs	USC	7
17	1938	Ollie Day— Al Krueger	USC	36
18	1941	Bob Robertson— Ralph Heywood	USC	20
19	"	Bill Musick— Bill Bledsoe	USC	5
20	"	Angelo Bertelli— Fred "Dippy" Evans	ND	17
21	1942	Angelo Bertelli— Creighton Miller	ND	48
22	"	Angelo Bertelli— Bob Livingstone	ND	12
23	1946	George Patterson— Leon Hart	ND	22
24	1948	Frank Tripucka— Leon Hart	ND	45
25	1949	Frank Spaniel— Leon Hart	ND	36
26	1954	Joe Heap— Jim Morse	ND	12
27	"	Jim Contratto-Chuck Griffith	USC	21
28	1955	Paul Hornung— Jim Morse	ND	78*
29	"	Jim Contratto— Jon Arnett	USC	64
30	"	Jim Contratto— Don McFarland	USC	12
31	1956	C.R. Roberts— Hillard Hill	USC	10
32	"	Bob Williams— Bob Wetoska	ND	10
33	"	Jim Conroy— Don Voyne	USC	15
34	1957	Bob Williams— Monty Stickles	ND	17
35	"	Bob Williams— Monty Stickles	ND	7
36	"	George Izo— Dick Prendergast	ND	8
37	1958	Don Buford— Hillard Hill	USC	41
38	"	Don Williams— Norm Odyniec	ND	21
39	1959	Ben Charles— Angelo Coia	USC	13
40	1961	Daryle Lamonica— Jim Kelly	ND	17
41	1962	Bill Nelson— Fred Hill	USC	14
42	1963	Pete Beathard— Mike Garrett	USC	12
43	1964	John Huarte— Jack Snow	ND	22
44	1964	Craig Fertig— Fred Hill	USC	23
45	"	Craig Fertig— Rod Sherman	USC	15

Series Touchdown Passes (Cont.)

46	1965	Troy Winslow—John Thomas	USC	8
47	1966	Coley O'Brien—Jim Seymour	ND	13
48	"	Coley O'Brien—Jim Seymour	ND	39
49	"	Coley O'Brien—Dan Harshman	ND	23
50	1968	Coley O'Brien—Joe Theismann	ND	13
51	"	Steve Sogge—Sam Dickerson	USC	40
52	1969	Jimmy Jones—Terry DeKraai	USC	19
53	"	Jimmy Jones—Sam Dickinson	USC	14
54	1970	Jimmy Jones—Sam Dickinson	USC	45
55	"	Joe Thiesmann—John Cieszkowski	ND	9
56	"	Joe Thiesmann—Larry Parker	ND	46
57	1971	Jimmy Jones—Edesel Garrison	USC	31
58	"	Mike Rae—Edesel Garrison	USC	24
59	1972	Tom Clements—Willie Townsend	ND	5
60	"	Tom Clements—Gary Diminick	ND	11
61	"	Tom Clements—Mike Creaney	ND	10
62	1973	Pat Haden—Lynn Swann	USC	27
63	1974	Tom Clements—Pete Demmerle	ND	29
64	"	Pat Haden—Anthony Davls	USC	7
65	"	Pat Haden—Jake McKay	USC	18
66	"	Pat Haden—Jake McKay	USC	45
67	"	Pat Haden—Shelton Diggs	USC	16
68	1975	Vince Evans—Shelton Diggs	USC	21
69	1976	Rob Hertel—Shelton Diggs	USC	6
70	"	Vince Evans—Randy Simmrin	USC	63
71	"	Rusty Lisch—Vagas Ferguson	ND	17
72	1977	Joe Montana—Ken MacAfee	ND	13
73	"	Joe Montana—Ken MacAfee	ND	1**
74	"	Rob Hertel—Calvin Sweeney	USC	14
75	"	Rusty Lisch—Speedy Hart	ND	4
76	1978	Paul McDonald— Kevin Williams	USC	30
77	"	Paul McDonald—Dan Garcia	USC	35
78	"	Joe Montana—Kris Haines	ND	57
79	"	Joe Montana—Pete Holohan	ND	2
80	1979	Paul McDonald—Dan Garcia	USC	12
81	"	Paul McDonald—Kevin Williams	USC	12
82	1984	Steve Beuerlein—Tim Brown	ND	11
83	1985	Terry Andrysiak—Joel Williams	ND	8
84	1986	Steve Beuerlein—Braxton Banks	ND	22
85	"	Steve Beuerlein — Milt Jackson	ND	32
86	"	Steve Beuerlein—Braxton Banks	ND	5
87	1987	Rodney Peete—John Jackson	USC	9

*Longest   **Shortest

Series Field Goals

NO.	YEAR	PLAYER	TEAM	YDS
1	1931	Johnny Baker	USC	33
2	1939	Milt Piepul	ND	29
3	1947	Fred Early	ND	29
4	1952	Bob Arrix	ND	27
5	1954	Sam Tsagalakis	USC	34
6	1960	Joe Perkowski	ND	31
7	1961	Joe Perkowski	ND	49
8	1963	Ken Ivan	ND	33
9	1964	Ken Ivan	ND	25
10	1966	Joe Azzaro	ND	38
11	1967	Ricky Aldridge	USC	22
12	1970	Vic Ayala	USC	19
13	1972	Bob Thomas	ND	45
14	1973	Bob Thomas	ND	32
15	"	Bob Thomas	ND	33
16	"	Bob Thomas	ND	32
17	1974	Dave Reeve	ND	20
18	1975	Dave Reeve	ND	27
19	"	Glen Walker	USC	35
20	1976	Glen Walker	USC	46
21	1978	Joe Unis	ND	47
22	"	Frank Jordan	USC	39
23	"	Joe Unis	ND	26
24	"	Frank Jordan	USC	37
25	1979	Chuck Male	ND	42
26	1980	Eric Hipp	USC	22
27	"	Harry Oliver	ND	30
28	"	Eric Hipp	USC	17*
29	1982	Mike Johnston	ND	40
30	"	Steve Jordan	USC	35
31	"	Mike Johnston	ND	47
32	1983	Mike Johnston	ND	30
33	"	Mike Johnston	ND	39
34	1984	John Carney	ND	45
35	"	John Carney	ND	45
36	1985	John Carney	ND	26
37	"	John Carney	ND	33
38	"	Don Shafer	USC	39
39	"	John Carney	ND	43
40	1986	Don Shafer	USC	48
41	"	John Carney	ND	33
42	"	Don Shafer	USC	60**
43	"	Don Shafer	USC	23
44	"	John Carney	ND	32
45	"	John Carney	ND	19

Series Field Goals (Cont.)

NO.	YEAR	PLAYER	TEAM	YDS
46	1987	Ted Gradel	ND	26
47	"	Ted Gradel	ND	32
48	1988	Quin Rodriquez	USC	26

*Shortest **Longest

Notre Dame Individual Scoring In Series, 1926-1988

PLAYER	TD	PAT	FG	TOTAL	YR(S)
Charles Riley	1	0	0	6	1926
Harry O'Boyle	0	1	0	1	1926
John Niemiec	1	0	0	6	1926
Ray Dahman	1	1	0	7	1927
John Chevigny	1	0	0	6	1928
Frank Carideo	2	3	0	16	1928-29-30
Albert Gerber	1	1	0	7	1929
Joe Savoldi	1	0	0	6	1929
Paul O'Conner	2	0	0	12	1930
Nick Lukats	1	0	0	6	1930
Charles Jaskwhich	0	3	0	3	1930-31
Steve Banas	1	0	0	6	1931
Marchy Schwartz	1	0	0	6	1931
Mike Layden	2	0	0	12	1934
Wally Fromhart	1	4	0	10	1934-35
Wayne Millner	1	0	0	6	1935
Bill Shakespeare	1	0	0	6	1935
Bob Wilke	1	0	0	6	1936
Nevin McCormick	1	0	0	6	1936
Andy Puplis	1	2	0	8	1935-37
Mario Tonelli	1	0	0	6	1937
Milton Piepul	2	1	1	16	1939-40
Benny Sheridan	1	0	0	6	1939
Bob Hargrave	1	0	0	6	1941
Steve Juzwik	1	2	0	8	1941
Fred "Dippy" Evans	1	0	0	6	1941
Creighton Miller	1	0	0	6	1942
Bob Livingstone	2	0	0	12	1942-46
John Creevy	0	1	0	1	1942
Coy McGee	2	0	0	12	1946
Leon Hart	3	0	0	18	1946-48-49
Fred Earley	0	7	1	10	1946-47
Gerry Cowhig	1	0	0	6	1946
Emil Sitko	4	0	0	24	1947-48-49
John Penelli	1	0	0	6	1947

Notre Dame Individual Scoring In Series, 1926-1988

Name					Years
Alfred Zmijewski	1	0	0	6	1947
Steve Oracko	0	4	0	4	1948-49
John Petibon	2	0	0	12	1949-51
Frank Spaniel	1	0	0	6	1949
Bill Barrett	1	0	0	6	1949
Bob Williams	1	0	0	6	1950
Vincent Meschivitz	0	1	0	1	1950
Johnny Lattner	6	0	0	36	1951-52-53
Neil Worden	2	0	0	12	1951-53
Bob Joseph	0	1	0	1	1951
Bob Arrix	0	0	1	3	1952
Joe Heap	1	0	0	6	1953
Ralph Guglielmi	0	5	0	5	1953
Pat Bisceglia	1	0	0	6	1953
Jack Lee	0	1	0	1	1953
Jim Morse	3	0	0	18	1954-55
Don Schaefer	1	3	0	9	1954
Paul Hornung	3	4	0	22	1955-56
Bob Williams	2	0	0	12	1956-58
Bob Wetoska	1`	0	0	6	1956
Ron Toth	1	0	0	6	1957
Monty Stickles	2	5	0	17	1957-59
Pat Doyle	1	0	0	6	1957
Jim Cotty	1	1*	0	8	1957-58
Aubrey Lewis	0	1	0	1	1957
Dick Prendergast	1	0	0	6	1957
Nick Pietrosante	1	0	0	6	1958
Norm Odyniec	1	0	0	6	1958
Gerry Gray	2	0	0	12	1959
Joe Perkowski	0	5	2	11	1960-61
Daryl Lamonica	3	0	0	18	1960-61
Bob Scarpitto	1	0	0	6	1961
Jim Kelly	1	0	0	6	1961
Joe Rutkowski	1	0	0	6	1961
Tom McDonald	1	0	0	6	1963
Ken Ivan	0	8	2	14	1963-64-65
Bill Wolski	2	0	0	12	1963-64
Jack Snow	1	0	0	6	1964
Larry Conjar	5	0	0	30	1965-66
Joe Azzaro	0	7	1	10	1966-67
Tom Schoen	1	0	0	6	1966
Jim Seymour	2	0	0	12	1966
Dan Harshman	1	0	0	6	1966
Nick Eddy	1	0	0	6	1966
Dave Martin	1	0	0	6	1966
Terry Hanratty	1	0	0	6	1967
Ron Dushney	1	0	0	6	1968
Scott Hempel	0	9	0	9	1968-69-70

Notre Dame Individual Scoring In Series, 1926-1988

Player	TD	PAT	FG/2pt	Pts	Years
Bob Gladieux	1	0	0	6	1968
Joe Theismann	3	0	0	18	1968-70
Bill Barz	1	0	0	6	1969
Denny Allan	1	0	0	6	1969
John Cieszkowski	2	0	0	12	1969
Larry Parker	1	0	0	6	1970
Andy Huff	1	0	0	6	1971
Bob Thomas	0	6	4	18	1971-72-73
Willie Townsend	1	0	0	6	1972
Gary Diminick	1	0	0	6	1972
Mike Creaney	1	0	0	6	1972
Tom Clements	1	0	0	6	1973
Eric Penick	1	0	0	6	1973
Wayne Bullock	1	0	0	6	1974
Dave Reeve	0	9	2	15	1974-75-76-77
Pete Demmerle	1	0	0	6	1974
Mark McLane	1	0	0	6	1974
Al Hunter	1	0	0	6	1975
Tom Lopienski	1	0	0	6	1975
Kris Haines	1	1*	0	8	1975-78
Vagas Ferguson	3	0	0	18	1976-79
Russ Lisch	1	0	0	6	1976
Dave Mitchell	1	0	0	6	1977
Joe Montana	2	0	0	12	1977
Tom Domin	0	1*	0	2	1977
Ken MacAfee	2	0	0	12	1977
Jay Case	1	0	0	6	1977
Speedy Hart	1	0	0	6	1977
Joe Unis	0	1	2	7	1978
Pete Buchanan	1	0	0	6	1978
Pete Holohan	1	0	0	6	1978
Chuck Male	0	2	1	5	1979
Jim Stone	1	0	0	6	1979
Harry Oliver	0	1	1	4	1980-81
Phil Carter	1	0	0	6	1981
Larry Moriarty	1	0	0	6	1981
Mike Johnston	0	4	4	16	1982-83
Allen Pinkett	5	0	0	30	1983-84-85
Tim Brown	2	0	0	12	1984-87
John Carney	0	6	8	30	1984-85-86
Steve Beuerlein	1	0	0	6	1985
Frank Stams	1	0	0	6	1985
Joel Williams	1	0	0	6	1985
Andy Heck	1	1*	0	8	1986
Braxston Banks	2	0	0	12	1986
Milt Jackson	1	1*	0	8	1986
Ted Gradel	0	2	2	8	1987

Notre Dame Individual Scoring In Series, 1926-1988

Tony Rice	2	0	0	12	1987-88
Mark Green	3	0	0	18	1987-88
Stan Smagala	1	0	0	6	1988
Reggie Ho	0	3	0	3	1988
Safeties	-	-	-	4	1954-59

*2-point conversion

134 ND players have scored against USC.
109 have scored touchdowns.

Southern California Individual Scoring In Series, 1926-1988

PLAYER	TD	PAT	FG	TOTAL	YR(S)
Morton Kaer	1	0	0	6	1926
Don Williams	1	1	0	7	1926-28
Russell Saunders	3	0	0	18	1927-28-29
Marger Apsit	2	0	0	12	1928-29
Jesse Hibbs	0	2	0	2	1928
Tony Steponovitch	1	0	0	6	1928
Lowrey McCaslin	1	0	0	6	1928
Gaius Shaver	2	0	0	12	1931
Johnny Baker	0	1	1	4	1931
Bob McNeish	1	0	0	6	1932
Ernie Smith	0	1	0	1	1932
Homer Griffith	2	0	0	12	1932-33
Irvine Warburton	2	0	0	12	1933
Lawrence Stevens	0	1	0	1	1933
David Davis	1	0	0	6	1935
Glenn Thompson	1	0	0	6	1935
Homer Beatty	0	1	0	1	1935
Dick Berryman	1	0	0	6	1936
Laurence Langley	1	0	0	6	1936
James Henderson	0	1	0	1	1936
Gene Hibbs	1	0	0	6	1937
Al Krueger	1	0	0	6	1938
Bill Anderson	1	0	0	6	1938
Phil Gasper	0	1	0	1	1938
Grenville Lansdell	2	0	0	12	1939
Ambrose Schlinder	1	0	0	6	1939
Robert Jones	0	2	0	2	1939
Bob Peoples	1	0	0	6	1940
Ralph Heywood	1	0	0	6	1941
Bill Bledsoe	1	0	0	6	1941
Bob Robertson	1	0	0	6	1941
Johnny Naumu	1	0	0	6	1946

Southern California Individual Scoring In Series, 1926-1988

Jack Kirby	1	1	0	7	1947
Bill Martin	2	0	0	12	1948
Dean Dill	0	2	0	2	1948
Jim Sears	2	0	0	12	1950-51
Frank Gifford	1	1	0	7	1950-51
Des Koch	1	0	0	6	1953
Sam Tsagalakis	0	3	1	6	1953-54
Aramis Dandoy	1	0	0	6	1953
Jim Contratto	1	0	0	6	1954
Chuck Griffith	1	0	0	6	1954
Ed Fourch	0	1	0	1	1954
Ellsworth Kissinger	1	3	0	9	1955-56
Jon Arnett	3	5	0	23	1955
C.R. Roberts	1	0	0	6	1955
Bob Isaacson	0	1	0	1	1955
Don McFarland	1	0	0	6	1955
Jim Conway	1	0	0	6	1956
Hillard Hill	2	0	0	12	1956-58
Rex Johnston	1	1	0	7	1956-57
Don Voyne	1	0	0	6	1956
Ernie Zampose	1	0	0	6	1956
Tom Maudlin	1	0	0	6	1957
Don Zachik	0	1	0	1	1958
Jerry Traynham	1	0	0	6	1958
Angelo Coia	1	0	0	6	1959
Ben Wilson	2	0	0	12	1962
Tom Lupo	0	1	0	1	1962
Fred Hill	2	0	0	12	1962-64
Craig Fertig	1	0	0	6	1962
Pete Beathard	1	0	0	6	1963
Dick Brownell	0	4	0	4	1963-64
Mike Garrett	2	0	0	12	1963-64
Rod Sherman	1	0	0	6	1964
John Thomas	1	0	0	6	1965
Tim Rossovich	0	1	0	1	1965
O.J. Simpson	4	0	0	24	1967-68
Rikki Aldridge	0	3	1	6	1967
Sandy Durko	1	0	0	6	1968
Vic Ayala	0	8	1	11	1968-69-70
Sam Dickerson	3	0	0	18	1968-69-70
Terry DeKraai	1	0	0	6	1969
Clarence Davis	2	0	0	12	1970
Bob Chandler	0	1*	0	2	1970
Pete Adams	1	0	0	6	1970
John Vella	1	0	0	6	1970
Edesel Garrison	2	0	0	12	1971

Southern California Individual Scoring In Series, 1926-1988

Player					Years
Mike Rae	0	7	0	7	1971-72
Sam Cunningham	2	0	0	12	1971-72
8ruce Dyer	1	0	0	6	1971
Anthony Davis	11	1*	0	68	1972-73-74
Chris Limahelu	0	7	0	7	1973-74
Lynn Swann	1	0	0	6	1973
Jake McKay	2	0	0	12	1974
Shelton Diggs	3	0	0	18	1974-75-76
Charles Phillips	1	0	0	6	1974
Glen Walker	0	5	2	11	1975-76
Ricky Bell	1	0	0	6	1975
Vince Evans	1	0	0	6	1975
Randy Simmrin	1	0	0	6	1976
Mario Celotto	1	0	0	6	1977
Frank Jordan	0	2	2	8	1977-78
Lynn Cain	1	0	0	6	1977
Calvin Sweeney	1	0	0	6	1977
Kevin Williams	2	0	0	12	1978-79
Dan Garcia	2	0	0	12	1978-79
James Hunter	0	1*	0	2	1978
Charles White	5	0	0	30	1978-79
Eric Hipp	0	8	2	14	1979-80
Michael Harper	5	0	0	30	1980-82-83
Marcus Allen	1	0	0	6	1981
Steve Jordan	0	5	1	8	1981-82-84
Todd Spencer	1	0	0	6	1981
Ryan Knight	1	0	0	6	1984
Don Shafer	0	4	4	16	1985-86
Lou Brock	1	0	0	6	1986
Leroy Holt	1	0	0	6	1986
Todd Steele	1	0	0	6	1986
Rodney Peete	1	0	0	6	1986
John Jackson	1	0	0	6	1987
Quin Rodriquez	0	2	1	5	1987-88
Scott Lockwood	2	0	0	12	1987-88
Randy Tanner	0	1*	0	2	1987
Safety	-	-	-	2	1950

*2-point conversion
114 USC players have scored against ND.
81 have scored touchdowns.

NOTRE DAME COACHES Vs. SOUTHERN CALIFORNIA

	G	W	L	T
Knute Rockne	5	4	1	0
Hunk Anderson	3	0	3	0
Elmer Layden	7	4	2	1
Frank Leahy	10	8	1	1
Terry Brennan	5	3	2	0
Joe Kuharich	4	3	1	0
Hugh Devore	1	1	0	0
Ara Parseghian	11	3	6	2
Dan Devine	6	1	5	0
Gerry Faust	5	3	2	0
Lou Holtz	3	3	0	0
TOTALS	60	33	23	4

SOUTHERN CALIFORNIA COACHES Vs. NOTRE DAME

	G	W	L	T
Howard Jones	15	6	8	1
Sam Barry	1	0	1	0
Jeff Cravath	6	1	4	1
Jesse Hill	6	2	4	0
Don Clark	3	0	3	0
John McKay	16	8	6	2
John Robinson	7	6	1	0
Ted Tollner	4	0	4	0
Larry Smith	2	0	2	0
TOTALS	60	23	33	4

Series Attendance

	G	ATT.	AVG.
At Los Angeles	32	2,504,087	78,253
At South Bend	26	1,402,202	53,931
At Chicago	2	198,924	99,462
TOTALS	60	4,105,213	68,420

Series Highs and Lows

MOST FIRST DOWNS
31	ND	1966
30	SC	1978
29	ND	1964
29	SC	1979
28	ND	1970
28	ND	1986
28	ND	1987

FEWEST FIRST DOWNS
1 SC	1936
1 SC	1950
4 ND	1933
5 ND	1928
5 ND	1938
5 SC	1952
5 ND	1975

MOST YARDS RUSHING
517	ND	1946
397	ND	1947
373	ND	1954
351	ND	1987
336	ND	1953

FEWEST YARDS RUSHING
-4	SC	1961
17	SC	1949
34	SC	1936
45	SC	1941
53	SC	1960

MOST YARDS PASSING
526	ND	1970
358	ND	1978
311	SC	1979
293	ND	1986
286	ND	1979

FEWEST YARDS PASSING
4	SC	1950
10	ND	1952
10	ND	1963
18	SC	1927
18	ND	1960
18	ND	1961

MOST TOTAL YARDS
623	ND	1946
591	SC	1979
557	ND	1970
538	SC	1978
535	ND	1979

FEWEST TOTAL YARDS
53	SC	1936
74	SC	1950
74	SC	1960
120	ND	1980
131	SC	1932

MOST PASSES ATTEMPTED
58	ND	1970
45	SC	1987
44	SC	1988
42	SC	1985
41	ND	1978

FEWEST PASSES ATTEMPTED
2 SC	1950
2 ND	1960
5 SC	1926
5 ND	1963
5 SC	1980

MOST PASSES COMPLETED
33	ND	1970
25	SC	1985
24	SC	1982
23	SC	1987
23	SC	1988

FEWEST PASSES COMPLETED
1 SC	1926
1 ND	1931
1 SC	1932
1 SC	1950
1 ND	1952
1 ND	1960
1 ND	1962

Series Highs And Lows

MOST TURNOVERS
10	ND	1946
9	ND	1967
8	SC	1952
8	ND	1970
7	SC	1949
7	ND	1955
7	SC	1984

FEWEST TURNOVERS
0 SC	1932
0 ND	1953
0 SC	1970

MOST PUNTS
13	ND	1932
13	ND	1933
13	SC	1938
12	ND	1931
12	SC	1932
12	SC	1933
12	ND	1935

FEWEST PUNTS
1 ND	1946
1 ND	1957
1 ND	1986
2 ND	1955
2 ND	1960
2 ND	1964
2 ND	1966
2 ND	1968
2 SC	1986

MOST YARDS PENALIZED
167	ND	1967
111	ND	1956
111	ND	1981
110	SC	1976
93	SC	1972

FEWEST YARDS PENALIZED
0 SC	1931
0 SC	1933
0 SC	1935
0 ND	1981
5 ND	1928
5 SC	1929
5 SC	1930
5 ND	1932